目次

序文　4

風景の中の木材　14
　倒立する家　16　キロットーヴィチャード
　山あいの家　22　サイア・バーバリス・トポザノフ・アルシテクト
　チュン邸　28　チュン・スタジオ
　アイランドハウス　34　アルキテクトスタジオ　ウィッジェダル・ラッキ・ベルガーホフ

変容する木材　40
　スーツケース・ハウスホテル　42　エッジ・アーキテクツ
　プトニー邸　48　トンキン－ズライハーグリア
　プレヌフ・ヴァル・アンドレの住宅　54　ドーフレスヌ, ル・ギャレ・エ・アソシエ
　ネンニングの住宅　60　クックロビッツーナハバール　アーヒテクテン

木材と匠の技　66
　カーサDMAC　68　ナザール・アーキテクトス
　ダニエルソン邸　74　ブライアン・マッケイーリヨン　アーキテクツ
　マウントヴュー・レジデンス　80　JMA　アーキテクツQLD
　KFNパイロットプロジェクト　86　ヨハネス＆オスカー・レオ・カウフマン

木材と自然　92
　チルマークの住宅　94　チャールズ・ローズ　アーキテクツ
　ランボー氏別荘　100　オラヴィ・コポーネン
　ケーラー邸　106　サルメラ　アーキテクチャー＆デザイン
　アカヤバ自宅　112　マルコス・アカヤバ

表皮としての木材　118
　軒の家　120　手塚建築事務所＆池田昌弘
　集合住宅II　126　ヴォークト・アーヒテクテン
　ギャロウェイ邸　132　ザ・ミラーーハル　パートナーシップ
　チャマルティンの住宅　138　フエンサンタ・ニエト＆エンリケ・ソベヤノ

持続可能性としての木材　144
　バンデイラ・デ・メロの住宅　146　マウロ・ムニョス　アルキテクチュラ
　シュタインヴェントナー邸　152　ヘルトゥル・アーヒテクテン
　パッシブハウス　158　ヨハネス＆オスカー・レオ・カウフマン
　マウラー自宅兼アトリエ　164　トーマス・マウラー　アーキテクト

インテリアとしての木材　170
リビングルーム
Great(Bamboo)Wall	172	隈研吾建築都市設計事務所
屋根の家	174	手塚建築事務所＆池田昌弘
ミカエリス邸	176	ハリー・レビン アーキテクツ
トレジャーパレス	178	エッジ・アーキテクツ
山あいの家	180	サイア・バーバリス・トポザノフ・アルシテクト
ランボー邸	182	オラヴィ・コポーネン
チュン・スタジオ	184	チュン・スタジオ
アカヤバ自宅	186	マルコス・アカヤバ
バンデイラ・デ・メロの住宅	188	マウロ・ムニョス アルキテクチュラ
パインの森別荘	190	カトラー・アンダーソン アーキテクツ
エッシンゲンの住宅	192	シュルーデ・アーヒテクテン
シュトゥットガルトの集合住宅	194	シュルーデ・アーヒテクテン
シャーレ・ピクテ	196	シャルル・ピクテ アルシテクト
サヴォア通り2世帯住宅	198	リトー・アルシテクト

キッチン
集合住宅Ⅱ	200	ヴォークト・アーヒテクテン
シャーレ・ピクテ	202	シャルル・ピクテ アルシテクト
ラトーレ邸	204	ギャリー・カニンガム アーキテクト
ウッドハウス	206	カトラー・アンダーソン アーキテクツ
ミカエリス邸	208	ハリー・レビン アーキテクツ
山あいの家	210	サイア・バーバリス・トポザノフ・アルシテクト
アイランドハウス	212	アルキテクトスタジオ ウィッジェダル・ラッキ・ベルガーホフ

ベッドルーム
スタジオ3773	214	ドライデザイン
サヴォア通り重層式アパート	216	リトー・アルシテクト
シャーレ・ピクテ	218	シャルル・ピクテ アルシテクト
トレジャー・パレス	220	エッジ・アーキテクツ
山あいの家	222	サイア・バーバリス・トポザノフ・アルシテクト
水没する家	224	GADアーキテクチュア
3つの時代にまたがる家	225	GADアーキテクチュア
フィンランドの住宅	226	ウッドフォーカス・フィンランド

バスルーム
トレジャー・パレス	228	エッジ・アーキテクツ
スーツケース・ハウスホテル	230	エッジ・アーキテクツ
バンデイラ・デ・メロの住宅	232	マウロ・ムニョス アルキテクチュラ
アイランドハウス	233	アルキテクトスタジオ ウィッジェダル・ラッキ・ベルガーホフ
3つの時代にまたがる家	234	GADアーキテクチュア
R邸	236	フェイファリック-フリッツァー アーヒテクテン
フィンランドの住宅	238	ウッドフォーカス・フィンランド
シャーレ・ピクテ	240	シャルル・ピクテ アルシテクト

テラス
縁側の家	242	手塚建築事務所
アヴァロン邸	244	コナー-ソロモン アーキテクツ
ネンニングの住宅	246	クックロビッツーナハバール アーヒテクテン
ハイン邸	248	クックロビッツーナハバール アーヒテクテン
水没する家	250	GADアーキテクチュア
Great(Bamboo)Wall	252	隈研吾建築都市設計事務所
マシューズ邸	254	JMA アーキテクツQLD

夢を持つため（ツリーハウス）　256
ポール・ミード・ツリーハウス	258	ハワード-フーティット-ミラー
リー・ツリーハウス	264	ジョセフ・リム アーキテクト
ハーディー・ツリーハウス	270	ユー・クワン エリア

主要木材カタログ　276
作品・建築家一覧　286

人間にとって木材は永遠の宝
序文
introduction

　人類の夜明けとともに建築材料として使われてきた木材は、さまざまな特性に恵まれ、大いなる万能性を発揮してきた。木材は構造部材として用いられるだけでなく、熱や音の絶縁にも有能で、しかも大変環境に優しい素材である。温もり、肌目、触感といった木材固有の特質については言うまでもなく、室内装飾において木材の果たす役割は事実上無限である。

　現代の思潮は、木材は再生可能な、枯渇することのない自然資源であるという見解で一致している。環境保護団体からの圧力により、伐採と製材のコンピュータ化、自動システム化が一層進展した。その結果木材副産物から数多くの製品が生み出され、この貴重な自然資源は最大限無駄なく活用されている。また集成材や合板の製造、木材修復技術、さらには木材を長期間保護し耐久性を高める防除薬剤の分野でも多くのめざましい進歩が達成された。

　こうした進歩により、現在木材はプレハブ工法の重要なエレメントとなっている。この工法においては、労働力の大半は工場や作業場で費やされ、その結果労働時間が節約され、最先端の機械の使用が可能となっている。それにより製造された製品は、軽量かつ全体的に再利用可能で、輸送が容易であり、しかも施工に特殊技能を必要としない。

Wood, which has been used for building since the dawn of man, is blessed with a variety of characteristics which afford it great versatility. Used for structural work, it is also effective for insulating against temperature and noise and is very ecological. Its uses in interior decorating are practically unlimited, not to mention some of its more subjective traits such as warmth, texture and touch.
Current thinking has it that wood as a raw material is a renewable natural resource of unlimited supply. Pressure from the ecology sectors has led to ever more computerized and automated systems of cutting and wood transformation. This in turn has afforded countless products that are made from wood by-products thus optimizing the use of this natural resource. Important advances have also been made in cementing and joining wood, in wood renovation, and in anti-pest products which grant long-term protection and conserve the wood.
Thanks to these advances wood is a key element in prefabrication construction. Here, the majority of the elaboration is done in the factory or workshop, thus saving time and allowing ultra-modern machinery to be used. This provides us with a light, totally recyclable product, that can be easily transported and whose installation does not require specialized labor.

ログキャビン

Log Cabin

　ログキャビンは木造建築のなかでも最古の歴史を誇り、その起源は北欧にあると考えられている。民族大移動の波とともに、その様式は良質の木材が豊富に見出される地域にあまねく広まっていった。当初は皮を剥いだ丸太を水平に積み上げ、端部または角で相互に接合するという単純な工法であったが、その後製材用ノコギリの出現とともに、ログ材は一定の形に成形され、標準化されるようになった。

　現在このタイプの建築システムでは、すべての部材が工場で成形されてキットの形に商品化され、現場で簡単に短期間で組み立てられるようになっている。最近ではさまざまな表面仕上げのものが選べるようになっており、滑らかに仕上げたもの、斧あとを残した荒々しい仕上げのもの、ステイン塗装したもの、年代を感じさせるもの、ペイント塗装したものなど種々用意されている。同様に外形も多種多様なものが用意されており、過去の単純な立方体のものからはるかに進化している。

This is the oldest of wood constructions whose origin would seem to be from northern Europe. With the waves of migration its use became extended as long as quality wood could be found in abundance. Initially, construction consisted of placing round trunks, without the bark, horizontally one atop the other and joining them at the ends or the corners. Later, with the appearance of sawmills, the size of the logs became uniform and standardized.

Nowadays, this type of building system is commercialized in kits that contain totally prefabricated parts which can be quickly and easily set up at the site. Presently a vast array of finishes are sold such as smooth, rough hewn, stained, antique look, painted, etc. Likewise, diverse shapes are available which are a far cry from the simple, square original ones.

在来軸組構法

the heavy framework

　この構法の基本は、基準寸法に則って成形され、堅固に組み合わされた、大きく重量のある柱と梁の構造である。この基本構造の上に、それよりも小さい梁、けたなどの副次的構造が組み立てられる。この構法はすでに新石器時代のヨーロッパと中国に見られ、その後北アメリカ、日本、東南アジアへと広がっていき、中世の終わり頃から19世紀にかけて最盛期を迎えた。近代的な軸組構法はヨーロッパでは16世紀末に、そして日本では18世紀末に現れた。その特徴は固定と接合に金物を用いて補強を加えることで、その結果強度が高まり、プレハブ化と自動化が図られるようになった。

In this system of building there is a well-braced structure of large, heavy pillars and girders in module-like sections. This supports another secondary structure of smaller girders. It appeared in Europe and China in Neolithic times and later spread to North America, Japan and Southeast Asia. It attained its maximum expression between the end of the Middle Ages and the nineteenth century. Its modern version appeared in Europe at the end of the sixties and in Japan in the eighties. It brought with it new fastening and joining systems that use steel, which afford more strength and facilitate prefabrication and automatization.

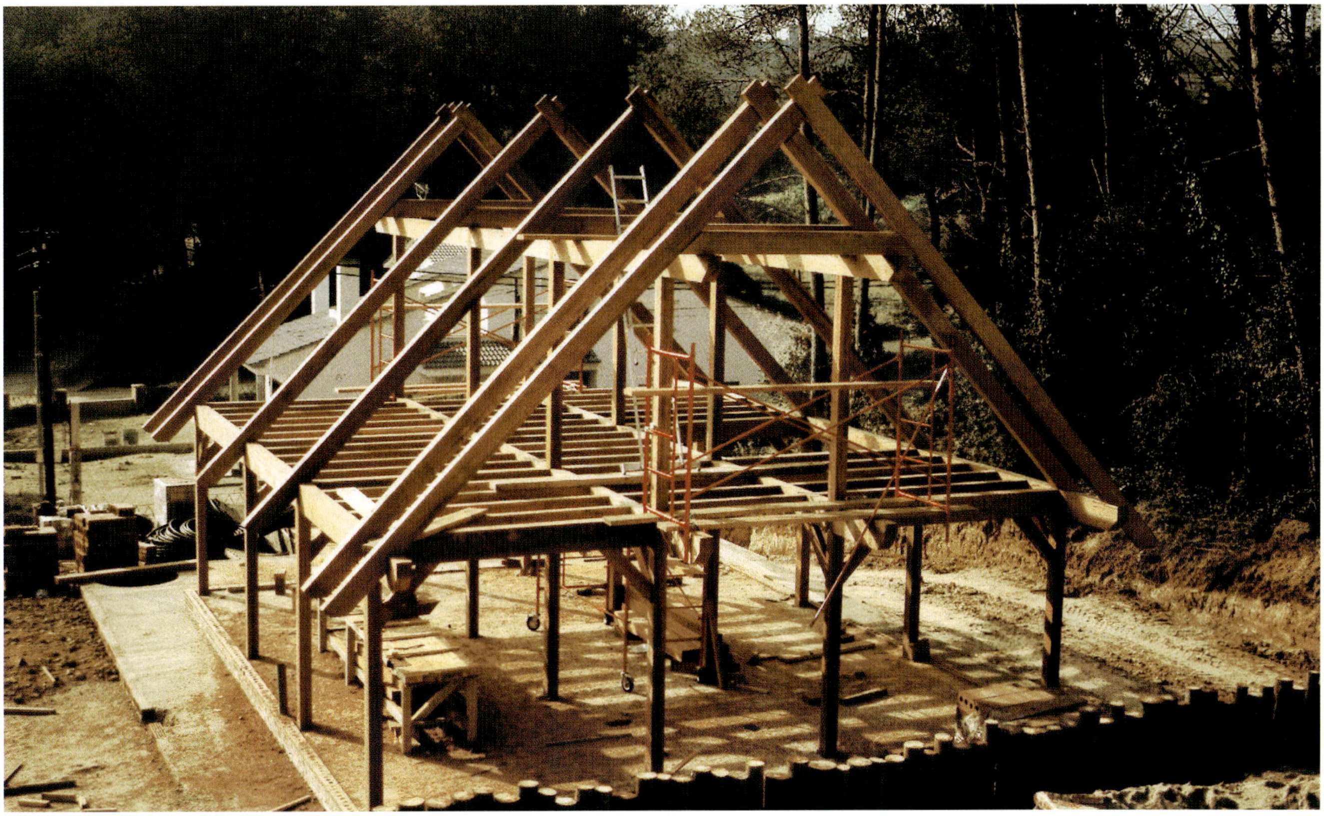

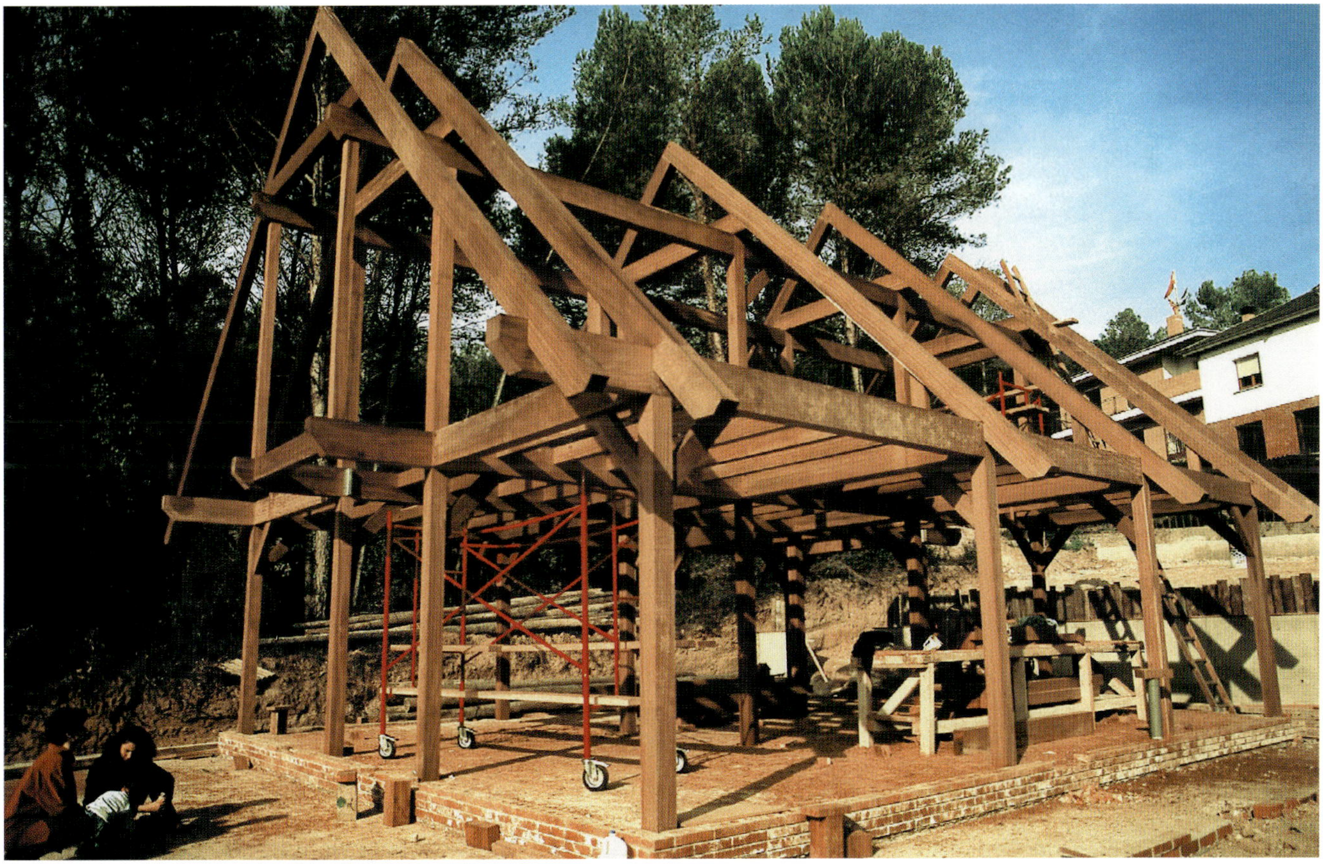

軽量枠組構法

the light framework

　在来軸組構法は19世紀アメリカにおいて新しい構法へと進化した。在来軸組構法においては、鉛直荷重を負担する構造材および被覆・屋根エレメントには、それぞれ異なった特殊な部材が必要とされるが、この新しい構法では、規格化されたパネルと壁がその両方の機能を果たす。パネルは釘またはステープルによって接合される。モジュール化されているため、高度な標準化が可能となるだけでなく、融通性に富み、プレハブ方式に最適である。20世紀後半に登場した木質パネルは、構造的枠組の考え方に革命をもたらしたが、なかでもそれを最も象徴しているのが合板パネルである。合板パネルの進化はまた、接着剤の開発と密接に関連している。

The heavy framework evolved towards this new system in the United States in the nineteenth century. It does not require specific materials for the load-bearing structures and the enclosing and roof elements but rather the same panels and walls serve the two functions. The panels are put together with nails or staples. This module-like system affords high standardization, great flexibility and ideally lends itself to prefabrication. Wood panels, which came on the scene in the second half of the twentieth century, proved to be a revolution in regards to the structural framework. The most emblematic of these is the plywood panel whose evolution is closely tied to the development of adhesives.

集成材構造

laminated wood

　接着剤で貼り合わせ製造される集成材は、20世紀初頭に登場した。最初はまっすぐな長尺梁を作るために開発されたが、その後湾曲した梁も作られるようになった。集成材構造は軽量枠組構法と同様の技術に基づいている。それはラミナと呼ばれるひき板を連結、接着して、ほとんど無制限といえる大きさのエレメントを作りだす。1910年のブリュッセル万国博覧会に登場して以降広く受け入れられ、特に中欧およびスイスで盛んに用いられた。1923年以降はヨーロッパ以外の国々にも普及し、1930年代の終わりには、その精度と強靭さが広く認識されるに至った。第2次世界大戦の勃発によって余儀なくされた鉄鋼の使用制限によって、集成材の利用はさらに進み、現在の地位を確立した。同時期に開発された合成接着剤を使用することによって、集成材はどんな場所でも使える素材となり、室内に限るという使用制限は不要となった。

Laminated wood using glues made its appearance at the beginning of the twentieth century where it was utilized for manufacturing straight beams of great length. Curved beams would appear later on. It is based on techniques similar to light framework; it uses small cross-sections to build elements of almost unlimited dimensions. Beginning with the International Exposition in Brussels in 1910, it enjoyed widespread acceptation especially in Central Europe and Switzerland. After 1923, it began to be used outside of Europe. By the end of the thirties, its quality was well-acclaimed. Due to the restrictions on steel imposed by the Second World War, its use became firmly and definitively established. At the same time, the invention of synthetic adhesives permitted laminated wood to be employed practically anywhere, without the former restrictions on indoor use.

01

Wood on the Landscape

Wood is an element that integrates to a high degree and its role in integrating into the landscape is very important. The projects in this chapter become the absolute masters of their environment as they establish a dialogue with it, a dialogue among equals, they create their own private garden, or they become an integral, almost necessary, part of the landscape

風景のなかの木材

木材はすべてを高い次元で統合する能力を持つエレメントであり、建築を風景と統合するときに果たすその役割はきわめて重要である。本章で紹介するプロジェクトはどれも、風景との対話、すなわち同等なもの同士の対話を確立することによって、またそれ自身の私的な庭園を創造することによって、あるいは風景のなかの必須の、ほとんど不可欠といえる構成要素となることによって、環境の絶対的な支配者となっている。

倒立する家
風景をつかまえて

キロットーヴィチャード
共同設計：アレキサンダー・ルノーブル
エマニュエル・ボードイン
撮影：ルック・ベーグリー

MAISON CONVERCEY
capture the landscape

グラショウーフランス―2001

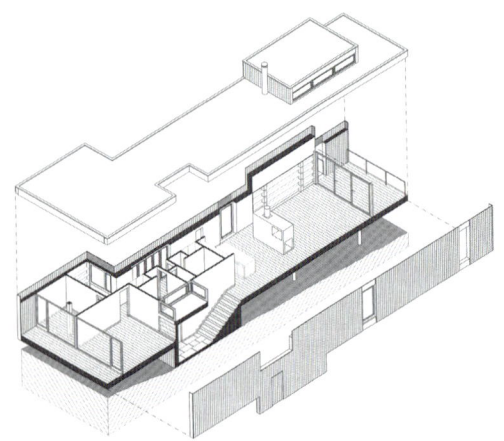

　建物は数本の柱で大地に手をついて倒立し、無垢な田園風景のなかに軽やかに浮かんでいる。内部から眺めると、景観は額縁に収められた1枚の完璧な風景画となり、設計の巧みさがうかがえる。建物は両端に向かって細長く引き伸ばされ、まるで万華鏡のようである。万華鏡を覗くと、限りなく広がる周囲の景観が次から次に現れてくる。

Elevated above the terrain by way of pillars, the building lightly flows over the unbroken countryside. From the inside, it is masterly designed to afford perfect views of the picture-framed exterior. The building, narrow and extending out to each end, takes on the appearance of a kaleidoscope through which we are afforded a vast array of views of the unfolding land around it.

　たった2週間という短期間で組み立てられた軽量鉄骨造の建物は、気持ちよさそうに木材にくるまれている。それによって本来ならばそのボリュームによって周囲を威圧するかもしれない建物を、完璧なまでに風景に溶け込ませている。ドア入口がこの建物が大地と接する唯一の場所であり、そこは緑の海に浮かぶ直方体がバランスを取り連結する支点の役割を果たしている。

A light steel structure, assembled in only two weeks, is delightfully clad with wood that perfectly integrates, what would seem to be rather stern volumetry, into its setting. The access to the door is the only contact with the terrain and it acts as a point of balance and connection for this tetrahedron that is floating on a sea of green.

部屋ごとにわずかにつけられている高低差、見事に計算された開口部、やむことのない室内と外界の対話、これらが風景への影響をできるだけ抑えてデザインされたこの建物を単調さからまぬがれさせている。内部の空間の流れは、ダイニングとリビングスペースの間の仕切りただ1カ所でさえぎられているだけである。

Slight variations in height for the different rooms, shrewdly calculated apertures, and the non-stop dialogue between interior and exterior, enrich the design which purposely subdues its impact on the setting. Inside, the spatial flow is only interrupted in order to delimit the dining and living room spaces.

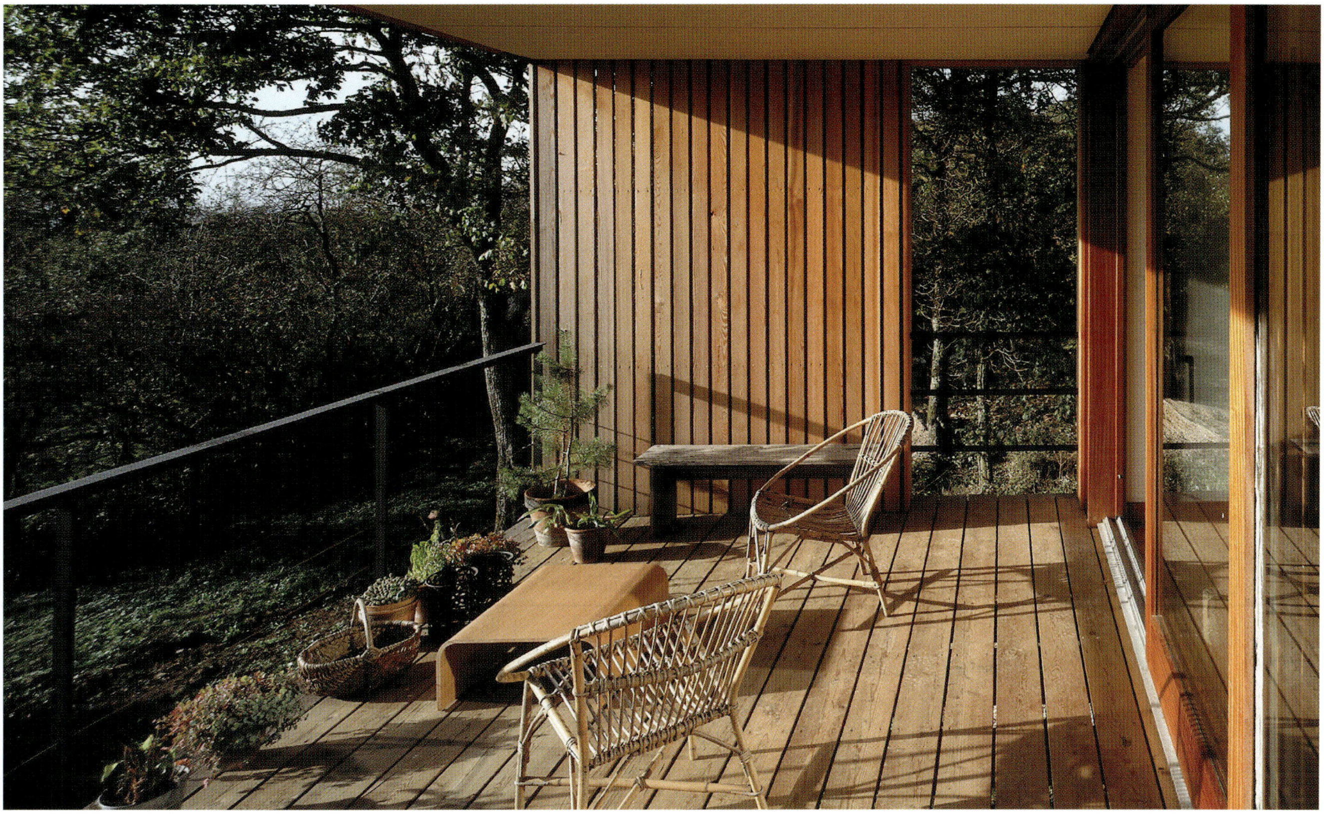

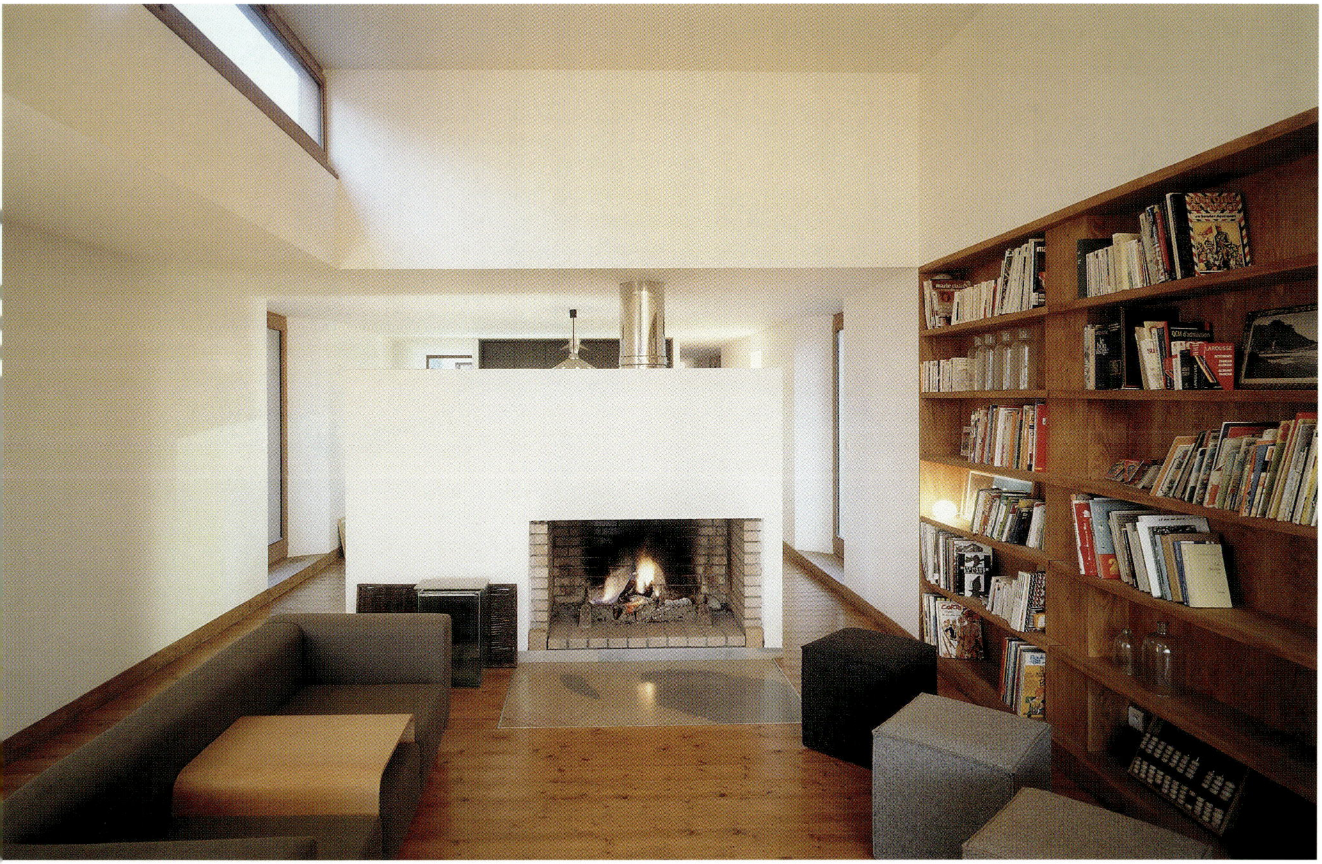

山あいの家
暖かい避難小屋

サイア・バーバリス・トポザノフ・アルシテクト
撮影：マーク・クレーマー, フレデリック・サイア

MAISON GOULET
warm refuge

サント・マルグリット・デュ・ラック・マッソン—カナダ—2003

　荒々しい厳酷の環境に屹立し、この住居の外観は避難小屋を想起させる。敷地は湖に向かって北から南へと傾斜しており、建物は東西に伸びる平らな石積みの基礎の上に建てられている。2基の巨大な石積みの煙突が、この木造建築物をしっかりと大地に固定している。亜鉛鉄板の外皮は、この建物にベルベットのような、あやうく冷たいと感じられかねない質感を与えているが、逆にそれが建物内部から発する暖かさを惹きたたせている。

Isolated in a rough and rugged setting, the outline of this dwelling brings to mind the image of a refuge. Placed on terrain that slopes down from north to south to the shores of a lake, the construction is placed on a flat, rocky plot that extends out from east to west. Two large stone chimneys seem to anchor the wooden structure to the terrain. A zinc covering confers it a velvet-like texture, almost cold, which contrasts with the warmth that emanates from the interior.

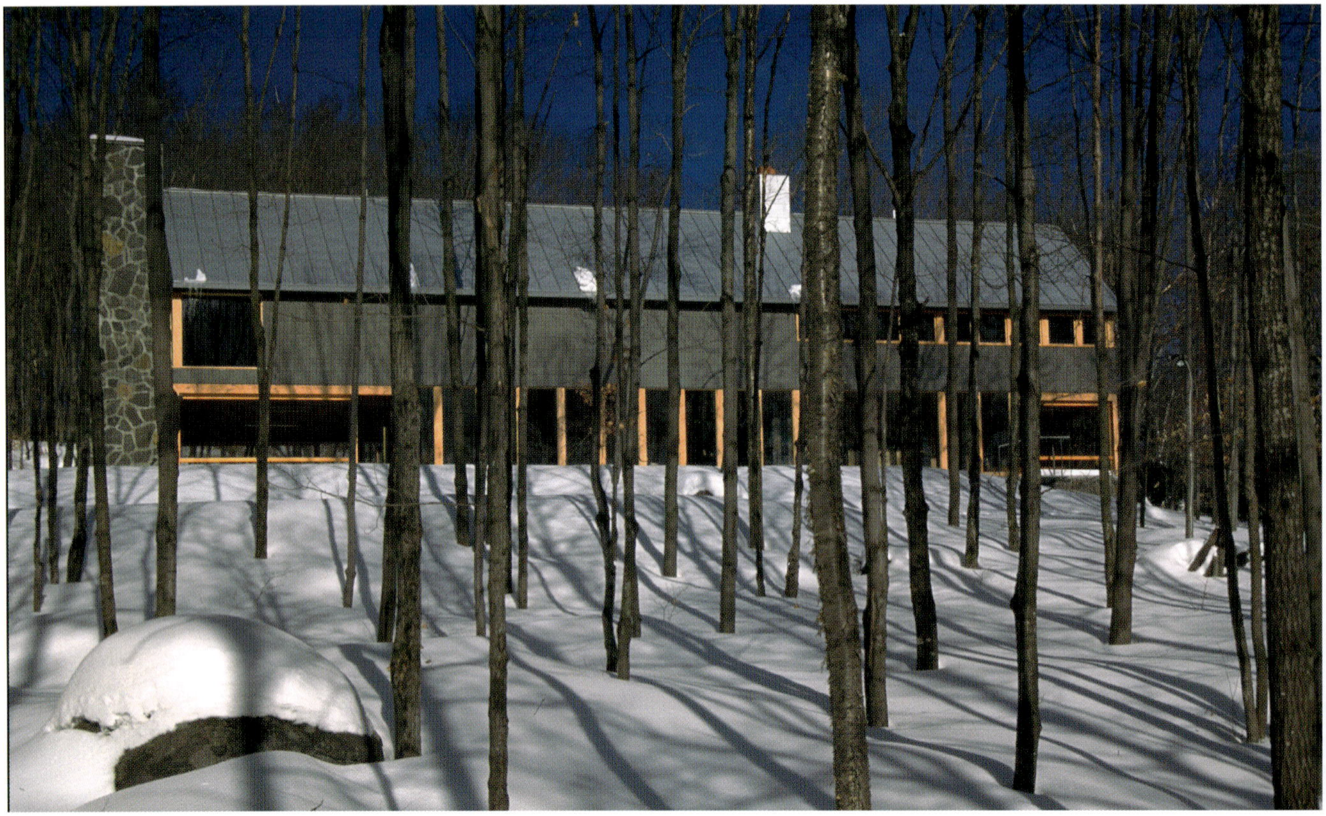

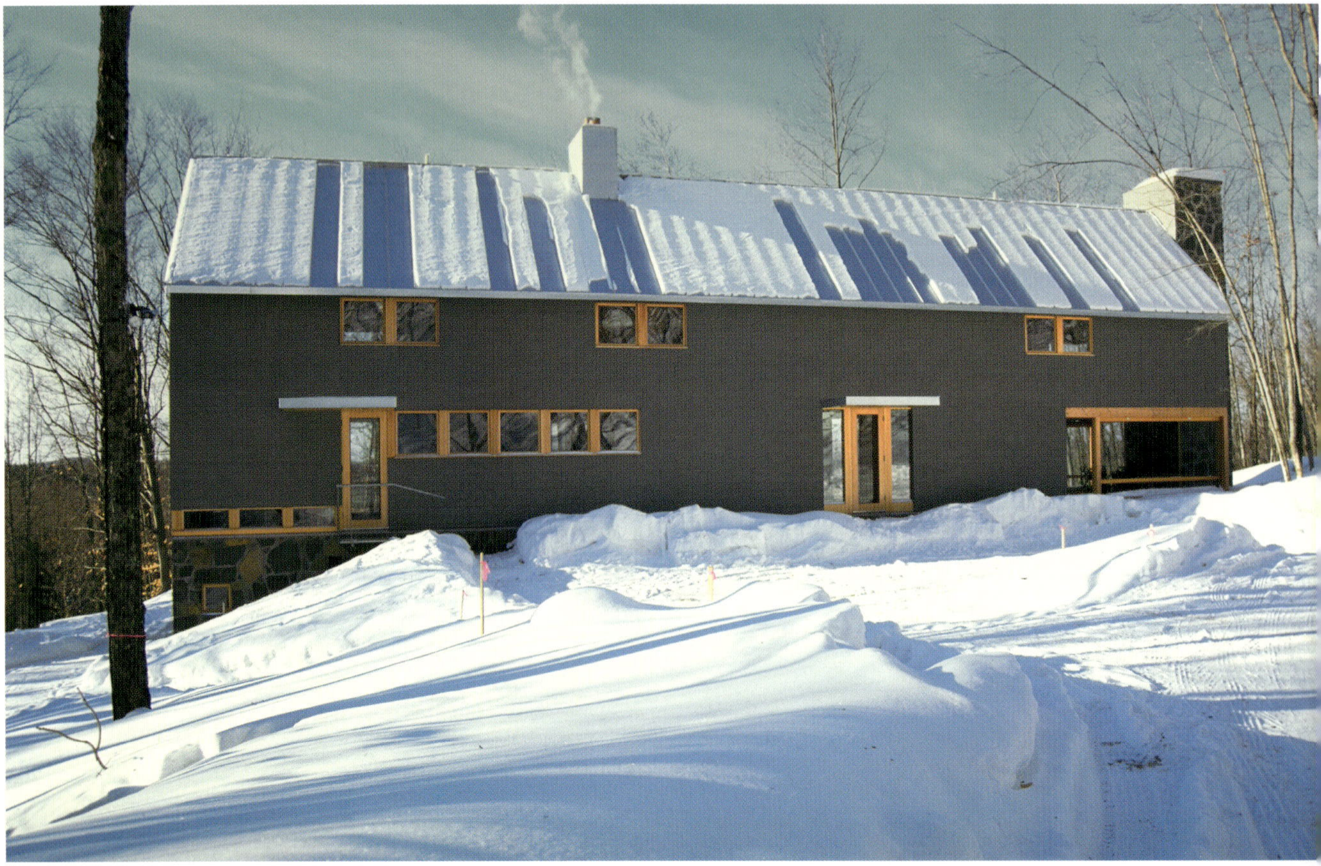

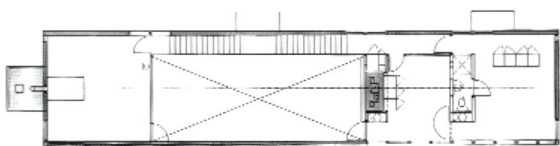

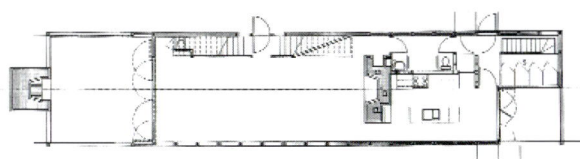

　天候の穏やかな日には大きなドアとガラス壁は開け放たれ、壁は溶解し、外部空間が内部空間へと越境することが許される。2階に上ると、両側に窓が調和よく開かれ、周囲の大地と湖へと下るスロープが見渡せる。

When the weather permits, the large doors and glass walls are opened, thus dissolving the walls and allowing the exterior spaces to prolong the interior ones. On the second floor, the windows on both sides are in harmony as they afford views of the surrounding terrain and the slope below.

建築は現場の地勢と気候に深く根を下ろし適応させられているので、最終的な結果については、さまざまな解釈を許容するものとなった。一見したところ、建物は伝統的な外観を保持しているが、無駄な細部装飾は省かれ、住む人を環境に結びつけると同時に、それから保護している。すなわちこの建物は郷愁と因習の暗がりを避けようと試みている。

As architecture deeply rooted in and conditioned by the topography of the site and the climate, the final result is open to interpretations. At first glance it is a traditional volumetry but lacking in superfluous details, that ties us to and protects us from its environment, as it attempts to avoid the gray areas of nostalgia and convention.

チュン邸
内省的な平面

チュン・スタジオ
共同設計：ジャミー・ブッシュ
ジョン・ブロディー
撮影：ティム・ストリート・ポーター

CHUN RESIDENCE
levels of introversion

サンタモニカ―カリフォルニア―2003

　H型に配置された住宅の通りに面した部分は、2階建ての横に長い擁壁構造になっている。万里の長城を彷彿とさせるその壁面は、通行人の視線から住人のプライバシーを守る役割を果たしているが、訪問者が内側の居間から眺めるとき、その中央部に2階まで吹き抜けの空間があるため、その壁は溶解しているように見える。その吹き抜けの空間は、石材を用いることによって重厚感を出した不透明な表側と、ガラスと木材で巧みに構成された透明な内側の間の変移点として機能している。

This residence with an H-shaped layout features a two-story bar construction facing the street that acts as a monument-like wall so as to grant the dwellers privacy from passers-by. However, for the visitor, gazing out from the inside, it would seem to dissolve as in the middle of it there is a two-story void. This functions as a transition between the opaque exterior, with its heavy use of stone, and the transparency of the interior spaces which are fashioned from glass and wood.

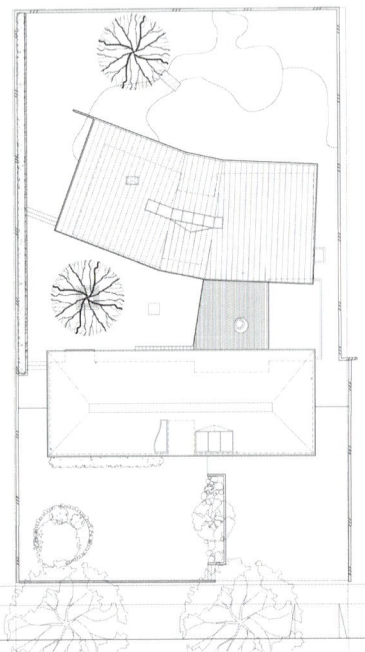

　プロジェクトは、外界で進行している事物からの影響を抑制し、それから切り離された独自の稀有な空間を創造するという試みであった。訪問者は、史跡を彷彿とさせる実物大の擁壁から内部空間へ、そして中庭へと進むとき、第1の感覚の変移を経験する。第2の感覚の変移はさらに大きく前進するもので、ガラスに覆われた室内と庭、特に日本庭園との間の対話を通して獲得される。

The project attempts to create its own unique world, controlled and removed from what is going on around it. The visitor's senses experience a transition as he goes from the life-size, monument-evoking walls outside, to the interior spaces and interior gardens inside. A second transition, an even larger step forward than before, is attained by way of the dialogue between the glassy interiors and the gardens, especially the Japanese garden.

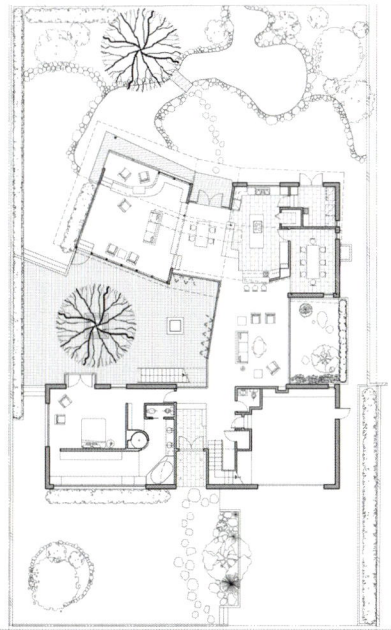
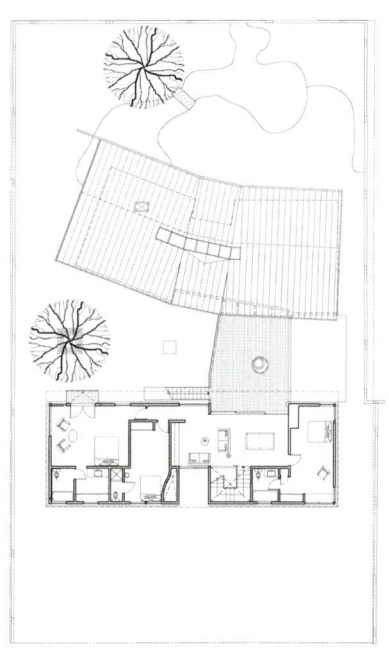

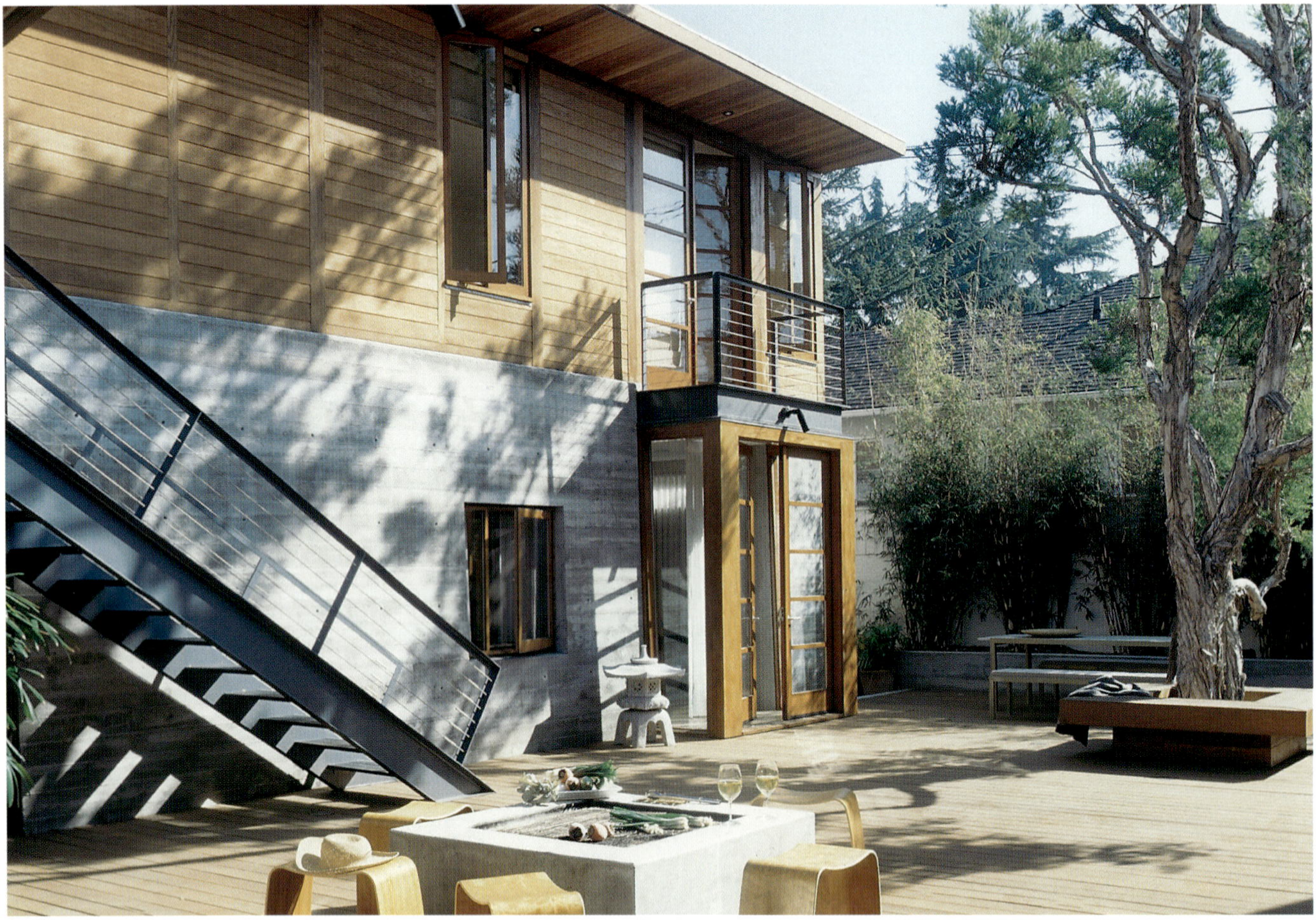

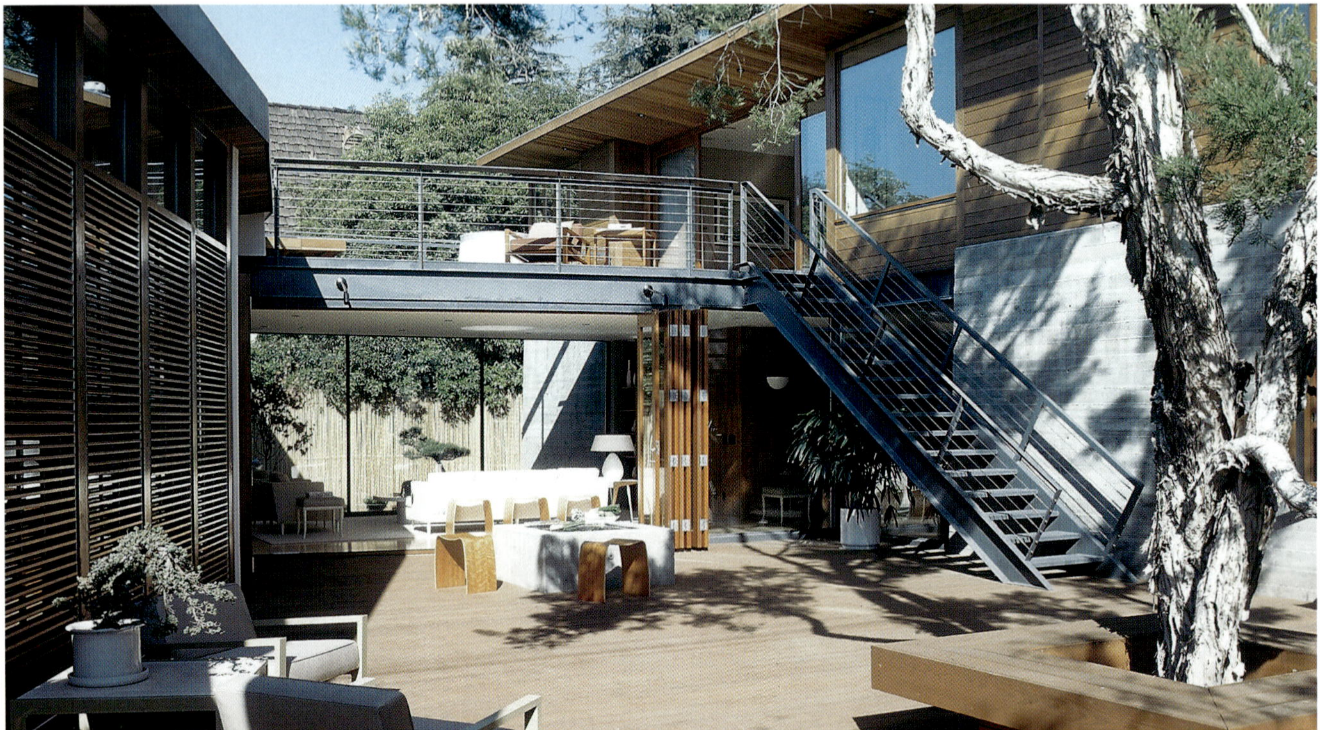

住居内部は訪問者にとって開放的になっており、キッチンがすべての部屋へ向かうハブの役目を果たしている。ガラスのカーテンウォールを多用することによって、空間は中心から外部に向かって漸進的に拡張し、そのまま日本庭園に到達し、人の心に優美と平安、そして静寂を沁み込ませる。

The interior of the dwelling unfolds for the visitor where the kitchen acts as the hub for all of the other rooms. Thanks to the abundant use of glass for the interior walls, the space would appear to expand out progressively from the center to reach out finally to the garden, which instills one with a sense of lightness, peace and silence.

アイランドハウス
自然を分界する

アルキテクトスタジオ　ウィッジェダル・ラッキ・ベルガーホフ
撮影：エイク・エリクソン―リンドマン

ISLAND HOUSE
island house

ストックホルム―スウェーデン―2002

　その建物はストックホルム群島のとある海岸に位置している。一見不毛の地のように感じられるが、彫刻を思わせる岩の造形、そしてオークやマツの木立が興趣を添えている。樹齢500年を超えると信じられている1本のオークが風景の高い位置の焦点になっている。

It is situated on the coast on one of the islands of the Stockholm archipelago. The rather barren land features sculpture-like rocks and oak and pine trees. An oak that is believed to be 500 years old is the centerpiece of the upper part of the terrain.

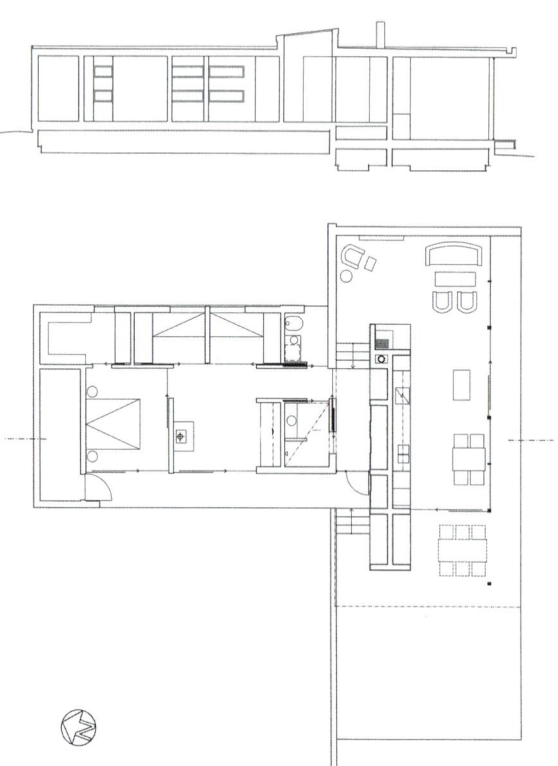

幼児2人を含む家族の要望は、荘厳な景観を十分生かしながらも、建築はあくまでも抑制的にというものであった。また住宅はやすらぎとリラクゼーションの場所として、そして団欒と友人を迎えるための場所として位置づけられた。

The inhabitants, a family with two small children, wanted the house to take full advantage of the magnificent panorama yet architecturally remain discreet. Likewise, the home was destined to be a place of comfort and relaxation, and a place for enjoyment and for receiving friends.

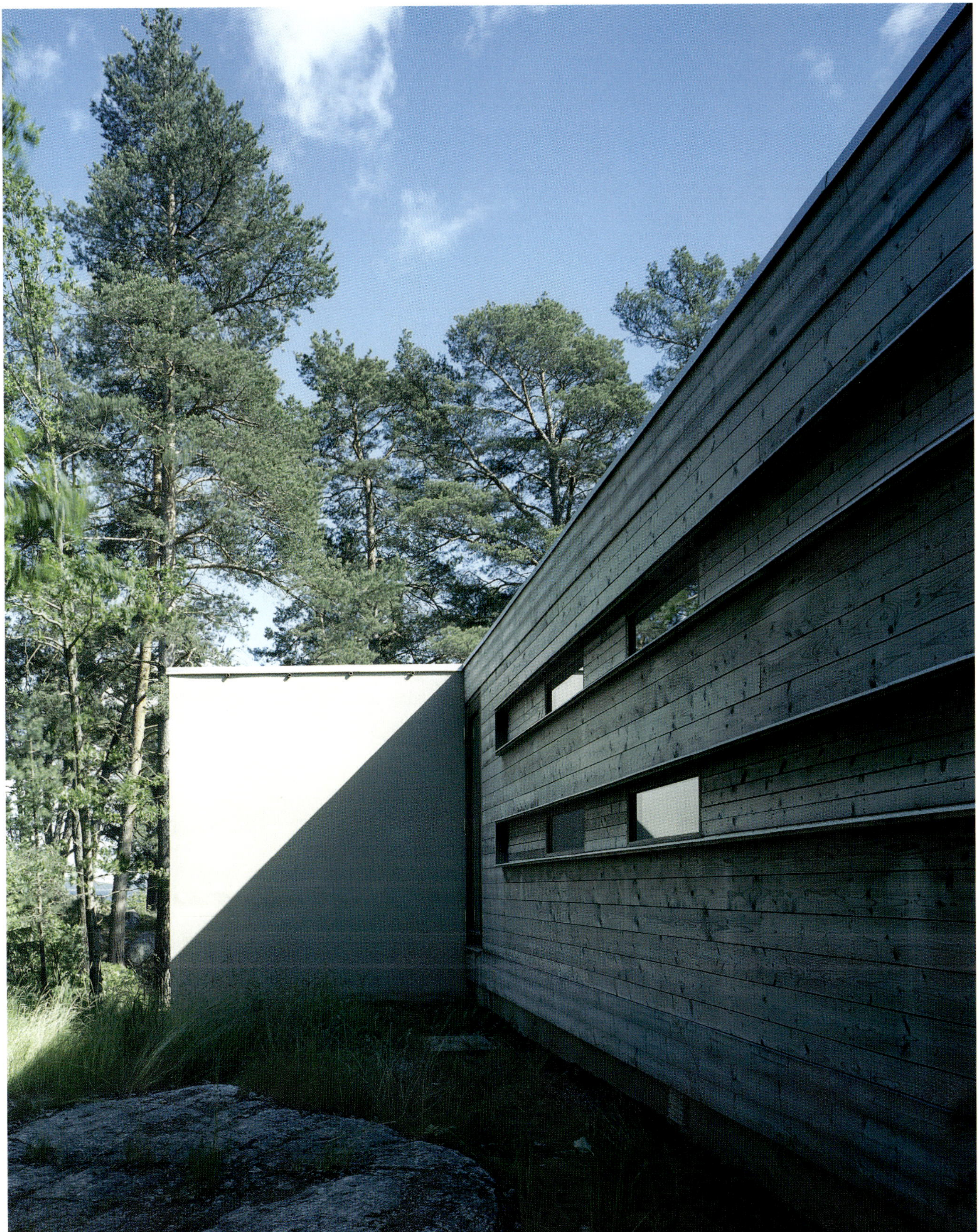

住宅は海岸からやや後方、わずかに高い場所に位置している。木立のなかに身を隠すように建てられているが、屋外テラスが海に向って延びている。住宅は、プラットホームと屋根、そしてその間に挟まれたスライドドアのあるいくつかの共用部屋で構成されている。プライベートな個室は、建物の後方、岩肌に囲まれた木立に向って配置され、樹齢数百年のオークがそれを護っている。

The house is placed slightly back and slightly raised from the coastline. Hidden among the tree trunks, with an open area of terraces it faces the ocean. The volume consists of a platform, the roof and several common rooms with sliding doors. The more private chambers are to the rear, facing the woods among the rocks and the centuries-old oak.

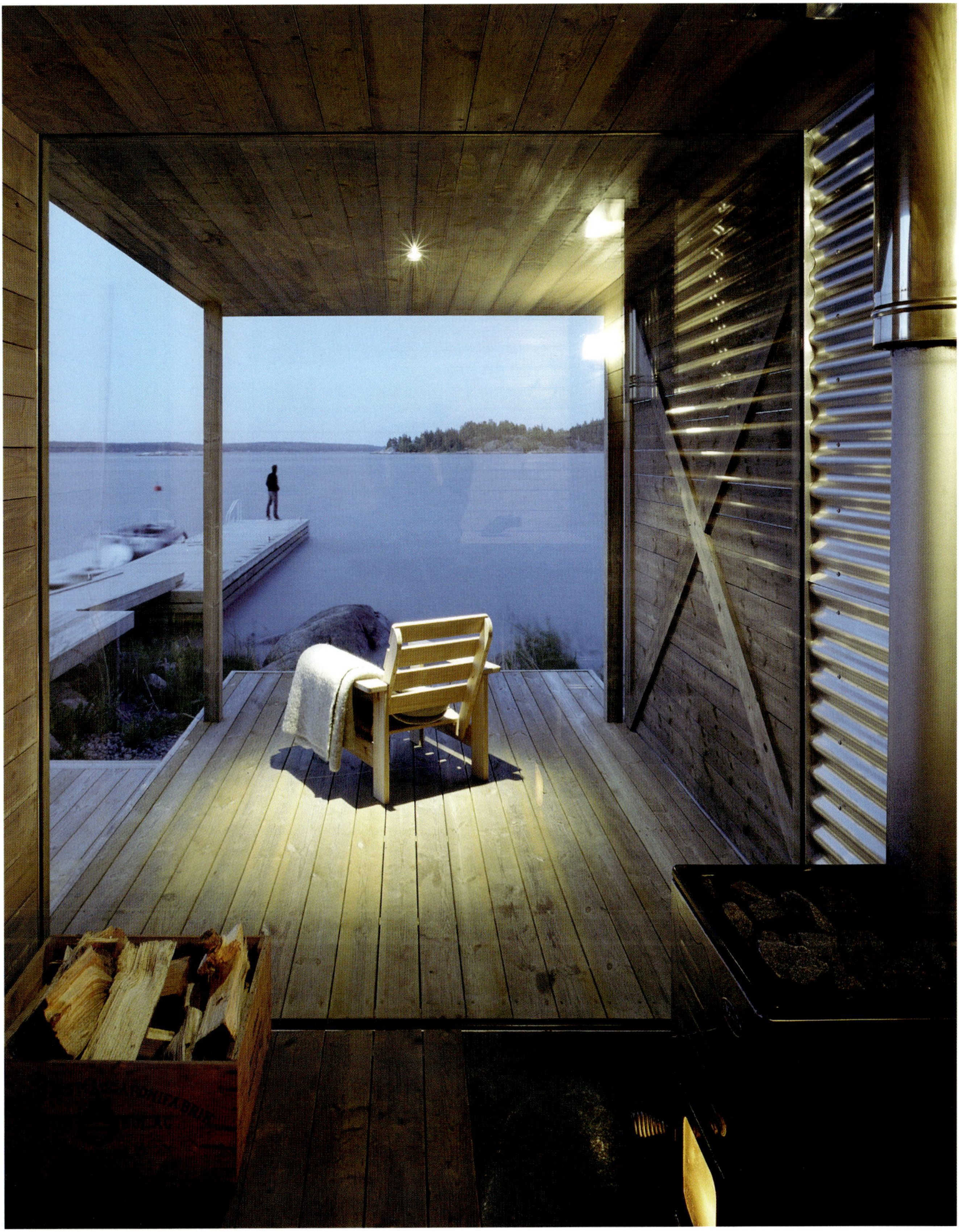

02

Changing Wood

A construction is normally considered to be something fixed and unchanging. The following projects exploit the versatility of wood. They are spaces that can undergo transformation, they are images created by wood that change with the passage of time, the seasons, the intensity of the sunlight, the inhabiting or not of the house, or the use that is made of it

変容する木材

建築は普通、固定したもの、変化しないものと考えられている。しかしこれから示すプロジェクトは、その主題に木材の変化を織り込んでいる。それは変容する空間であり、時の流れ、季節の移ろい、陽射しの変化、居住あるいは不在、そしてその使用の中で変化していく木によって創造されたイメージである。

スーツケース・ハウスホテル
変幻自在の感覚

エッジ・アーキテクツ
共同設計：アンドリュー・ホールト、ハワード・チャン、ポパイ・ツァン、イー・リー
撮影：淺川 敏、ハワード・チャン、ゲーリー・チャン

SUITCASE HOUSE HOTEL
versatile sensation

八達嶺　水完―北京―中国―2001

　このプロジェクトは、アジアの若手建築家12人を招いて行われた、万里の長城沿いに12棟の別荘を建設するというコンペのなかで実現されたものである。設計思想は、いくつかの水平面によって構成された澄明で純粋な空間を創造するというものであった。それはまた、レジャー空間としての使用はもちろん、1日を通して起こりうるさまざまな使用に完璧に対応できるものでなければならなかった。そして木材がすべての機能を統合するエレメントととして選ばれた。

This project was part of a competition for twelve young promising Asian architects, which entailed the design of twelve communitarian residences at the foot of the Great Wall. The proposal was for a clear and pure volume with levels inside. It need be extremely adaptable to diverse uses during the day including use as a leisure space, where wood would become the unifying element.

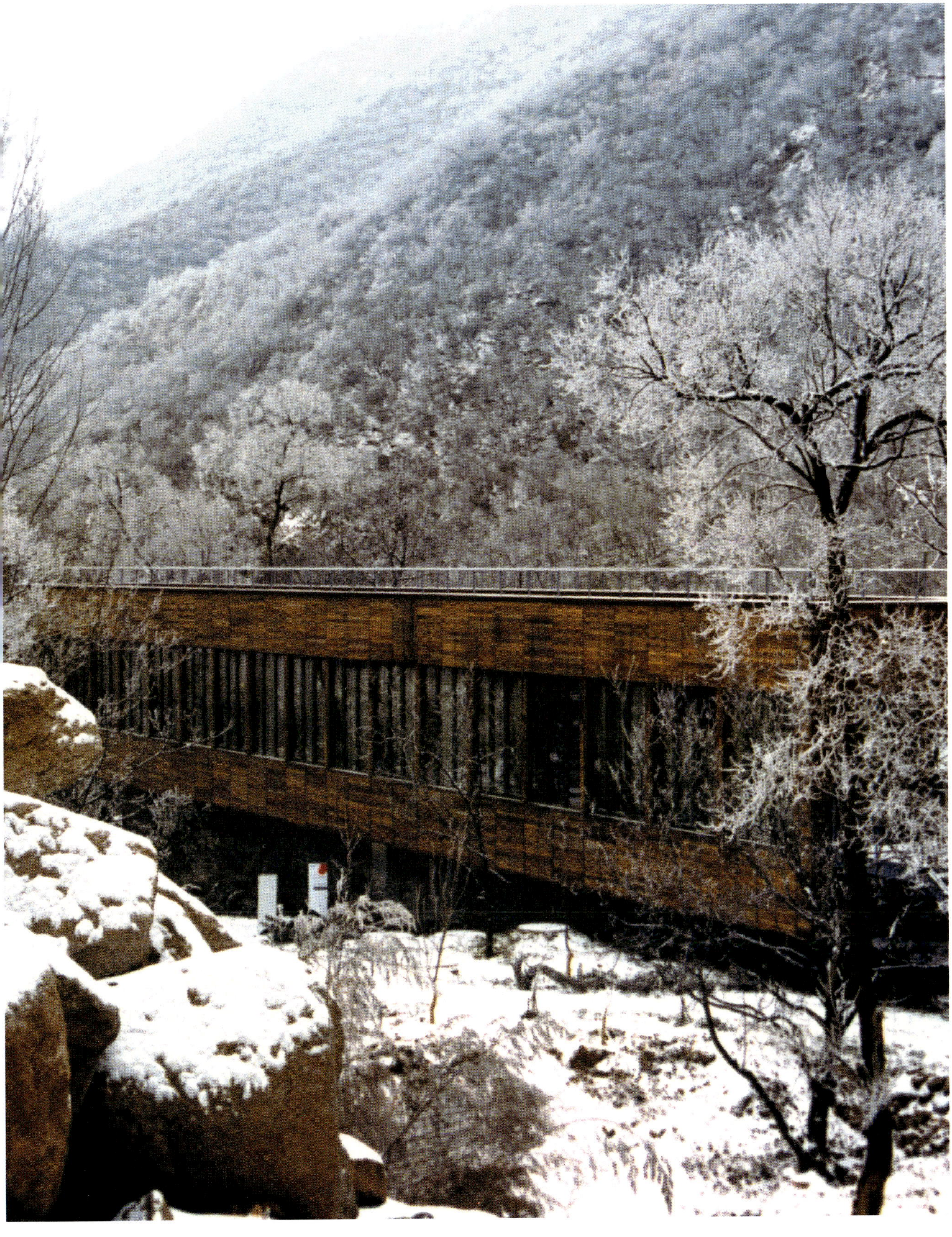

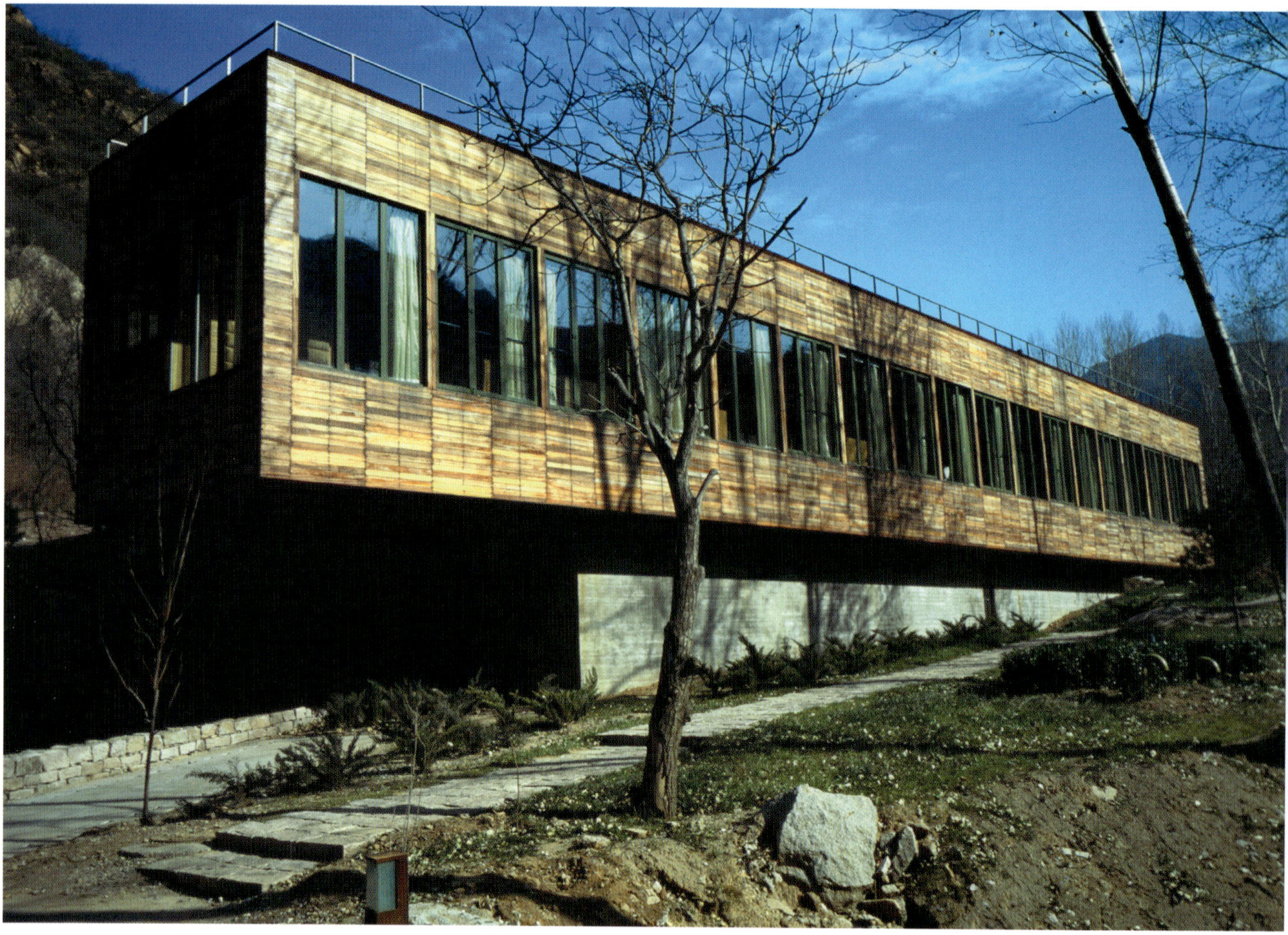

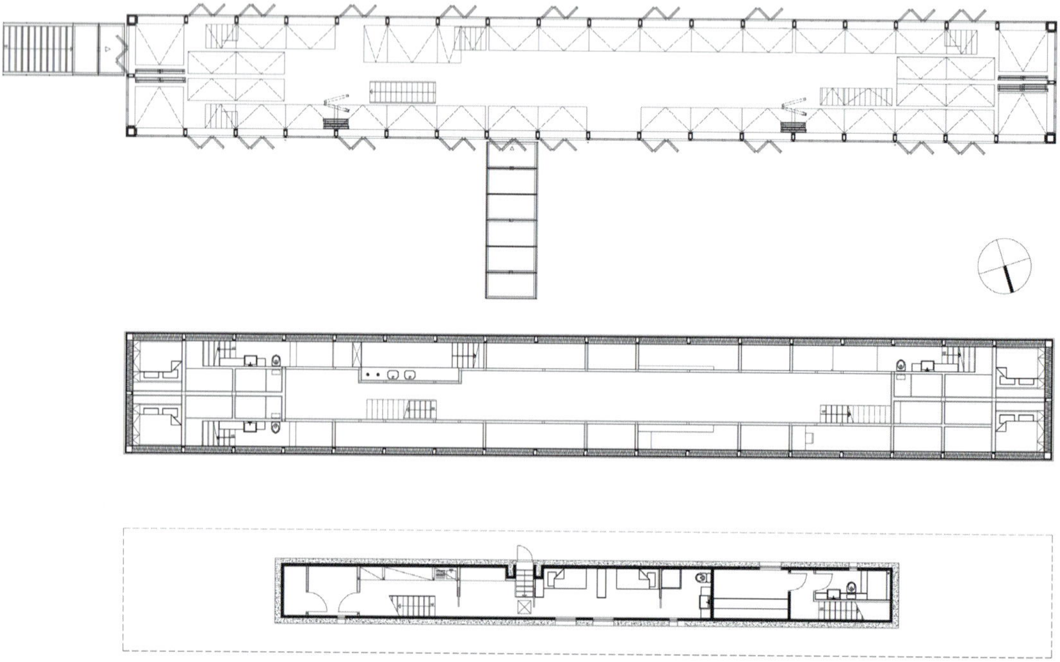

住居は3階構成になっており、内部空間はさまざまな用途に柔軟に対応できるようになっている。昼間、最上階は完全に開放され、全長44メートルの広々としたホールが出現する。夜になるとその空間は、音楽を楽しむ空間、読書する空間、瞑想する空間、入浴あるいはサウナのための空間へと、いくつかの小さな空間に分割される。新たな住人が到着すると、それらの空間は再度開放されたり、あるいは就寝のための空間として準備されたり、あるいはパーティーの会場になったりする。

Consisting of three levels, the interior space is very malleable to diverse uses. During the day the upper level opens completely and evokes the sensation of an open hall of 44 meters in length. Later, this same area can be delimited into smaller spaces for listening to music, for reading, meditating, bathing or having a sauna. Later, with the arrival of more of the residents, the space can be reopened, or it can be made ready for sleeping or having a party.

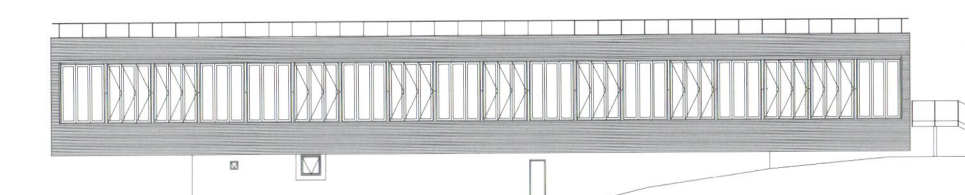

内部空間の可変性とは裏腹に、ファサードは同一形状の窓の連続という構成になっており、垂直な層により包装されているようである。そのことによって室内の様相が絶えず変移しているにもかかわらず、外観の同一性は保たれている。天井、壁、床、家具、すべてのエレメントが木材で覆われることによって、住宅内部の境界線はすべて曖昧になり、穏やかなものにされている。

As a reflection of the free internal distribution, the facade consists of series of identical windows, like a wrapping of vertical layers, which affords a sensation of exterior uniformity while the internal organization is undergoing constant change. The interior, the furniture, the structure and all of the elements are clad with wood, which diffuses and softens the limits of the house.

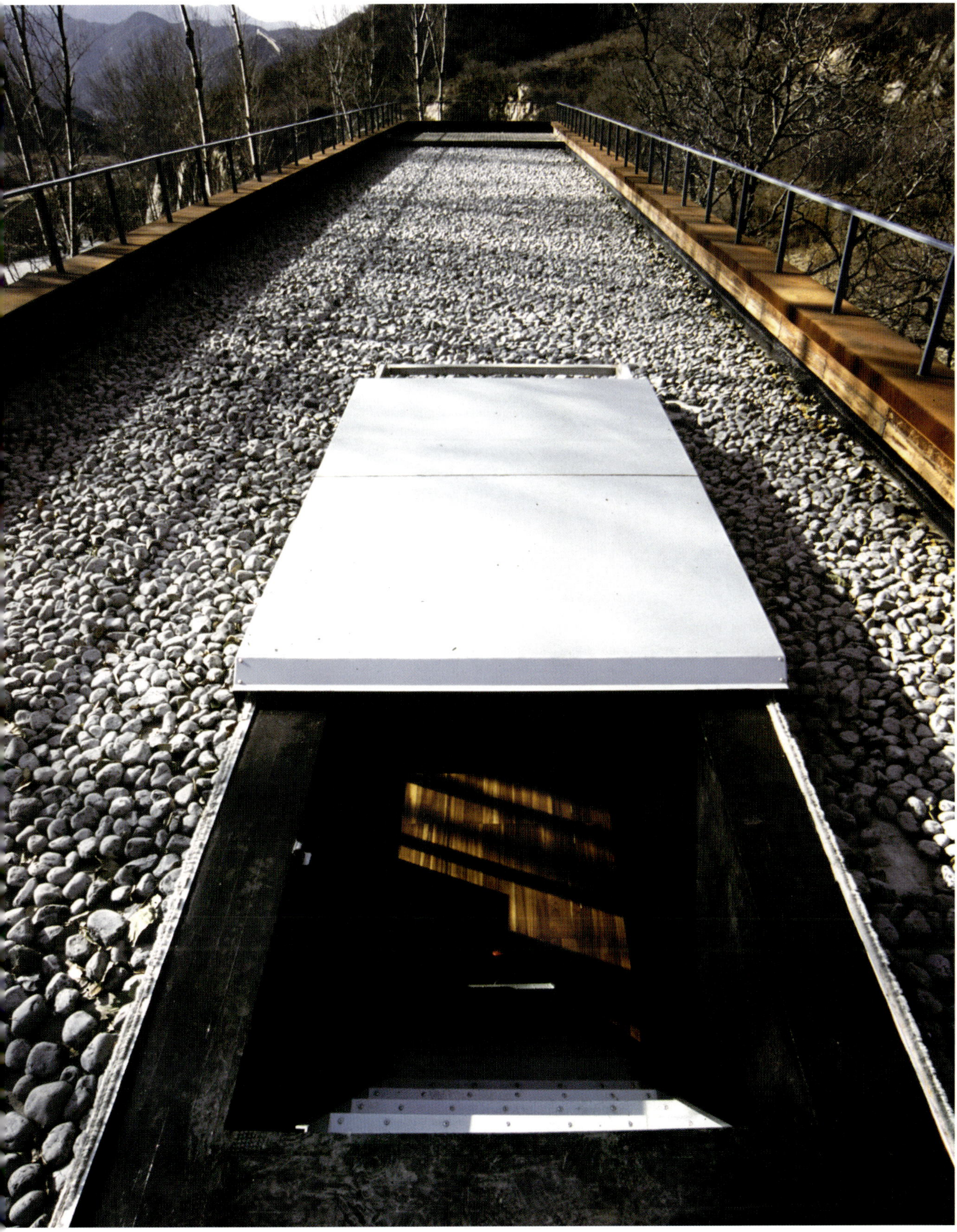

プトニー邸
二重人格の家

トンキン―ズライハーグリア
撮影：パトリック・ビンガム・ホール

PUTNEY HOUSE
double personality

シドニー―オーストラリア―2001

　この表現力に富み、遊び心に満ちた、それでいて落ち着いた雰囲気を持つ古典的な住宅は、周囲の都会的環境のパターン化された受動性と絶交するかのように誇らしげに立っている。住宅はシドニー湾にそそぐパラマッタ川の河岸に位置し、北側の光と南側の影が住宅の形を規定している。それは開放的であると同時に内向的であり、北に向っては微笑み、南に向っては敬虔に頭を垂れる。

As it dares to break with the passivity and uniformity of its urban setting surrounding it, this expressive, playful, contained and classical dwelling proudly rises up. On the banks of the Parramatta River in the Bay of Sydney, the light of the north and the darkness of the south define the duality of its forms, which are both open and timid, as it happily smiles to the north and politely bows to the south.

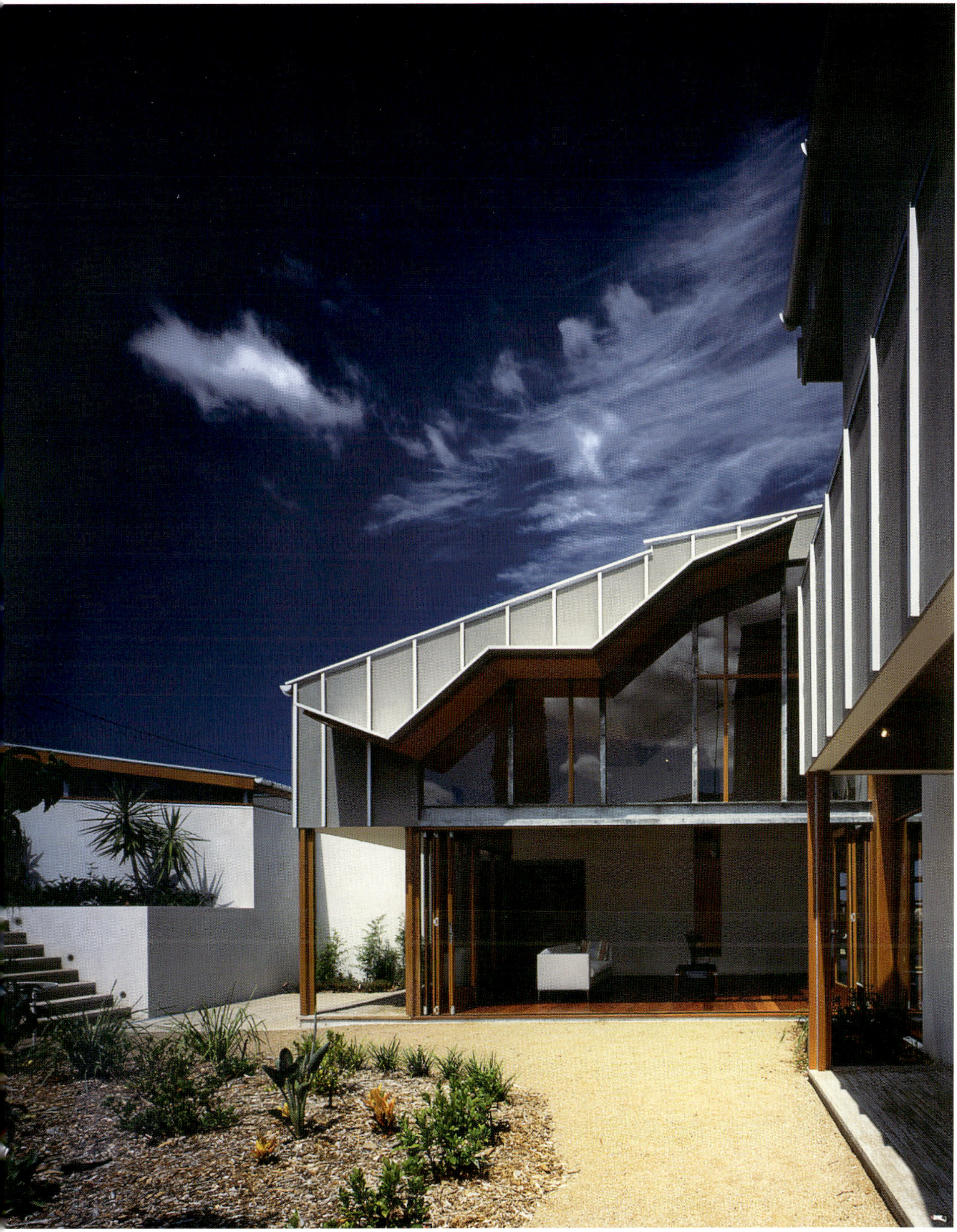

さまざまなタイプのリビングルームが、河岸の北側に立つこの家を統一する中庭に向って開かれており、その最大のものは2階吹き抜けになっている。住宅南側には3つの玄関ホールがあり、訪問客は昔風の別荘に来たような感覚を持つ。裏玄関ともいうべき入口からは、玄関フロアを経て、階上の主寝室、スタジオへと向うことができる。

Different living rooms open out onto a courtyard that conforms the house on the north side of the bank, the largest being of double height. The south side affords access to three halls so that one has the sensation of being in a classical villa. A kind of back porch affords access to the floor above where the main bedrooms and studio can be found.

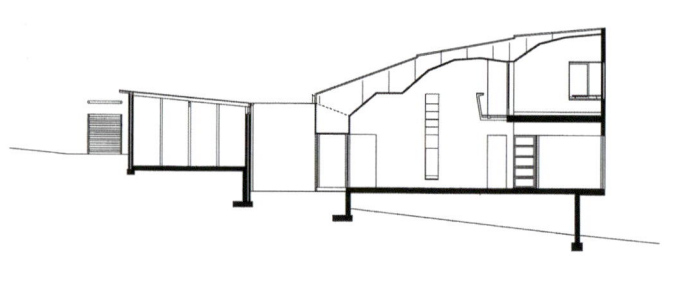

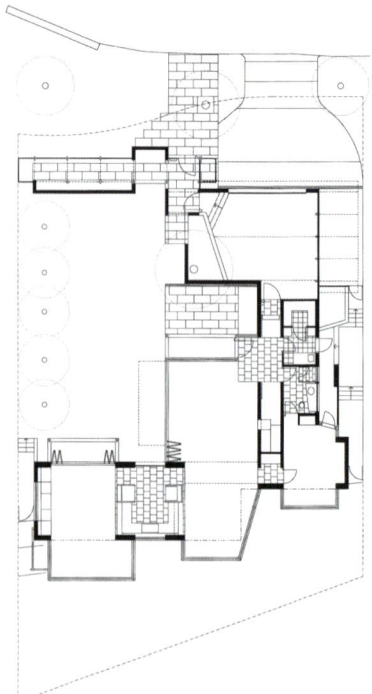

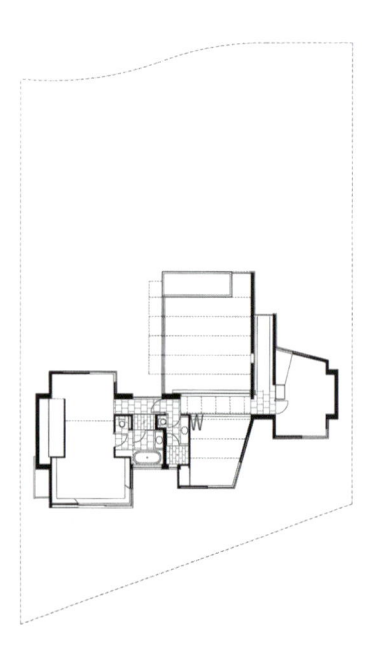

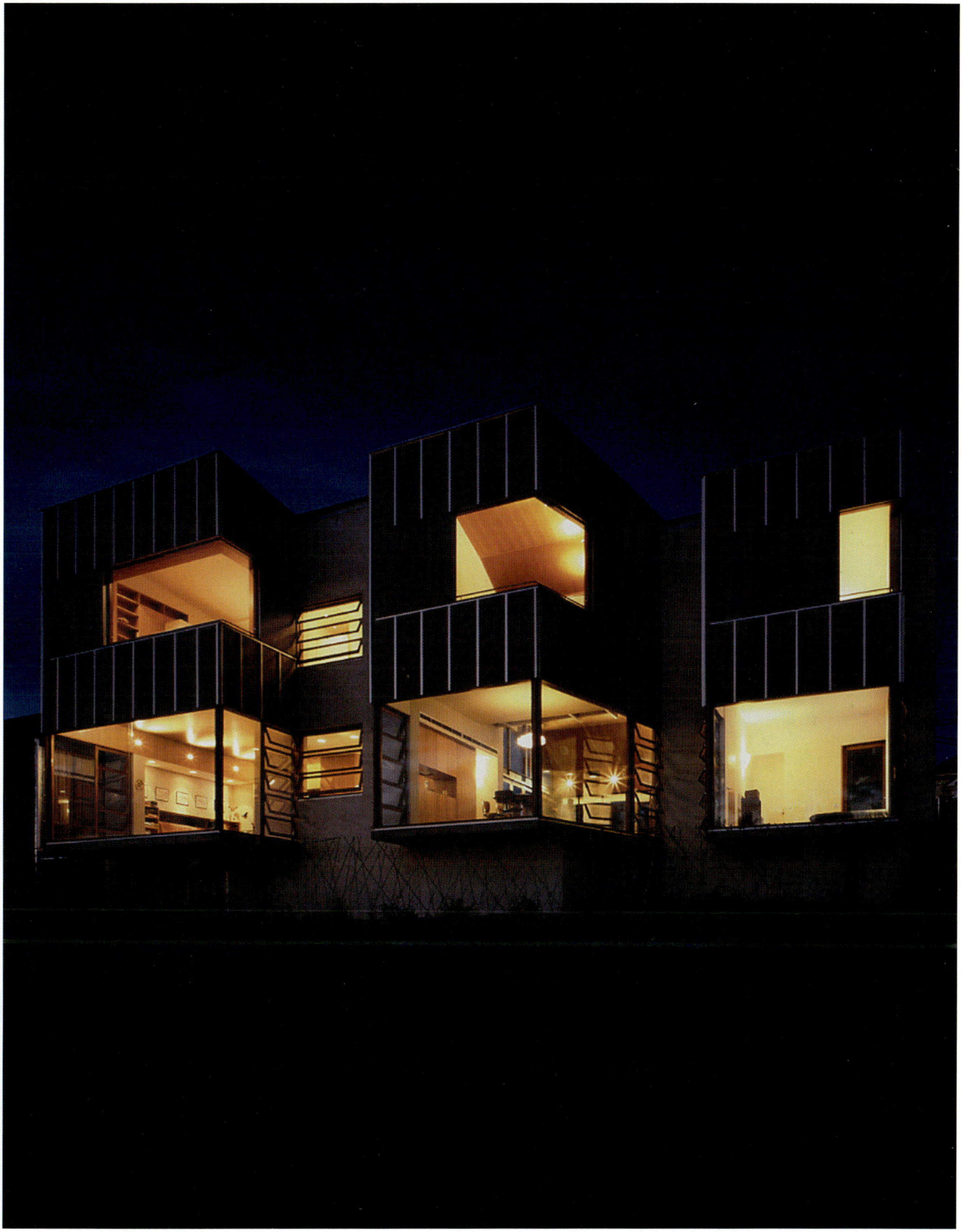

北側に面した屋根は三角形を基調に構成されており、南側のまっすぐ水平な線で統一されたファサードとは好対照をなしている。木の葺き材によって覆われた天空を指さすように造形された屋根の頂きが、この家に安らかな日影を与えている。壁は開け放たれ、精巧にしつらえられた枠のないガラス窓を通して、室内にいながら魅力的な外界の景色を心ゆくまで堪能することができる。

The roof facing the north draws triangles which contrast with the straight, uniform horizontalness of the opposite facade. The vertexes pointing up drawn by the wood-clad roof grant the home shade. Frameless windows subtly placed in the walls allow the exterior landscape scenes to be enjoyed by captivating gazes from within.

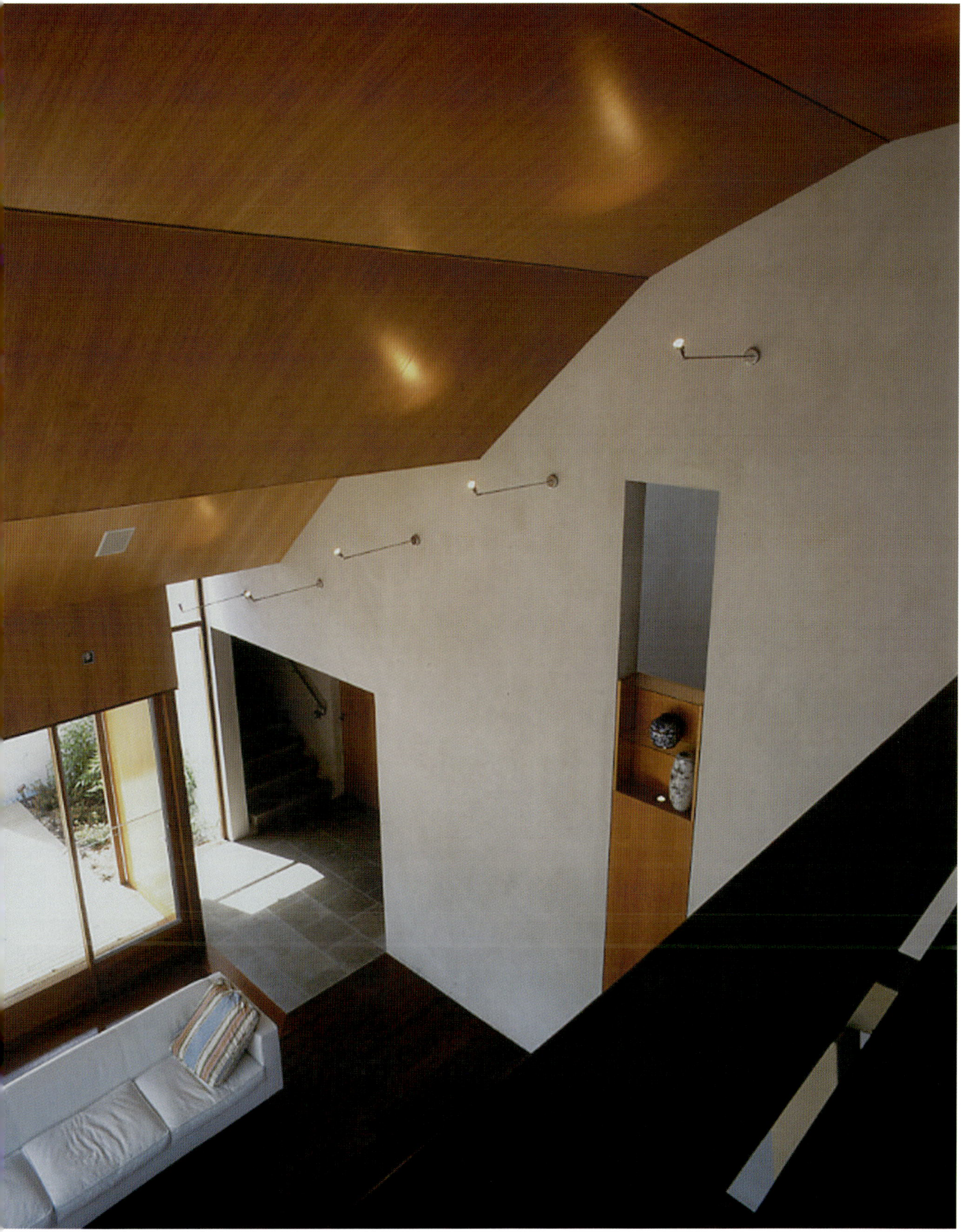

プレヌフ・ヴァル・アンドレの住宅
存在と不在の間で

MAISON PLÉNEUF-VAL-ANDRÉ
between presence and absence

ドーフレスヌ, ル・ギャレ・エ・アソシエ
共同設計：エコーボア, ギルデ・ダラス
撮影：スティーブン・ルーカス

イトゥ―フランス―2002

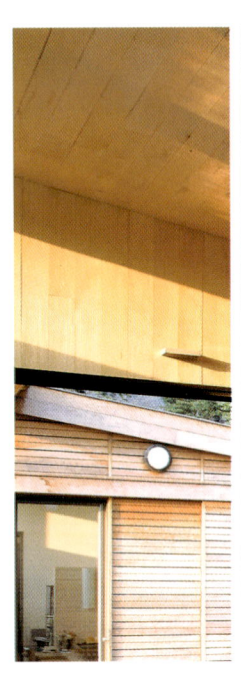

　建物は2つの様相を持つことを求められた。1つはゲストハウスで、控え目でありながらそれ自身完結したプロジェクトでなければならなかった。もう1つは主たる居住部分を含むもので、さらに完全性が求められた。建物は、2つのボリュームに分かたれているが、それにもかかわらず、相互に依存しながら真に1つの統一された外観を保持している。地面の上に浮かぶプラットホームのようなテラスがハブとなって両者を結んでいる。

Undertaken in two phases, first was the guest house, a discreet yet no less complete project. Phase two was the more complete project involving the main residence. Nonetheless, the two buildings really can be seen as one unitary project of mutual interdependence where the terrace, a kind of platform atop the terrain, is the hub.

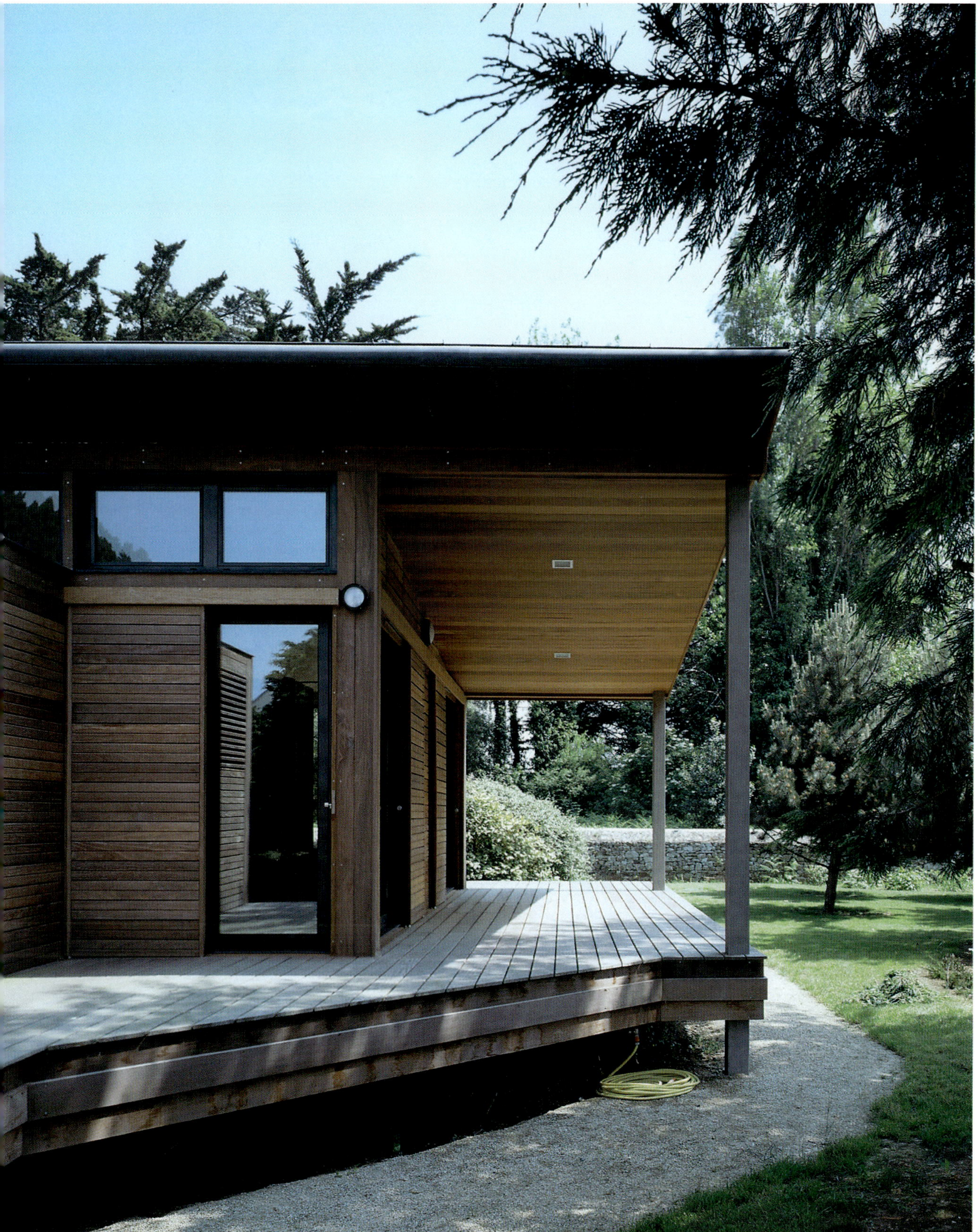

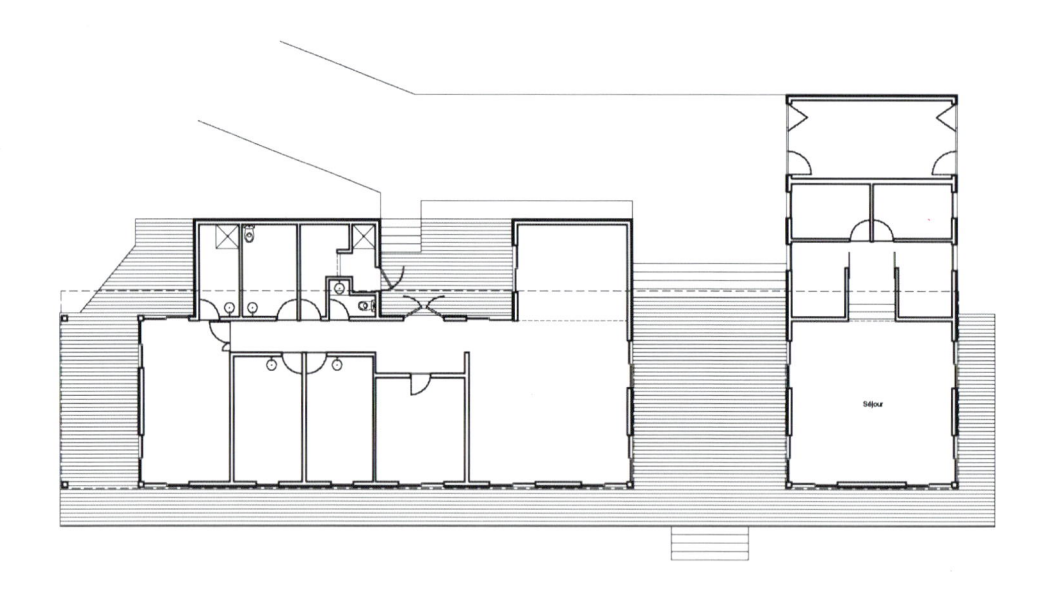

常時使用されない住宅には、ある種のジレンマがある。住人がいるときは、それは周囲の環境に対して開かれ、透過性があり、太陽を室内に招き入れるものでなければならない。一方住人不在のときは、それは外部に対して放棄された家という印象を与えてはならず、同時に外界の作用因子から保護されていなければならない。解は、可変式のファサードにするというものであった。それは自在に開閉することができ、ある時は外界に開かれた透過性を持つ住宅となり、またある時は不可侵の単一な塊、モノリスとなる。

A residence that is not in constant use can pose the following dilemma; when occupied it must open out to the surrounding environment, be permeable and let the sun in. When not in use it should not take on the appearance of being abandoned and should be protected from the outside elements. The solution devised was to have moving facades that could be opened and closed at will so as to afford a permeable, open dwelling, or an impenetrable massive monolith.

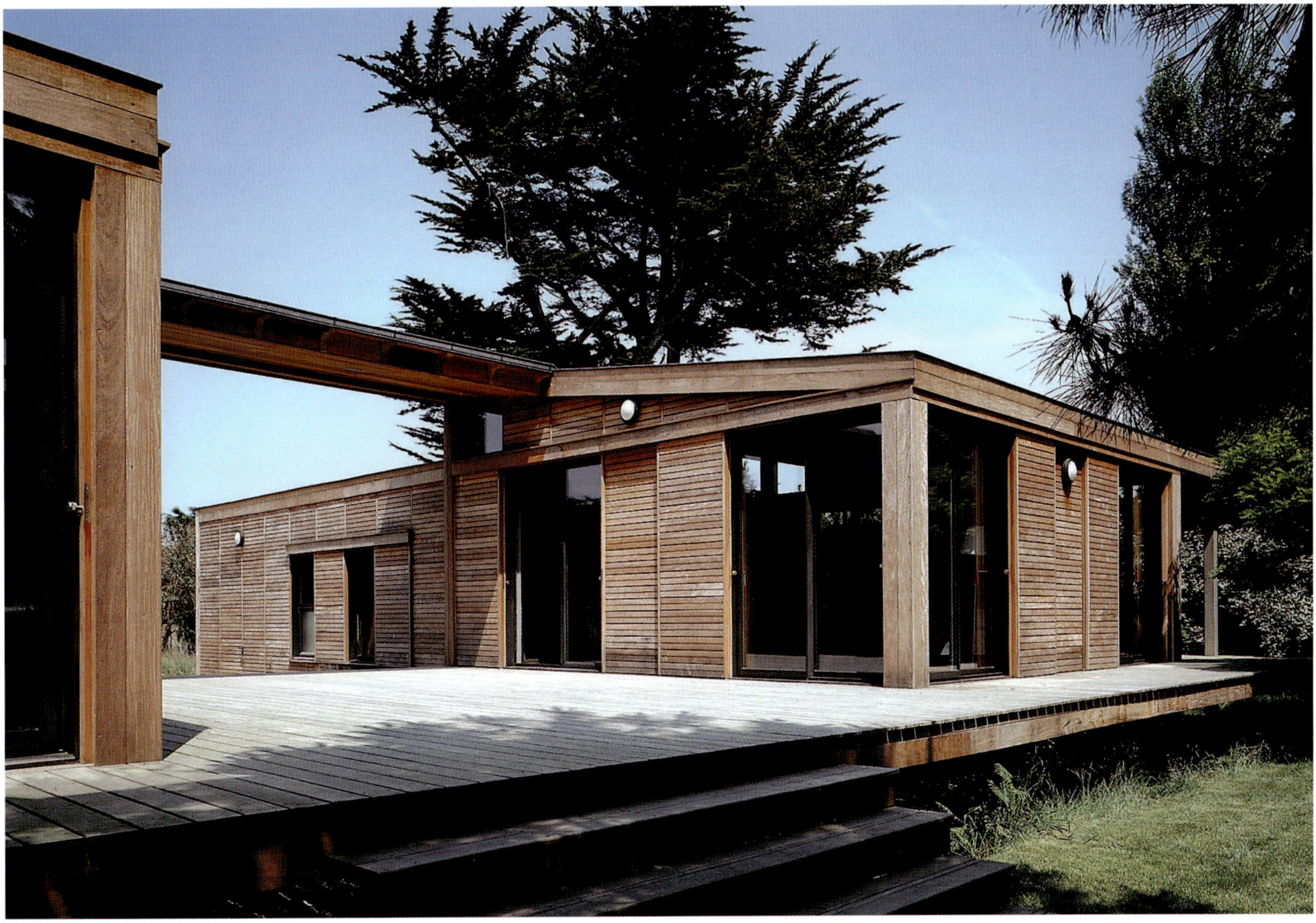

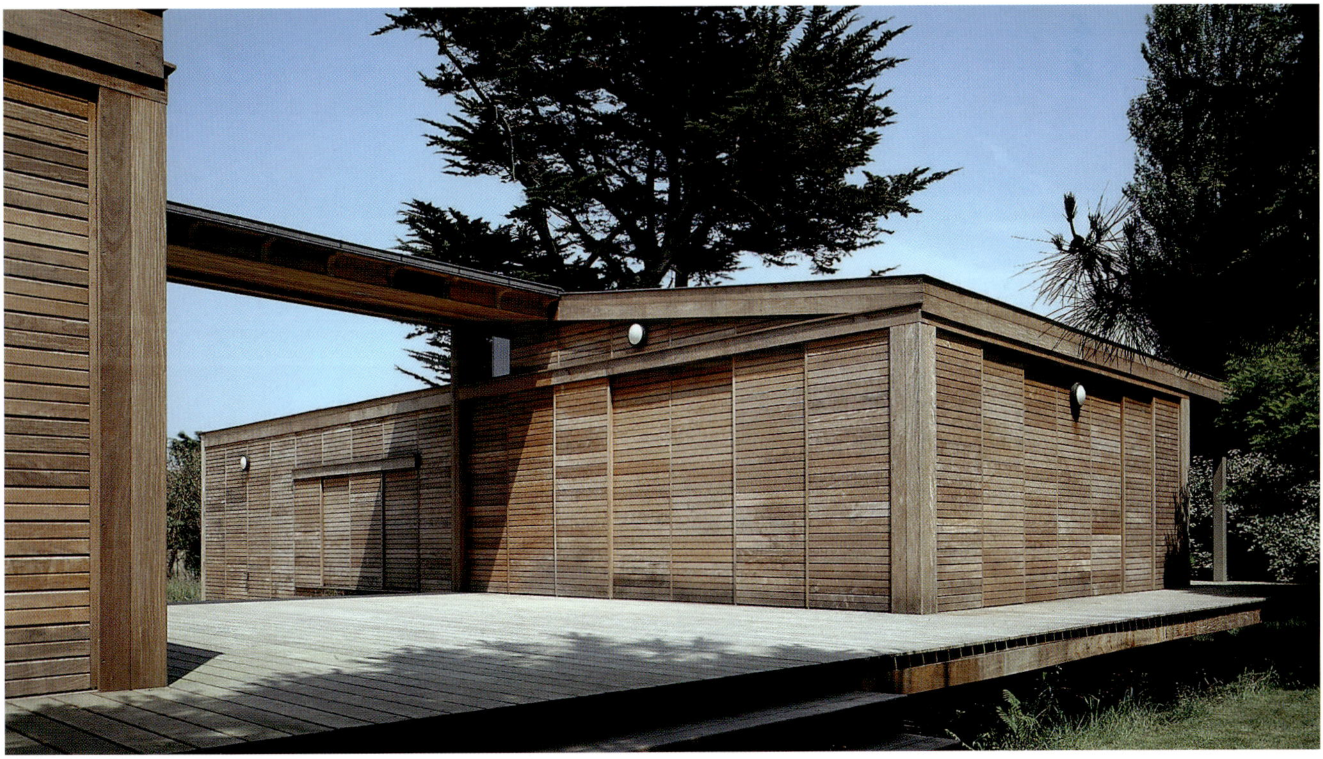

短期間に建設する必要性と、周囲の環境に融合させたいという願いから、住宅にはケルト、ファー、クマロの木材を使用することとした。その結果、非常に調和のとれた美しさが出現した。実用的な観点から、サービスルーム（キッチン、バスルーム）は北向きに、そしてベッドルームとデイルーム、およびテラスは南向きにすることによって、大きな窓を透過してくる日光は、住宅の後部にまで到達することができる。

The need for quick construction and the desire to coalesce the house with its setting dictated the use of kerto, fir and coumarou wood, which resulted in very harmonious aesthetics. With an eye to practicality, the service rooms (the kitchen and bathrooms) are oriented to the north and the bedrooms, the day areas and the terraces to the south so that the light shining in through the large windows can reach to the back of the house.

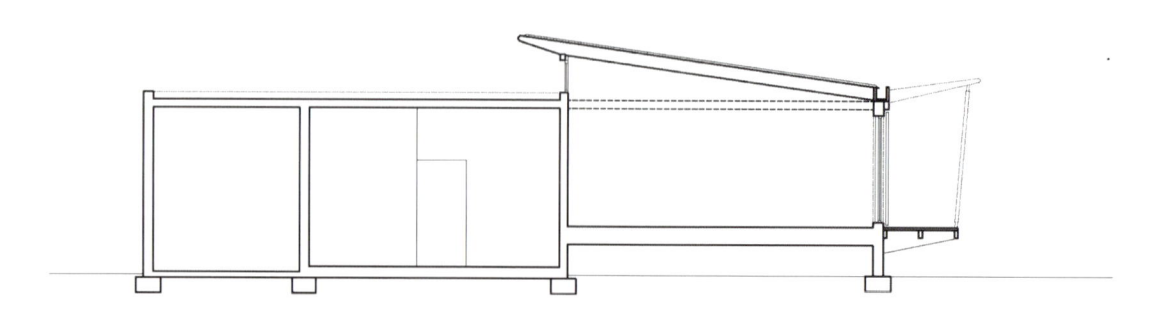

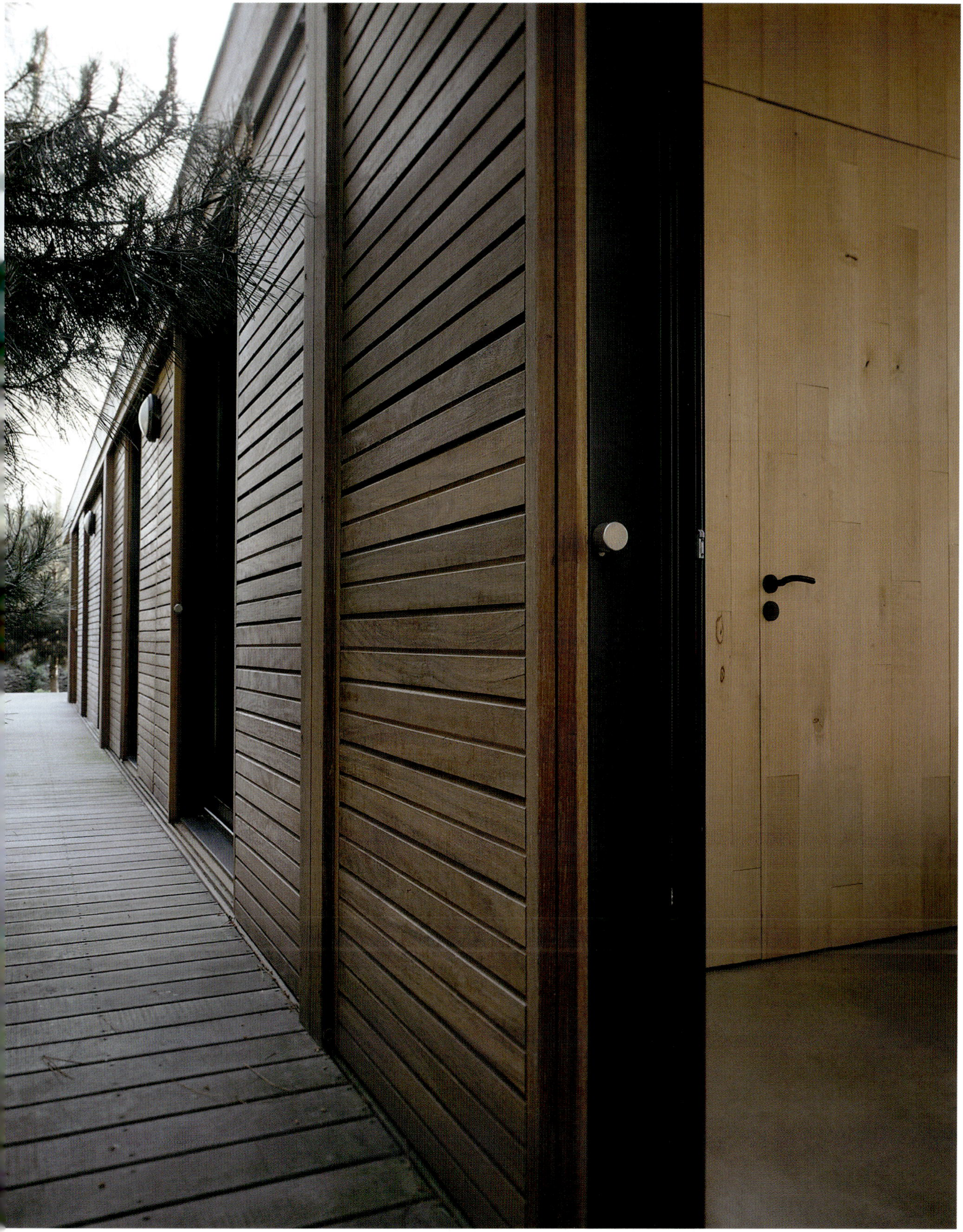

ネンニングの住宅
文脈的でしかも順応性のある家

クックロビッツーナハバール アーヒテクテン
共同設計：クリスチャン・ムーンズブルガー，
サスキア・ジェーガー，マルカス・クックロビッツ
撮影：ハンスピーター・シース フォトグラフィ

HAUS NENNING
contextual and adaptable

ヒッティサウ―スイス―2002

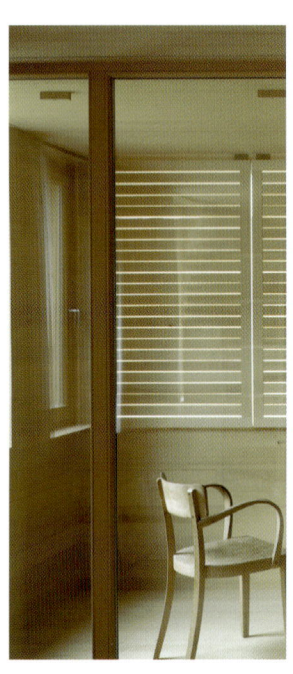

　大工が自宅として自ら建築したその住宅は、村のメインストリート沿い、教会の隣りにひっそりとたたずんでいる。3階建てになっており、1階には小さな店と共有スペース、そして通路がある。その上の2、3階は南向きになっており、家族の住居部分になっている。吹き抜け階段で仕切られた北向きの部分には、家族のさまざまな世代が住まうための、独立した、しかし統合されている部屋がある。

Built by and for a carpenter, the building sits alone next to the church on the main street of a village. The plan includes three floors. The ground floor has a small shop and common areas and accesses. The two floors above, oriented towards the south, house the family residence. Facing the north separated by the stairwell, there is an independent yet integrated apartment for housing different generations of the family.

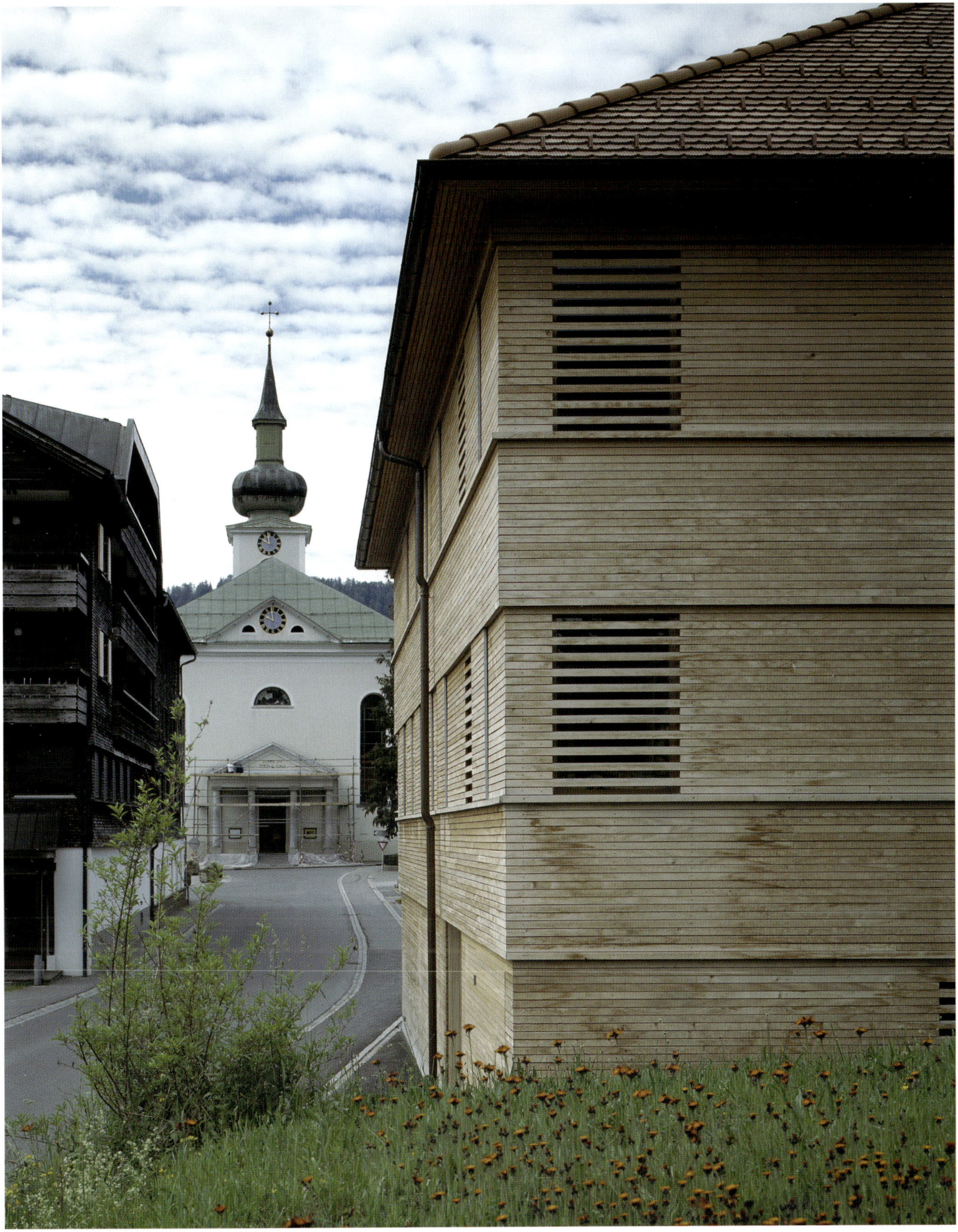

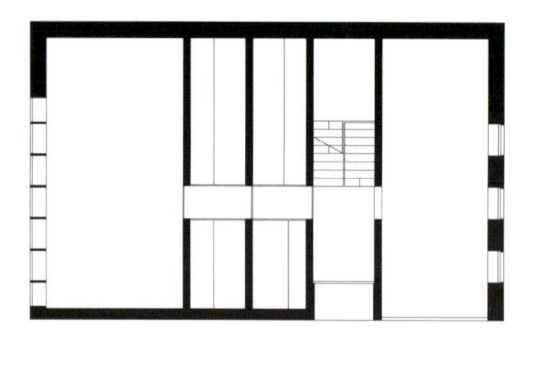

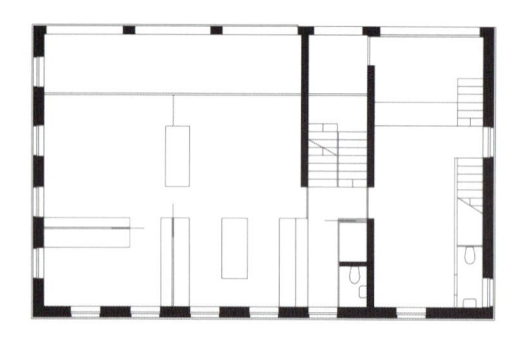

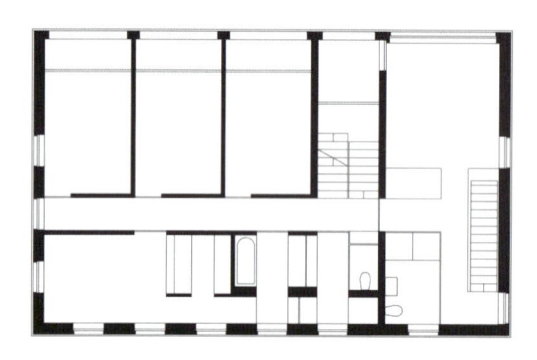

ファサードのわずかな変化とスライド式のよろい戸によって、住宅は厳酷な気候から防護されている。格調高い構成とディテールの美しさ、そして何よりも建築材料に無垢材を使用することによって、この住宅は独特の気高さを漂わせている。よろい戸をスライドさせるだけで、簡単に開口部の大きさを変えることができる。

The slight variations on the facade and the sliding shutters afford protection from the inclemency of the weather. The house acquires a distinct flavor thanks to details in the formal composition and to the use of solid wood in the construction. Variations in the size of the openings are easily attainable thanks to the sliding shutters.

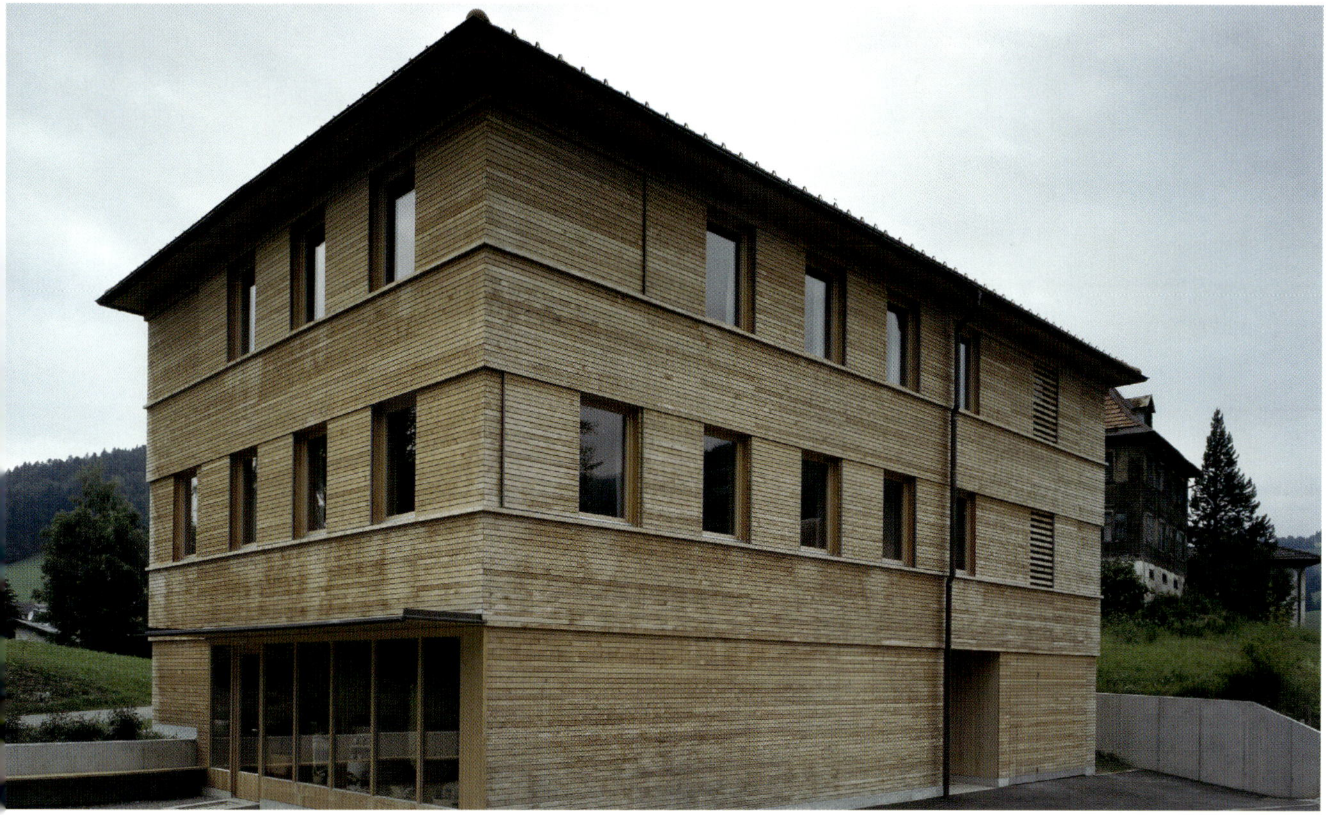

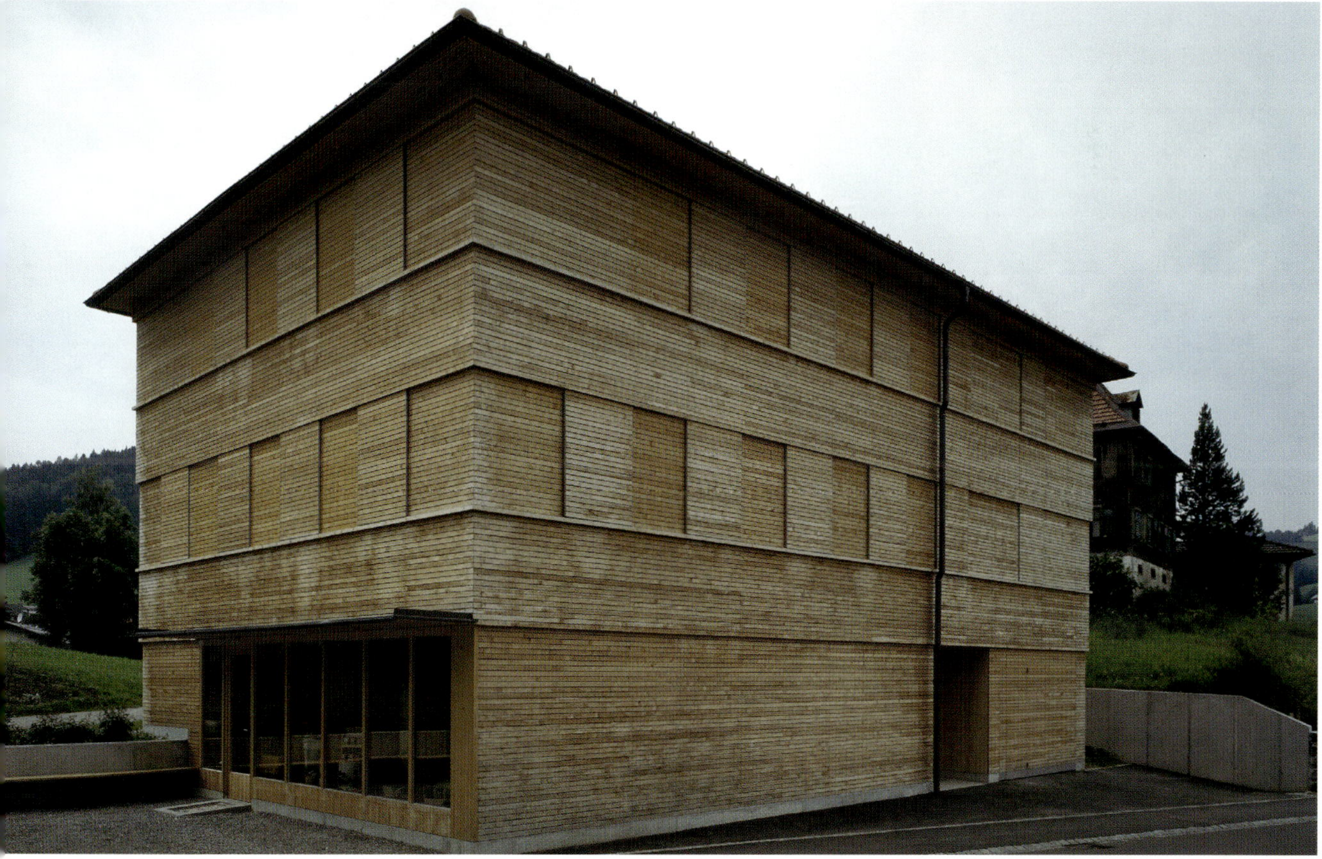

この地域では木造3階建ての住宅はめずらしくないが、この住宅は独自の風格を漂わせながら、しかも決して奢ってはいない。住宅は周囲の環境に美しく溶け込んでいるため、観察者はじっくり鑑賞しようと次に訪れたときに初めてその本当の美しさに心打たれる。

Though the three-story wood house is typical of this area, the house evokes unique character but without being brazen. The house fits in beautifully with its setting and is only striking if the observer decides to contemplate it for a second time.

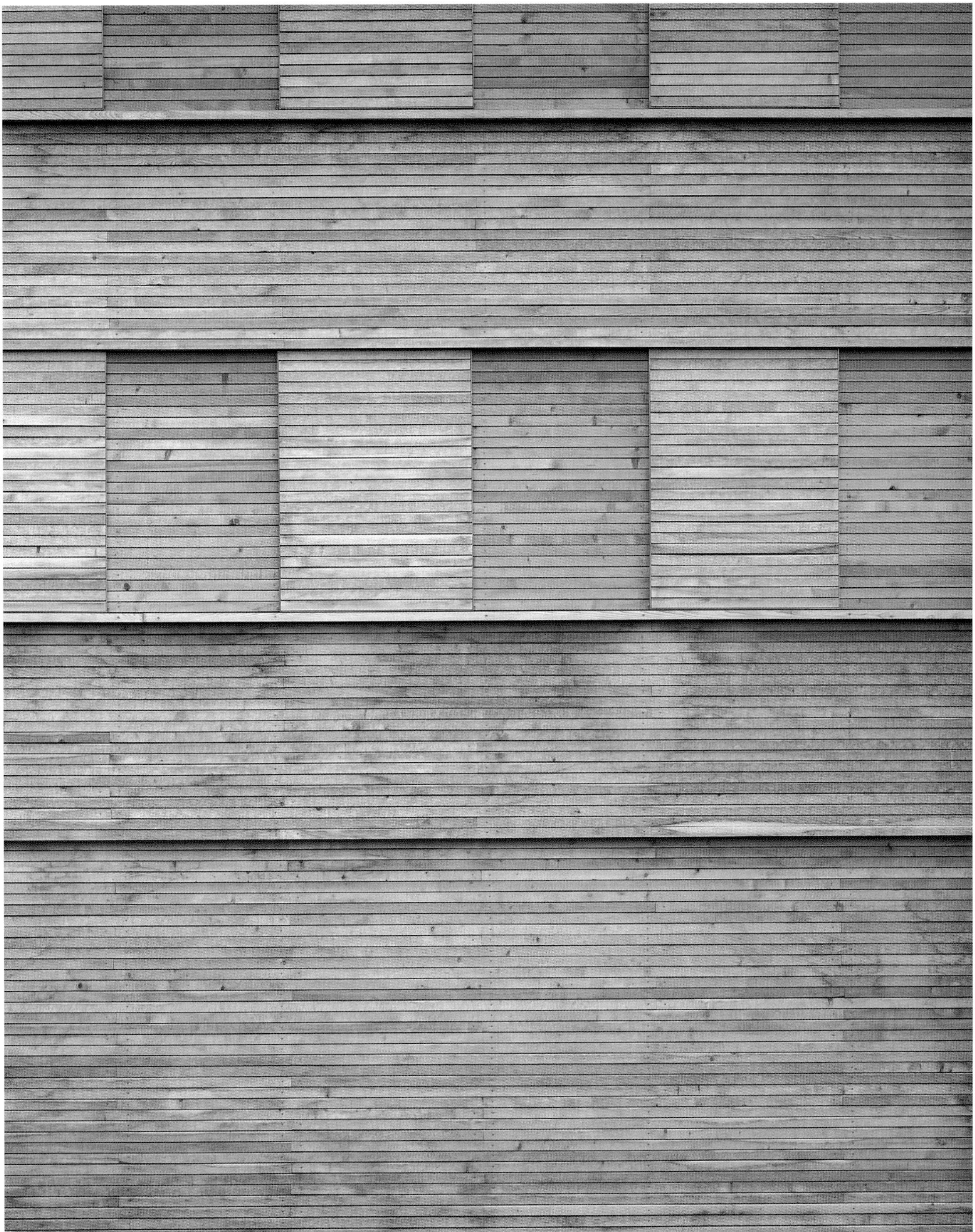

03

Expert Wood

There are occasions when the designer and the woodworker join hands and the fruit of this collaboration are projects where both space and the materials are dealt with, with the same expertise and delicateness. Though sited at very different places, the execution of the following four projects reflects the aforementioned because they have innovated, recuperated or systematized, or simply because they have employed wood in a highly expert way

木材と匠の技

設計者と大工の棟梁が手をたずさえて建築を行う場合がある。そのコラボレーションの成果は、空間と材料の両面から深く掘り下げられ、匠の技と設計の繊細さが結合した建築物である。環境は非常に異なっているが、以下の4つのプロジェクトはどれもこのようなコラボレーションの成果をとてもよく表現している。それらは革新的であり、活力に満ち、合理的である。そして何よりも木材を生かすことにおいて卓越している。

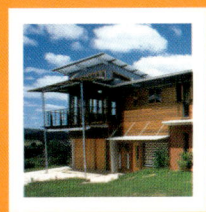

カーサDMAC
材料を知りつくして

ナザール・アーキテクトス
共同設計：ドミンゴ・ゴンザレス，
ホアキム・バラーリン
撮影：ダニエル・ナザール

CASA DMAC
knowing the material

ヴァルロマーネ―バルセロナ―スペイン―2002

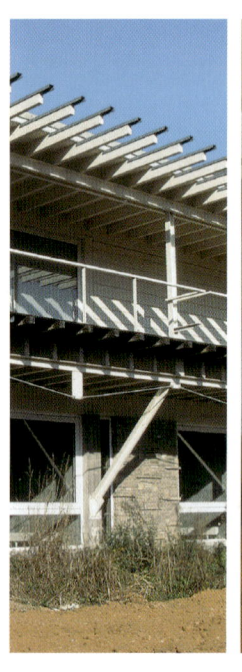

　非常に強い直線指向が見るものの心をとらえる。建物は大地を截然と分界して立ち、南に向けて開かれ、風景と光のなかに浸かっている。背部は北側を向いているが、そこにはただ建物への入口があるだけである。自然の傾斜を利用して建てられているため、入口を入ったところが2階になり、そこがリビングルーム、キッチンなど家族が集うデイエリアになっている。直接大地に接している1階には、プライベートな部屋が並んでいる。

The project is conceived with a very linear orientation in mind. It divides up the terrain and opens out to the south to soak in the vistas and the light, and turns it back on the north, which is only for affording access to it. By taking advantage of a natural slope access is direct to the second floor which is used for the day areas. The bottom floor, in direct contact with the terrain, is then reserved for the more private rooms.

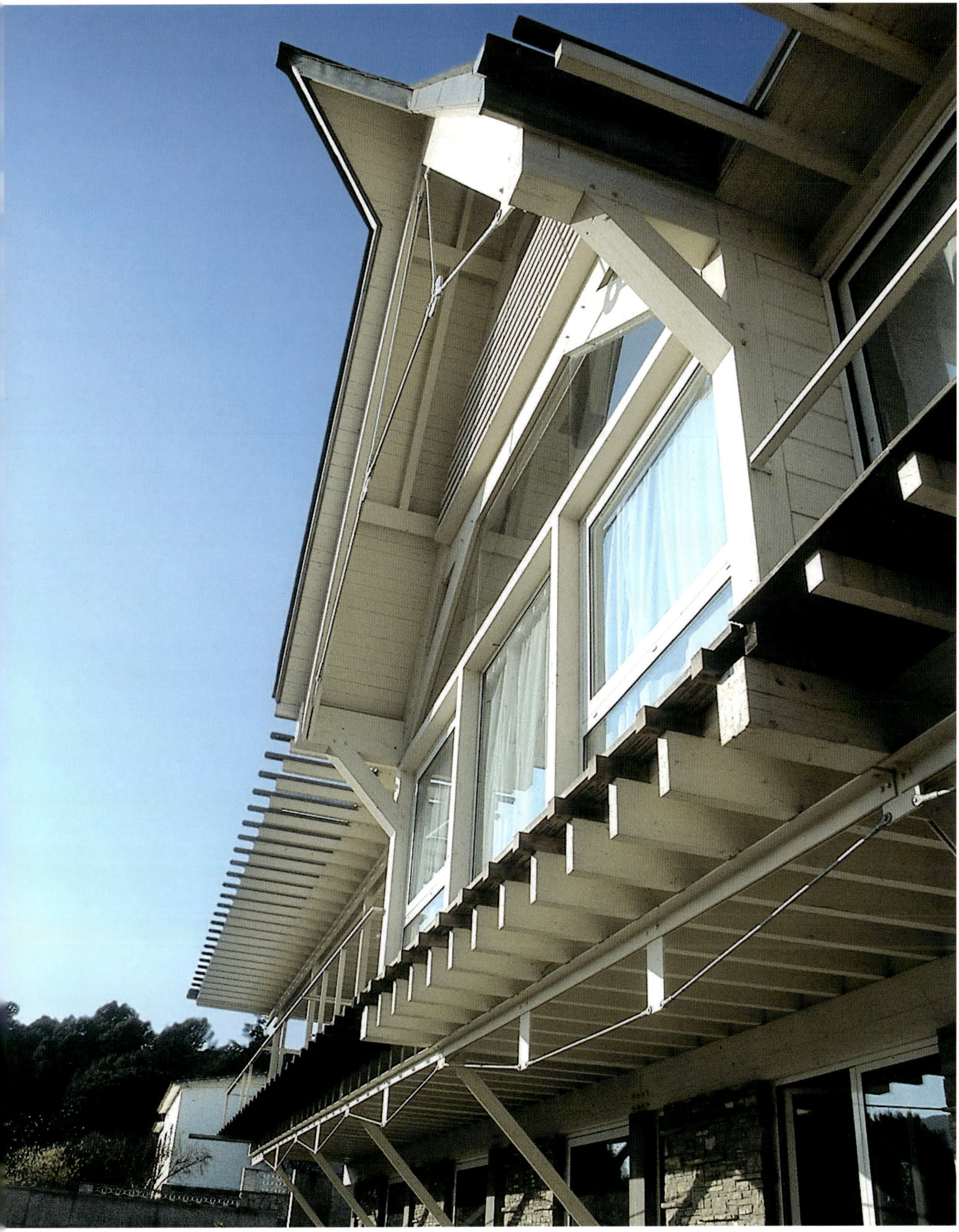

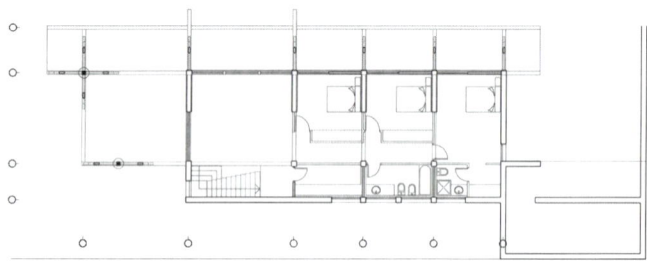

南向きのテラスは、客船のデッキを想起させる。縁甲板と下見板の線が遠近法を作り出し、甲板の上の梁の線をなぞっている。リビングルームがデッキの連続性を断ち切り、ファサード前面まで押し出されている。住居への入口は本石積みの壁に沿うように造られている。その壁は建物と外界を屹然と仕切ってはいるが、正面の外観のせいで、開放的な感じを賦与されている。

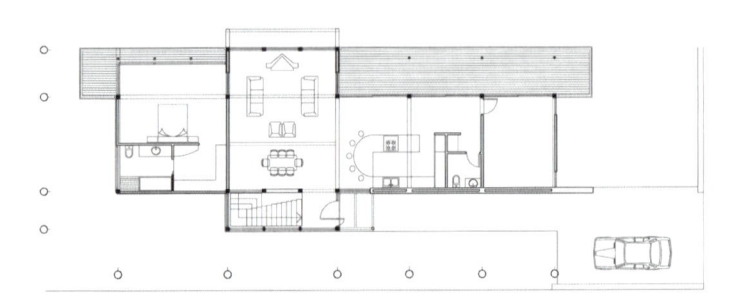

The terrace brings to mind the deck of a ship. The layout of the pavement and the lines on the wall that fade into the distance trace the beams on the ship's deck. The living room stands out on the facade and breaks the continuity of the terrace and the deck. The entrance to the dwelling is parallel to a rough stone wall which delimits the exterior but, thanks to the front, is endowed with an open character.

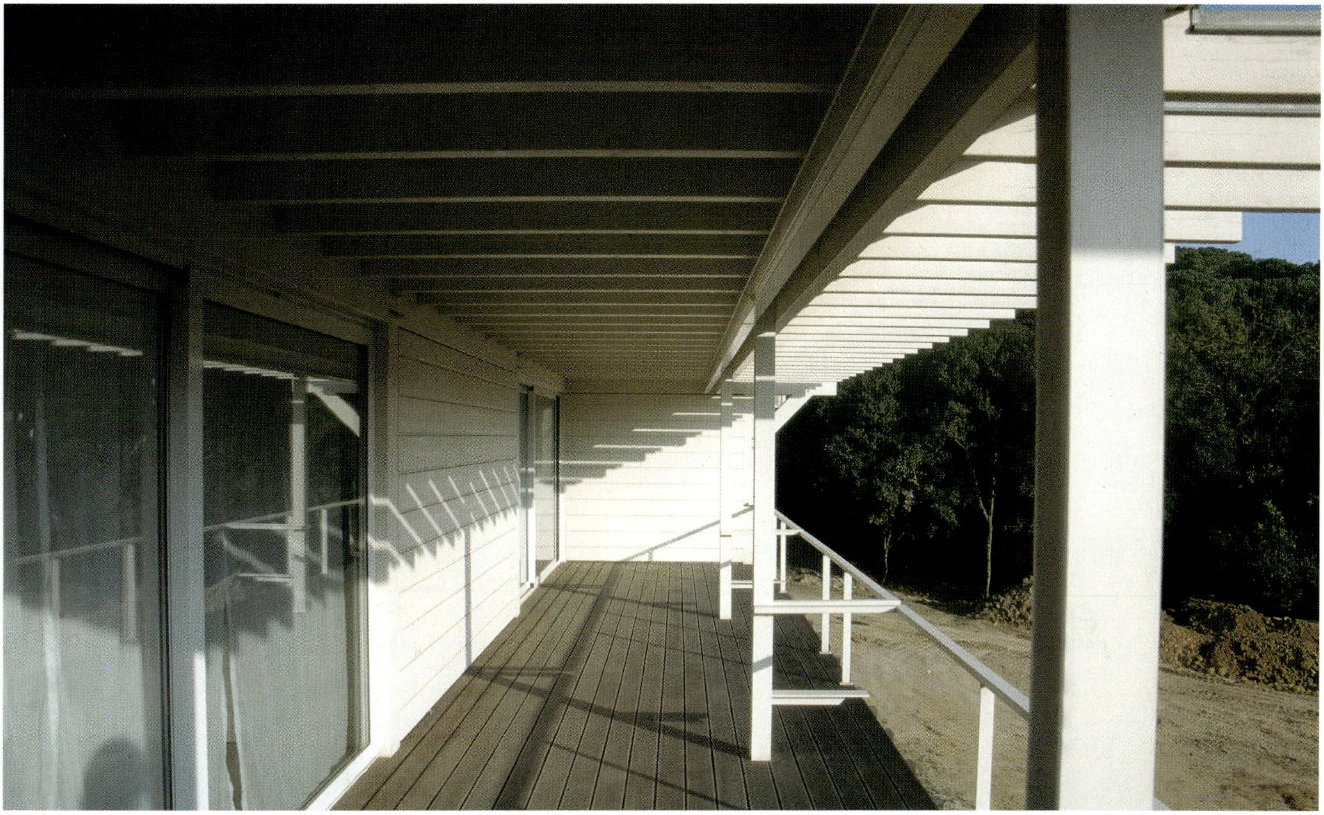

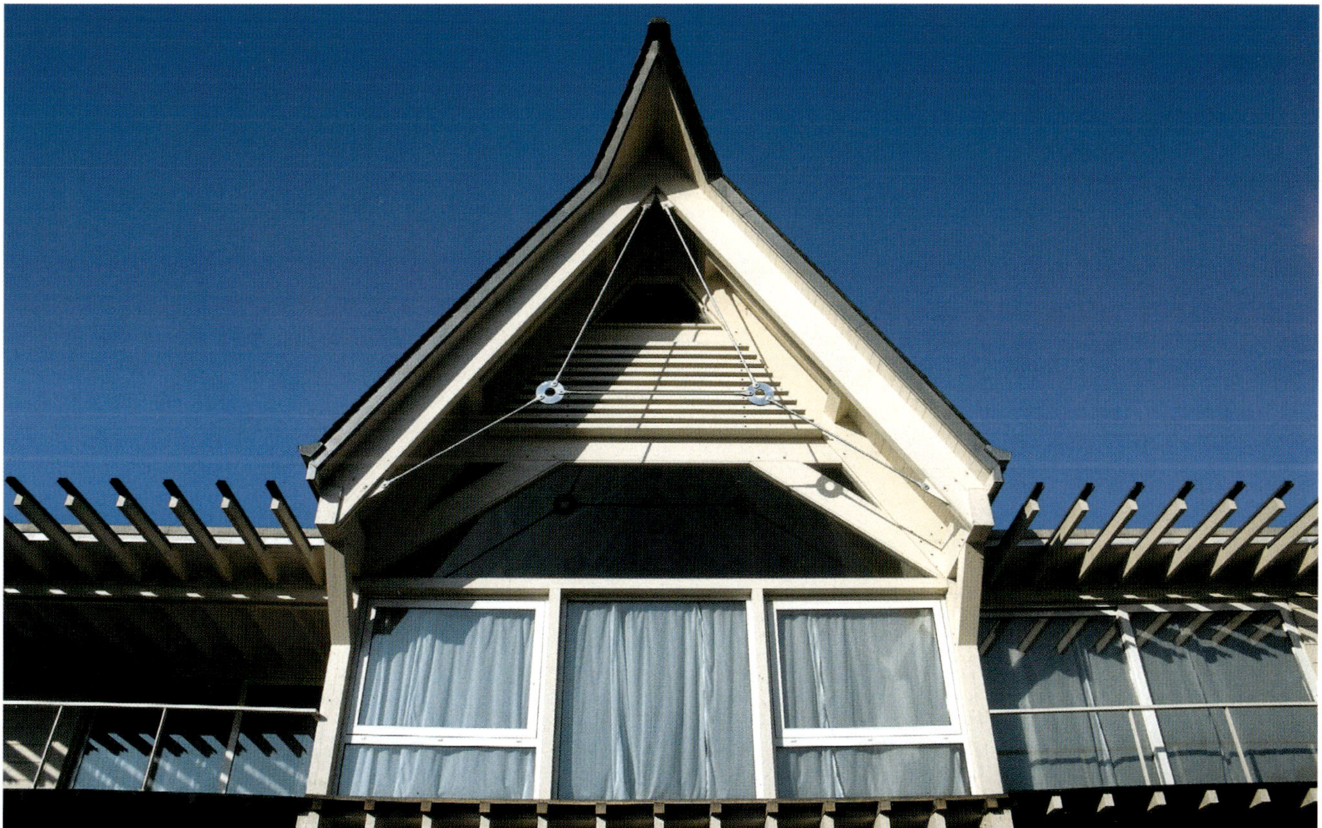

間仕切壁が天井まで達していないことによって、空間の連続性が強調されており、どんなに離れた角からでも屋根小屋組みの壮観な高さを臨むことができる。計算されつくした大梁の位置と、金属性のタイロッドの効果的な使用が、視覚的な興趣を生み出している。金属の構造物を白く塗装し、その上に無垢板を張った階段は、白く塗装したれんがの壁に対して片持ち状に昇っており、木材とれんがという2つの素材を構造的に結び付けている。

The fact that the dividing walls do not reach all the way up to the ceiling highlights the continuity of space and affords ample vision of the roof structure even from the most remote corners. The careful placement of the girders and the striking use of metal tie rods is a delight. The stairs consist of a metal structure painted in white and clad with solid, white-lacquered wood, which is up against a wall of white brick, thus structurally connecting the wood and the bricks.

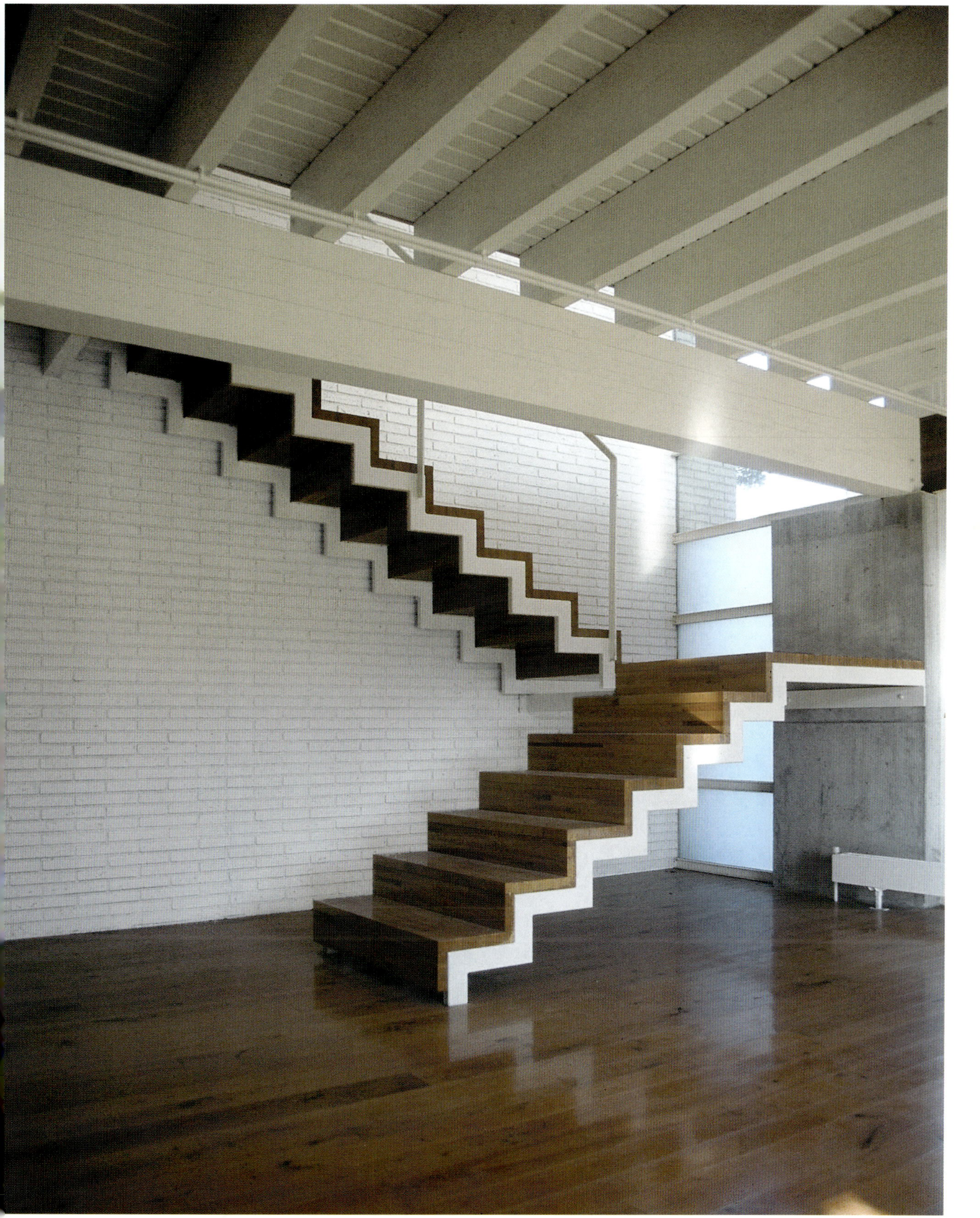

ダニエルソン邸
海に浮かぶ家

ブライアン・マッケイーリヨン アーキテクト
共同設計：トレバー・デイビーズ, ブルーノ・ウェーバー
ダリル・ジョナス
撮影：オンディーヌ・プレール

DANIELSON HOUSE
naval construction

スメルトブルック―ノバスコティア―カナダ―1998

　断崖の淵に立つこの建物は、気象学者の夫と風景画家の妻2人のための住宅で、つましい予算で建設された。孤立、そして純粋に機能的な計画、これは現在ますます広まりつつある人生観、ライフスタイルを表現している。それはわれわれの社会を覆っている日常的な喧騒に対する決然としたアンチテーゼである。

Placed on the edge of a cliff, it was built on a modest budget for a couple in which the man is a meteorologist and the woman a landscape painter. The isolation and the clear functional program are representative of an attitude and a lifestyle that has become ever more popular and is the response to the everyday absurdity of our society.

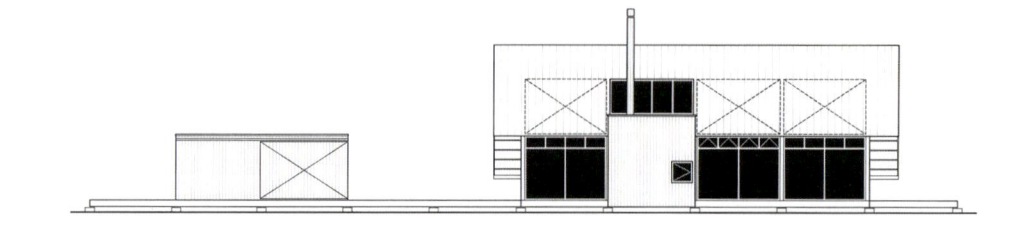

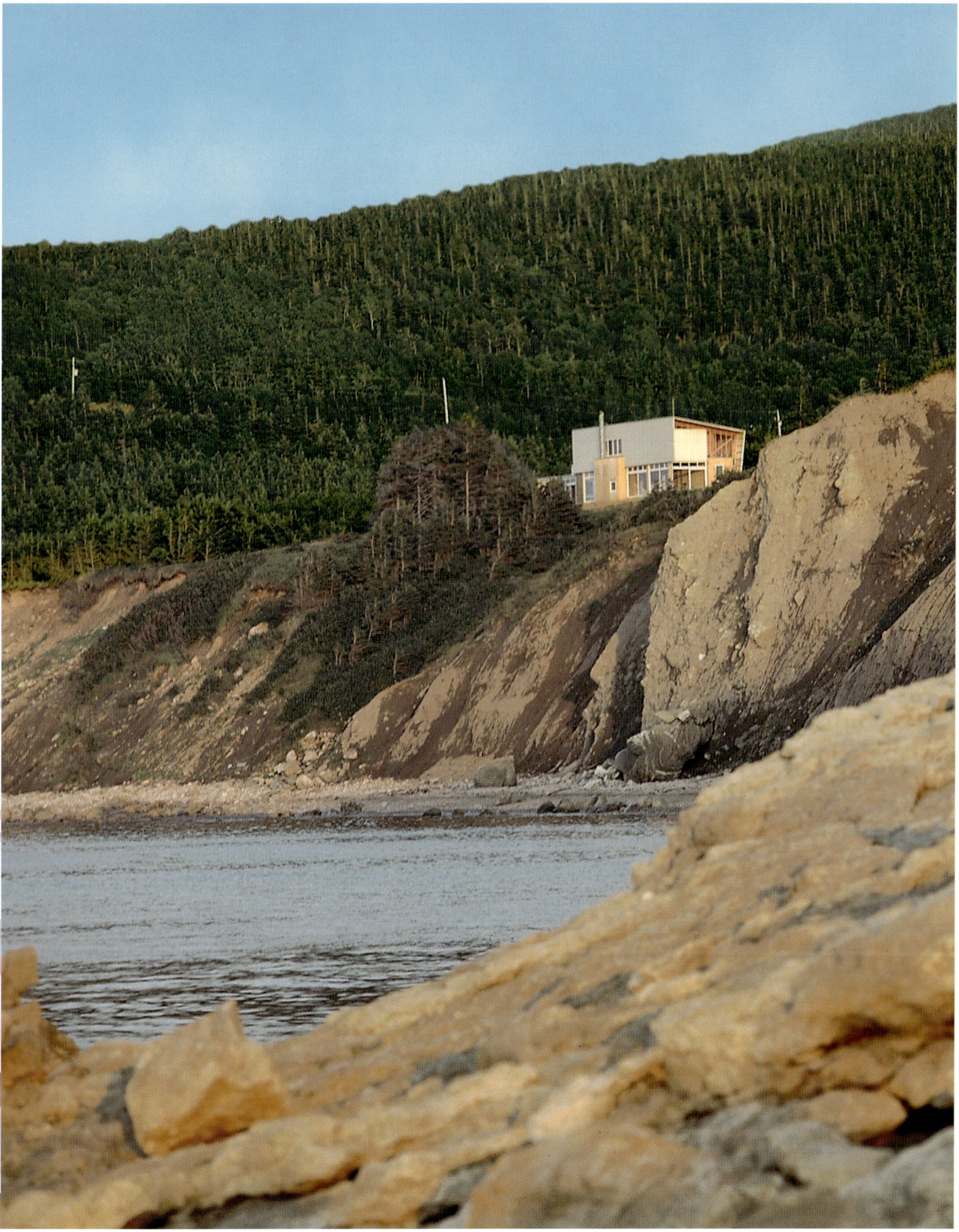

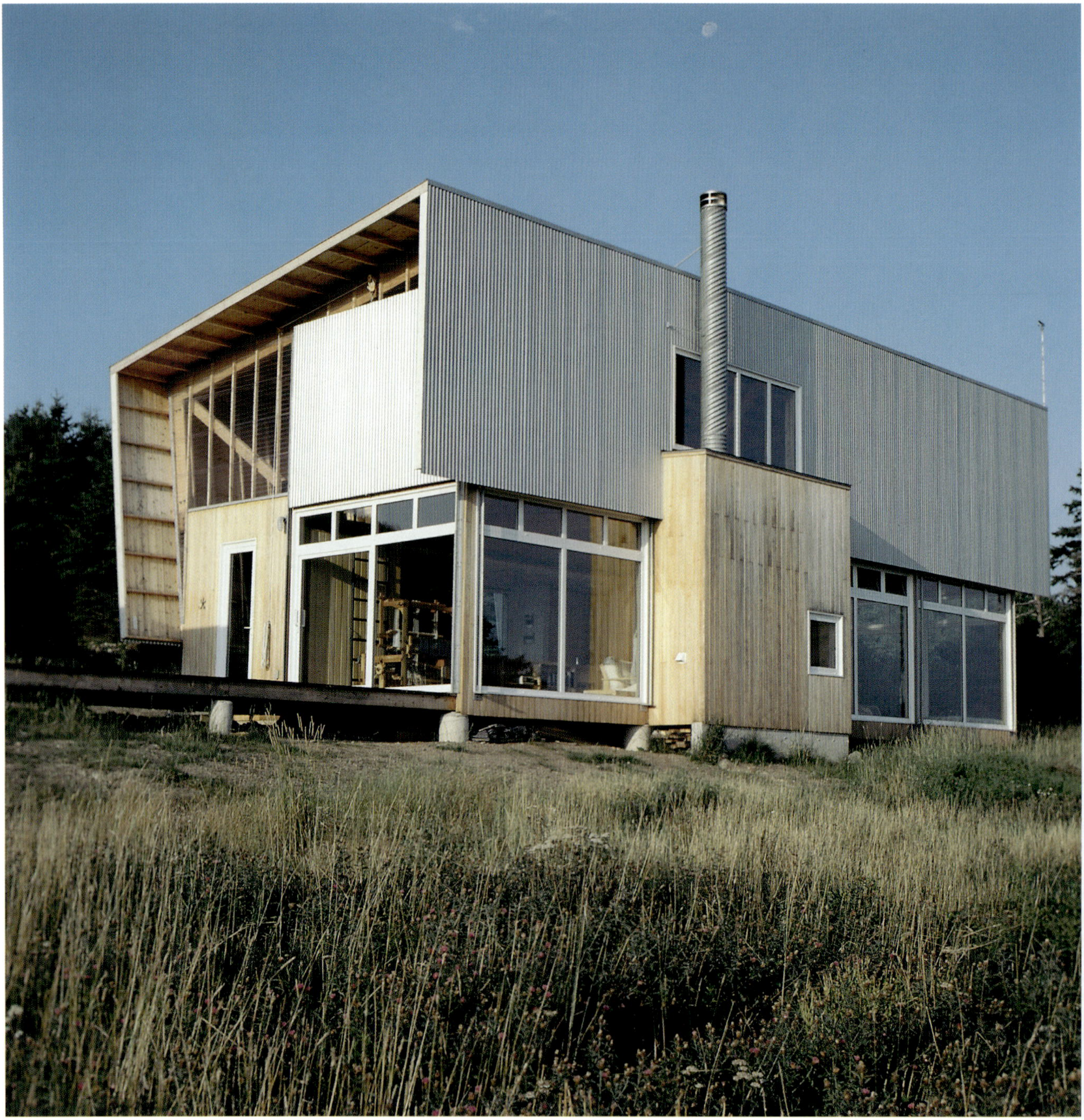

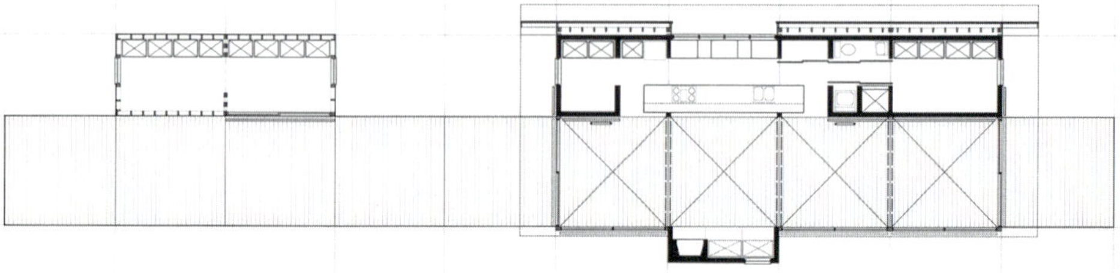

水平線に呼応するように設けられた木のプラットホームの上に、2棟の建物は構築されている。居住棟と供給設備を収納する別棟が並列して建てられているため、その間に広い空間が創りだされている。天気のよい日には、リビングルームの壁が開かれてその空間まで延長され、眺望を独占することができる。

The project consists of two volumes placed atop a wooden platform that establishes a relationship of horizontalness with the sea. The service areas are situated laterally and there is a space between this zone and the other so that when weather permitting, the living areas may be opened to also take advantage of this space.

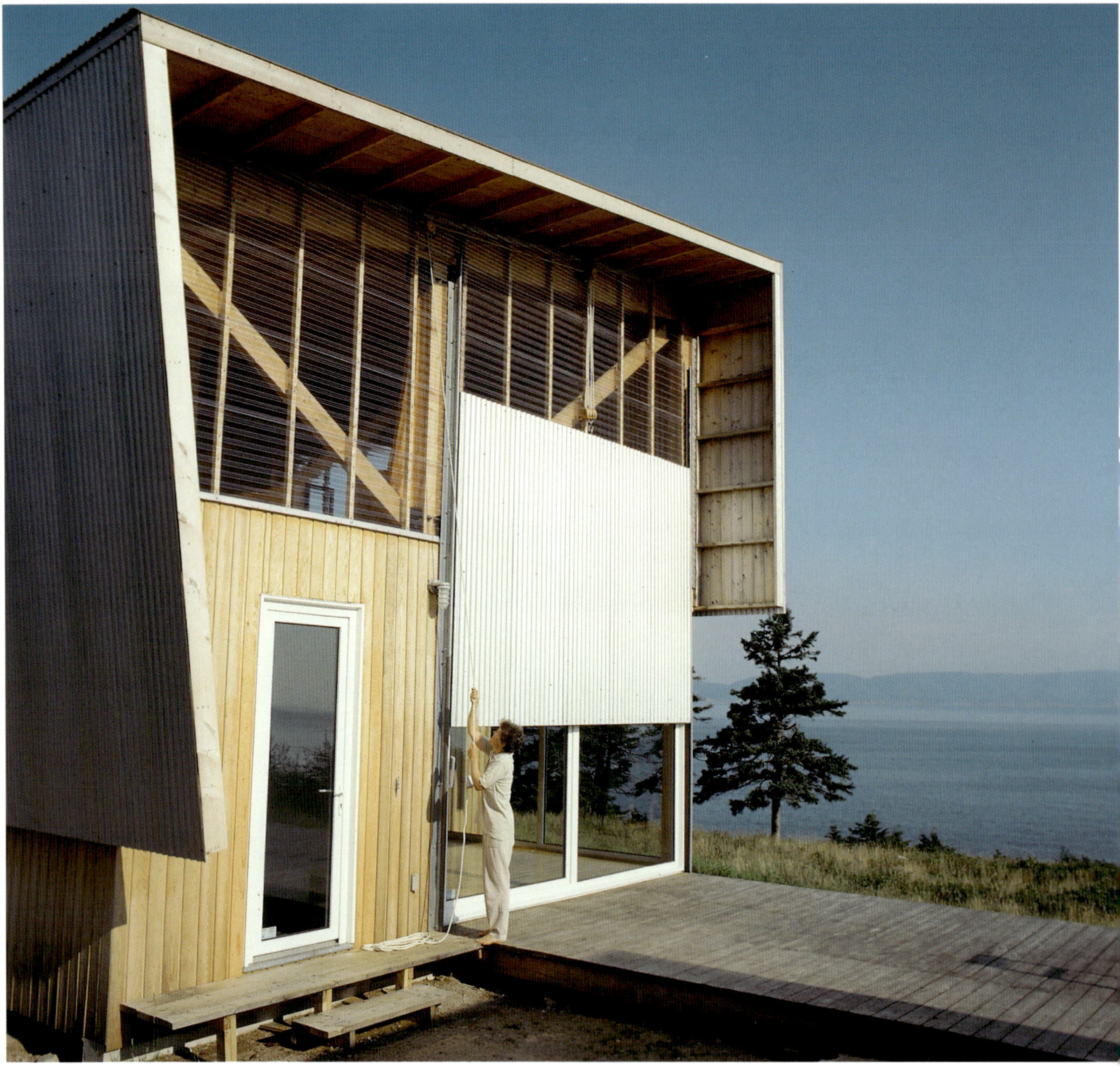

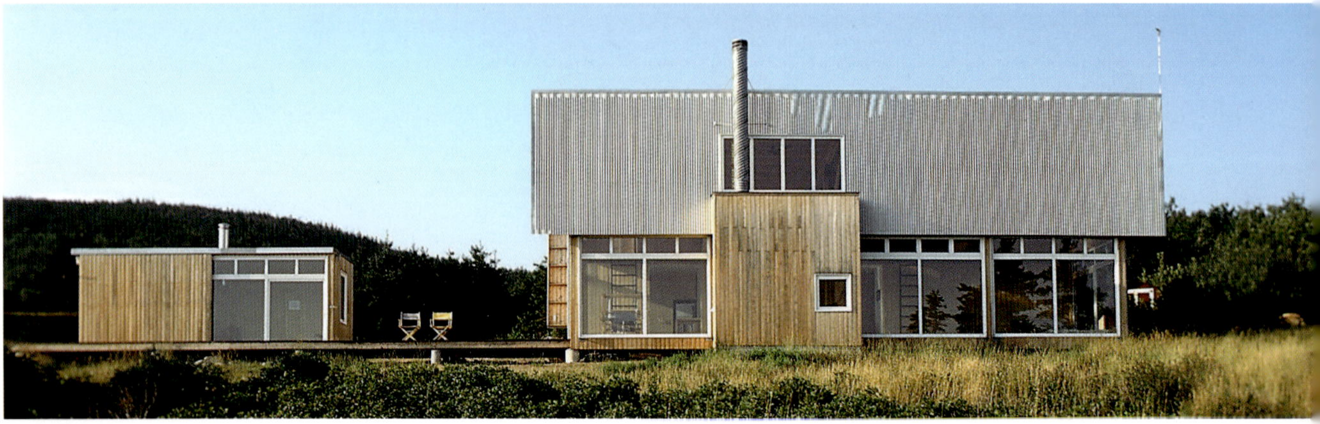

予算を最大限有効に活用するため、できるかぎりプレハブ方式と作業場における組み立てに頼った。積層材の筋かい、さまざまな質感と仕上げを持つ大梁や柱、これらによって表現力に満ちた、独特の美しさが生み出された。建物は軽量で可動式の構造を持ち、客船のように、ある時は大地の上を、またある時は海や氷の上を航行する。

So as to make the most of the available budget, prefabrication and assembly in the workshop are profusely used. Likewise, laminated wood cross-sections, and wooden girders and pillars with diverse textures and finishes confer it a high degree of aesthetic expressiveness. The result is a building that is like a vessel with a light and mobile structure whose habitat could be the land, the water or the ice.

マウントヴュー・レジデンス
よみがえった環境

JMA アーキテクツ QLD
共同設計：ジョー・ケース，スティーヴ・ガスリー
撮影：ジョン・メインワーニング，ピーター・ハイアット

MOUNTVIEW RESIDENCE
recuperated environment

ケニルワース―サンシャインコースト―オーストラリア―2001

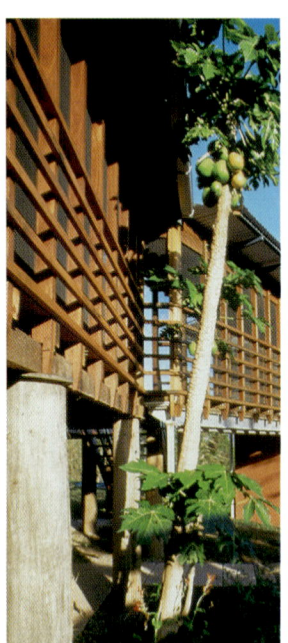

　建物は、過ぎ去りし日の生活様式と、消滅することを拒否した風景のパラダイムの再解釈である。全体はいくつかの建物によって構成されており、あるものは新たに建てられ、あるものは改修され、かつての植民地時代の聚落をほぼ忠実に再現するイメージが生み出されている。さまざまな断片が大地の上に行き当たりばったりに置かれているように見えるが、これは樹木と地形を尊重し、周囲の環境と一体化するためである。

Mountview is the reinterpretation of a way of life of bygone years and the paradigm of a landscape that refuses to disappear. The project consists of the construction and remodeling of several buildings so as to convey an image akin to a rural colony where the different pieces are placed on the terrain haphazardly, so as to respect the trees and topography and to coalesce with the site.

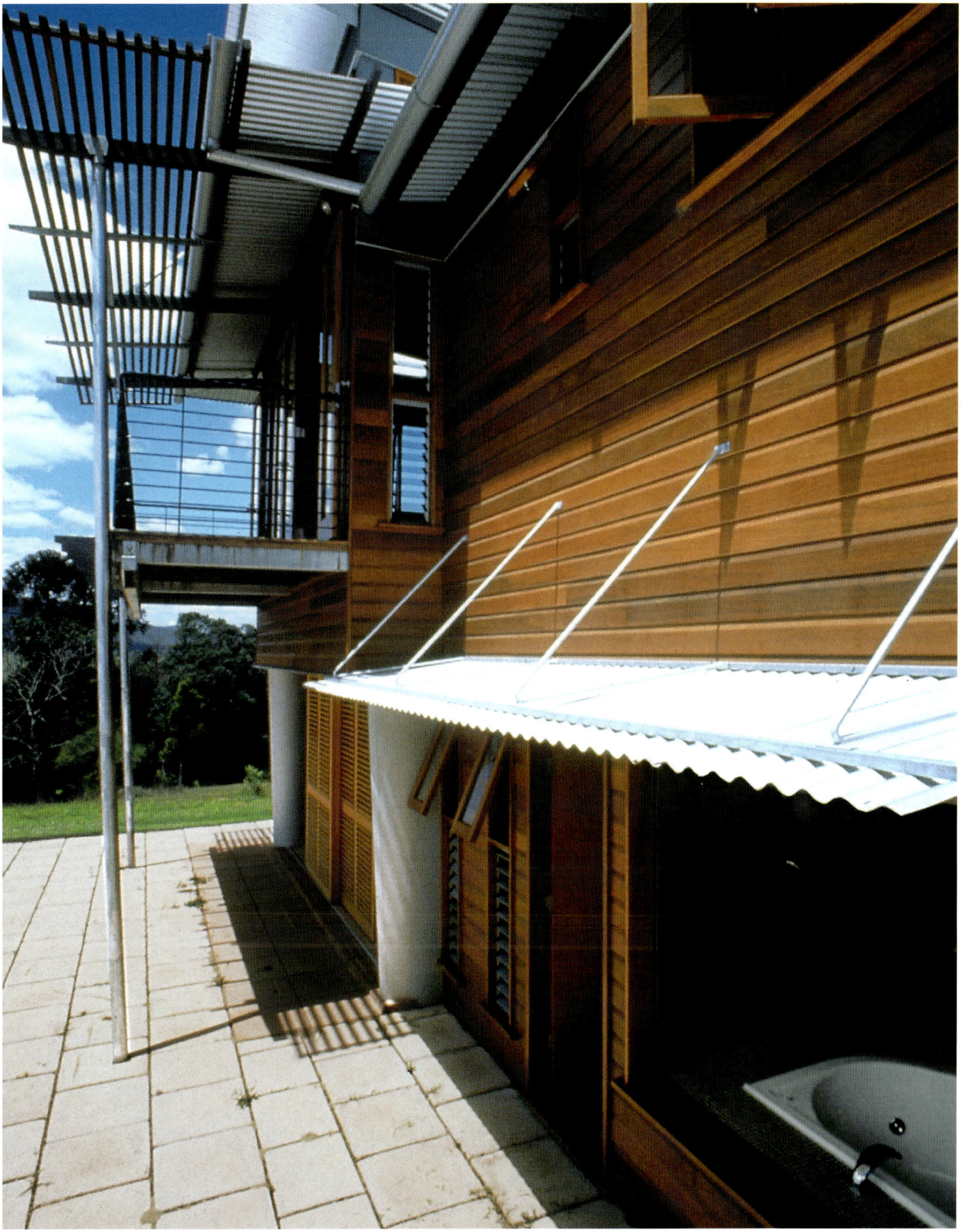

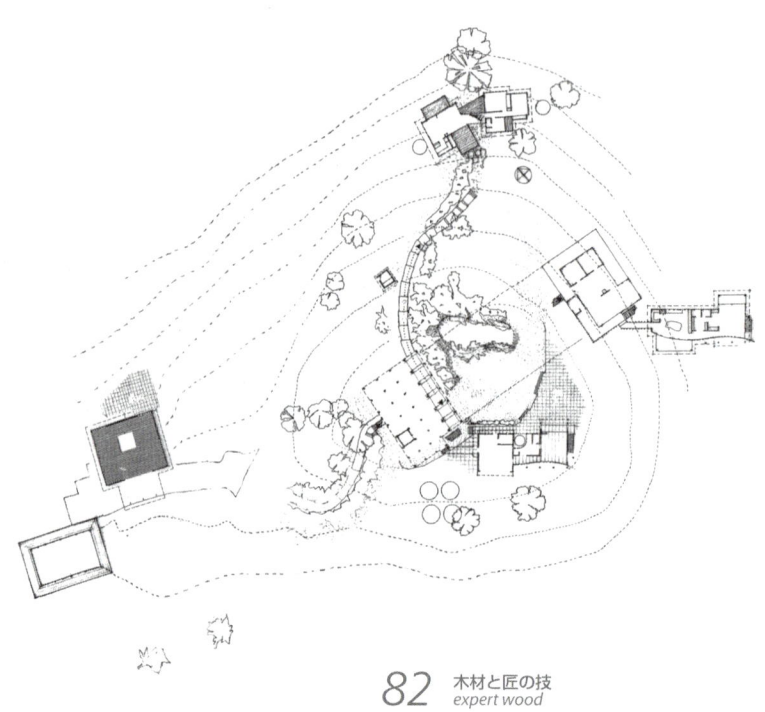

82 木材と匠の技
expert wood

1890年建造当時の木材の大部分は、シロアリの被害のため朽ちていた。改修は建物の外観はできるだけそのままの状態で残すというものであったが、内部の改造は大胆に実行された。間仕切り壁の大半は撤去され、ルーバー付きのスライド式の壁に取り替えられた。また内装は全面的に再仕上げがほどこされた。

Termites destroyed much of the original woodwork dating from 1890. The rehabilitation meant minimal changes to the exterior of the building whereas inside the modifications are more striking. Most of the interior dividing walls were eliminated and replaced by sliding ones with louvers and all of the interior was refinished.

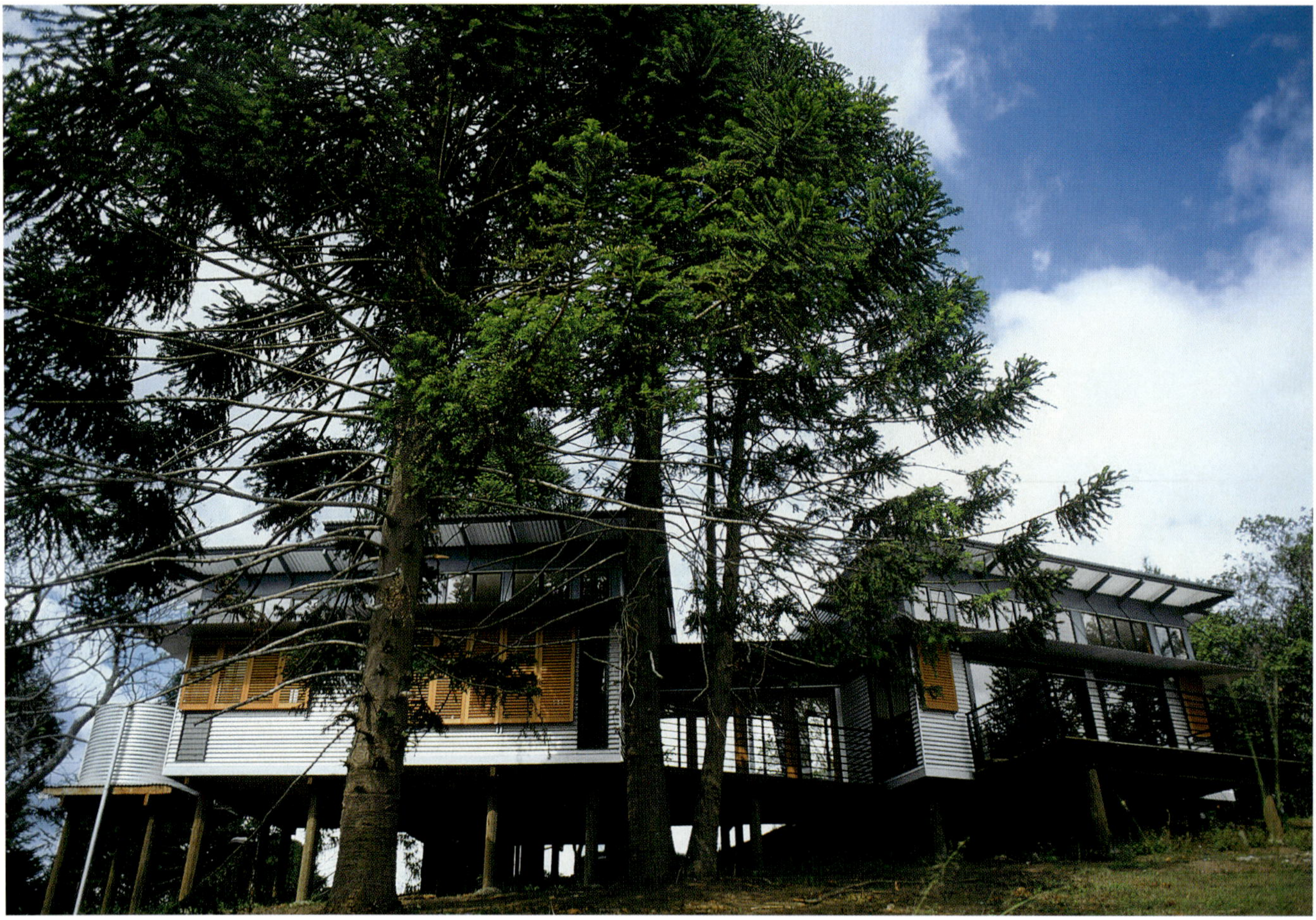

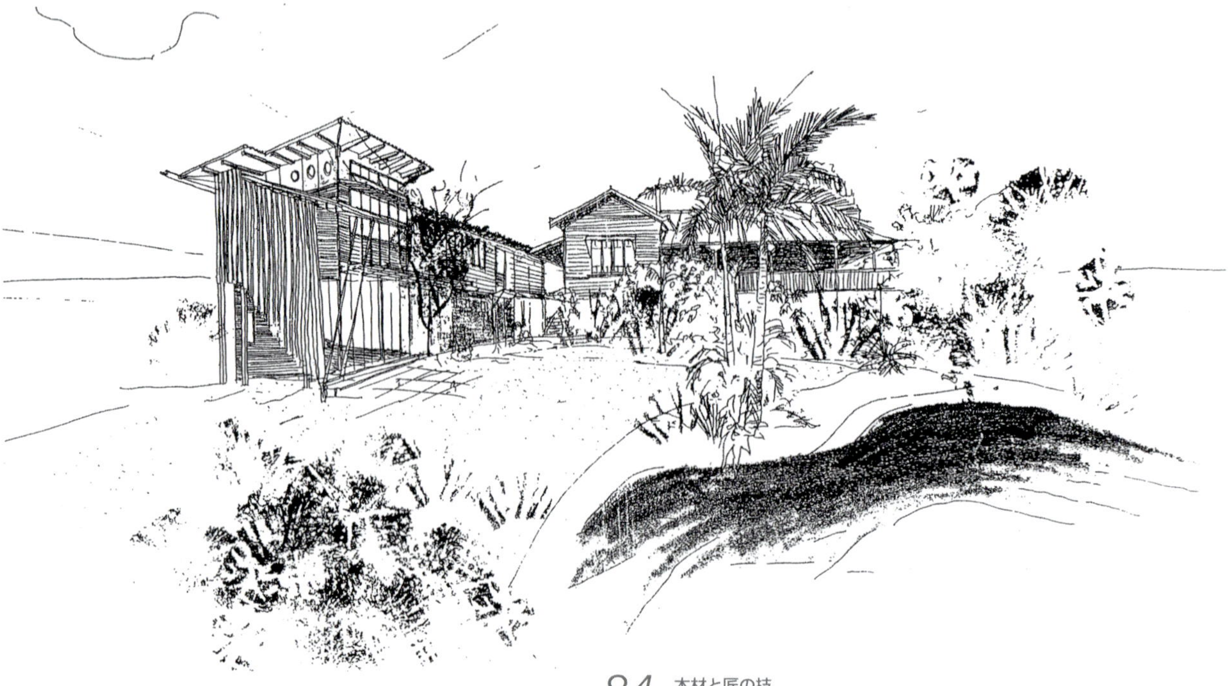

両サイドのファサードに大きな開口部を設け、大きな窓を設置し、屋根を新しいものと取り替えることによって、夏には快適な換気が得られ、冬には家全体が温室に変化する効果が生まれた。改修によって室内は外向的となり、広々と眺望を堪能できるものとなった。それは外界から身を護ることに汲々としていた、かつての内向的な建物とは根本的に異なった建物に生まれ変わった。

The apertures on both facades, the large windows and the new roofs were chosen so as to provide ventilation in the summer and to transform the house into a greenhouse in winter. After the rehabilitation, the interiors are extroverted, airy and endowed with vistas, which is a radical change from the original introversion fashioned to protect it from the exterior.

KFNパイロットプロジェクト
システムとしての木材

ヨハネス&オスカー・レオ・カウフマン
撮影:イグナチオ・マルティネス

PILOTPROJECT KFN
wood system

アンデルスバッハ―オーストリア―1997

　この2世帯住宅はKFNシステムにとって事実上のパイロットプロジェクトである。それは一定のモジュールに基づくシステムによって住宅を建てるという、建築家と工務店によるコラボレーションの成果である。モジュールは2.7mのファサードを持つ5×5mのもので、かなり自由に配置し組み合わせることができる。キッチンやバスなどの水回りをはじめ、全部で24のモジュールが用意されている。

This house for two families is in fact a pilot project for the KFN system, which stems from the collaboration between architects and a carpenter's workshop in order to make dwellings from a system of fixed modules. The modules are 5 x 5 meters with facades of 2.7 meters and can be placed and combined with great freedom, including wet zones (kitchen and baths), up to a total of 24 modules.

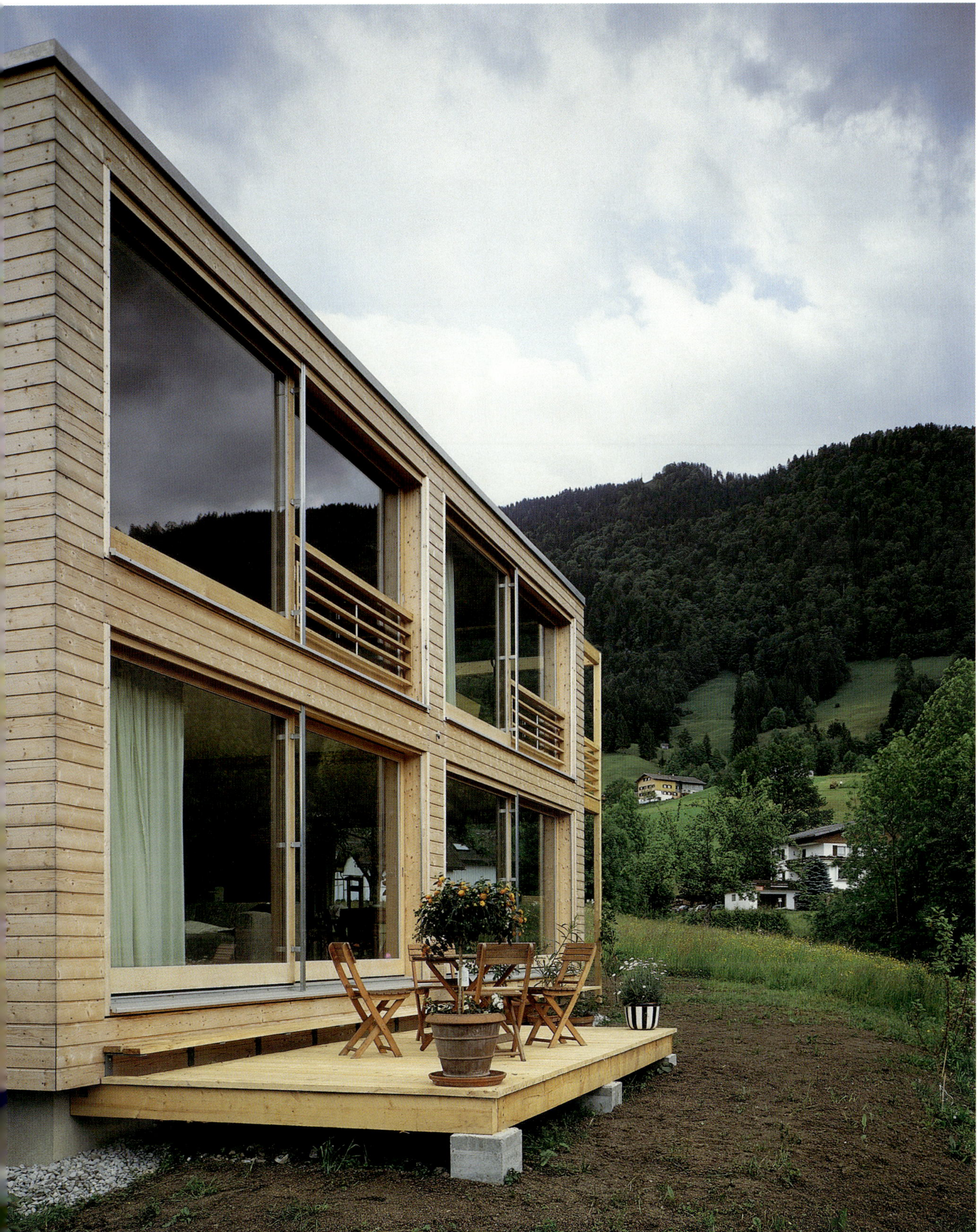

建築家は事務所で設計図を作成し、工務店はモジュールとそれ以外の部分を製作する。そしてその間に現場では基礎工事が行われる。次に「キット」が現場に搬入され、幼児用玩具が合体されるように組み立てられる。このシステムは短い工期と建築費の縮減を保証するだけでなく、形の美しさ、住まいの快適さをも確かなものにする。

The architects draw up the plans in their offices, the modules and other parts are manufactured in the workshop and at the site the foundations are laid. The "kits" are then delivered to the site and assembled, as if they were a child's toy to be put together. This process guarantees reduced construction times and costs while at the same time providing an aesthetically pleasing and comfortable home.

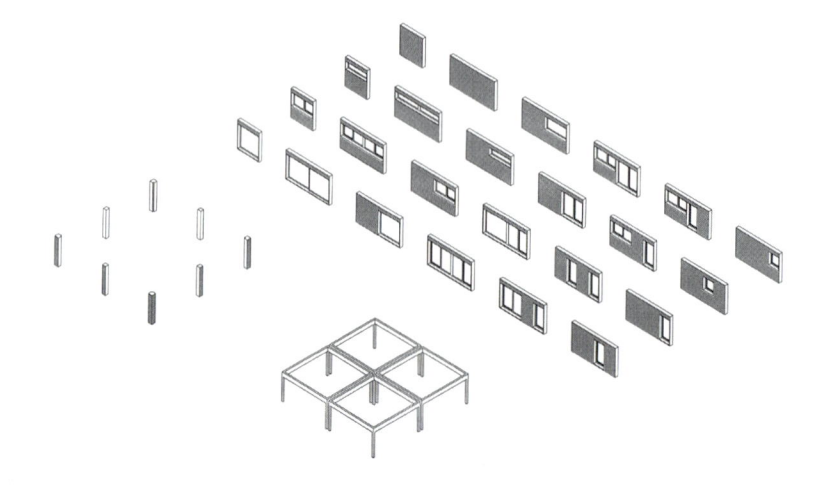

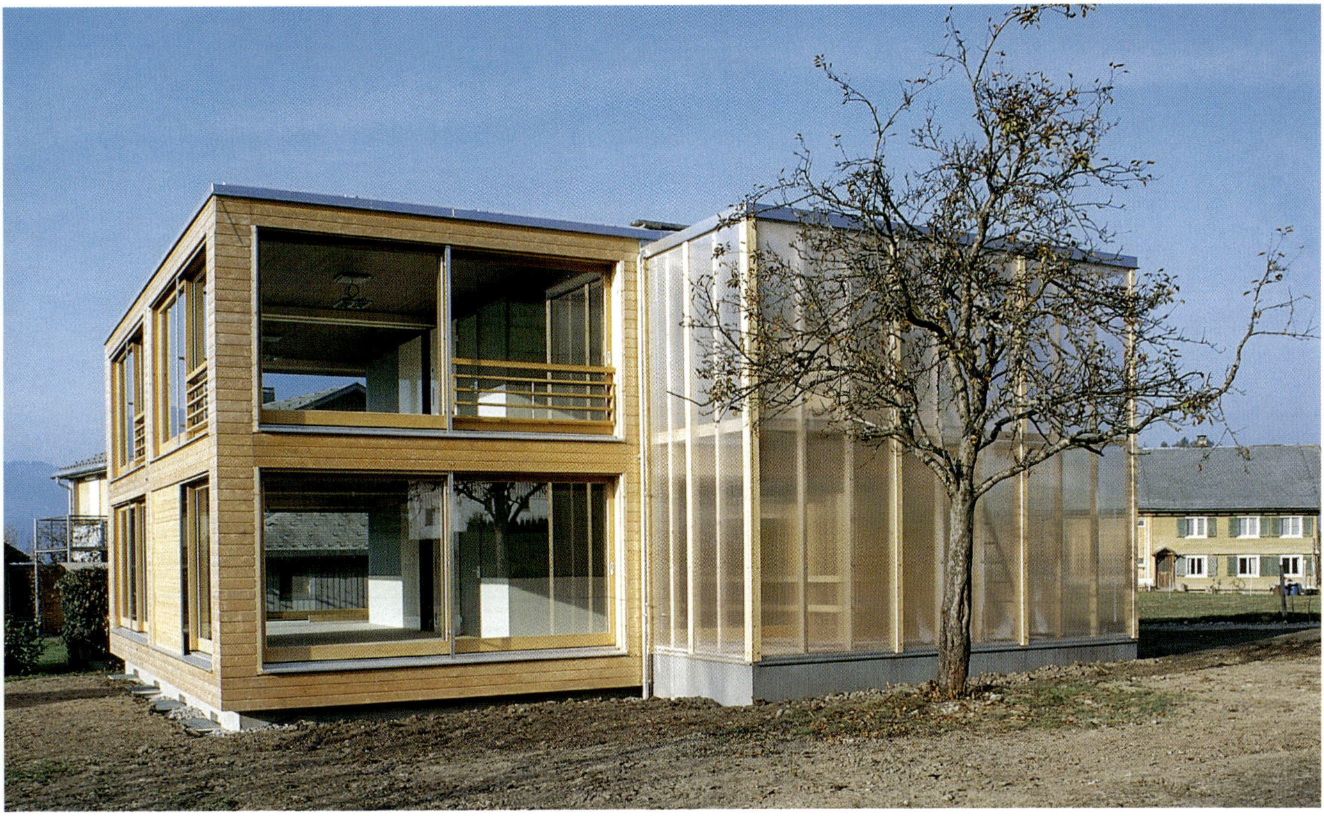

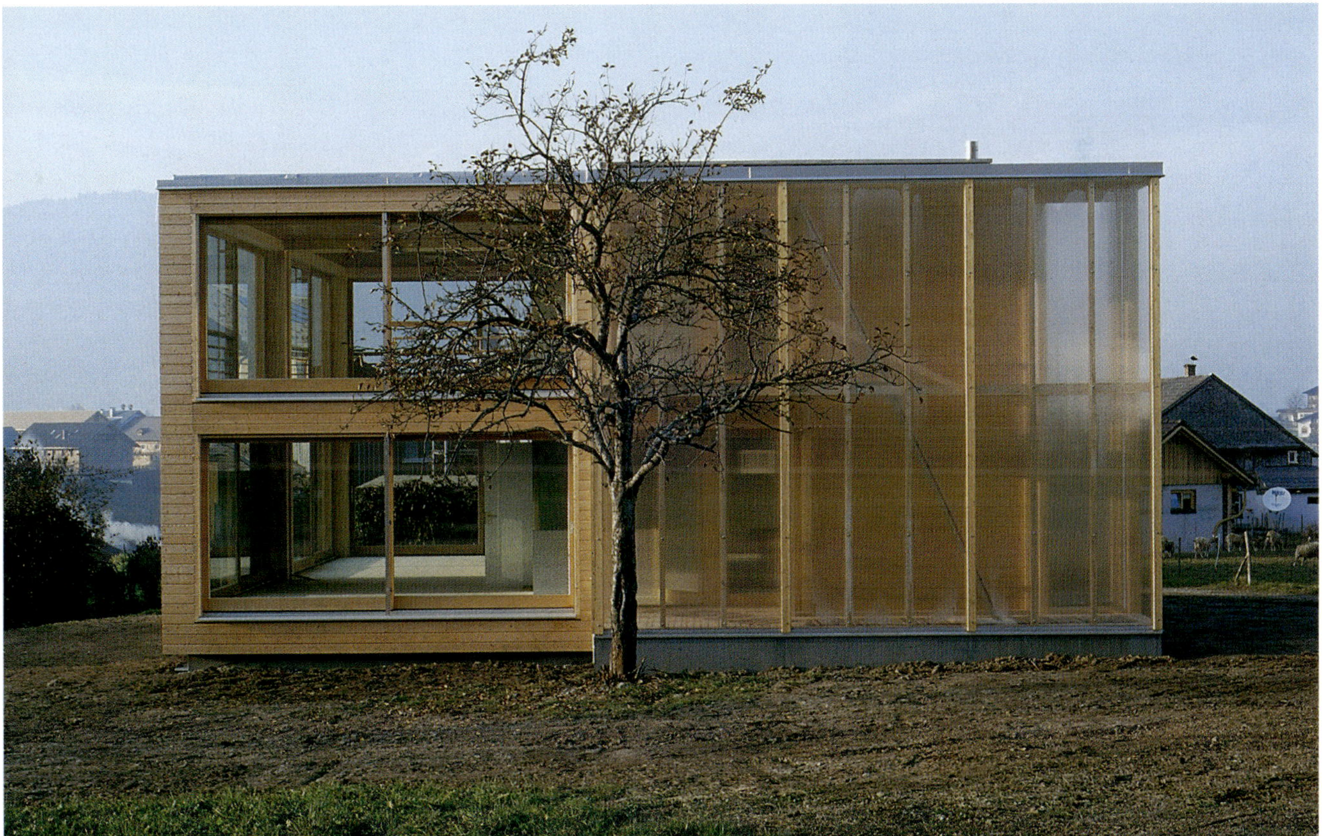

住宅の構造材にはスプルースが用いられ、それ以外のファサードやインテリアモジュールにはさまざまな仕上げのものが用意されている。概して木質パネルや合板のものが好まれている。システムは床暖房設備やリサイクル木材燃焼ヒーターなど、環境に対する配慮が多くなされている。施工の単純さはログキャビンに近いものがあるが、デザイン性には、はるかに多くの配慮がほどこされている。

The framework of the house is made of spruce whereas the other facade and interior modules can be in any type of finish though preferably wood panels or plywood. The system includes other ecological features such as radiant-floor heating and recycled wood-burning heaters. The simplicity of execution is akin to the log cabin but with greater attention to design.

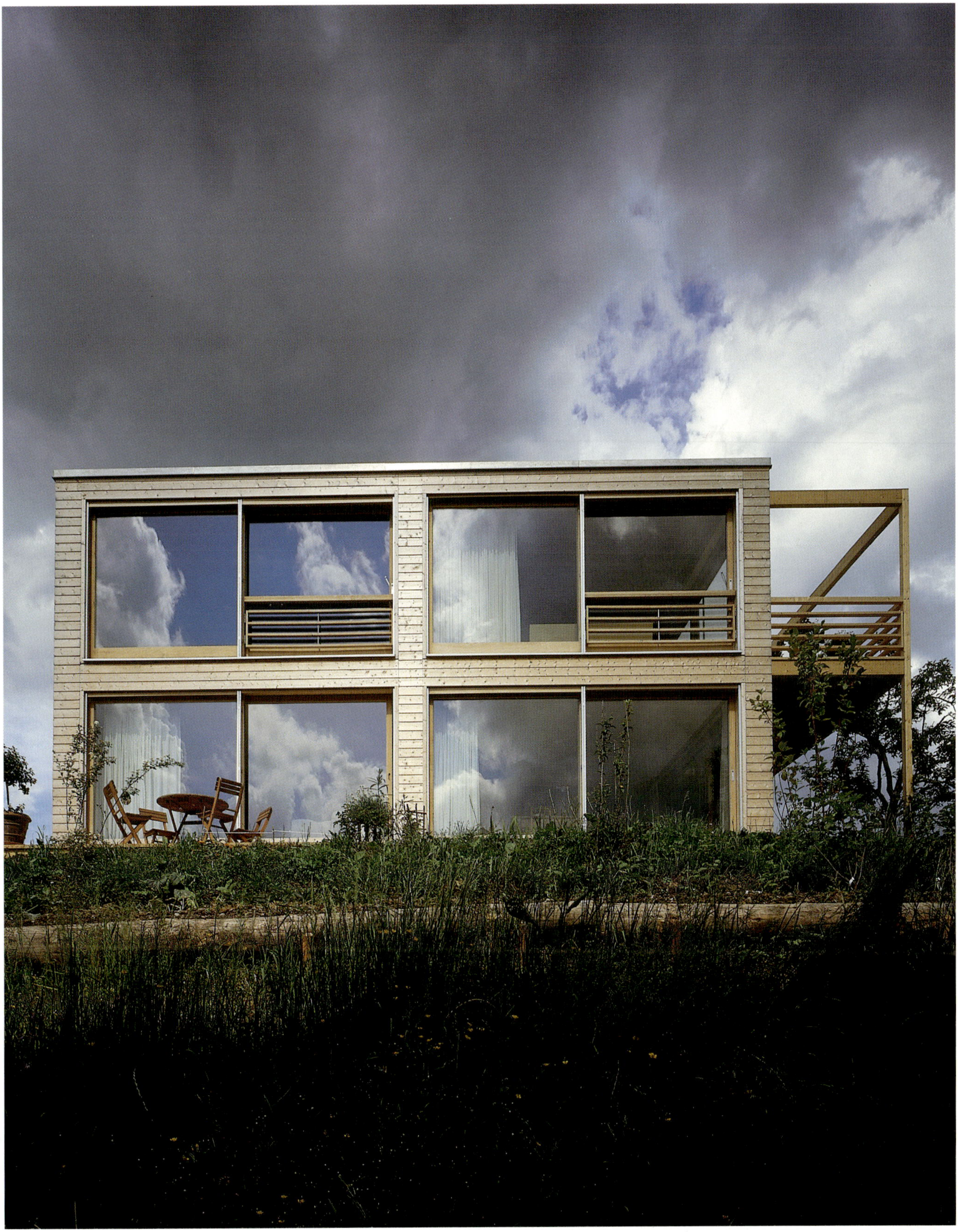

# 04

Wood and Nature

Unlike with other materials, construction with wood allows for a harmony with nature in which there are neither winners nor losers. In the following four projects characterized by great respectfulness, the environment marks the limit instead of being a place that will be spoiled by the construction

木材と自然

他の材料とは異なり、木材を用いた建築には自然との調和が約束される。そこには勝者もなければ敗者もない。これから紹介する4つのプロジェクトは、どれも自然に対する敬虔な態度がよく表現されている。環境は建築物によって毀損される場所となるのではなく、ただ結界を印すだけである。

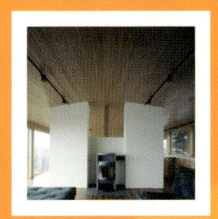

チルマークの住宅
林間の空き地

チャールズ・ローズ アーキテクツ
撮影：チャック・チョイ アーキテクチュラルフォトグラフィー

CHILMARK RESIDENCE
a clearing in the woods

チルマーク—マサチューセッツ—アメリカ—2001

施主によって選ばれた敷地は、非常に大きな困難を伴なう場所であった。そこは林間の不定形な小さな空き地で、建物は周囲を取り巻く豊かな植生の間隙を縫うように配置されなければならなかった。建設中、環境を毀損することがないように、何度も緻密な測量が繰り返された。

The site chosen by the proprietor turned out to be a true challenge. A small clearing in the woods of non-uniform dimensions obliged the layout to adapt to the scant space left free by the luxuriant vegetation. During the construction, strict measures were taken to assure that the environment was not harmed.

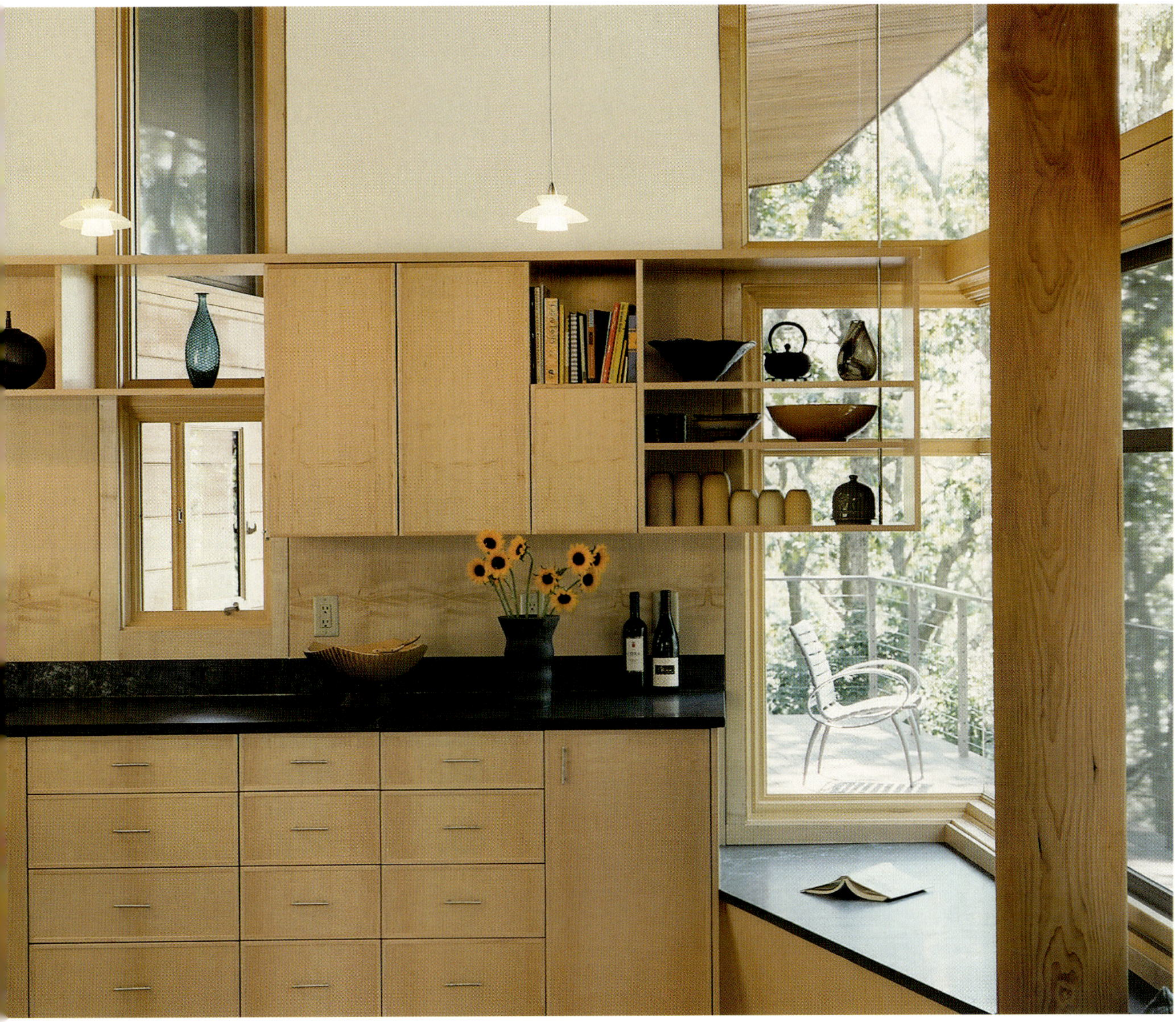

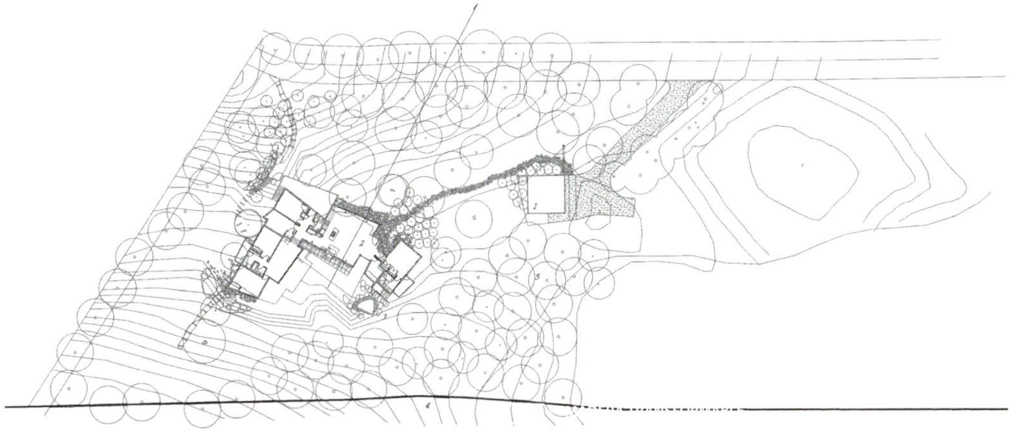

住宅は3つの部分から構成されており、中央の大きな部屋が両脇に主寝室と客室を従える格好になっている。客室は必要のないときは閉めておくこともできる。中央部分は光に溢れた単一の現代的な空間となっており、シーダー材を使用することによって暖かな雰囲気が全体に満ちている。そこにはリビング、ダイニング、キッチンが配され、家族が集う憩いの場所となっている。

The dwelling is laid out in three parts where a large room joins the master bedroom with the wing for the guests, which can be closed when is not necessary. At the center, one sole modern space with abundant light endowed with warmth thanks to the use of cedar, houses the living room, dining room and kitchen.

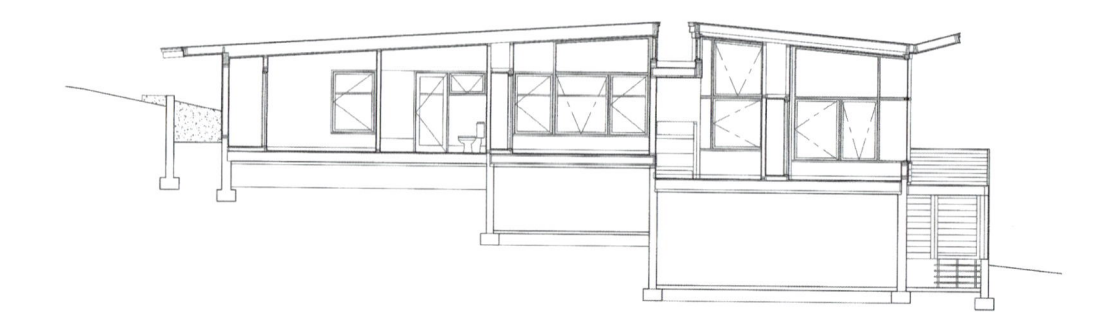

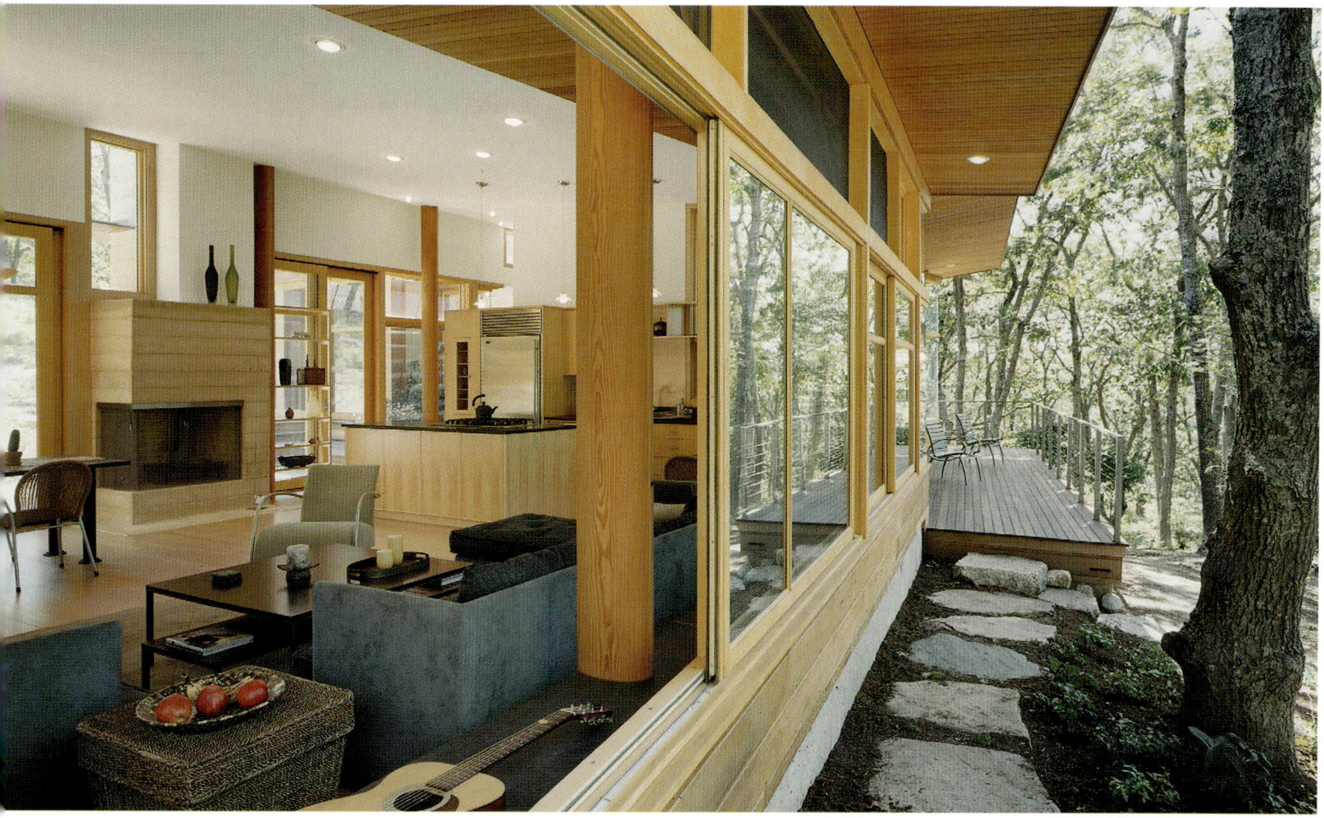

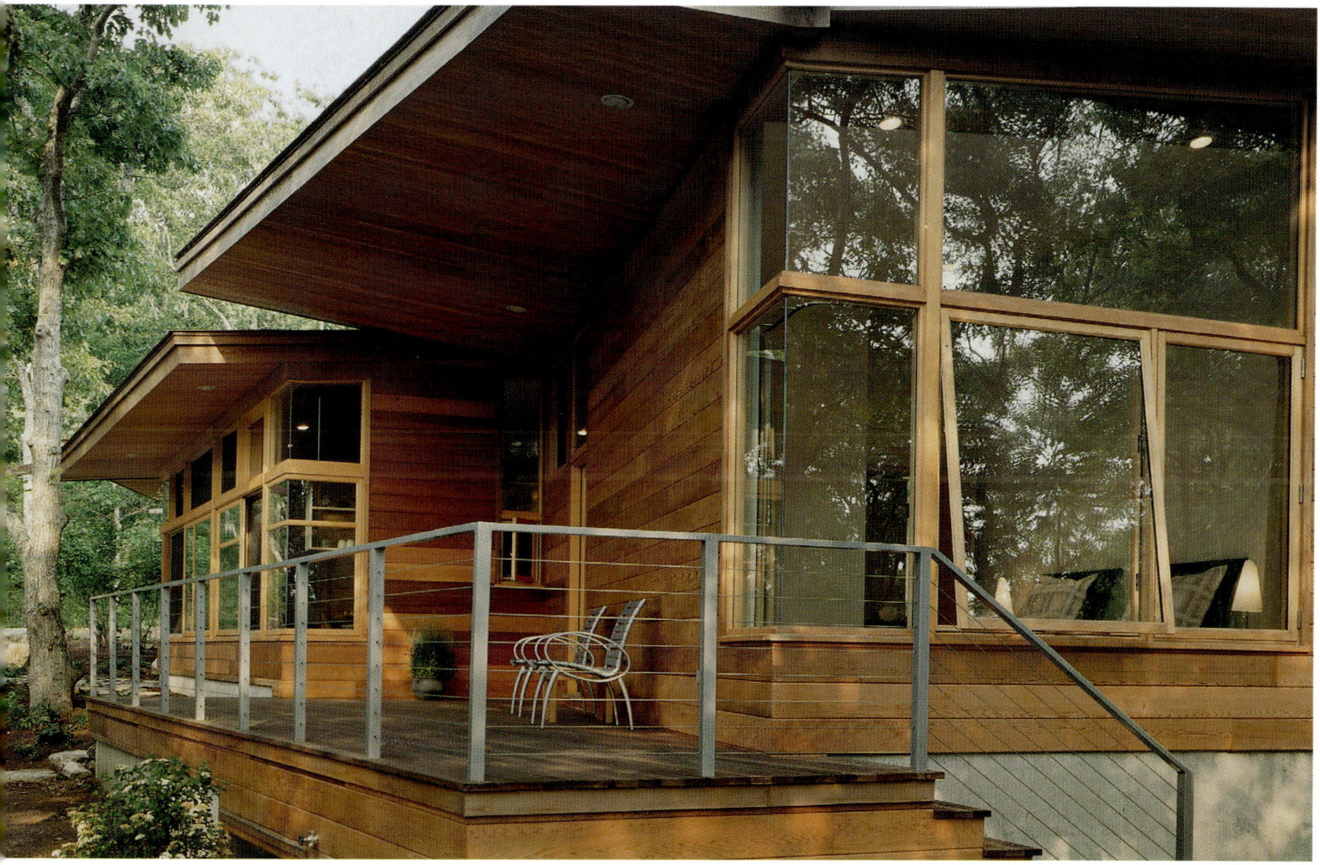

住宅内部の長円形の柱と大きなスライドドアによって、外壁は不要となり、住宅内部の空間と森林の風景、そしてその下に広がる海が連結されている。テラスと屋根の水平な広がりが、住宅と外界の間の障壁を消滅させるというこの家のコンセプトをさらに一層明確なものにしている。

The elliptical pillars in the interior and the large sliding doors allow the dividing walls to be done away with, so that the inhabitants can connect the space of the residence to the woodsy landscape and the ocean that lies below. The terraces and the roof accentuate this feeling of eliminating the barriers between interior and exterior.

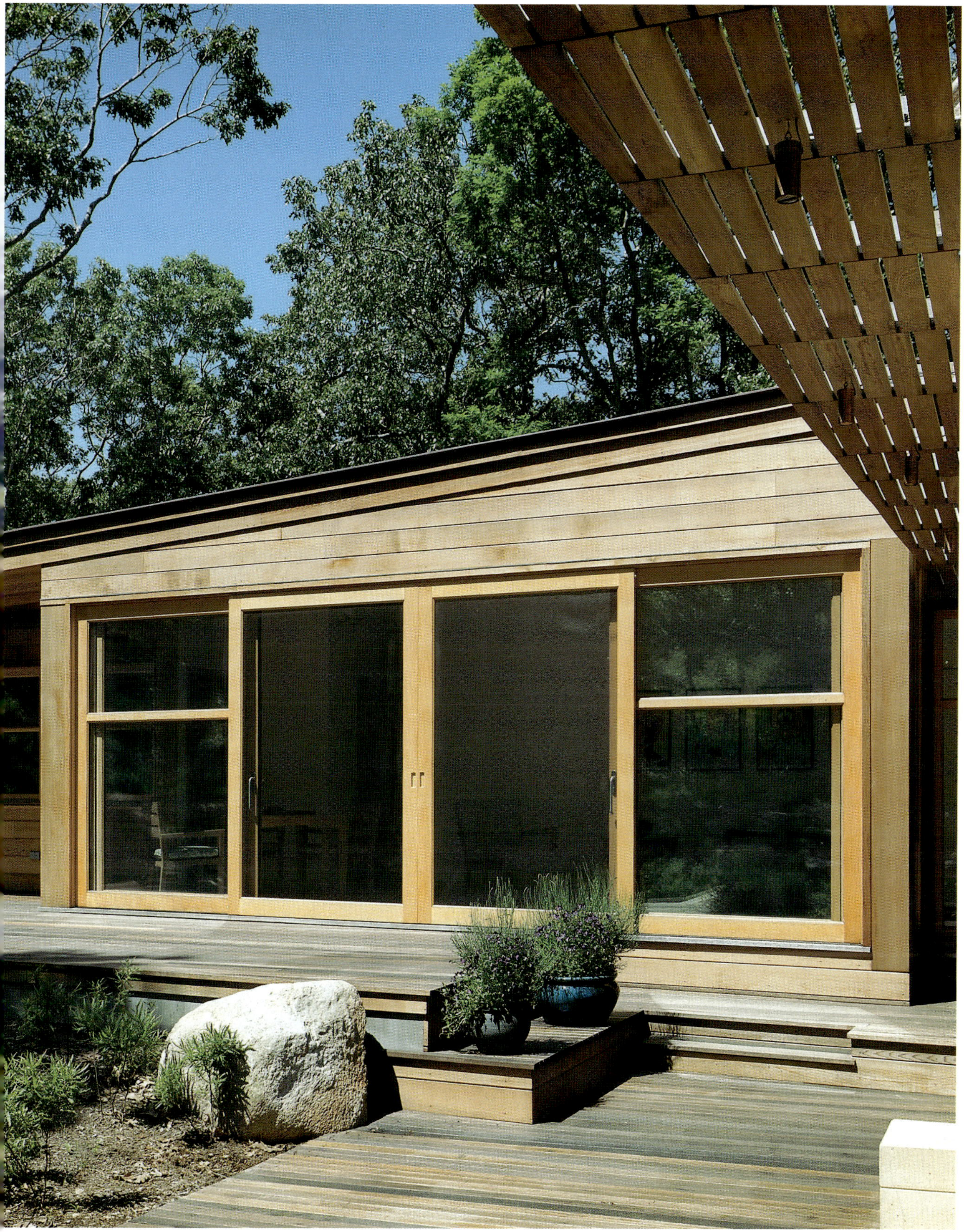

ランボー氏別荘
自然を分界する

オラヴィ・コボーネン
共同設計：オスカリ・ラウッカネン
撮影：ユシ・ティアニエン

VILLA LÅNGBO
limiting nature

ロングホルメン―ケミオ―フィンランド―2000

　別荘は島の北端、森が海に落ち込む場所に位置し、風に曝されている。それは海上から木の間隠れに見ることができ、また逆に別荘のどの部屋からも海の眺めを楽しむことができる。もともとは農場の一部として建てられており、居間のいくつかは、貯蔵や作業のための場所に転換することができる。

Located on the far western end of the island and exposed to the winds, it is at the edge of the woods. It can be partially seen from the sea, and from within any room, vistas of the sea can be delighted in. Originally built as part of a farm, some of the rooms for living can be converted into areas for storage or production.

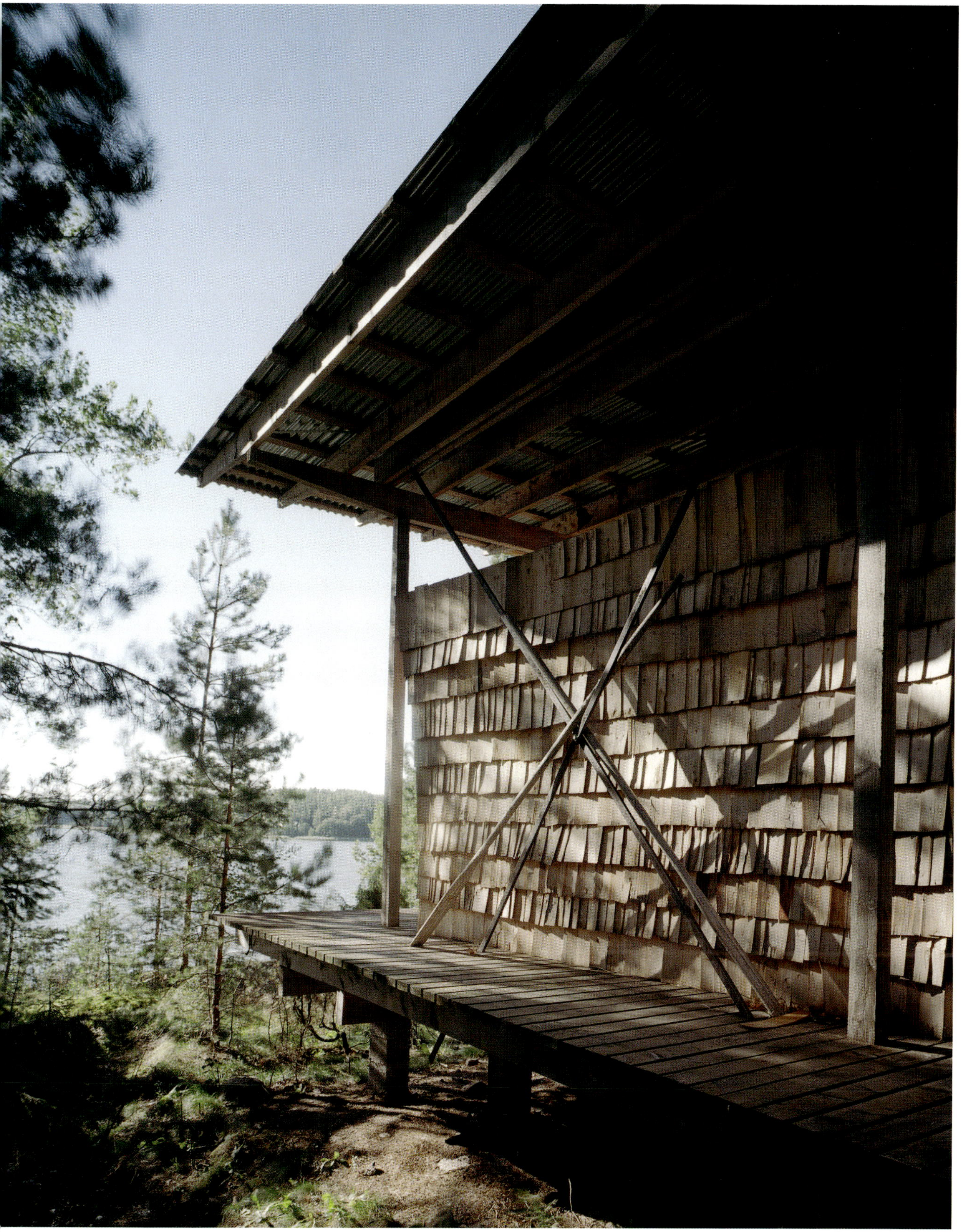

環境に対する人間の影響を最小限に抑えるという思想に基づいて、建物と周囲の環境の間の障壁は溶解させられている。光、感覚、自然との結びつきに従って個々に決定されたさまざまな外皮にくるまれ、個室と団欒の部屋が木のプラットフォームと屋根の間に配置されている。単純な構造がレイアウトの自由さを可能にしている。

Built with the idea to limit the impact of man in the environment, the building dissolves the barrier between the construction and the setting. The different enclosures which are defined individually in relation to light, sensation and the connection with nature, include both private and common areas and are distributed throughout a platform and under a roof. The simple structure easily affords variation in the layout.

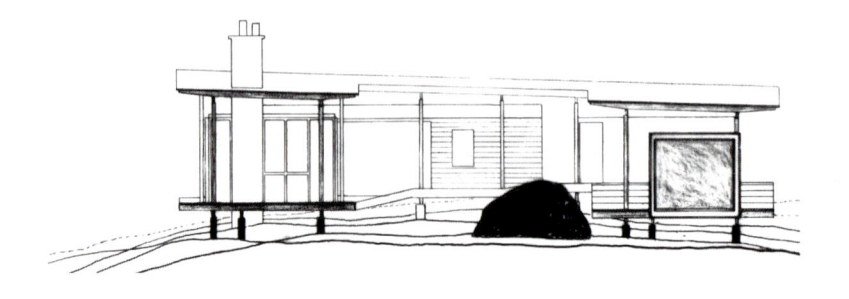

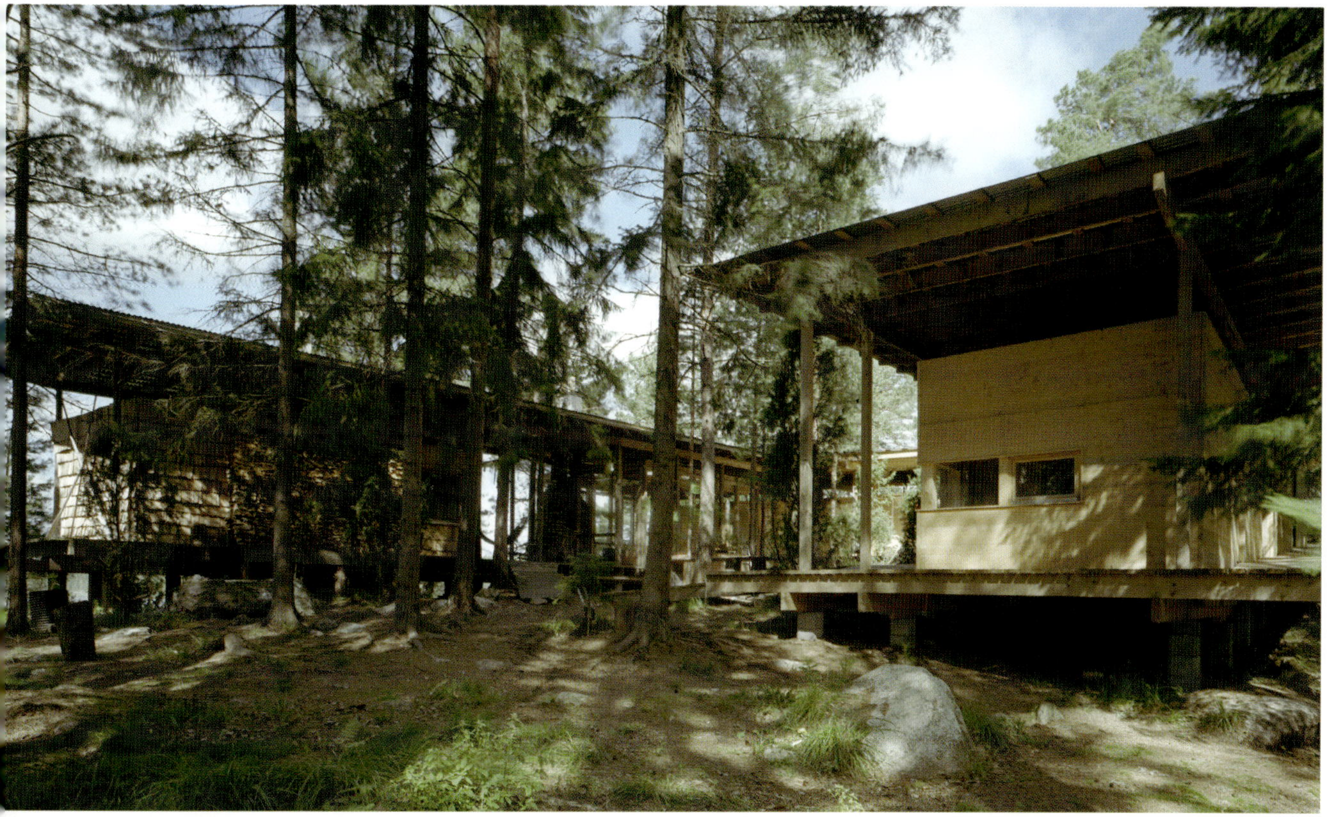

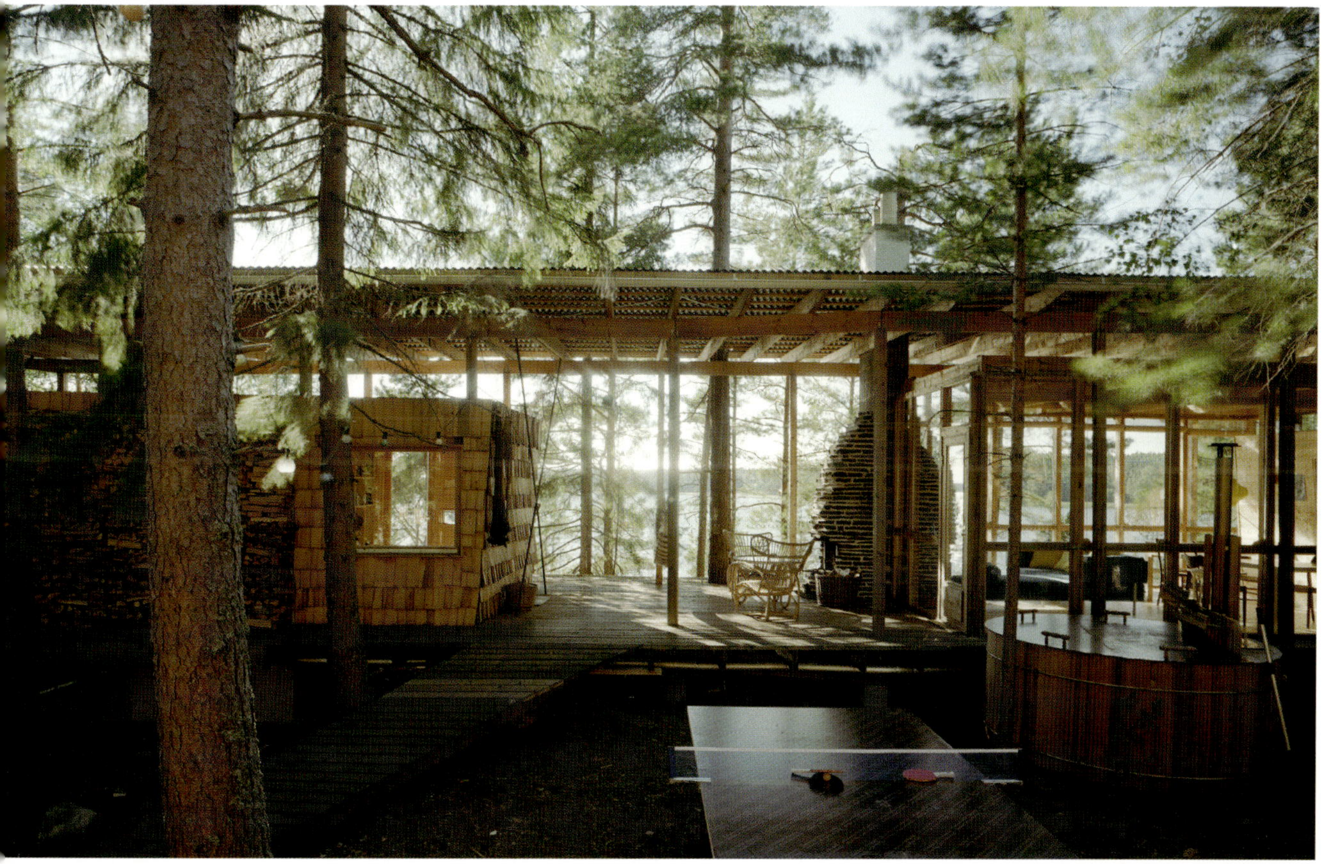

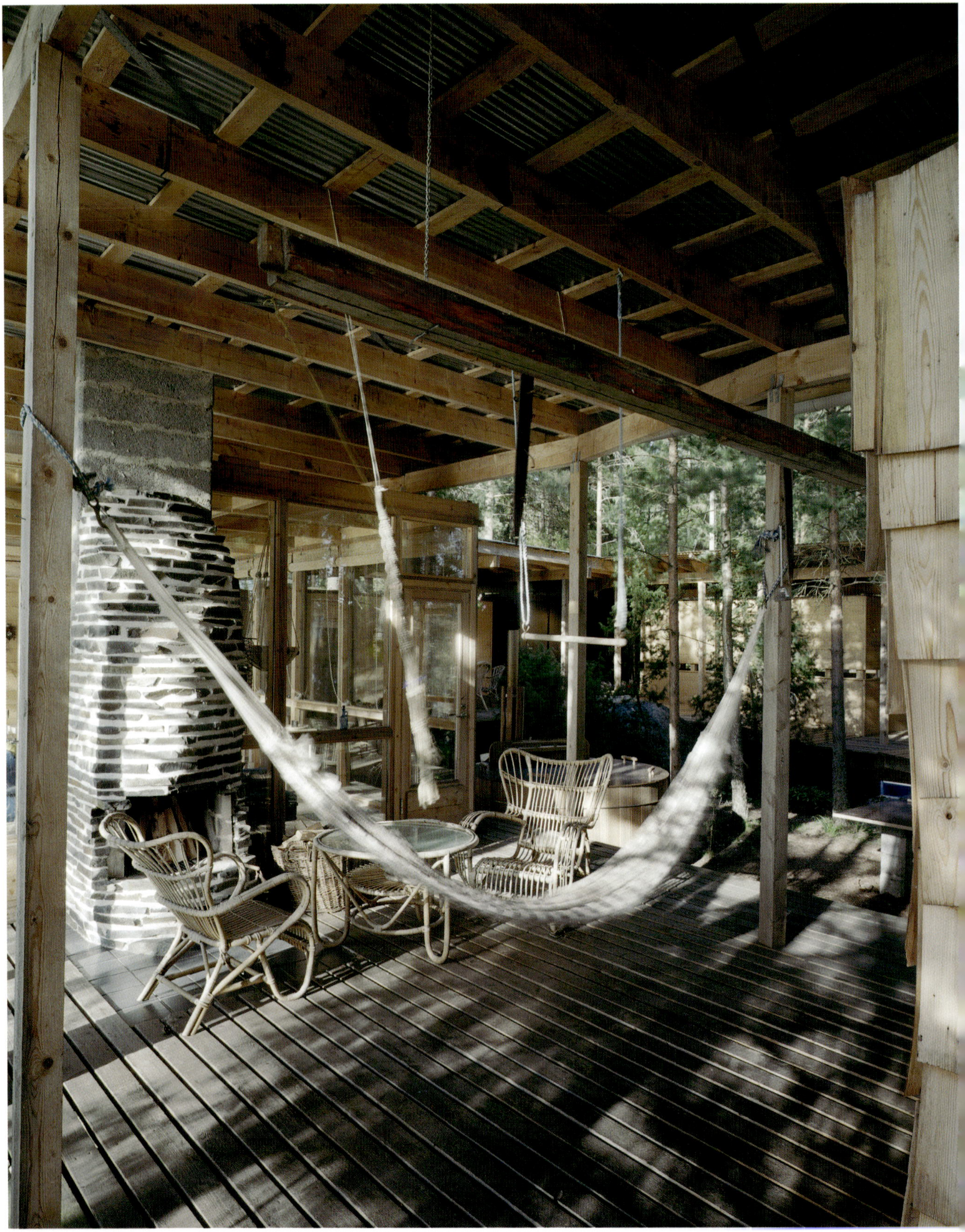

海が凍る時期があるため、年間をとおして利用することは不可能である。というよりも、スキーまたはボートで来ることができるときだけ、利用することができる。使用されている材料はいずれも再生利用が可能であり、木材はすべて近くの森から伐りだしたものである。建築は手作業で行われ、資材は馬によって搬入された。こうしてできるかぎり周囲の環境に変化をきたさないように配慮がなされた。

Due to periods when the sea is frozen, it is not always possible to access the building all throughout the year but rather only when it can be reached by using skis or boats. All of the materials utilized are recyclable, the wood comes from the immediate area and the construction was done manually. The materials were transported there by horse and the setting altered as little as possible.

ケーラー邸
鷹が舞い下りる家

サルメラ アーキテクチャー＆デザイン
撮影：ピーター・バスティアネリーケルツ

KOEHLER RESIDENCE
eagle's nest

シルバーベイ―ミネソタ―アメリカ―2003

　現代的なものにとらわれず、しかも思想を声高に主張することもなく、この家は最も野性的で、最も険しい自然の淵に建てられている。それはスペリオール湖の絶景を眺望できる急峻な断崖の上に位置している。

While fleeing from modernity but without renouncing its concepts, this dwelling was built on the wildest and most daring edge of nature. It is located atop a precipice with a daring view of Lake Superior.

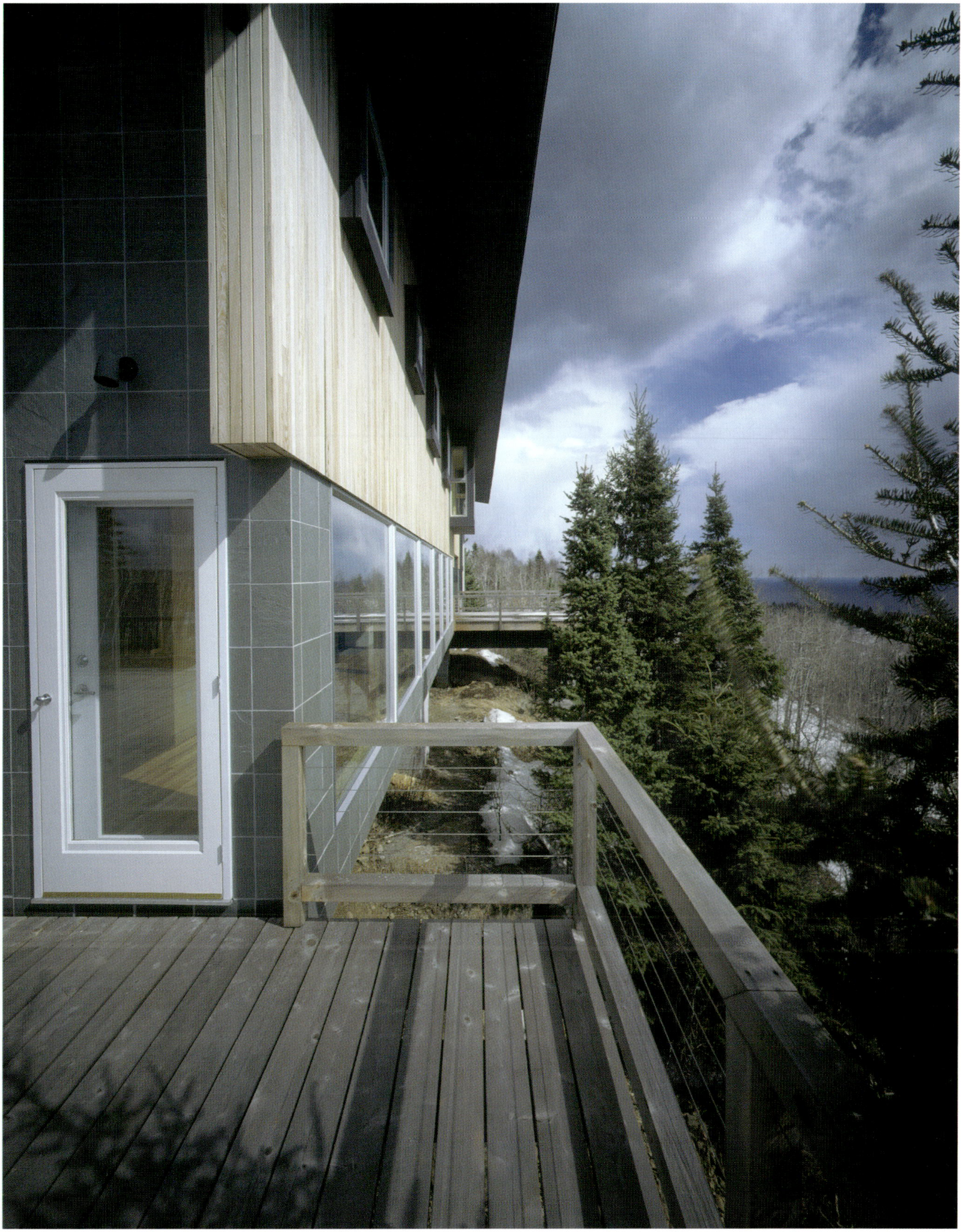

住宅を取り巻く森から伐り出したチェリー、メイプル、サイプレスの木材が住宅の内と外を飾っている。窓、天井、階段、クローゼットはメイプルから作られ、床材にはメイプルとチェリーが使われている。再生利用したサイプレスのファサードが周囲の風景との連続性をもたらし、積層材の梁が住宅を固い岩盤に連結している。

The bark from the surrounding cherry, maple and cypress trees decorates the interior and exterior of the house. Maple is used for the windows, ceilings, stairs and closets whereas maple and cherry are used for the floors. The facade of recycled cypress is a continuation of the landscape that surrounds it, together with the laminated wood beams that connect the house to its solid rock roots.

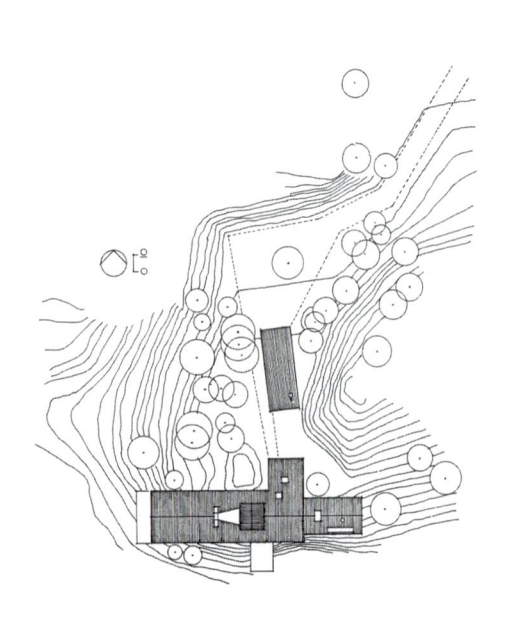

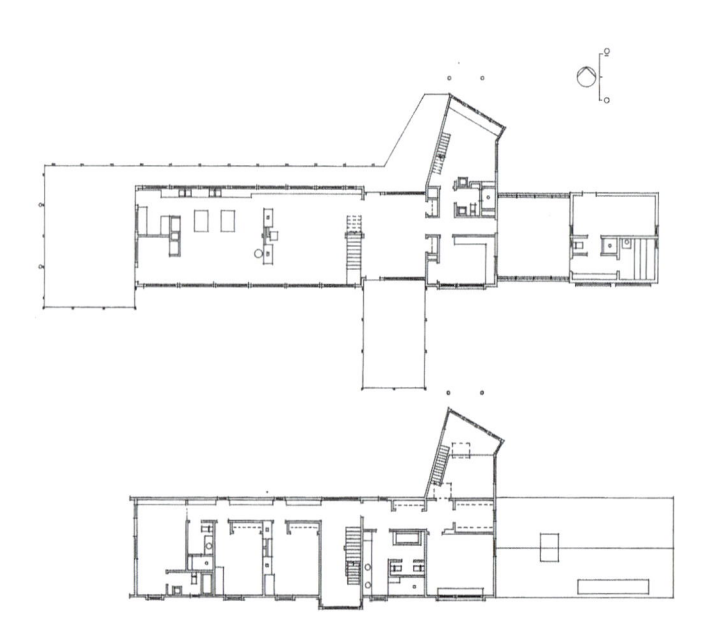

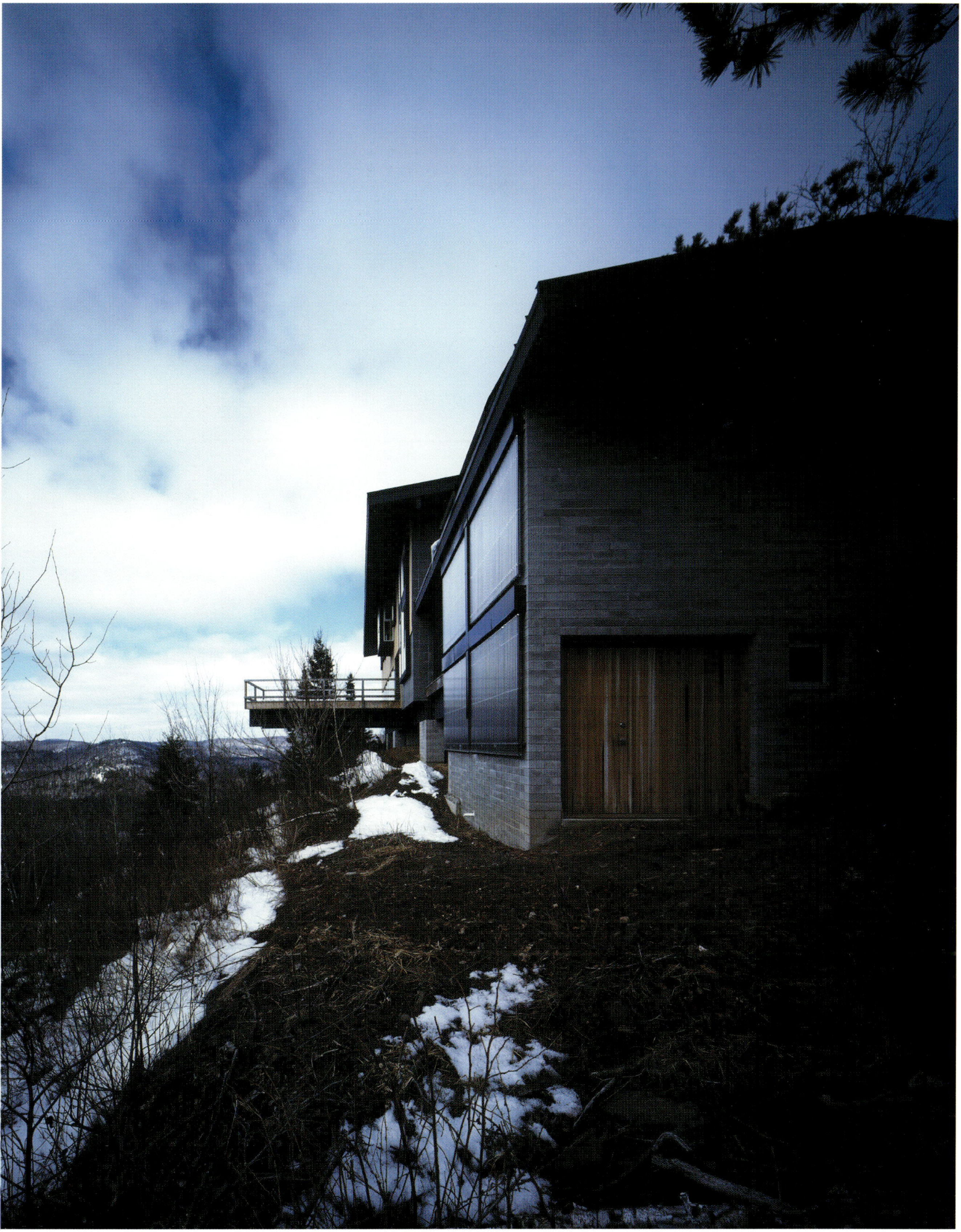

空っぽで裸の室内は、昇ってくる朝日の最初の光線を待ちわび、木々からこぼれる影と遊びたがっている。家族の集うスペースは日光が豊かに入り込む場所に配置され、一方画家の仕事場には、木々の葉に濾過された柔らかな光線が入る。木材が生みだす質感と、太陽の動きがもたらす明暗法が、この自然のふところに抱かれた住宅の美しさを物語っている。

The empty, nude interior eagerly awaits the coming of the first rays of the sun and the shadows of the trees. The more oft-used areas of the house are privileged with direct sunlight whereas the studio where the artist works, receives more filtered and subdued light. The textures of the wood and the chiaroscuro of the passing day attest to the beauty of this sheltered dwelling in the midst of nature.

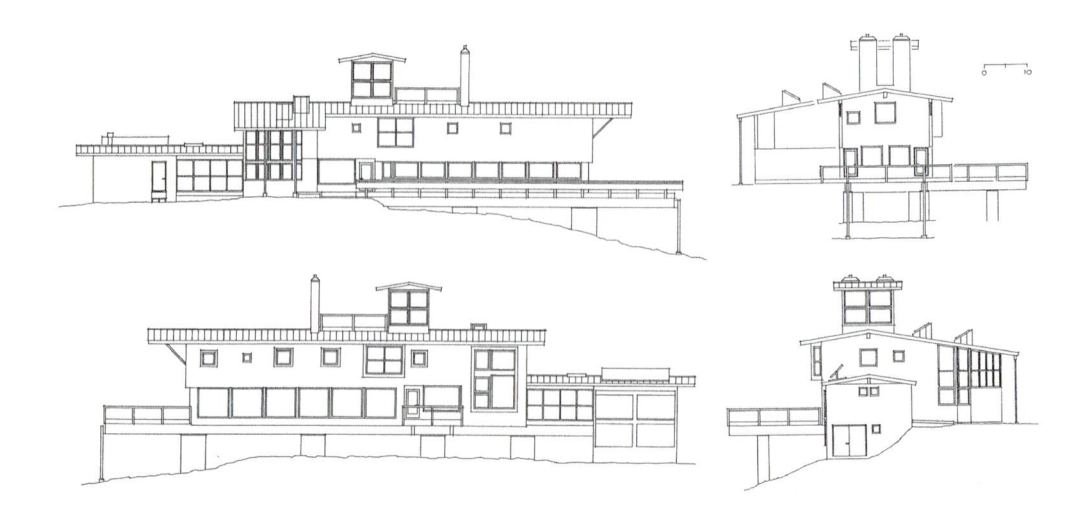

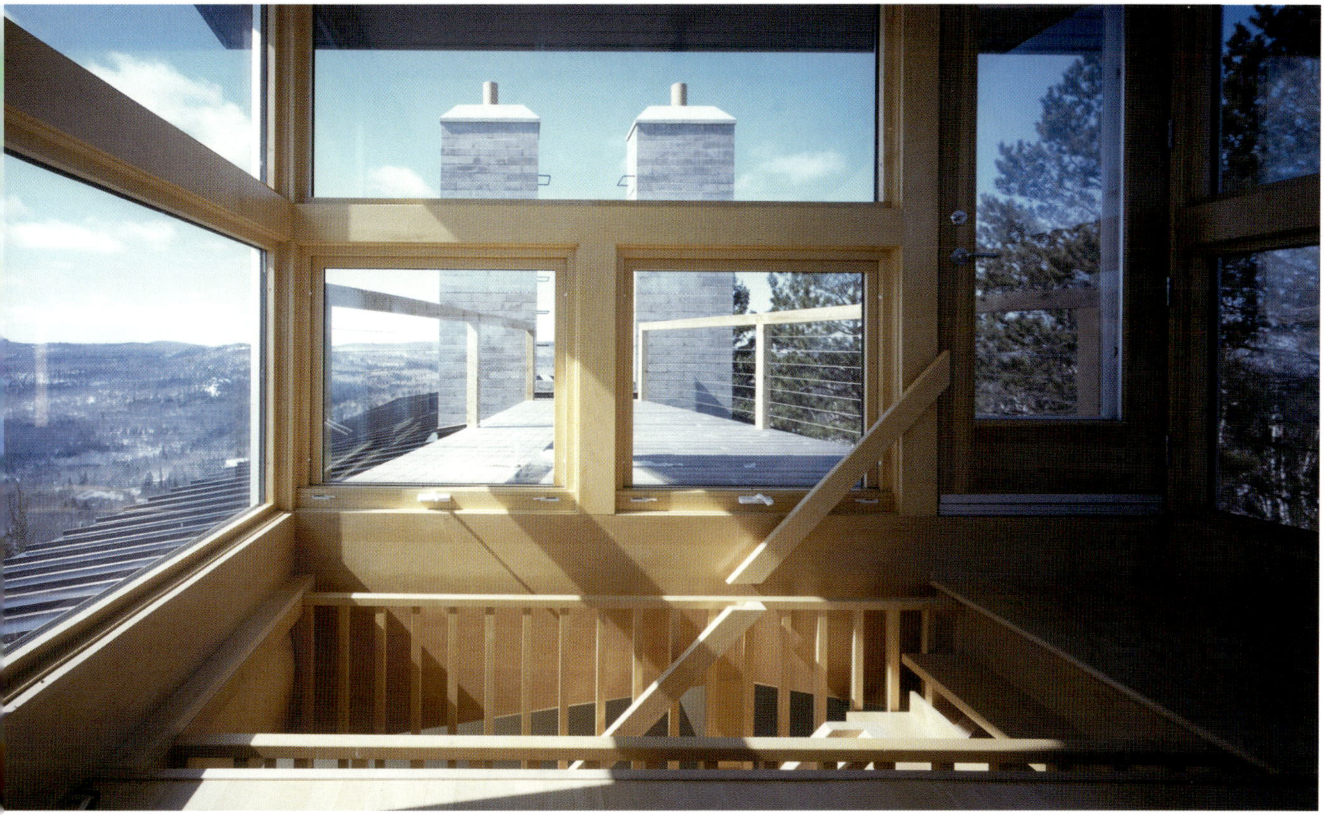

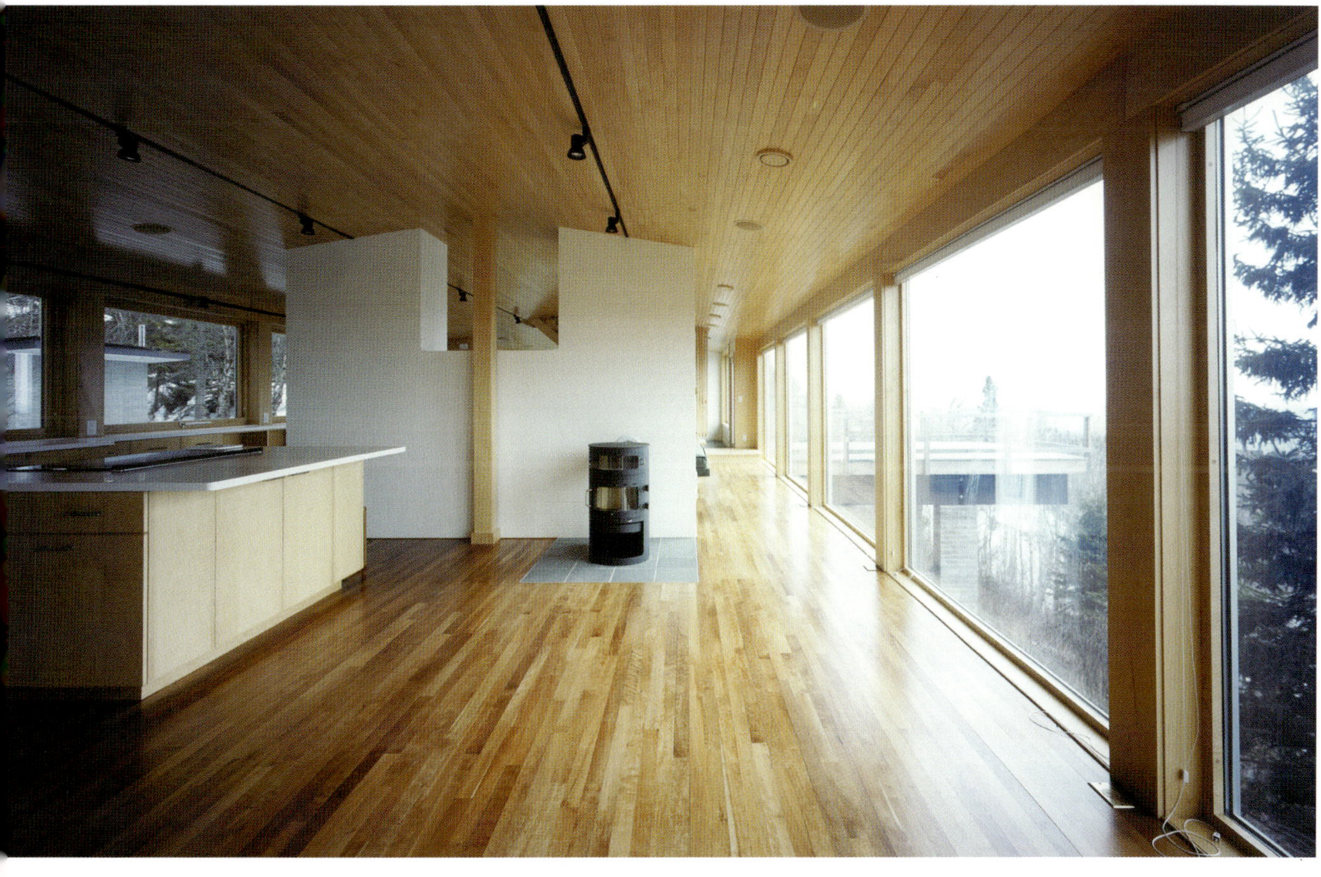

アカヤバ自宅
樹上生活の家

マルコス・アカヤバ
共同設計：マウロ・ハルーリ，スーリー・ミゾベ，ファビオ・ヴァレンティム
撮影：ネルソン・コン

CASA ACAYABA
arboreal life

ティジュコパーヴァ―ガラヤ―ブラジル―1997

　この住宅は、環境を傷つけることなしに、いかに傾斜地に建物を建築するかという問いに対する1つの解答である。場所は、海岸線から150mしか隔たっていないにもかかわらず、海抜が70mある地点である。大西洋に面する海岸線上の森の中、木々の間にわずか3本の基礎柱が打ち込まれ、その上に6角形の建物が建てられている。その3角形を基本とした構造は、あたかも1本の木のように枝を広げ、木製の柱と梁、鉄骨、ケーブル、ターンバックルによって相互に固定しあっている。

This house is a model for constructing on slopes without harming the environment. Though only 150 meters from the beach, it is 70 meters above sea level. Placed in the midst of a woods on the Atlantic coast, the foundation consists of but three pillars placed among the trees which provide a hexagon. The triangular structure which spreads out like another tree, is fit together with wood pillars and beams, steel, cables and turnbuckles.

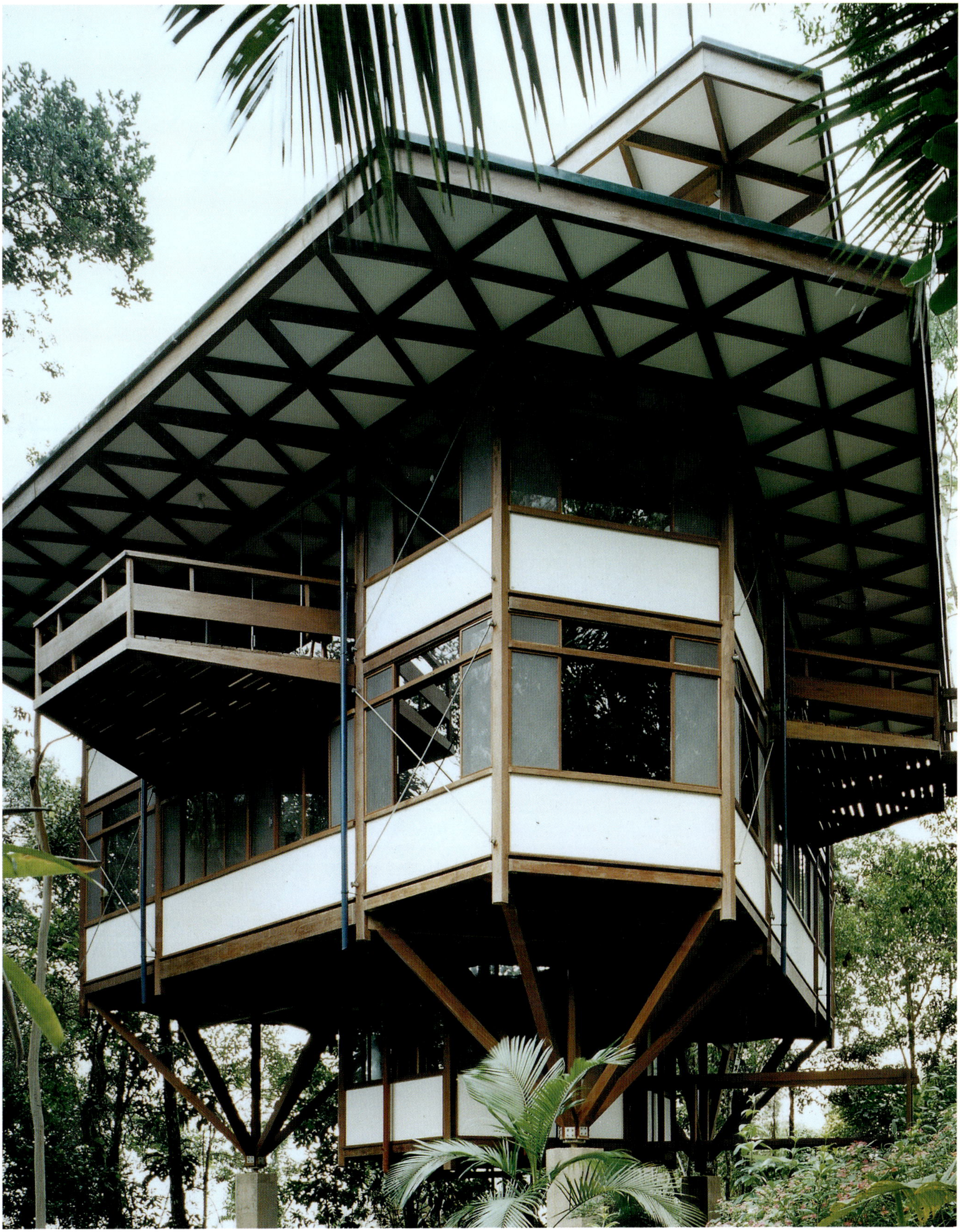

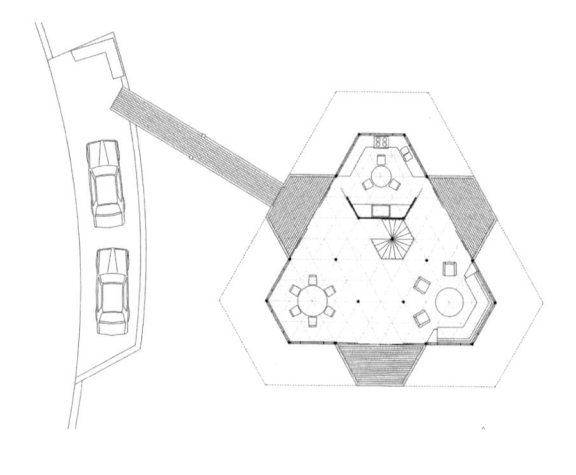

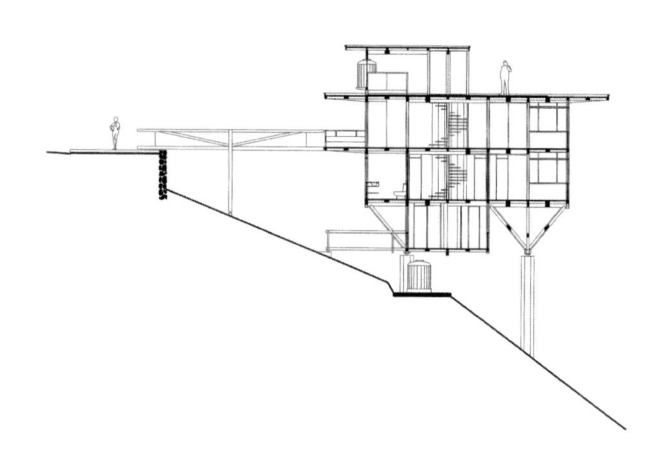

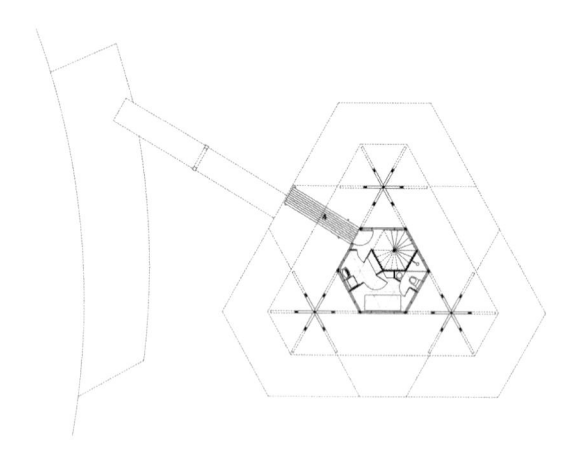

大きく張り出した軒によって熱帯特有のシャワーから守られているデッキは、いわば屋外リビングルームである。森の頂点に位置するその場所からは、丘の頂と海の両方の景色を楽しむことができる。独立した構造のキャットウォークを通り、デイエリアとキッチンのあるメインフロアーへと入る。その上の階は寝室となっており、下の階は供給設備室である。

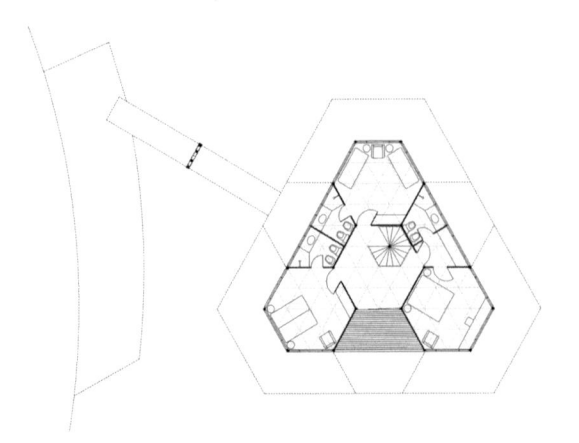

The deck, with protection for the tropical rains, is like an open-air living room. There, at the tops of the trees, one is afforded views of the top of the hill and the ocean. An independent catwalk provides access to the main floor which houses the day areas and the kitchen. The upper floor contains the bedrooms whereas the lower, the service areas.

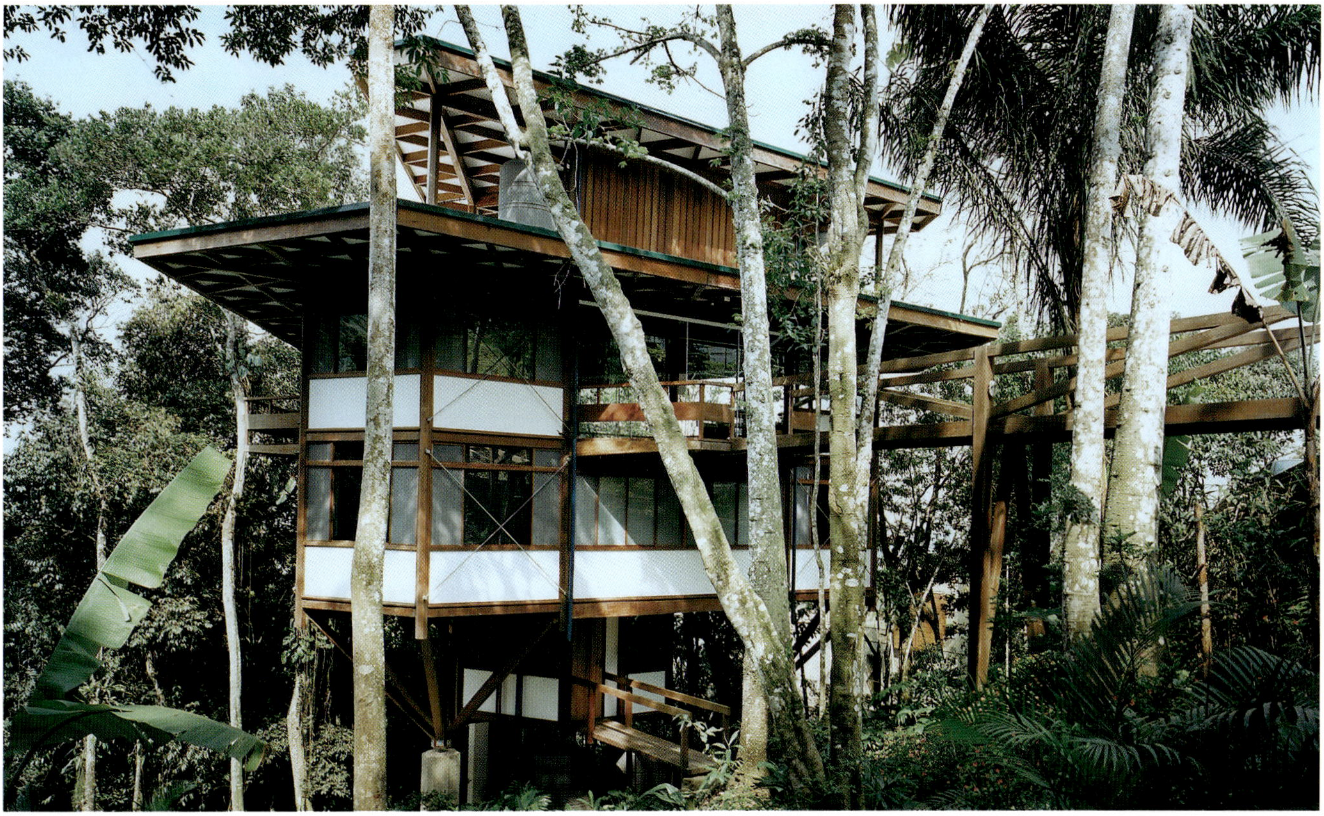

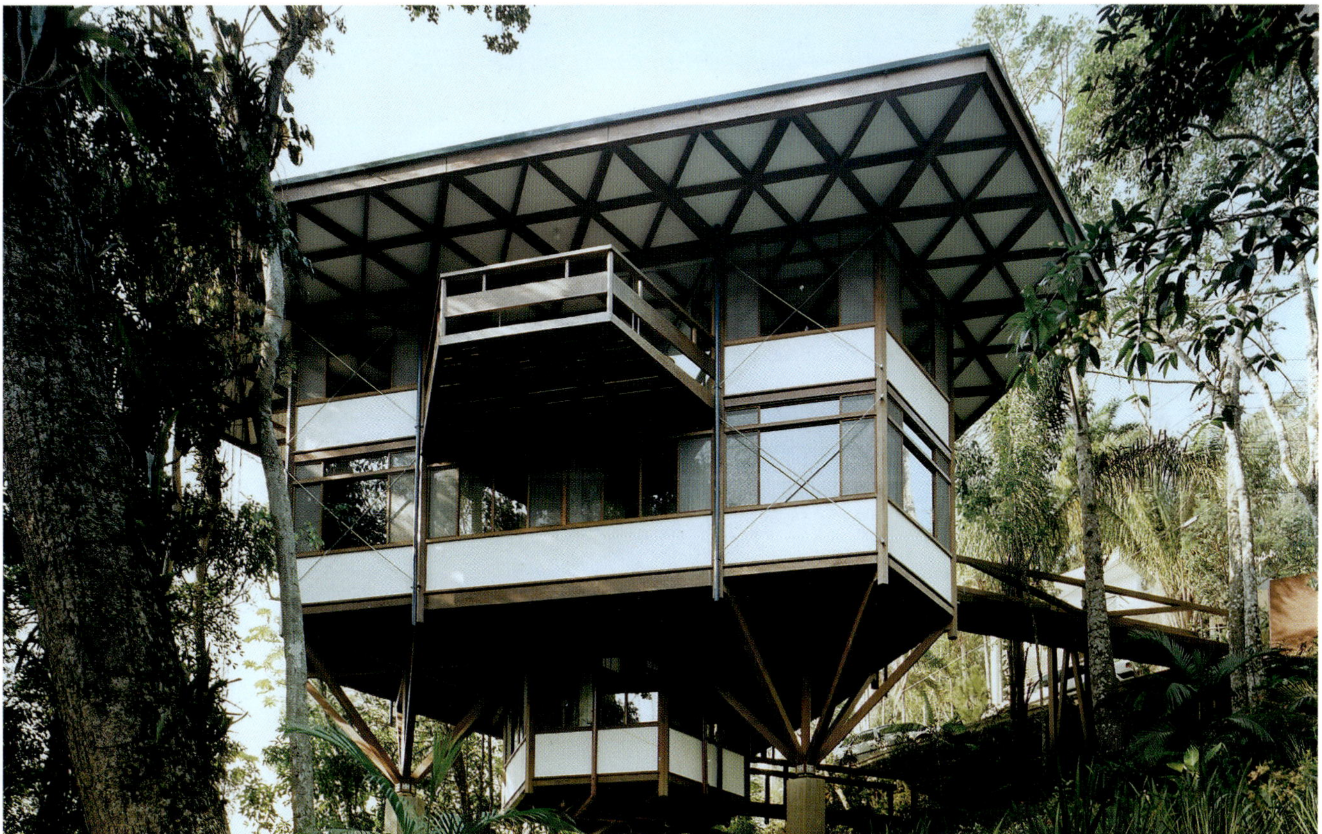

コンセプトは、種々の軽量の部材を作業場で製作し、たった4人の手で4ヵ月で現場に建築でき、しかも環境に対する影響を最小限に抑えるというものであった。3角形を基本とすることによって、構造は堅固なものとなり、内部空間と外界との会話が豊かなものとなった。各ファサードがバルコニーの連続のような感覚を与えている。

The concept was to fashion the different light construction pieces in the workshop, which allowed the entire building to be constructed in four months by only four people and with minimal environmental impact. The triangular geometry of the structure, by nature rigid, affords greater communication of the spaces with the exterior, as the facade gives the sensation of a series of balconies.

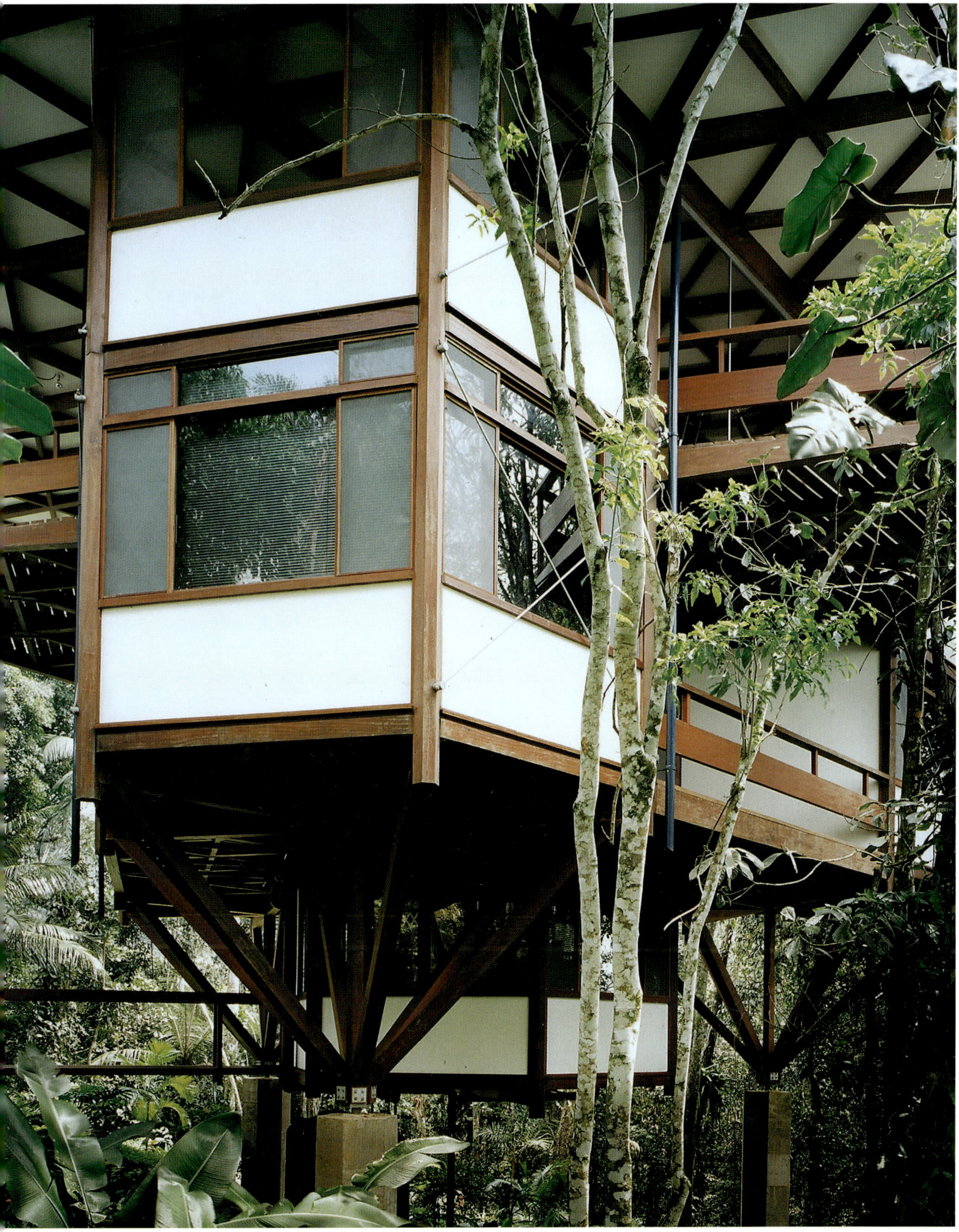

05

Wood in the Skin

At times the value of wood does not lie in its strength or load-bearing qualities. Simply the visual touch it confers a building can enrich it aesthetically. Four projects of very distinct origin feature this and serve as an example of the aforementioned

表皮としての木材

時に木材の価値が、その強度、耐荷重性に置かれていない場合がある。木材は、それがもたらす視覚的触感だけで、建物を美しく豊かなものにすることができる。それぞれ非常に異なった風土に建つ以下の4つのプロジェクトは、このことを如実に示す良い例である。

軒の家
防護するオーバーハング

手塚建築事務所＆池田昌弘
撮影：木田勝久

EAVE HOUSE
protective overhang

東京—日本—2002

　6月初旬に始まり、それからおよそ1ヵ月間東京を包み込む梅雨が、この家の形象を強く規定している。この雨の降り続く蒸し暑い季節、住まいは雨が降り込むのを避けながら、爽やかな風を室内に導きいれることを切望する。屋外に突き出したデッキ部分を蓋う5mの軒が、気候が提示するこの問題に対する解であった。

The monsoon that starts at the beginning of June and envelopes the city of Tokyo for one month strongly marks the character of this house. During this hot season of heavy rains the interior of homes need refreshing gusts of wind and at the same time protection from the rainwater. A five-meter eave around the open part of the residence attempts to afford a solution to this problem posed by the climate.

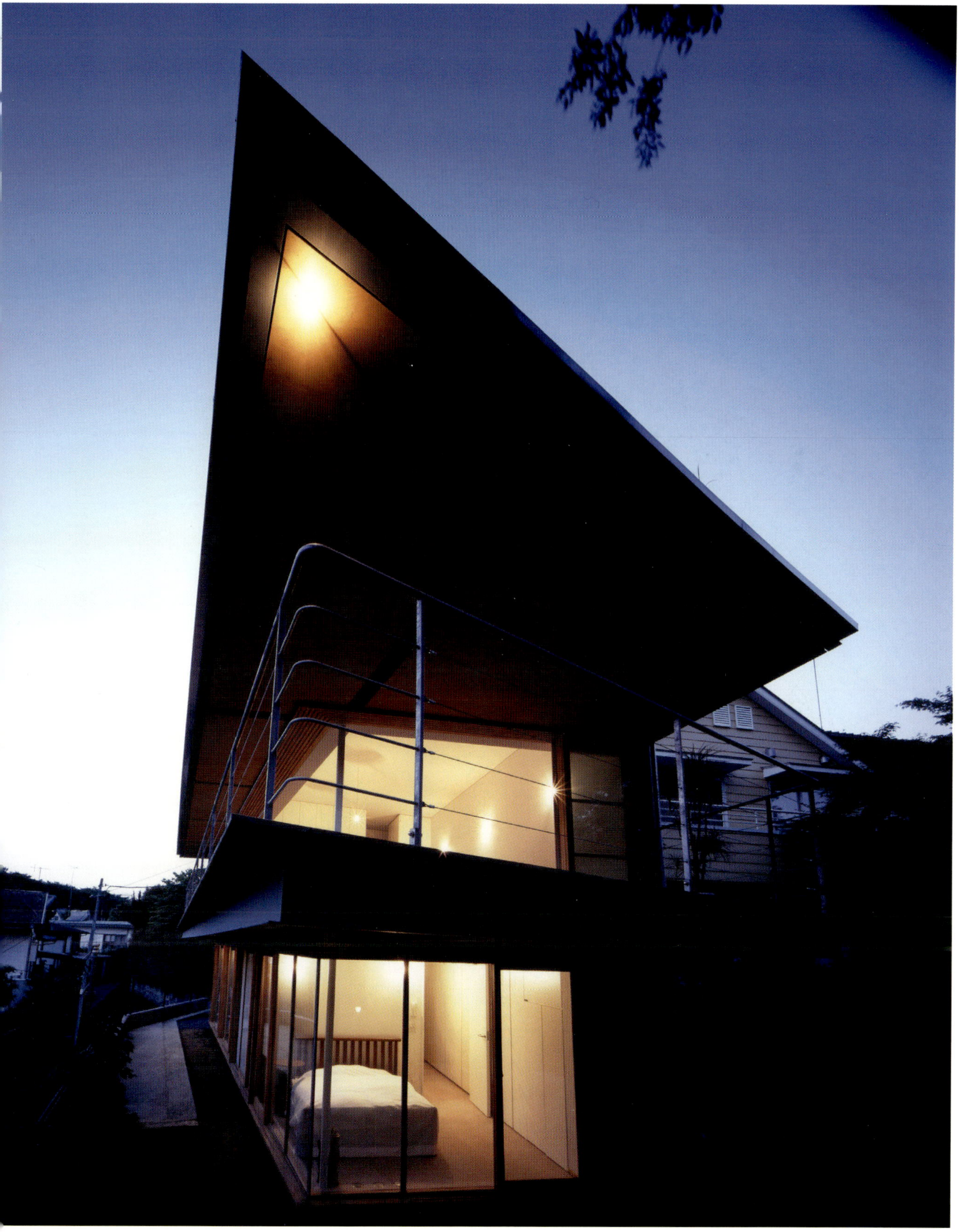

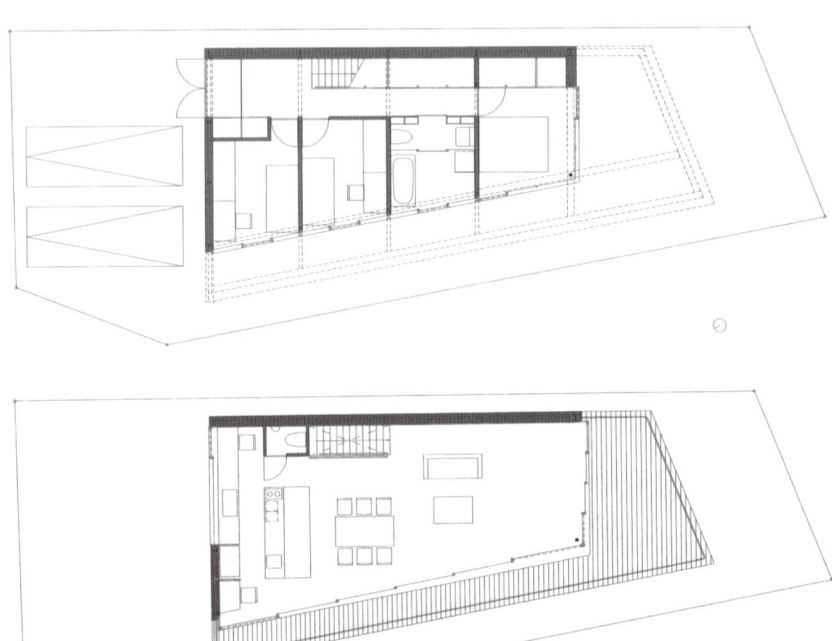

122 表皮としての木材
wood in the skin

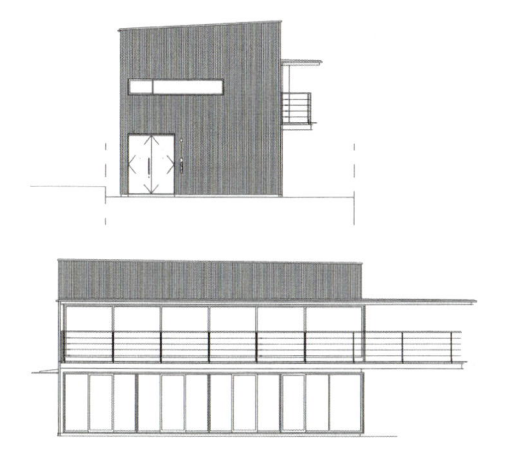

軒とデッキに挟まれた空間は、日光の室内への直接放射と雨の降り込みを抑えるため、高さを控え目にしている。スライディングドアをすべて開くと、ファサード一番外側の角に位置する柱は空に向ってむきだしになる。こうして内部空間は外側の軒の端まで拡張される。

The intermediate space of the house provides a height of slight dimensions in order to control the influx of direct sunlight and splashing from the rain. A pillar situated at the most open corner of the facade becomes open to the sky when the sliding doors are drawn, which lengthens the interior space and extends it to the edge of the eave outside.

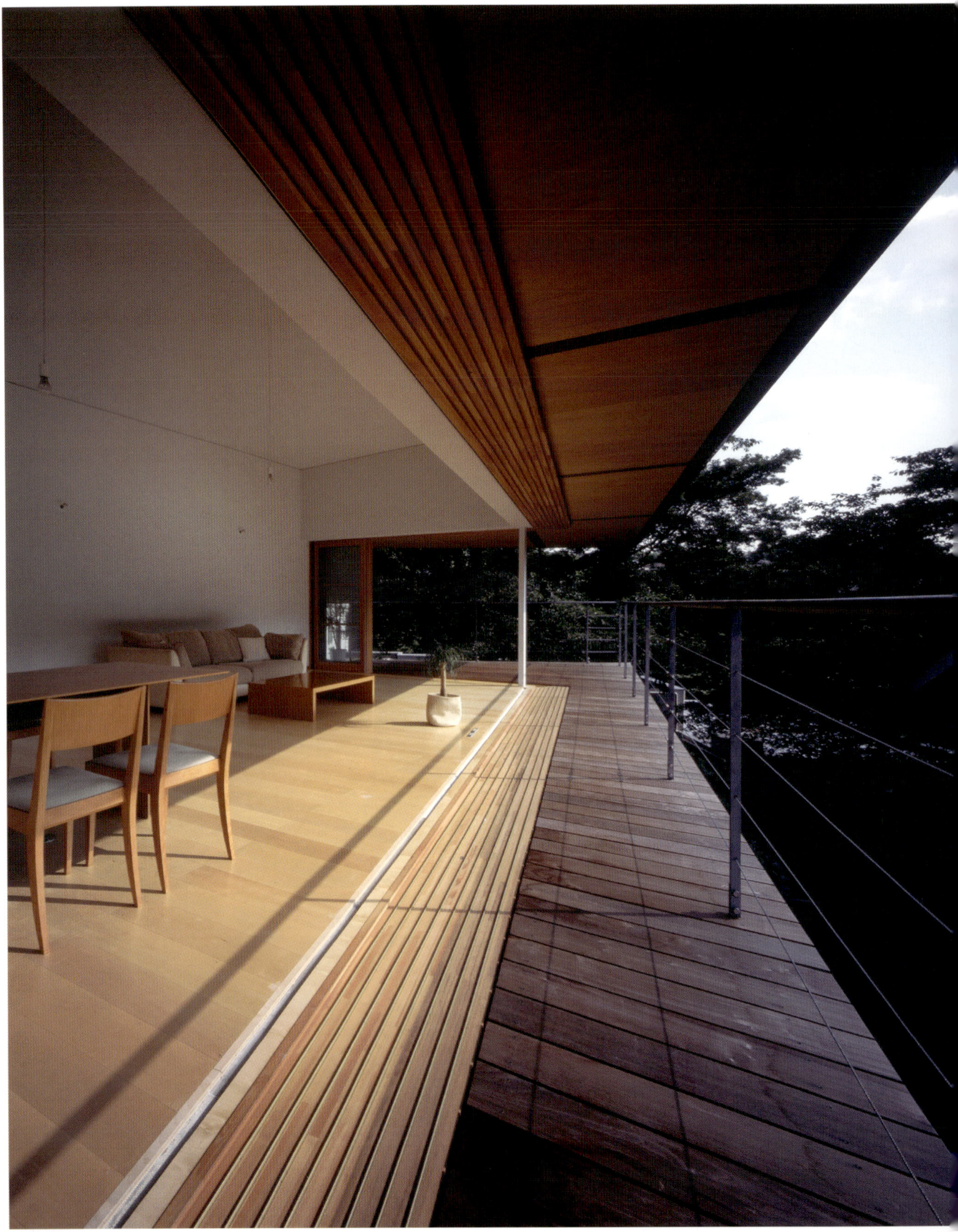

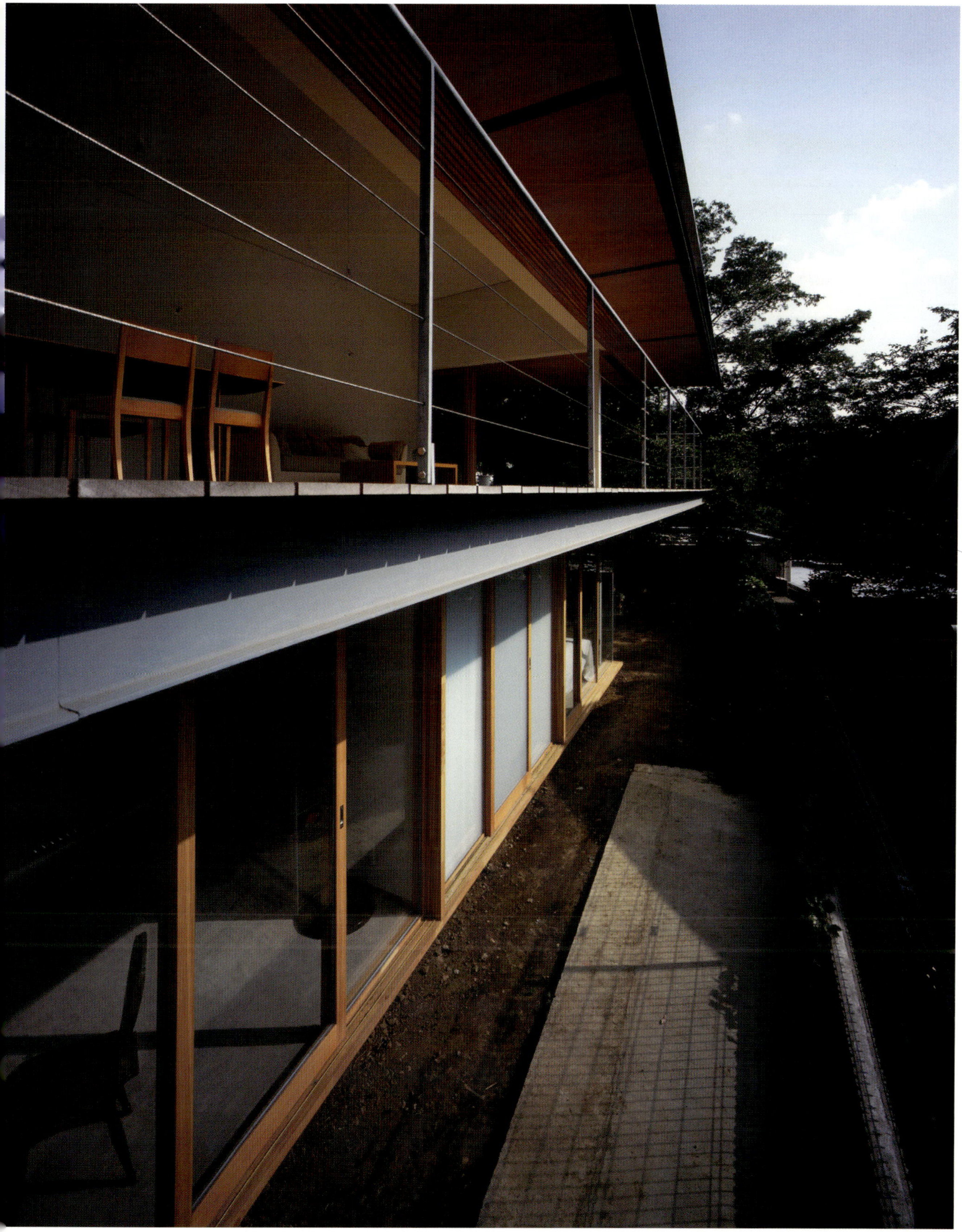

集合住宅 II
村の新しい住人

ヴォークト・アーヒテクテン
共同設計：マルセル・クノブランチ,
アントネーラ・シレノ, マーク・リヒティ
撮影：ドミニク・ビュットナー

MEHRFAMILIENHAUS II
new in the neighborhood

ムーヘン―スイス―2004

この集合住宅の構造を決定する最も重要な要素は環境であった。敷地は1813年建築の貴族の館を囲むように形づくられた村の中にある。現代美術の言語を用いながら、地元の材料を使用し、ボリュームを適度に抑えることによって、建物は周囲の強固に団結した環境との同化、統合を提示している。

The setting is the principal compositional element for this apartment block. It is placed in a neighborhood whose hub is a country house dating from 1813. By way of contemporary art language which makes use of local materials and sensible volumetries, it proposes the integration and assimilation with a consolidated setting.

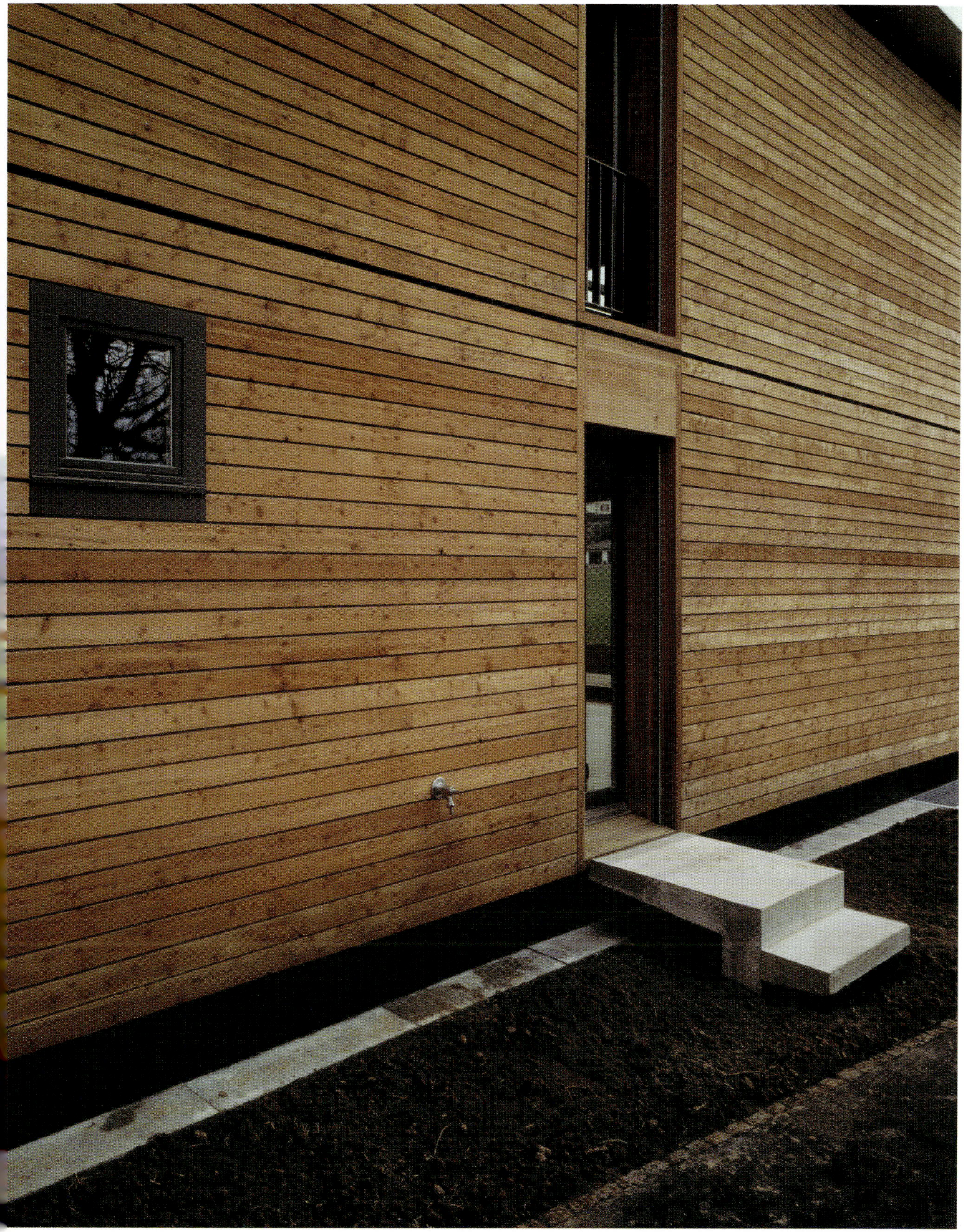

建物は2タイプの間取りの住宅4戸からなっている。ファサードは地元産出の木材、ラーチの無垢板のパネルで被覆されている。適度なボリュームとファサードの容姿が、周囲の小さな家々との同化を約束している。

The building houses four small apartments of two different types. The facade is a skin of untreated larch panels, the local wood. The volume and the facade grant an assimilation with the small buildings in the setting.

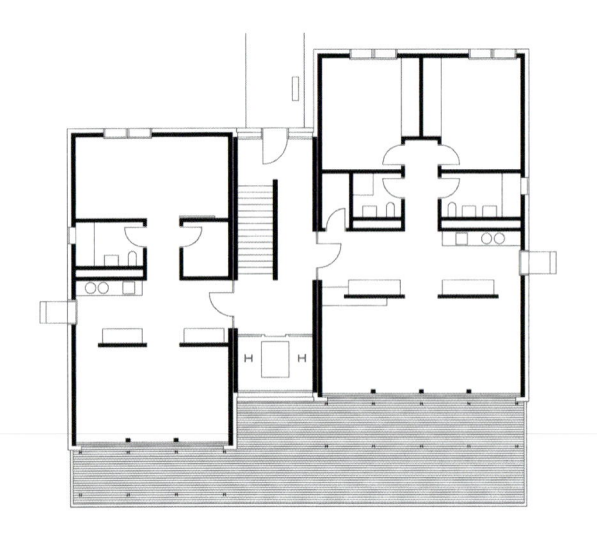

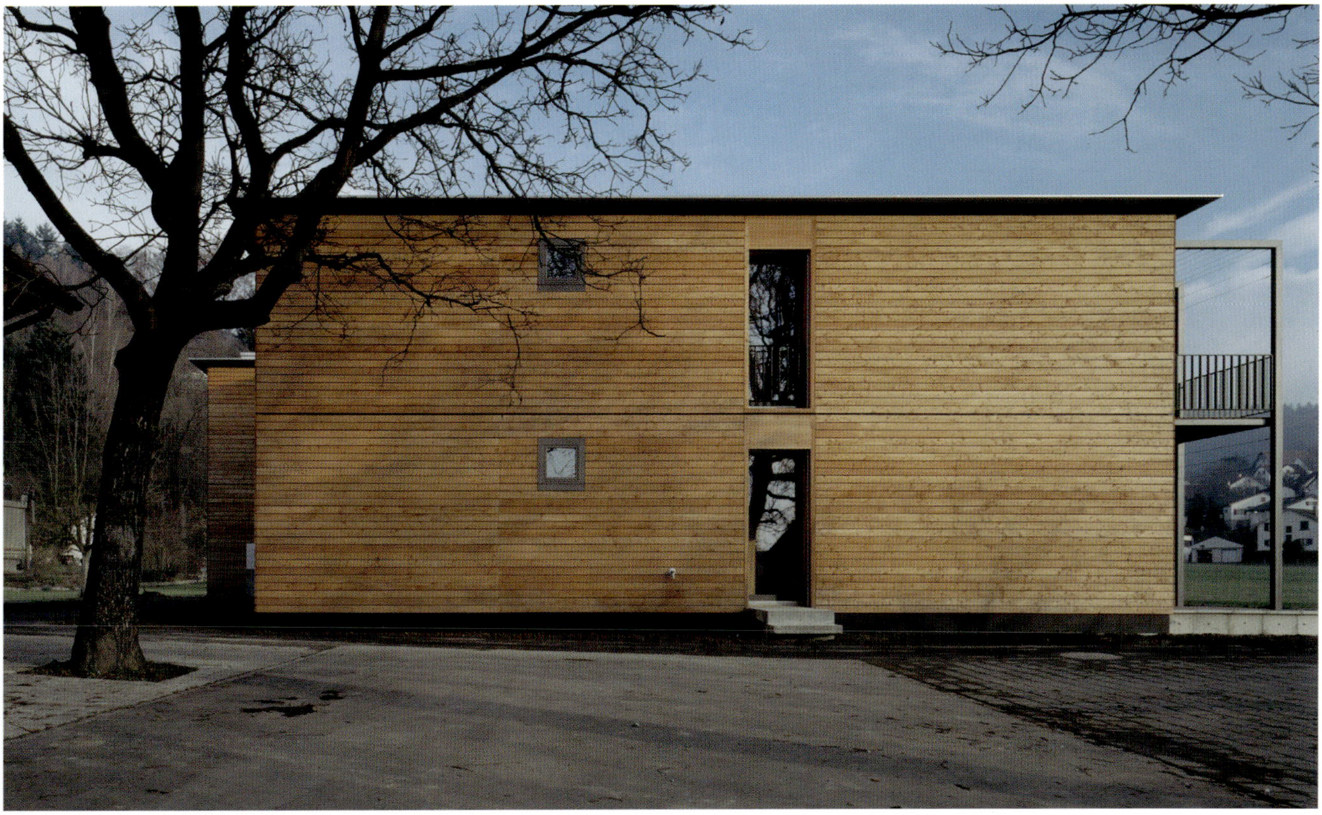

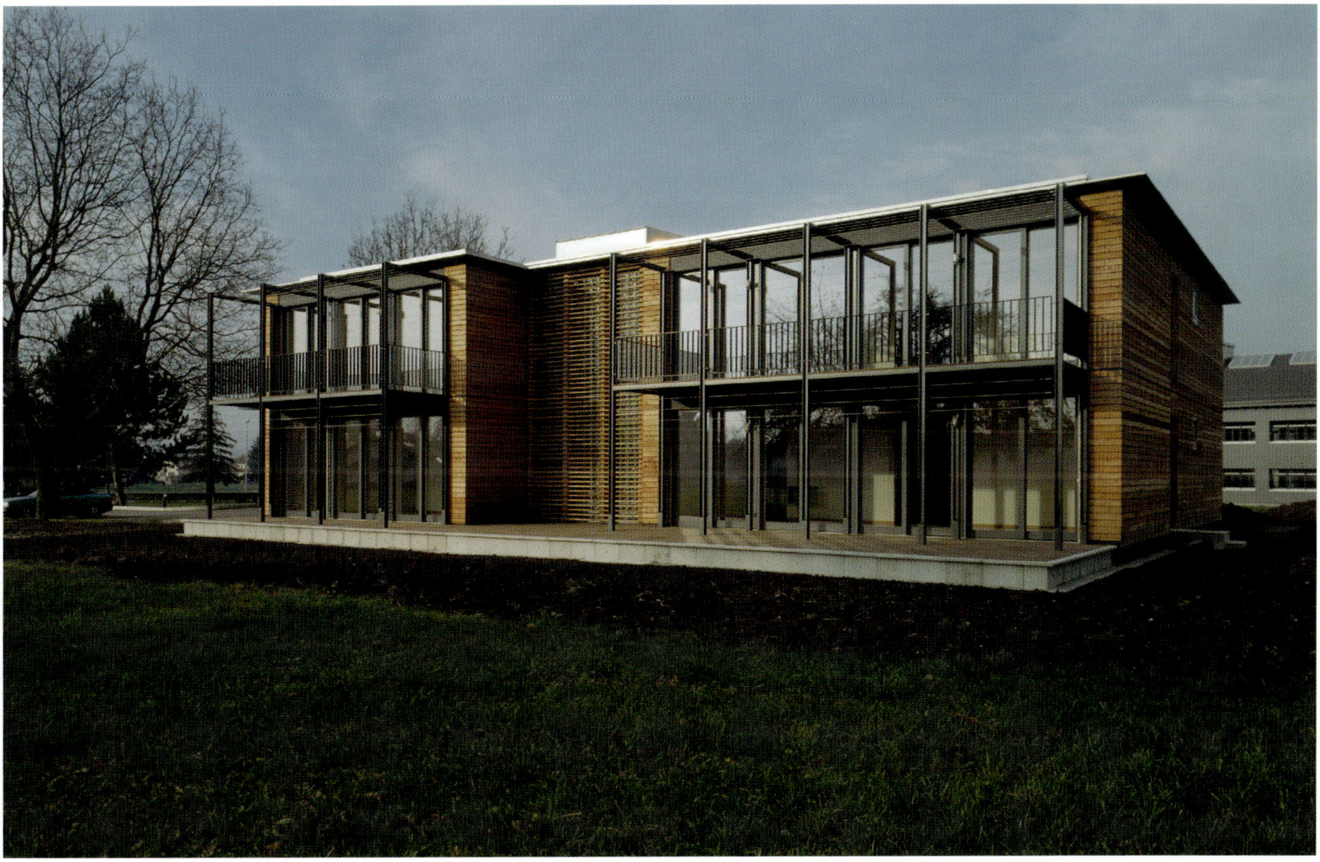

木材はファサードとバルコニーにおいて特別重要な役割を果たし、個々に分かれている金属の構造体を結びつけている。また吹き抜け階段では段板となって、ガラスブロックと鉄筋コンクリートを落ち着いた雰囲気のなかで統合し、共有スペースに調和をもたらしている。木材はまた床材として寄せ木張りに用いられ、さらには玄関、キッチンのすべての家具の材料となることによって集成材とリノリウムを融和させている。

Wood is of special importance in the facades and balconies where it is used in a separate metal structure, and in the stairwell with the steps that combine glass block and reinforced concrete in a relaxing atmosphere in harmony with its semi-public use. It is also used in the parquet wood floors and for all of the furniture of the entryway and kitchen, which combines treated wood and linoleum.

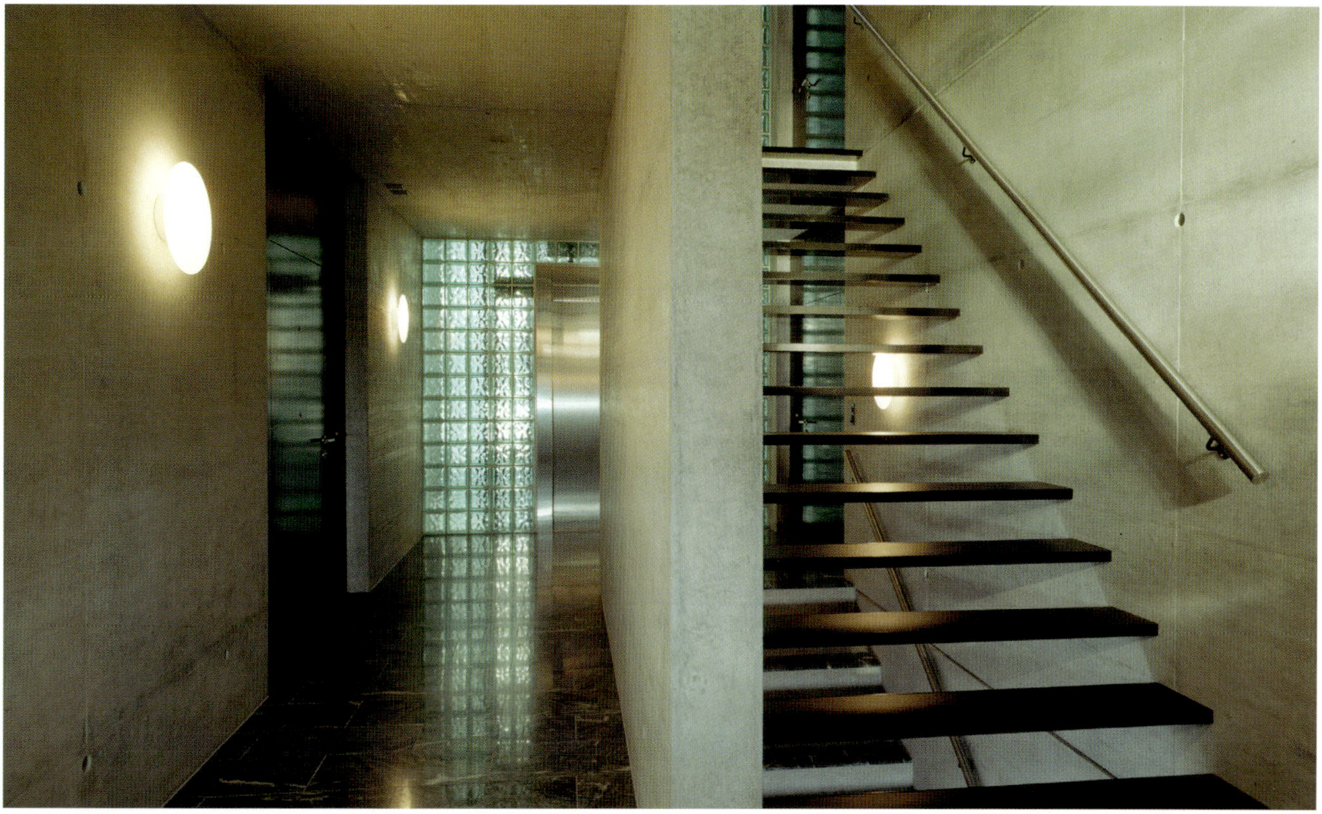

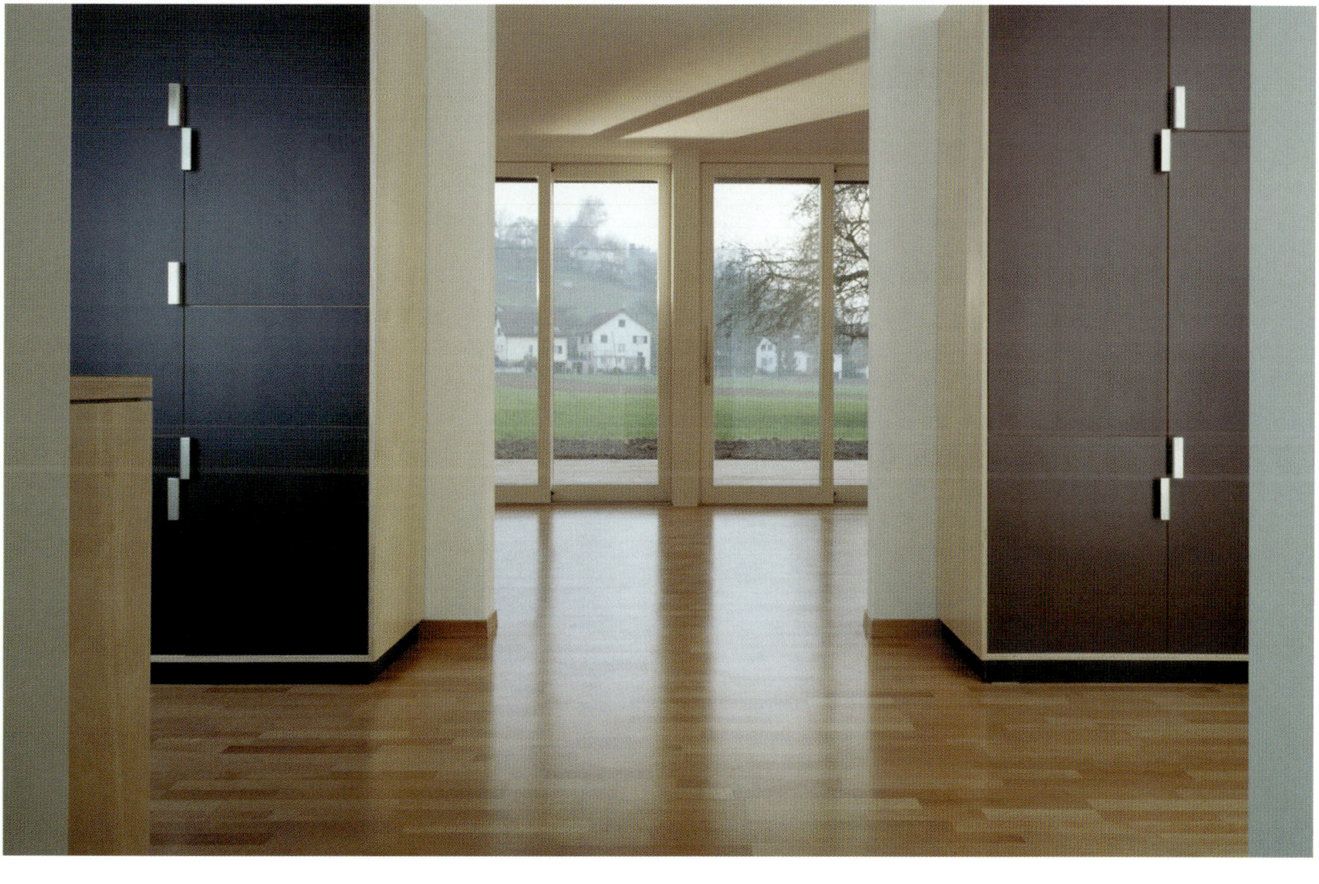

ギャロウェイ邸
豊かなる木材

ザ・ミラー―ハル パートナーシップ
共同設計：ロバート・ハル，ペトラ・ミシェリー
ブライアン・コート
撮影：ベンジャミン・ベンシュナイダー

GALLOWAY RESIDENCE
wood in abundance

マーサーアイランド―ワシントン州―アメリカ―2003

　住宅はワシントン湖の湖岸、段丘のような印象を与えるこんもりと木のおい繁った丘に位置し、湖を一望に治めている。住宅へは1本の橋が掛けられ、2階入口へと通じている。家の中へ入ると、中央に木と鉄とコンクリートでできた階段があり、1階のデイエリアへと降りて行く。すると湖がすぐ目の前に大きく開ける。

This residence is placed on wooded hillside that gives the impression of being terraced, on the shores of Lake Washington. It is privileged with a panorama of the lake. A bridge provides access to it at the upper level. Once inside, a central staircase of wood, steel and concrete descends down to the day areas on the lower floor, which open out to the shore of the lake.

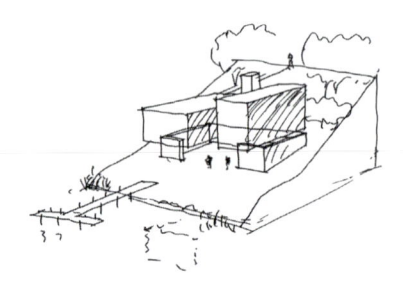

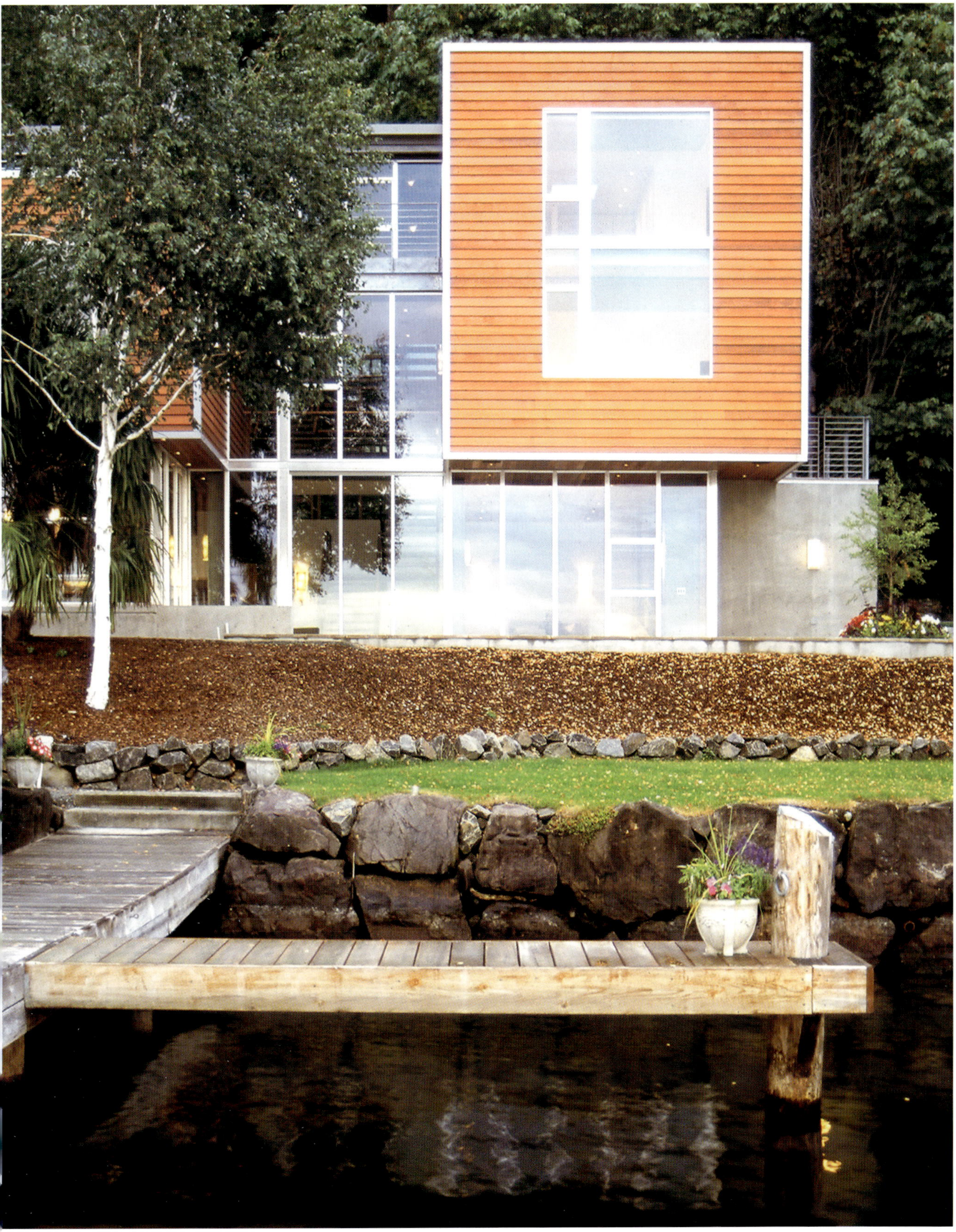

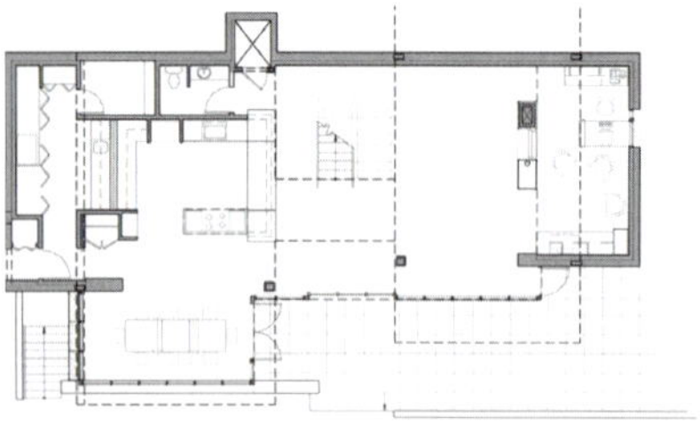

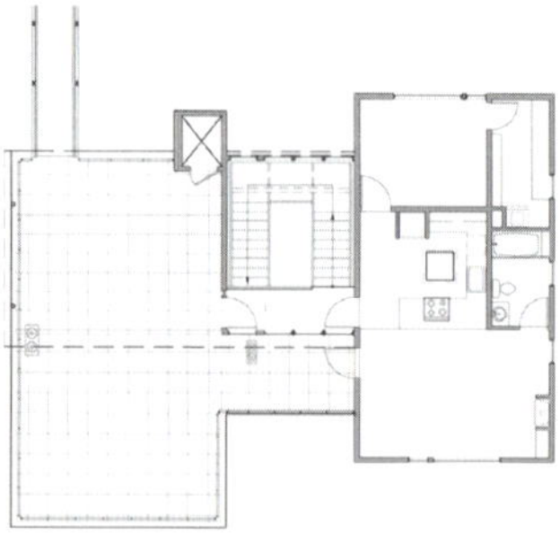

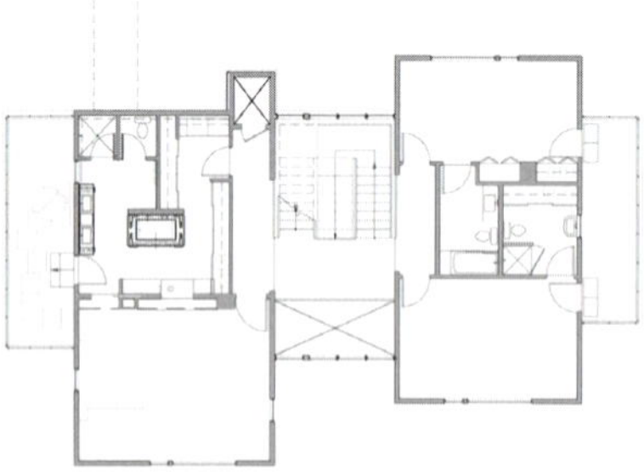

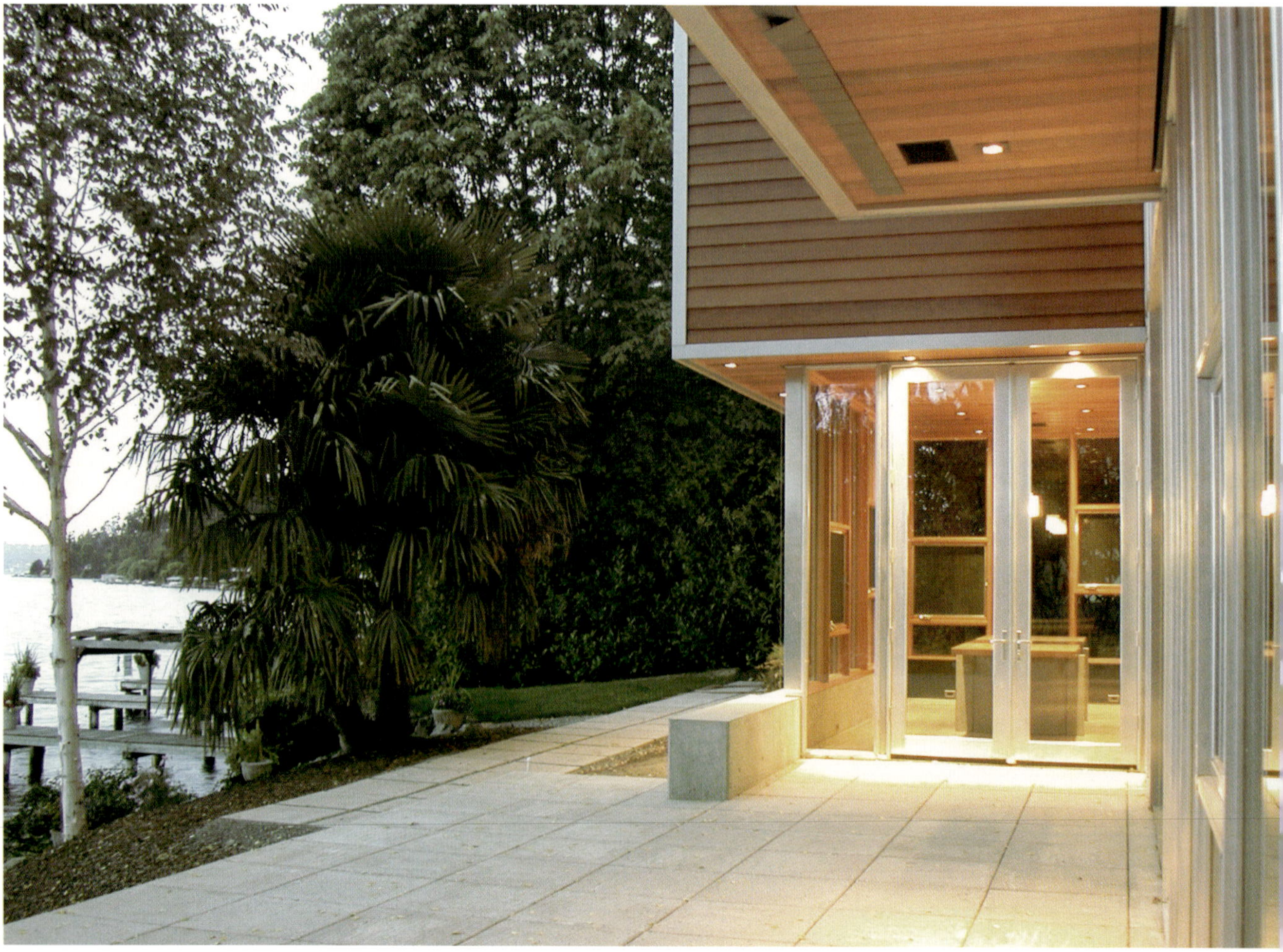

木で覆われた2個の巨大な箱が、一体成形された打放しのコンクリート壁の上に載っている。2階と3階に最もプライベートなゾーンが置かれ、客室は屋根平面の下に位置している。2個の箱はイエローシーダーの羽根板で覆われ、底面も側面も同様となっており、ボリューム全体に一体感が醸し出されている。

Two large boxes wrapped in wood perch atop a continuous bare cement wall. Here, on the second and third floor are situated the most private zones. A guesthouse has been designed under the roof plan. The boxes are clad with yellow cedar slats as are too the base below and its sides, which confer continuity to the volume.

木材による被覆、鉄、打放しコンクリート、これらの素材の組み合わせが、建物全体に強い澄明感をもたらし、森や湖との一体感を奏でている。窓わく外側は艶消しのアルミニウムを使い、内側はアップルと竹が使われている。中央の階段はパティオとなって、家全体に自然換気をもたらしている。

The combination of materials used for this building are the wood covering, steel and bare concrete, which draw the volumes with striking clarity and play with the duality of the vistas of the woods and the lake. Matt finish aluminum is used for the windows and in the interior apple wood and bamboo are the choice. The central staircase is like a patio, which provides the house with very good natural ventilation.

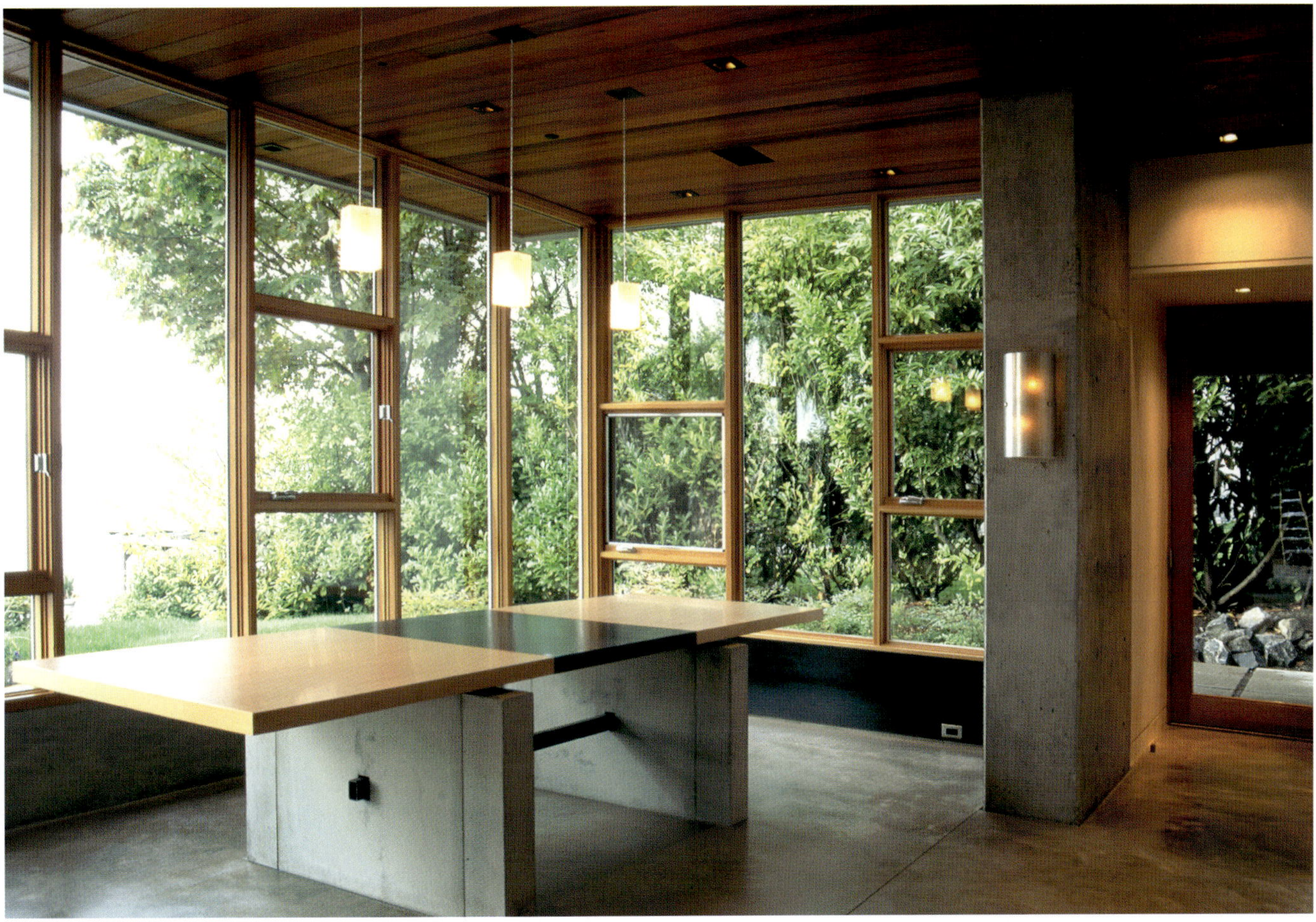

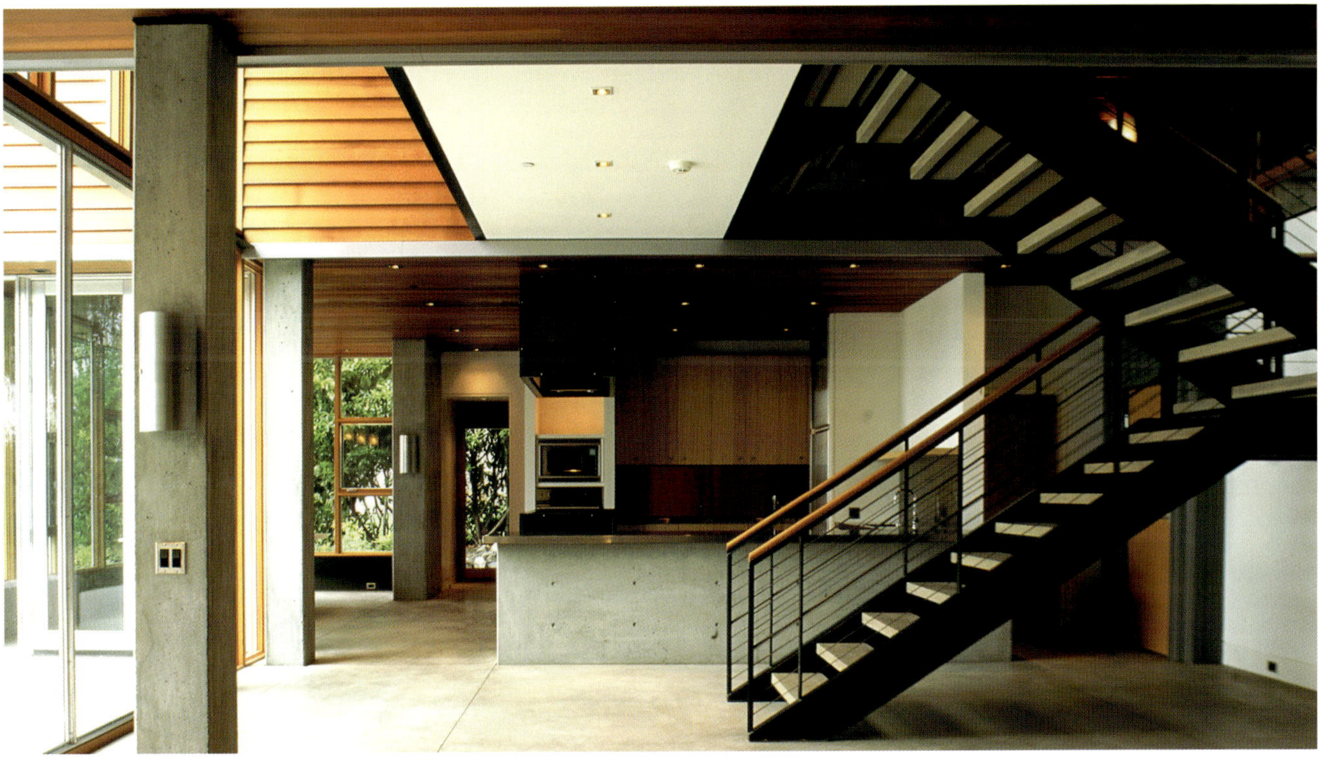

チャマルティンの住宅
第2の表皮

フエンサンタ・ニエト＆エンリケ・ソベヤノ
共同設計：カルロス・バレステロス，
マウロ・ヘレーロ, フアン・カルロス・レドンド
撮影：ルイス・アシン, 鈴木久雄

CASA EN CHAMARTÄN
a second skin

マドリッド―スペイン―2002

　1950年代から続く旧い住宅地域に新しい建物を建てるという望みは、旧い建物の取り壊しを禁ずる条例によって断たれた。そのため建築家は、2つの方向から徹底的にリフォームを行うことにした。その1つは、旧い建物の全体を木の新しい表皮で覆うこと、そして2つ目は、建物の頂点から底面まで「脊柱」を通すということであった。

The desire to build a new home in a residential area dating from the 1950's came up against regulations that prohibited the demolition of the original edifice. Consequently, the architects came up with an in-depth transformation along two lines: a new wooden envelope to cover all of the former building and a new "spinal column" from top to bottom of the structure.

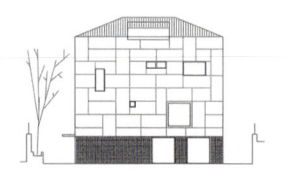

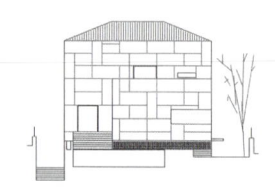

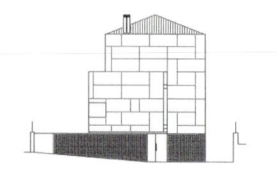

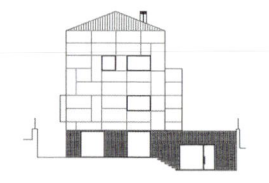

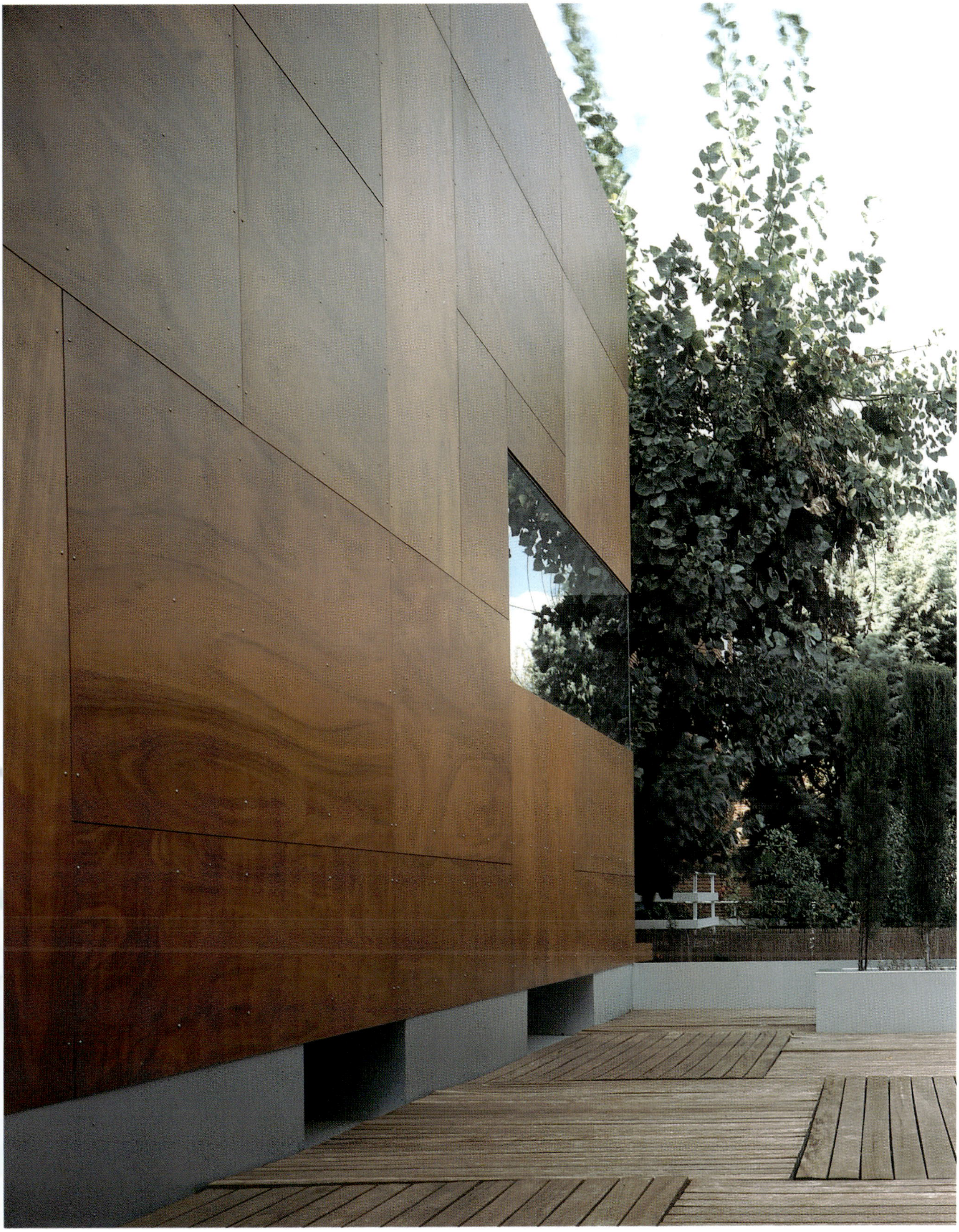

新しい包被は、高密度ベークライト処理された木質パネルの表皮である。その表皮はアルミニウムレールによって壁に固定されているが、通気層を設けてあるので、壁は換気ダブルスキンファサードになっている。地表面階はアルミニウム波板、そして屋根は銅板で被覆している。

The new envelope is a skin consisting of high-density bakelite-treated wood panels. Aluminum rails fasten it to the walls but with an air chamber so that the walls become ventilated facades. The ground floor is covered with corrugated aluminum and the roof with copper.

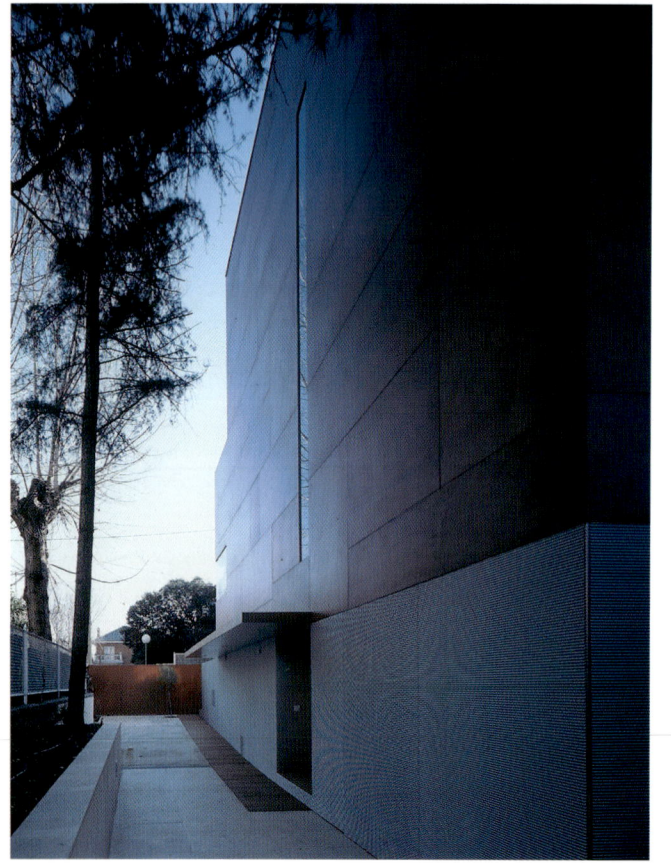

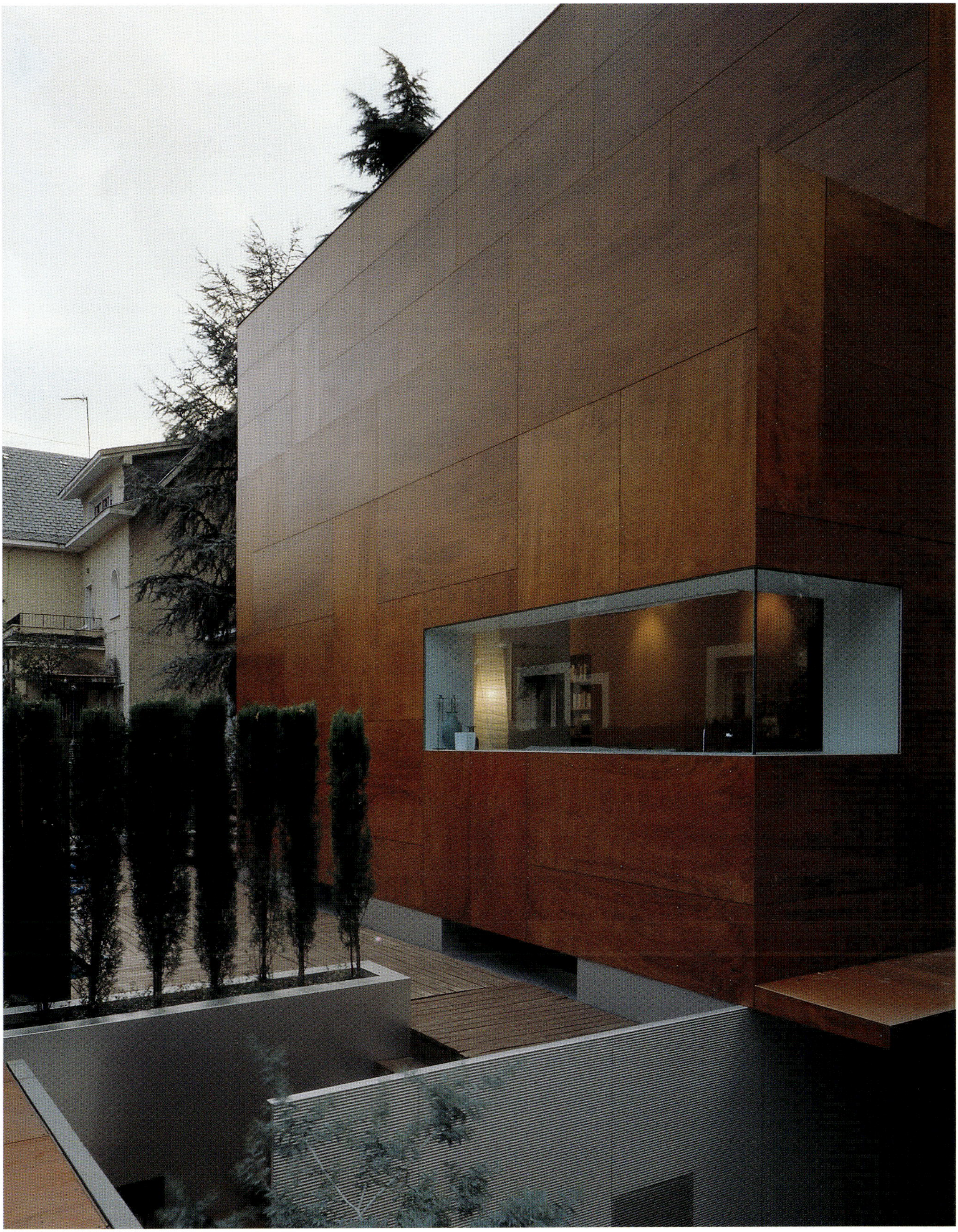

室内では、前述した「脊柱」がセントラル家具ユニットとなって、メインスペースに必要なさまざまな要素、すなわちクローゼット、書棚、収納棚、電化製品、さまざまなユーティリティ、ダクト、配線および配管、を最大限収容している。これによって床およびフロアスペースが自由に使えるようになった。包み、集める、これはすべての問題に共通する簡明な解決法であろう…そして人生そのものの。

In the inside a central furniture unit, the "spinal column", concentrates a maximum number of elements that serve the main spaces: closets, bookcases, shelves, electronic devices, and diverse utility and service ducts, tubes and pipes, thus freeing the floors and floor space for other uses. Wrap and concentrate, simple solutions to common problems… or maybe even a lifestyle?

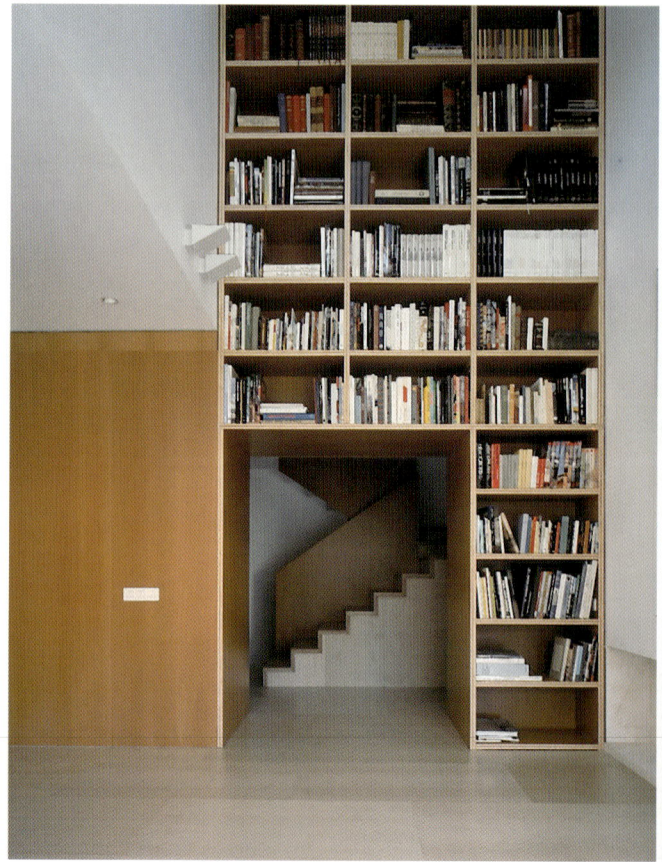

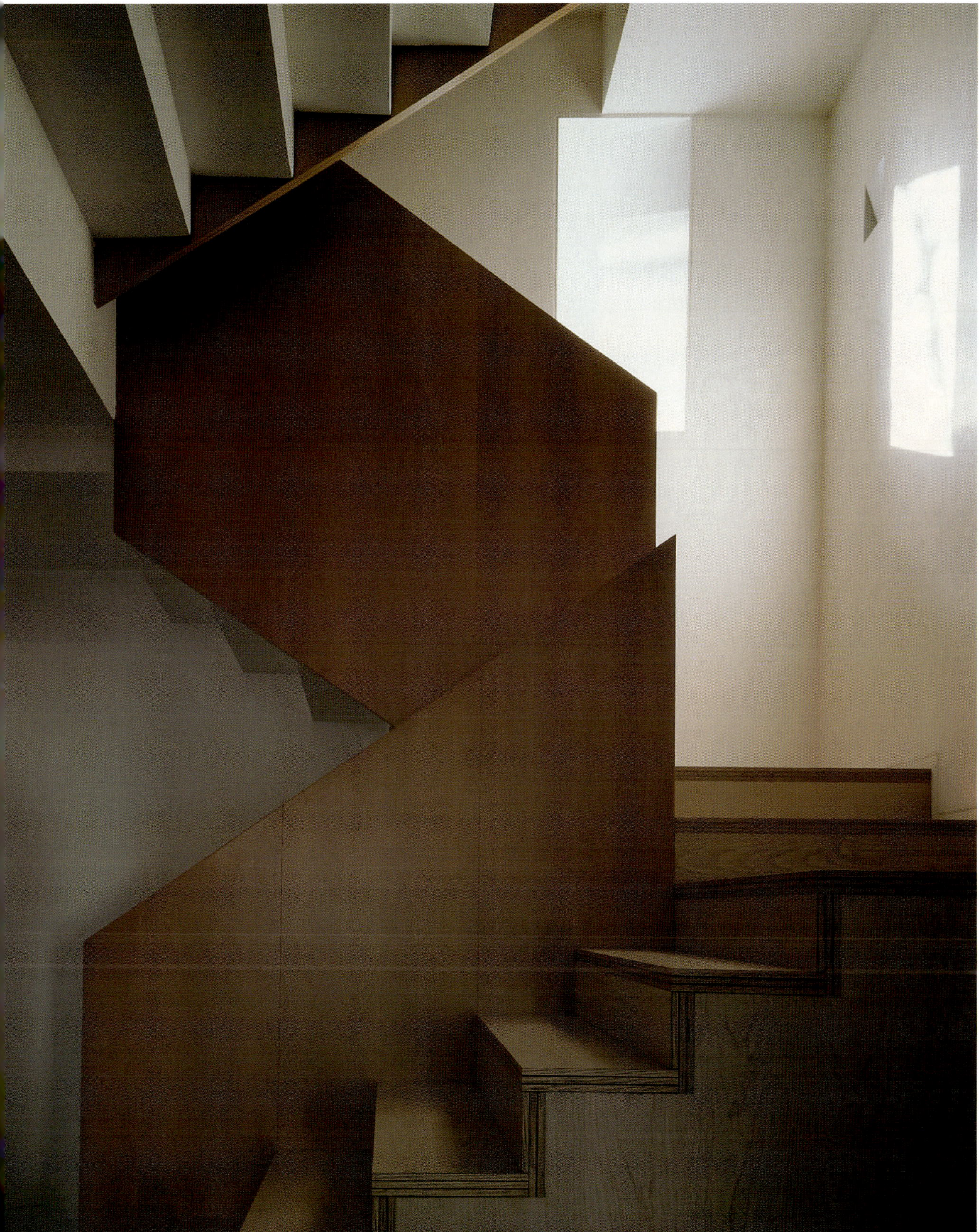

06

Sustenible Wood

Wood is a material that is renewable, ecological, recyclable and whose use is sustainable. Following, are four projects that incorporate the concept of sustainability as one element in the design. Whether in Brazil or Central Europe, respect for the environment, energy savings and the awareness that the planet which we inhabit can be used up, now pervade thinking

持続可能性としての木材

木材は再生可能で、環境を害さず、再利用できる資源である。そしてその利用は持続可能である。以下の4つのプロジェクトは、デザインの大切な要素である持続可能性という概念を具象化したものである。ブラジル、ヨーロッパと地域は異なっていても、環境に対する深い配慮、省エネルギー、そしてわれわれの住んでいる惑星は枯渇することもありうるという認識、これらが建築思想の中に充溢している。

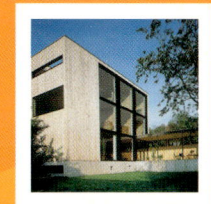

バンデイラ・デ・メロの住宅
快適さと持続可能性の共存

マウロ・ムニョス アルキテクチュラ
共同設計：アンドレア・フェルトリン
エデュアルド・ロペス, ビビアン・アルベス,
ファビアナ・タヌリ
撮影：ネルソン・コン

イツー―ブラジル―2003

CASA BANDEIRA DE MELLO
comfortable and sustainable

　サンパウロから40キロメートルの距離にあるこの建物は、2人の幼児を持つ若い夫婦のためにデザインされたものだが、ただ4人が週末を過ごすためだけのものではなく、来客をもてなし、パーティーを開き、親戚が寄り合うことができる場所として考えられた。そしてたぶん、夫婦の永久の住まいとなることまでも視野に入れられていたであろう。必然的に、建物の配置は2つのウイングを持つものとなった。1つは家族のための、そしてもう1つは来客のための。

Located 40 kilometers from Sao Paolo, it was designed for a young couple and their two small children as a weekend retreat but also as place to receive guests, have parties and family reunions and even perhaps with an eye to being their future permanent residence. Logically, the distribution calls for two wings, one for the family and one for guests.

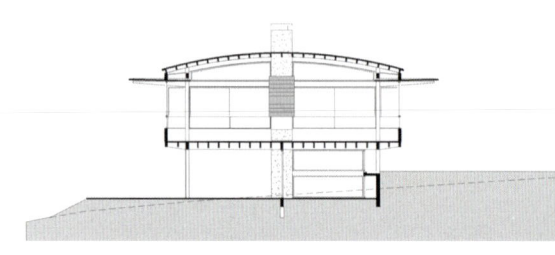

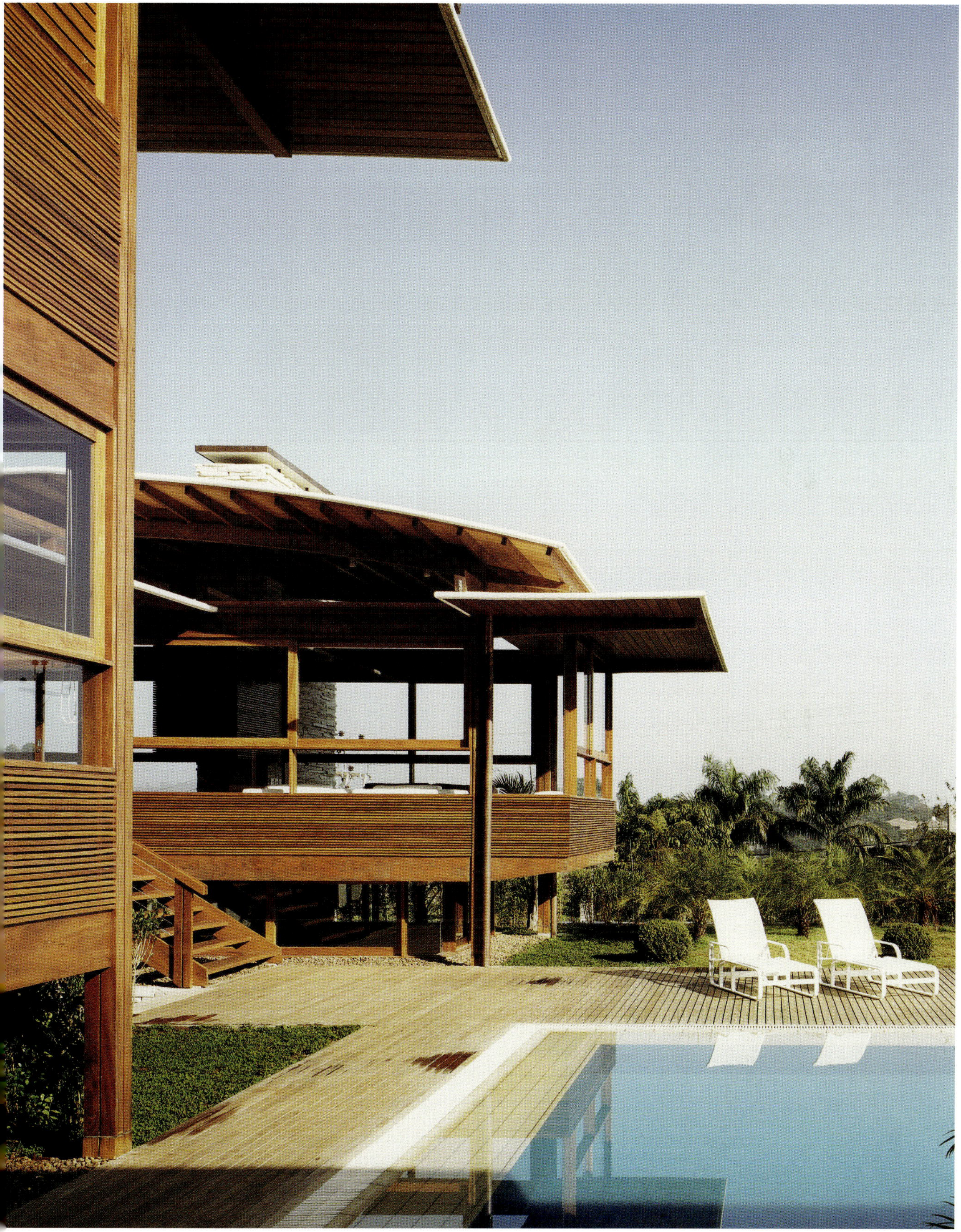

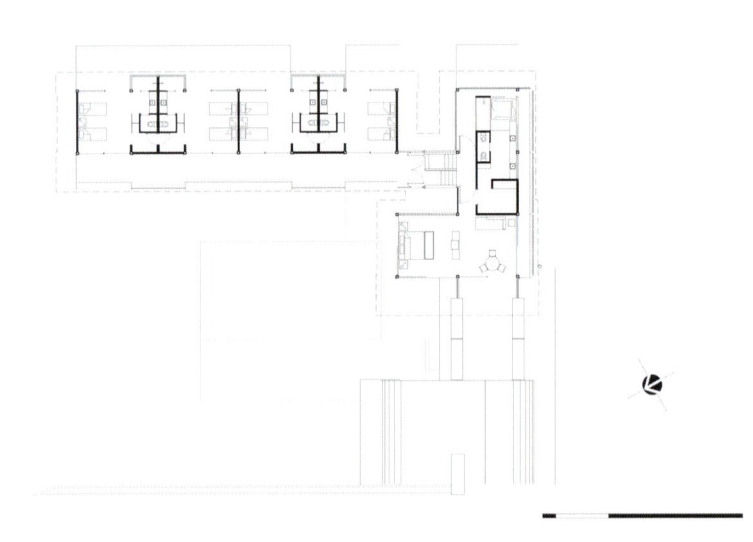

住宅は通りからとてもよく目立つ一方で、住人のプライバシーも確保されており、地形的要因(トポグラフィー)がプロジェクトの前面にでている。張り出し玄関同様に、リビングルーム、ベッドルームへの通路など、熱帯性気候の利点を最大限生かし、広々とした空間を満喫することができる。日光がこれらの半屋外空間に流れ込むとき、それに隣接する部屋も同様にたっぷりとそれに浸かることができる。

The topography comes to the fore in the project as the house is prominently visible from the street while at the same time affording privacy to those inhabiting it. Open spaces akin to porches, such as the living room and the access to the bedrooms, can be enjoyed, thus taking full advantage of the tropical clime. When the sun flows into these intermediate spaces, it likewise generously bathes the adjacent rooms.

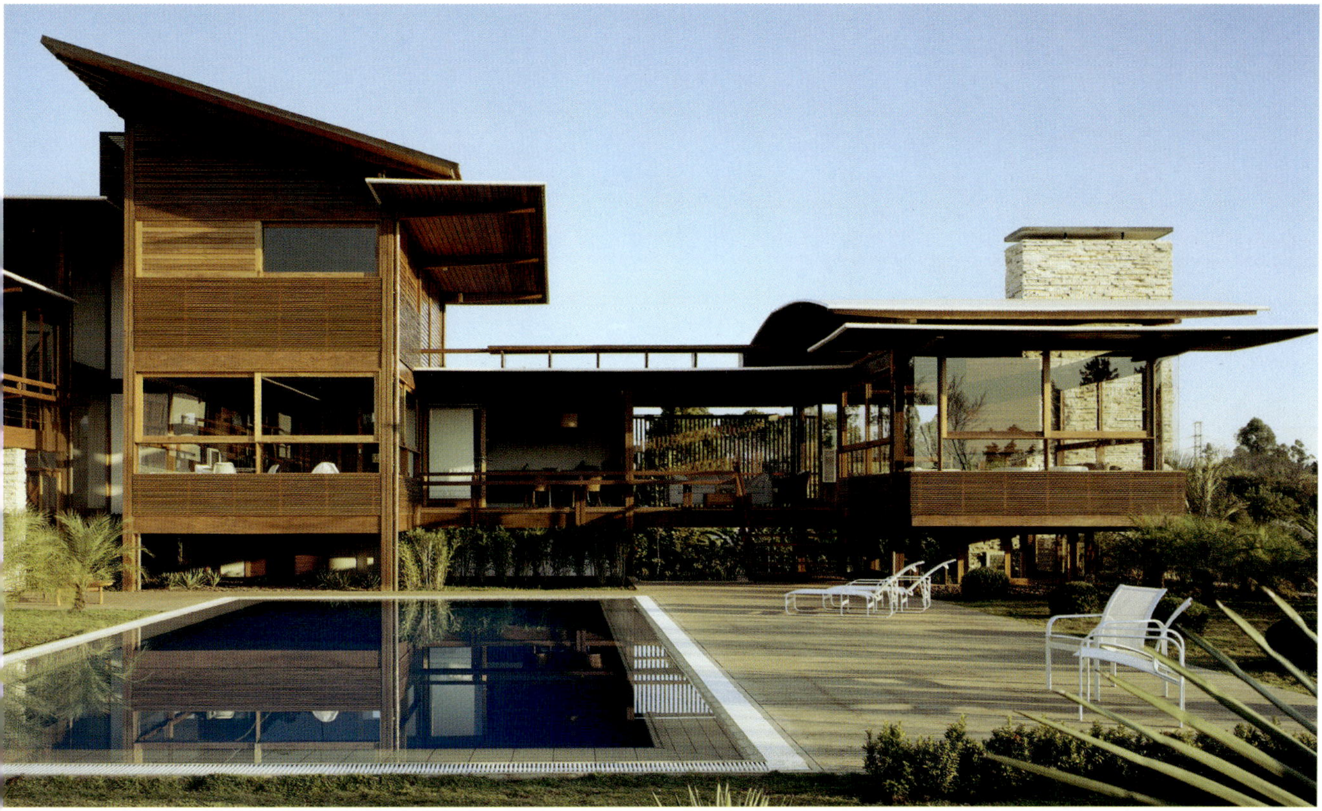

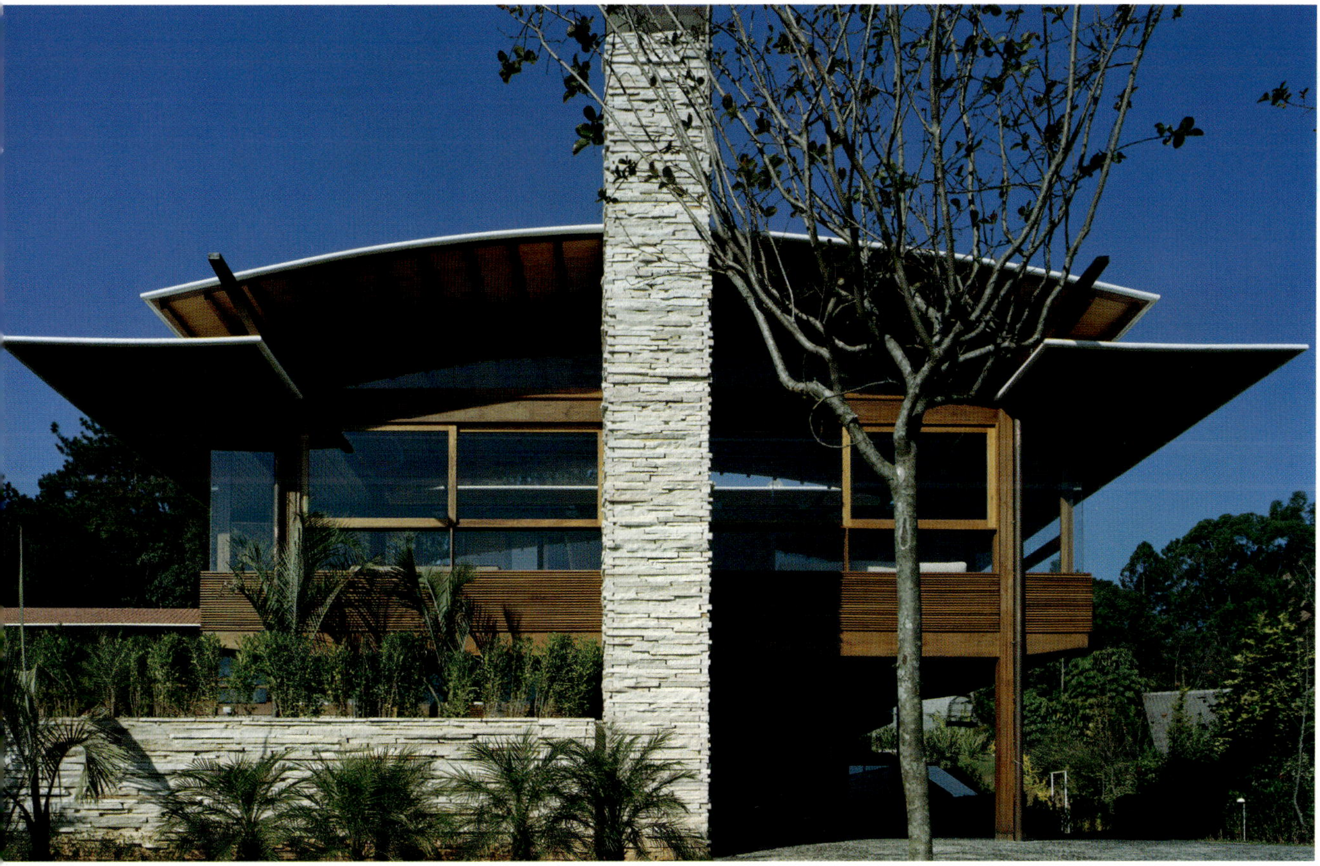

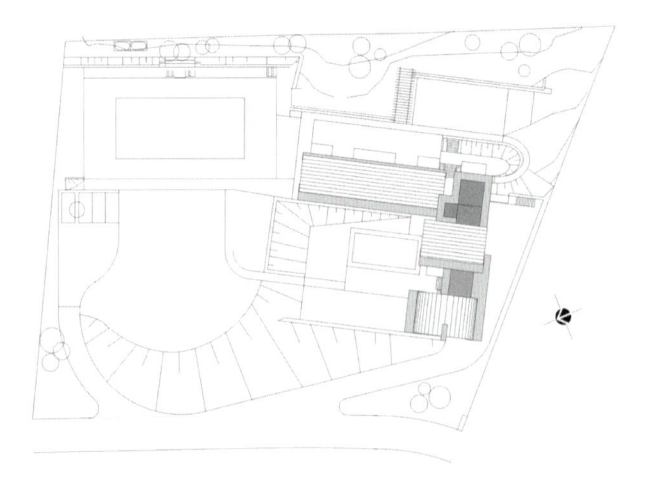

住宅の構造は、すべて環境保護団体によって認証されたクマル材からできており、それらは工場で成形加工され、現地ですばやく組み立てられた。受動換気、自然光の取り入れ、太陽熱利用、ポーチによる日陰の活用、渡り廊下など、設計に組み入れられたさまざまな配慮が、この家のエネルギー効率を非常に高いものにしている。

The structure of the house, totally of coumarou wood with environmental certification, was cut and prepared in workshops and assembled at the site with great speed. Features of the project design such as passive ventilation, natural light, taking advantage of the hot sun, the shade provided by porches and breezeways, improve the energy efficiency of the house.

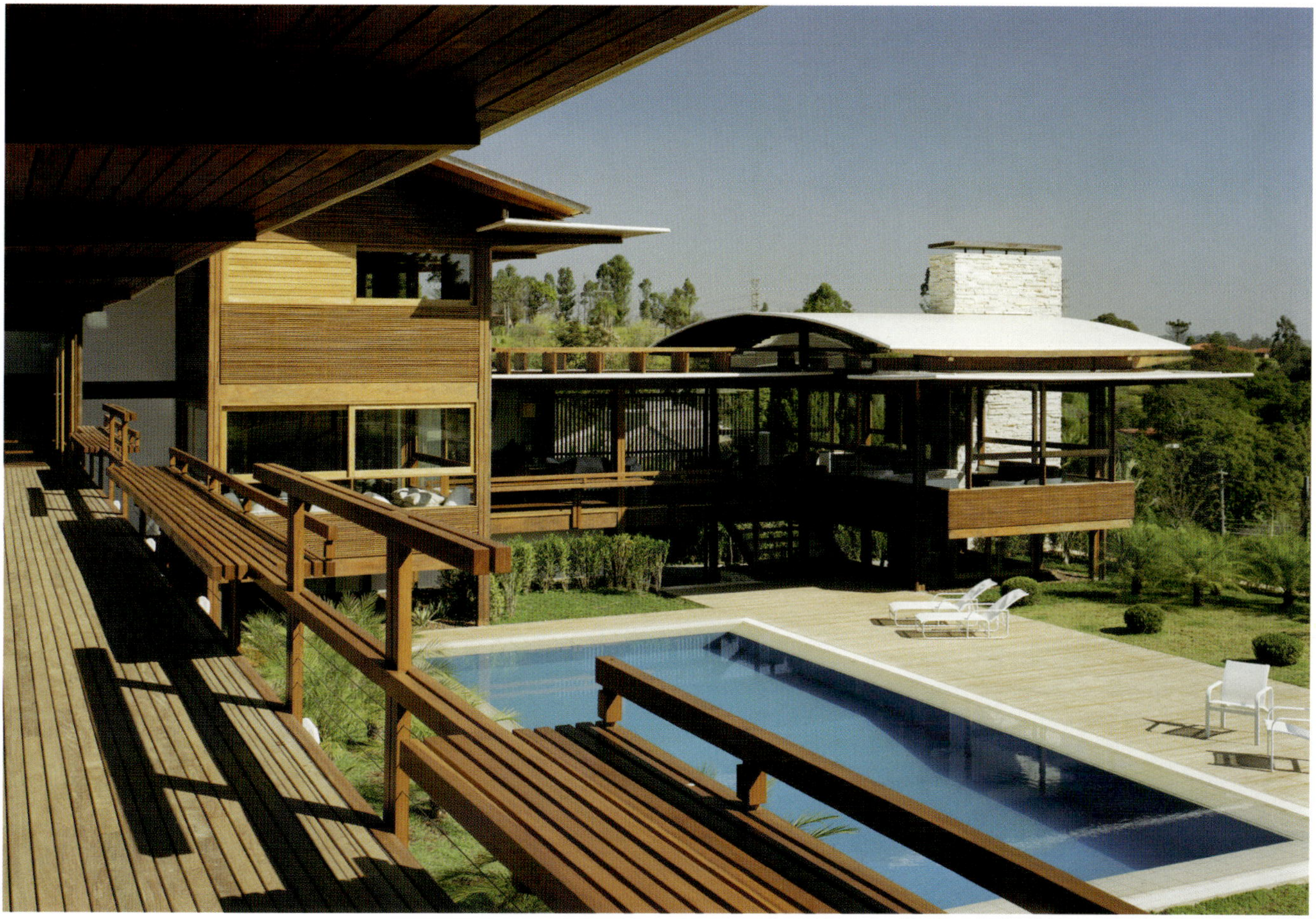

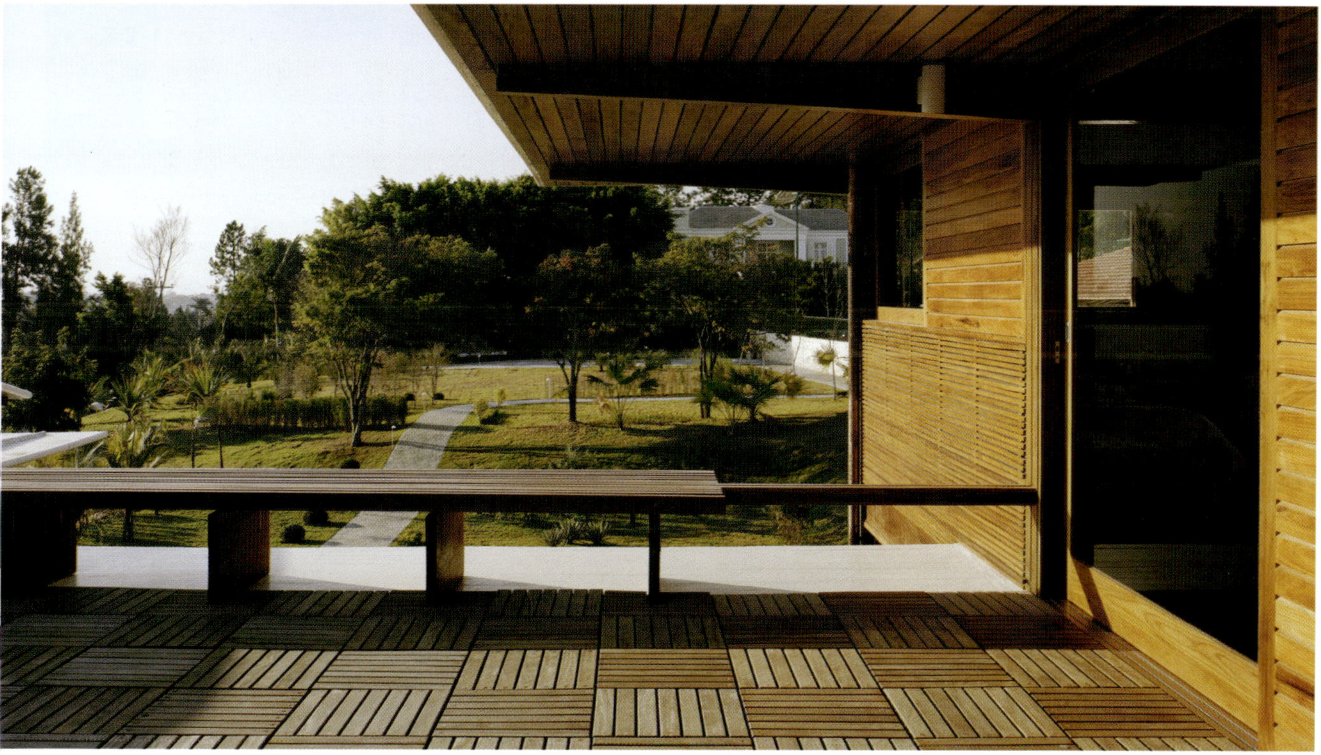

シュタインヴェントナー邸
神々の住む空間

ヘルトゥル・アーヒテクテン
共同設計：ミヒャエル・シュレッケンフックス
撮影：ポール・オット

STEINWENDTNER Haus
divine atmosphere

ステイヤー―ムンクホルツ―オーストリア―2003

　低予算の戸建て住宅としてデザインされたこの住宅は、庭の自転車用ガレージとガーデンツール用倉庫が鉄でできている以外は、ほとんどすべて木でできている。狭い敷地を最大限有効に活用するため、1階部分は、デイエリアの各部を結ぶ移動スペースは統合され、通路のない平面プランになっている。

Designed as a low-cost one-family home, it is totally made of wood, except for the two volumes sitting in the garden, the garage for bicycles and the shed for the garden tools, which are made of steel. To compensate for the lack of surface space, the transit areas that connect the day areas on the lower floor are integrated, which results in a floor plan without passageways.

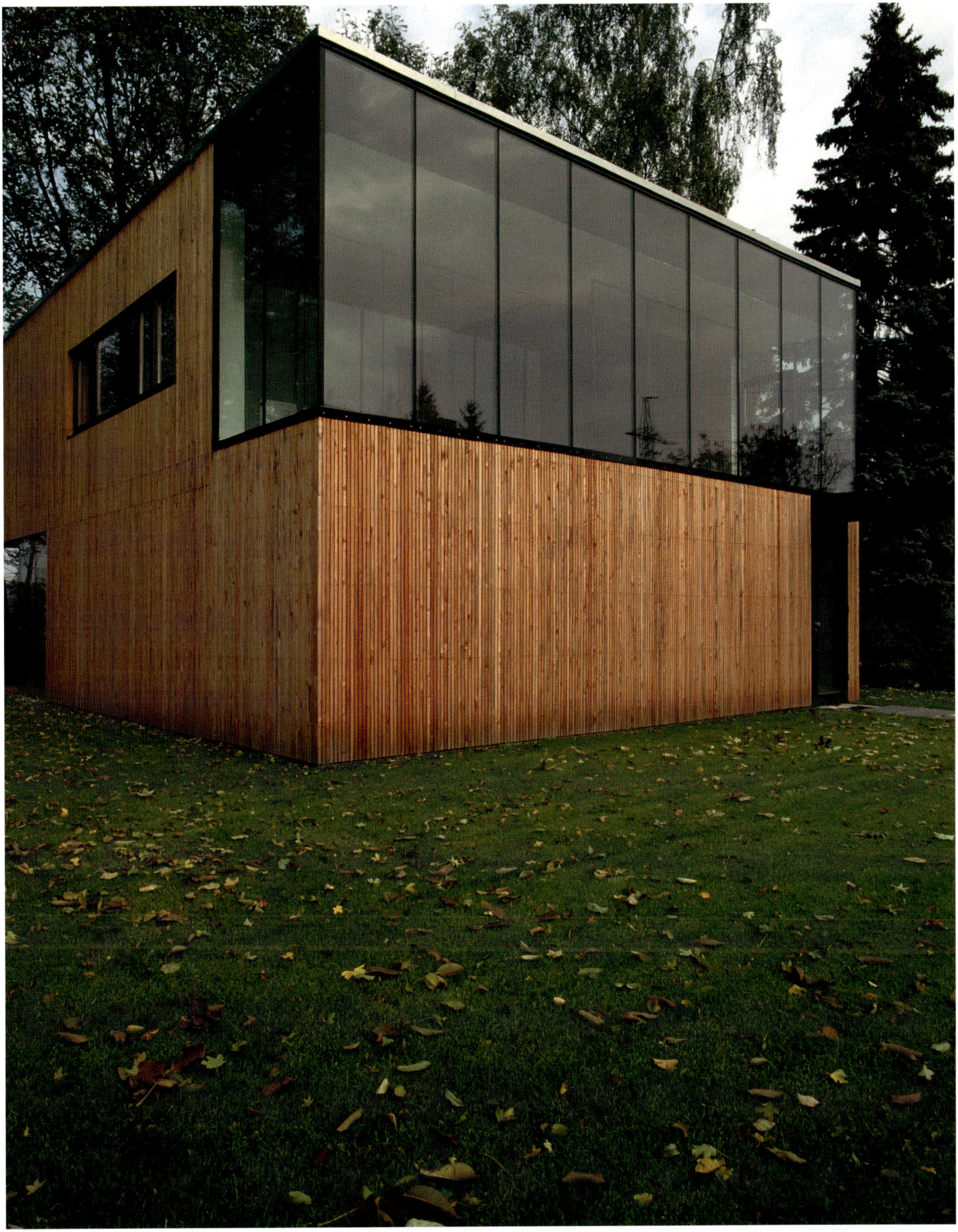

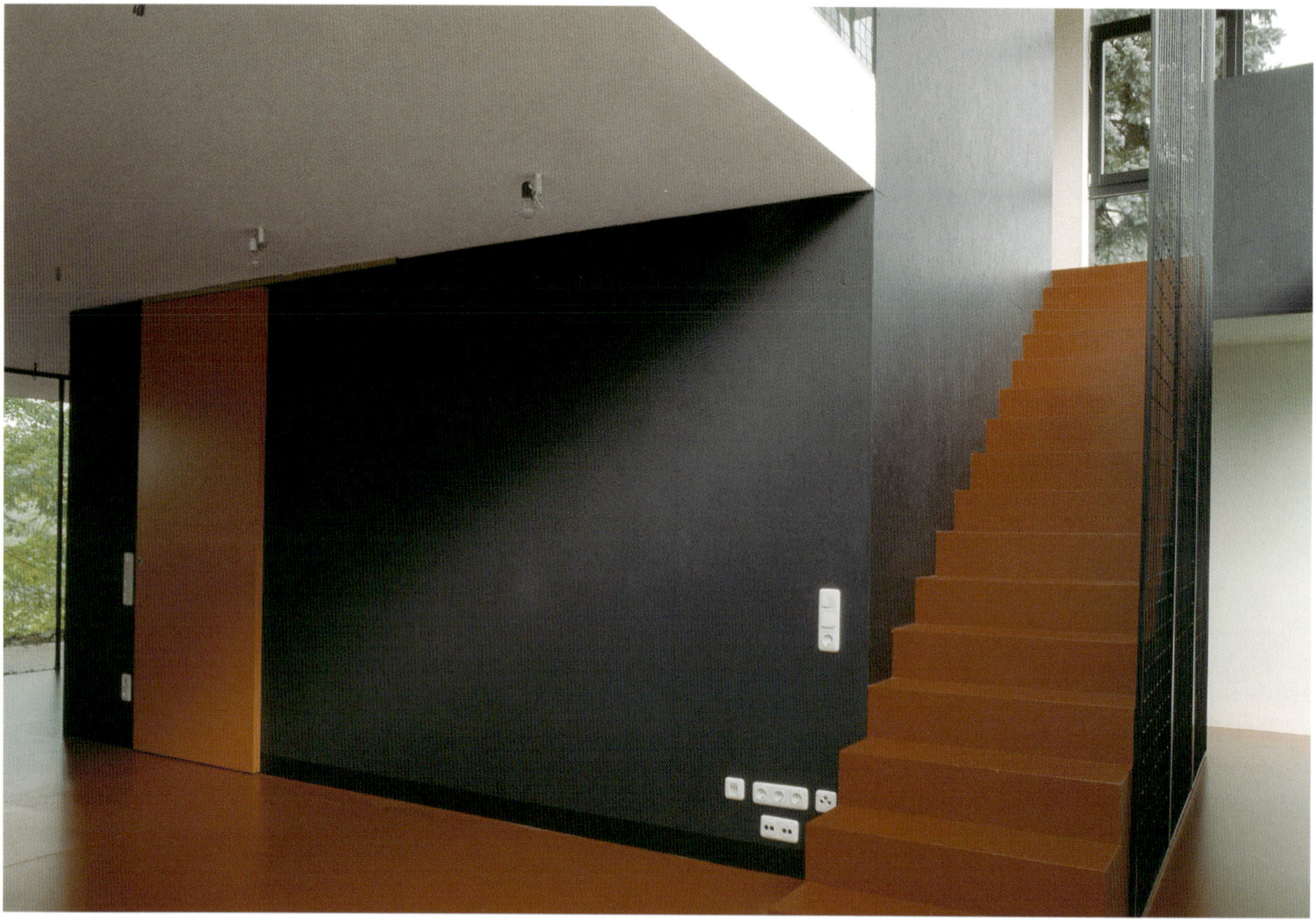

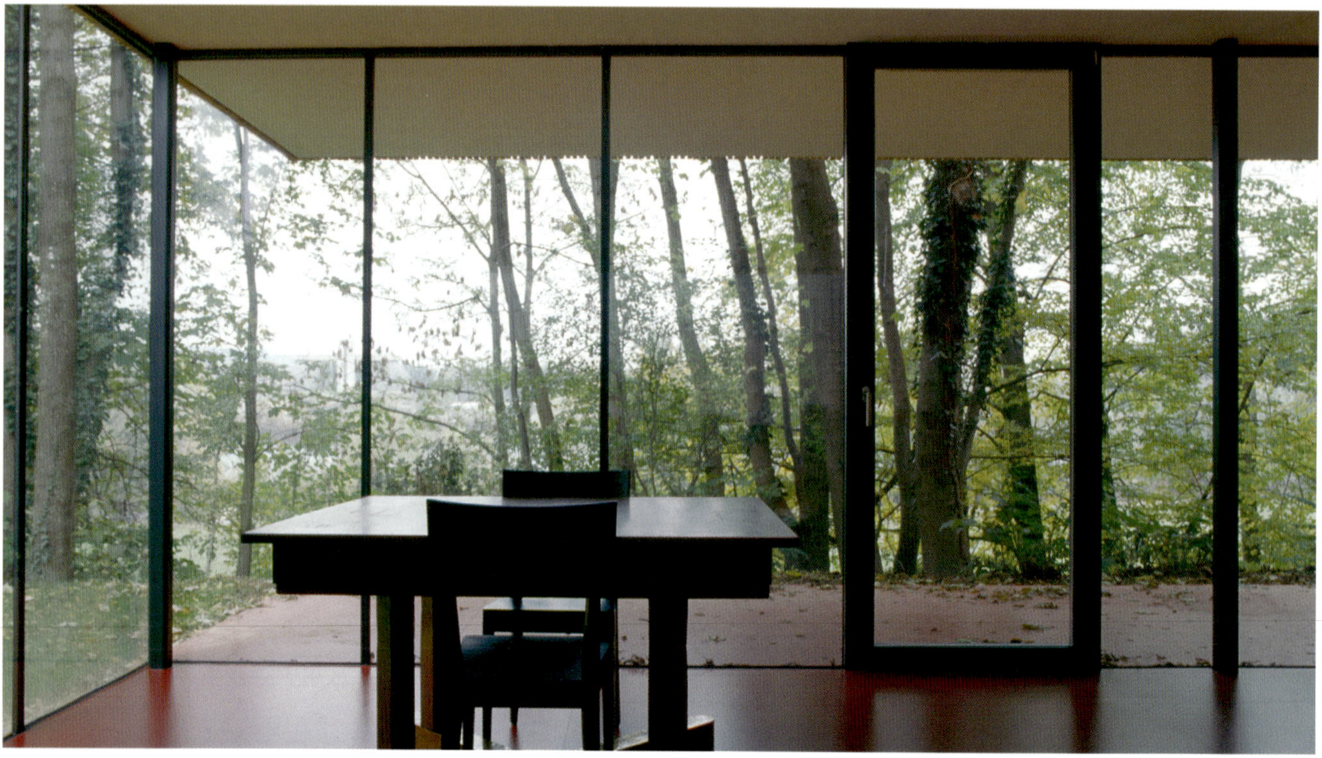

住宅内部に入ると、誰もがそのたっぷりとしたボリュームに驚き、外部からは決して想像できない広々とした空間を味わうことができる。最頂部のガラスパネルを通して、南からの日光が霧のようにリビングルームに降り注ぐ。これによって通りからは内部が見えなくなり、内省的な雰囲気が創造される。それこそまさにクライアントが望んでいたことであった。

Once inside the dwelling, one becomes aware of the general volumetry of the building and enjoys a feeling of spaciousness that is impossible to anticipate from the outside. Through the glass panels at the top, sunlight from the south filters in like mist into the living room areas. This blocks the view in from the street and creates an ambience of introversion, just exactly what the proprietor wanted.

北側では、建物からえぐるように切り出されたテラスを通して、リビングルームは直接、隣接する森の緑へと延長する。室内に氾濫する光、森や他の部屋を通して濾過された光、これと遠い神秘に満ちた聖なる場所に注ぐ光との類推、これがこのプロジェクトを通しての前提であった。

On the north side the living room expands out to the green of the adjoining woods thanks to the terrace, which is cut from the building. The analogy of the light that floods the house, a light which is filtered through the trees or other rooms, to the light to be found in sacred places, distant and full of subtleties, was a premise throughout the project.

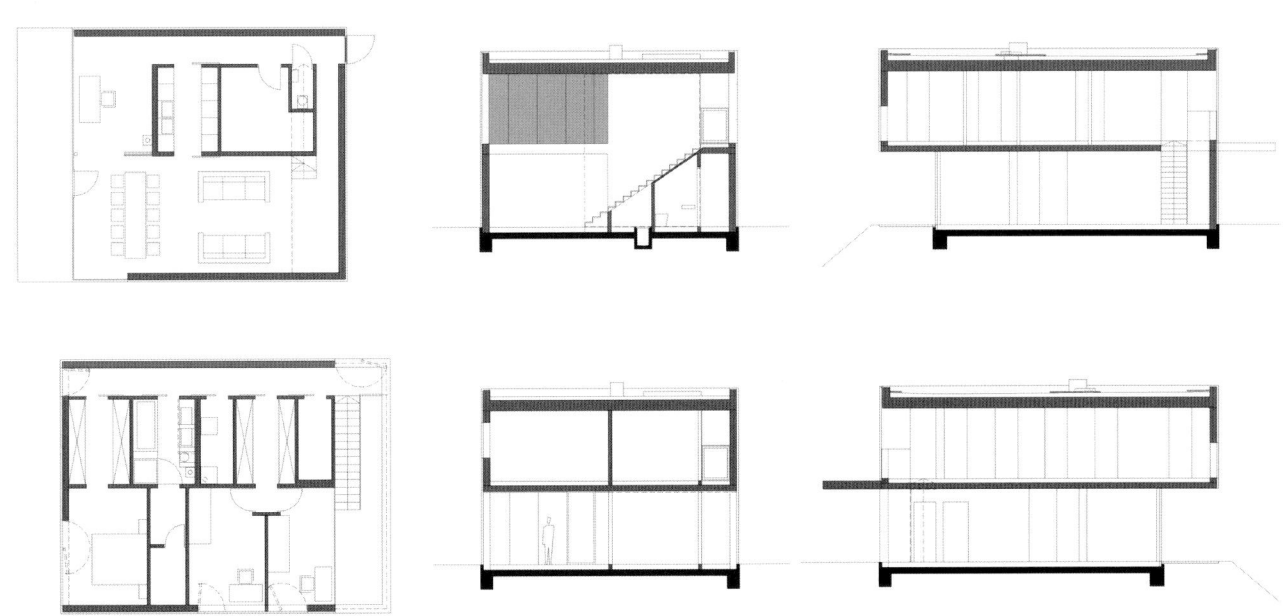

157 持続可能性としての木材
sustenible wood

パッシブハウス
エネルギーを捕まえて

ヨハネス&オスカー・レオ・カウフマン
撮影:イグナシオ・マルティネス

PASSIVEHAUSANLAGE
energy trapper

ドルンビルン―オーストリア―2003

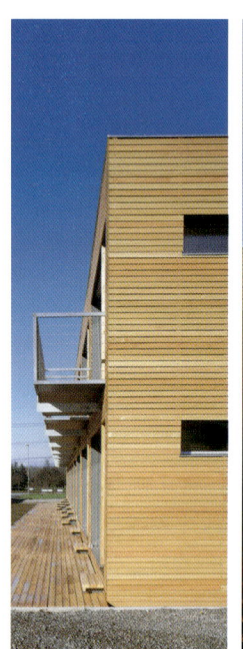

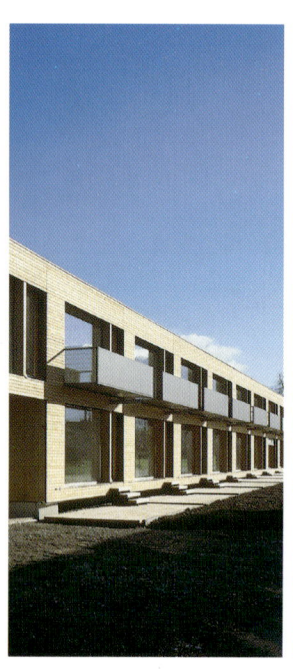

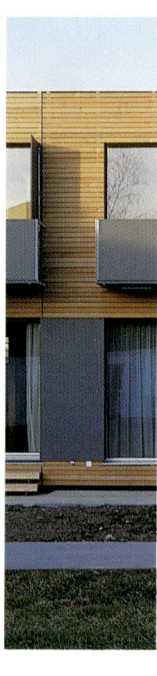

　この複合住宅は、横一列に並ぶ1戸の賃貸住宅と9戸の住宅から構成され、地下にはガレージが完備されている。建物はすべて木造であるが、これは新しい試みである。というのもつい最近まで、防火基準により各戸の間に耐火壁を設けることが義務づけられていたからである。建物は並列に建てられているいくつもの棟からなる大きな住宅地域の一部を構成している。全体として見ると、建物は一連の個性的なファサードから構成される市街地の景観である。

The complex consists of one apartment and nine dwellings in a row complete with an underground garage. It is all built in wood which is a novelty as until now fire restrictions obliged the use of fire walls between each residence. It is part of a much larger residential area arranged in rows. Seen in its entirety, it is a cityscape made up of series of distinct facades.

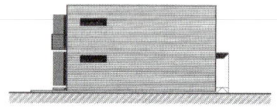

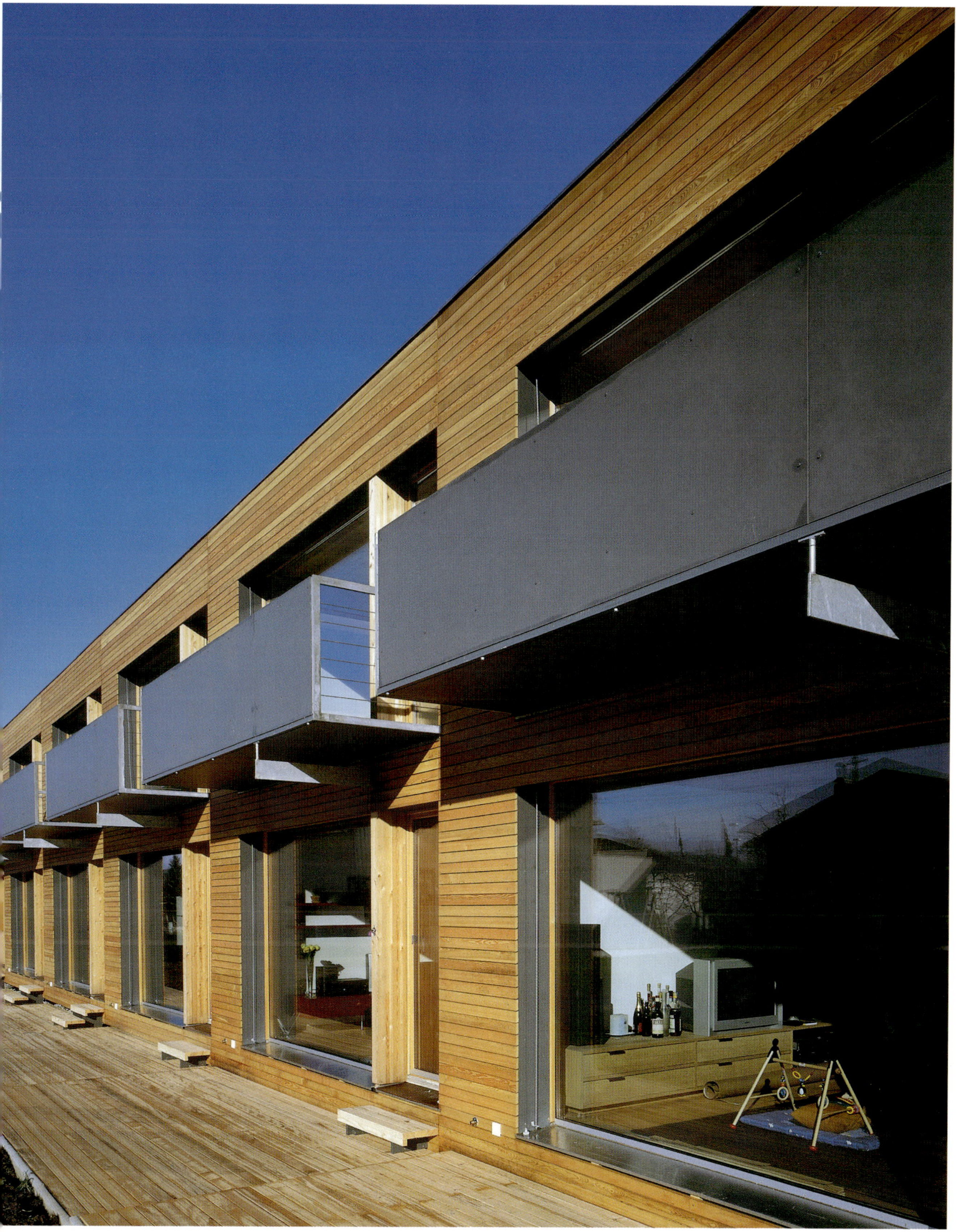

最小限の空間を最大限利用するという合理的な設計によって、建物は少ない予算で建設することが可能であった。空間は小さいが開放的で、各戸の持ち主の基準に合わせてレイアウトを決めることができる。平面プランは柔軟性があり、将来にわたって、間仕切壁内部のレイアウトの変更が可能である。

The rational design makes use of the least possible space, thus reducing costs. The spaces are small but open and lend themselves to be redrawn according to the criteria of each homeowner. The floor plan is flexible and allows for modifications in the walls in the future.

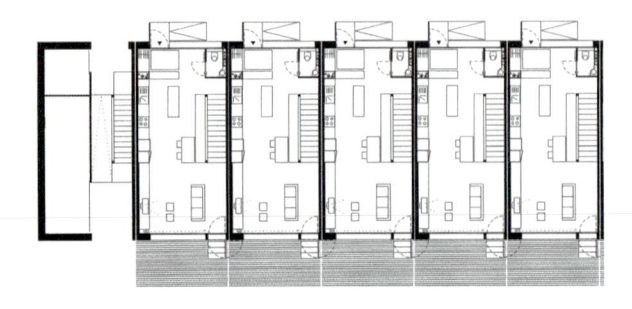

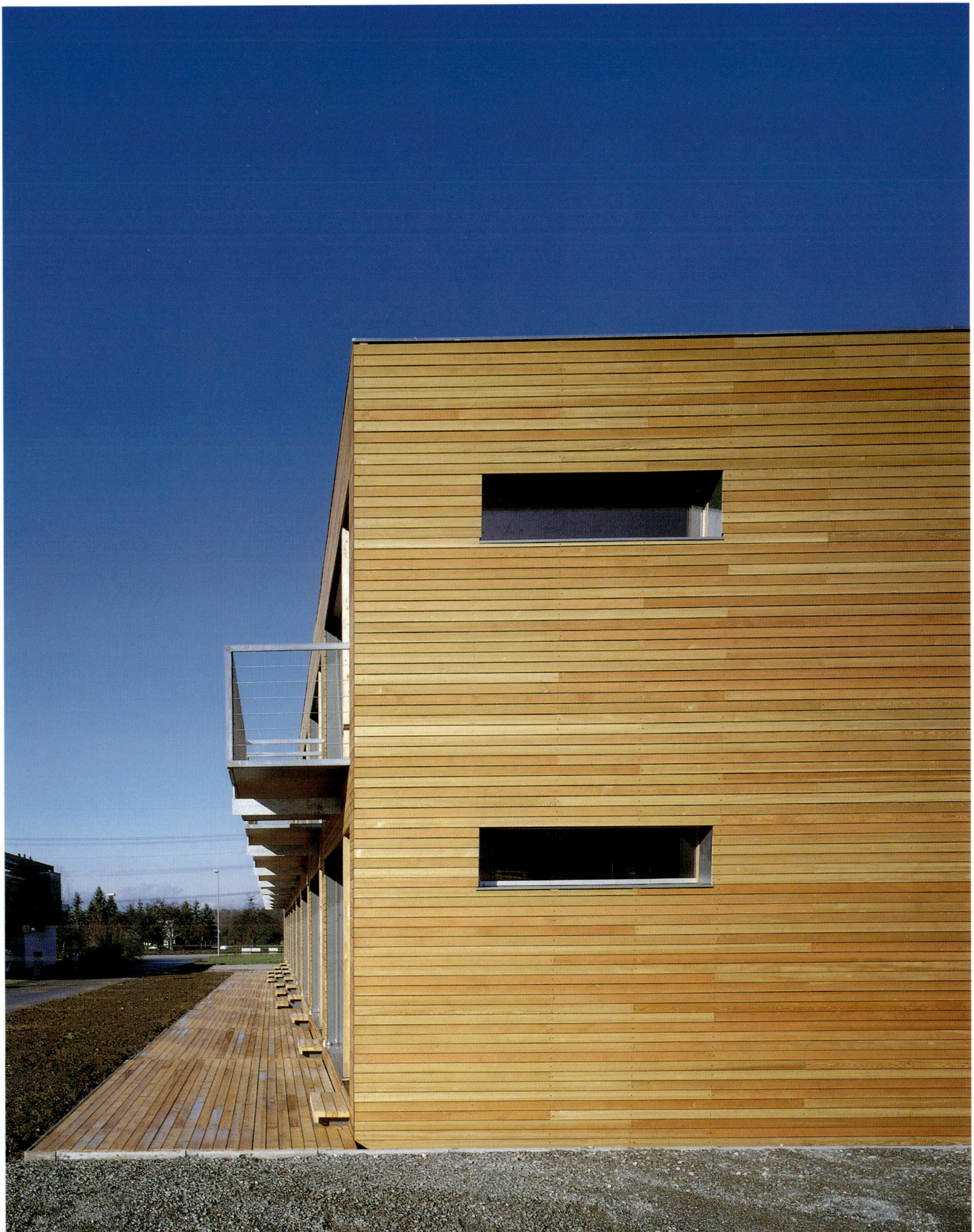

デザインは環境への配慮ということを最重要視している。各戸は完全に絶縁されており、空気の流入と排出は厳重に管理され、暖房は非常に効率が良く、ガラスと天窓は日光とエネルギーを受動的に捕捉し、屋根には通気層が設けられている。その結果この建物の光熱費は、通常の60〜80％で済んでいる。

Concerns for ecology are prominent in the design. The homes are perfectly insulated, the influx and outflow of air is tightly controlled, the heating is highly efficient, the glass and skylights passively capture light and energy, and the roof is ventilated. The final result is buildings whose energy costs are 60-80% less than normal.

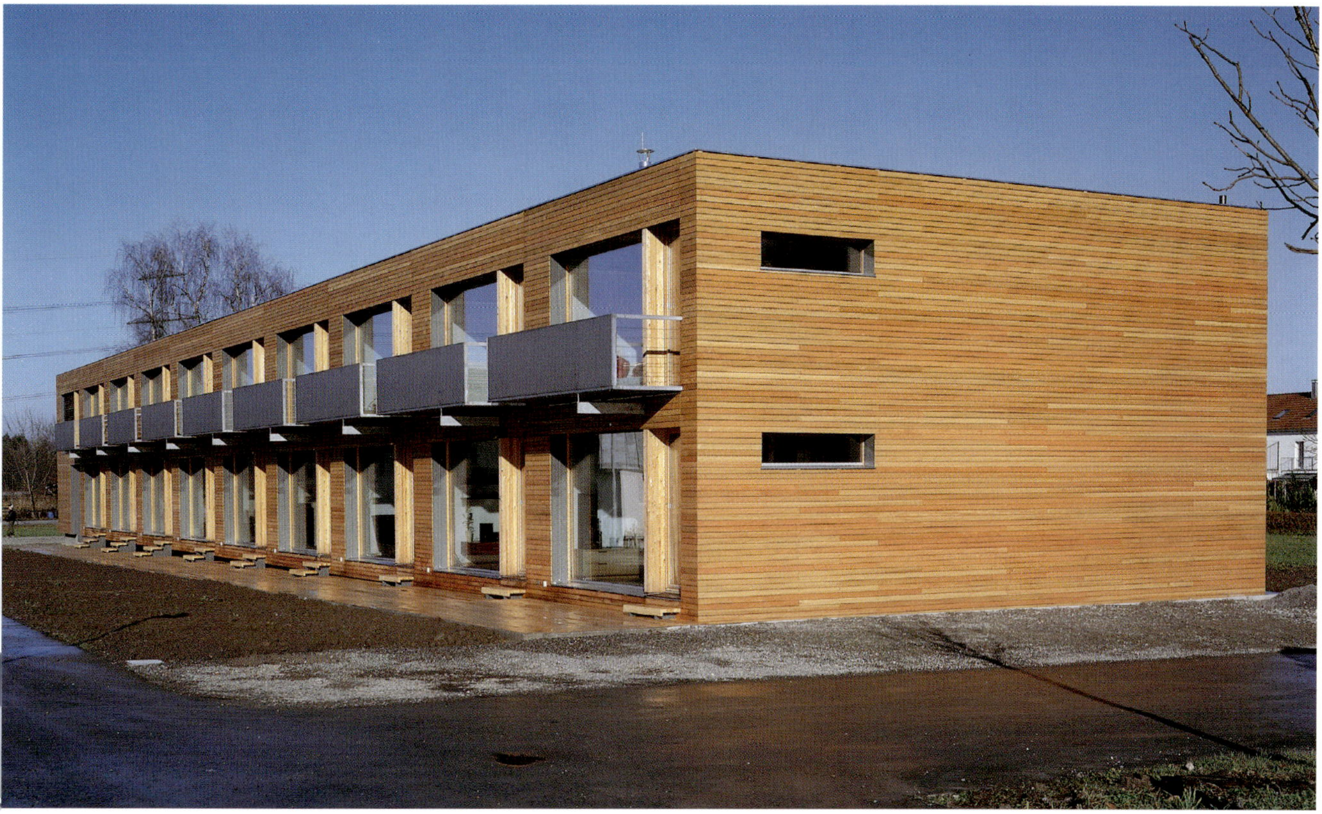

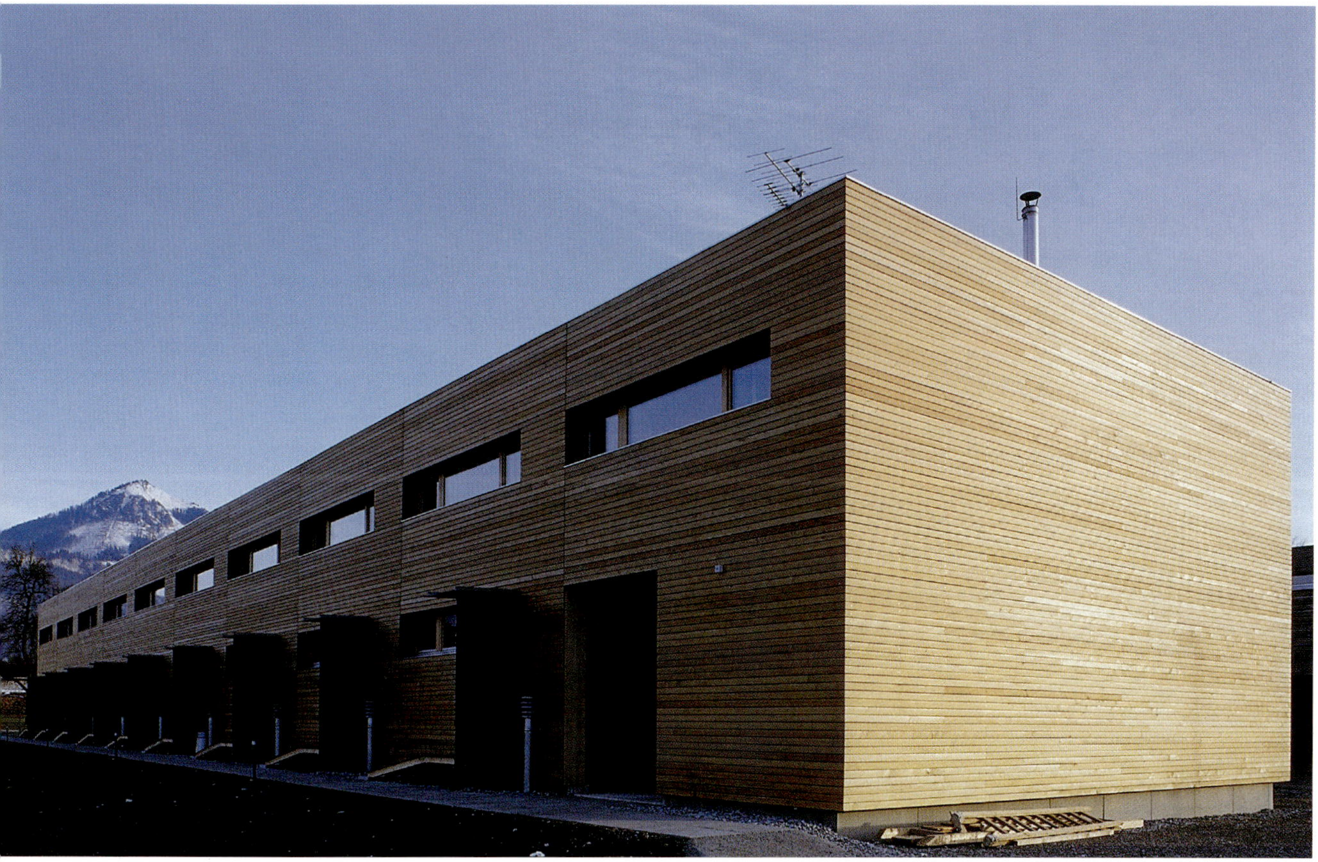

マウラー自宅兼アトリエ
優美な簡潔さ

トーマス・マウラー アーキテクト
撮影：フランチェスカ・ジョヴァネッリ

WOHNHAUS MIT ATELIER MAURER
elegant simplicity

ランゲンタール―スイス―2001

　住宅件建築事務所のこの建物を設計したのは、建築家自身である。以前は工業が栄えた地区に位置し、建物は格調高く木の立方体で整然と構成され、優美な簡潔さを漂わせている。建築事務所は地階に置かれ、1階がリビングスペース、2、3階が寝室になっている。正面のポーチがデザインの独創性を証明している。

Designed as a family residence and an architectural studio, the architect is also the creator of this project. Located in a formerly industrialized area, formally it consists of rotund cubic wooden forms that convey elegant simplicity. The studio is situated in the basement, the common areas on the ground floor and the bedrooms on the two upper floors with a porch at the front that grants a brushstroke of originality.

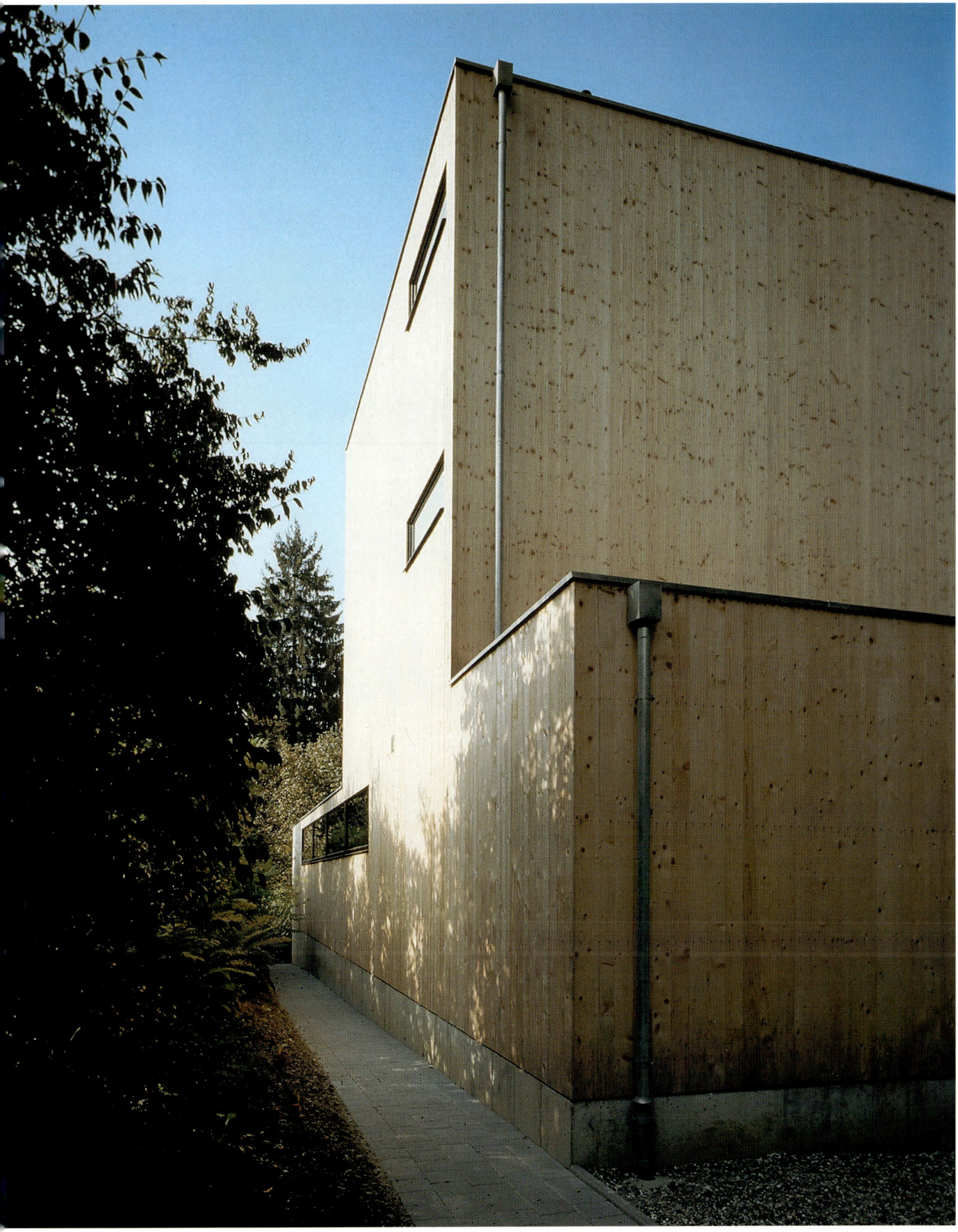

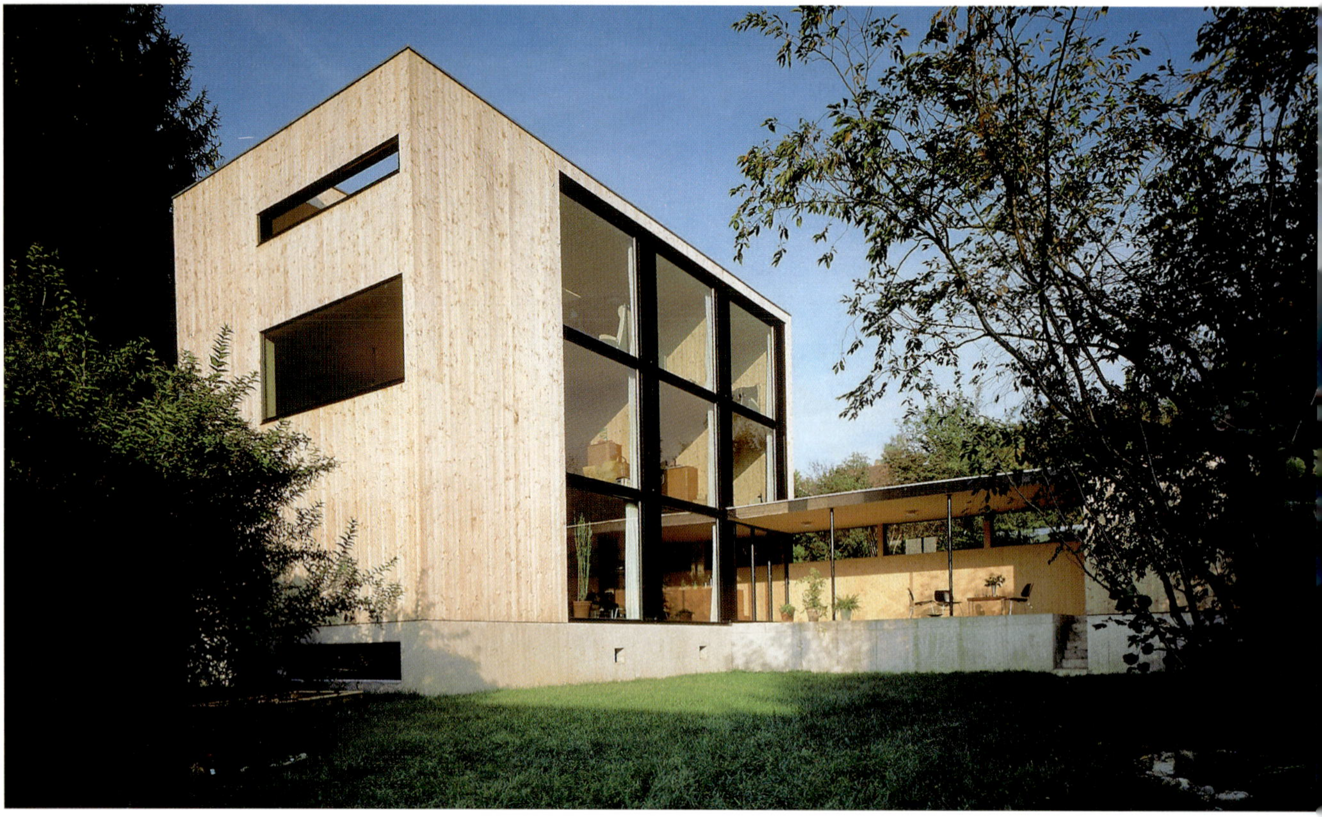

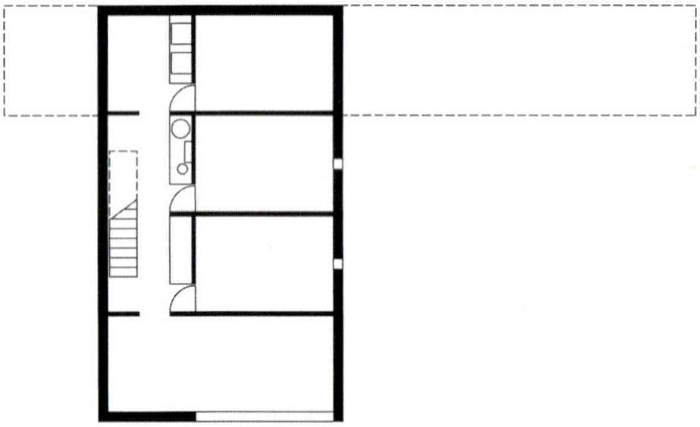

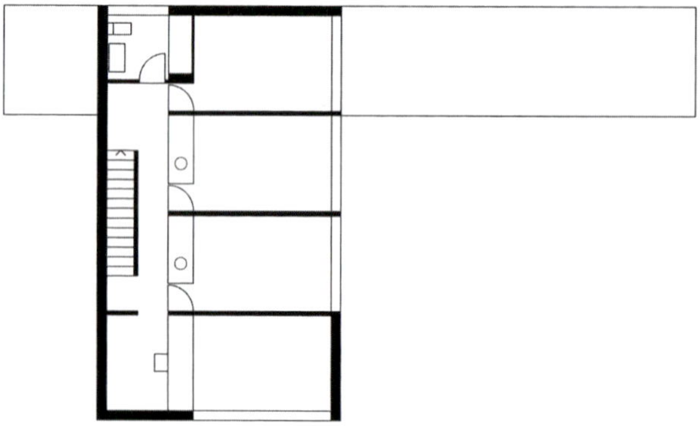

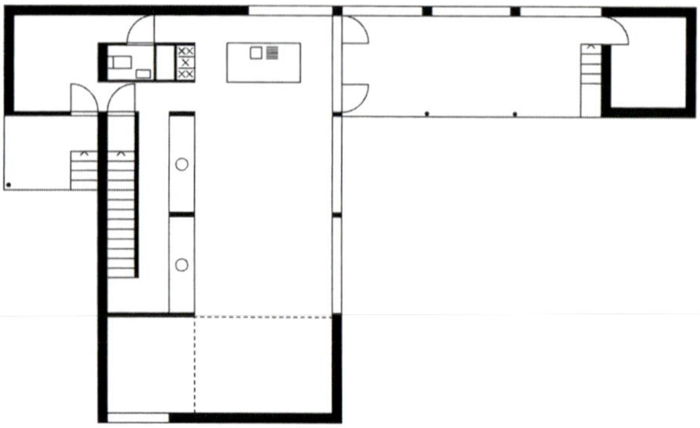

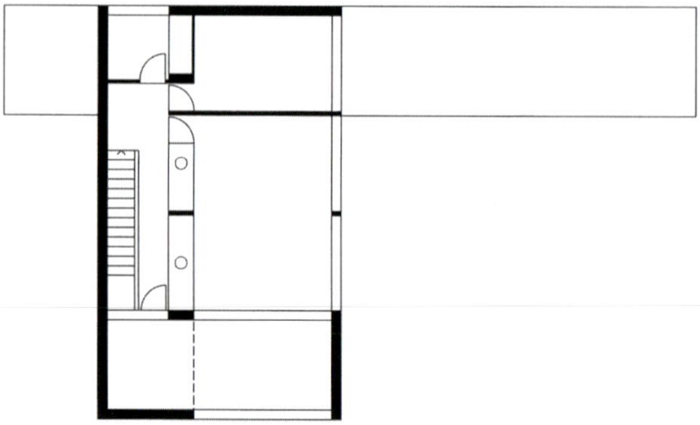

鉄筋コンクリートの基礎の上に、ファー材で作られた建物が直立している。建物は明確に南北方位指向を示しており、窓のない北側は頑なに閉ざされているが、南側は対照的に完全に開放され、日光にゆったりと浸かっている。その中間にサービスエリアがあり、バス、キッチンなどの水まわりと、階段が配置されている。移動式パネルを動かすことによって、各部屋を仕切ったり開放したりすることができる。

Reinforced concrete forms the base on which is erected a building made of fir wood. With a clear north-south orientation, the windowless north facade is in stark contrast to the south which is completely open so as to soak in the sun. In between the two, is the service zone that houses the wet areas (bath, kitchen) and the stairs. By way of movable panels, the rooms can be opened up or closed off.

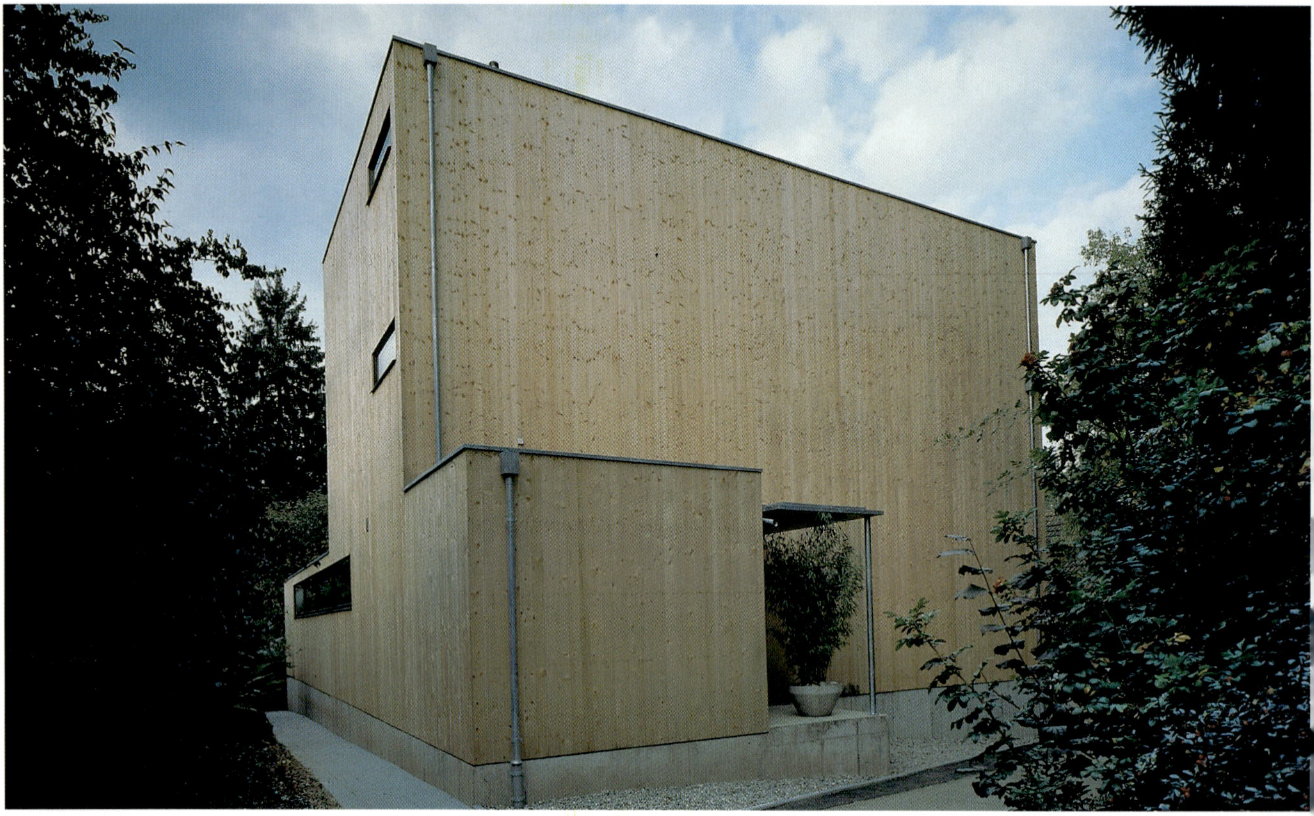

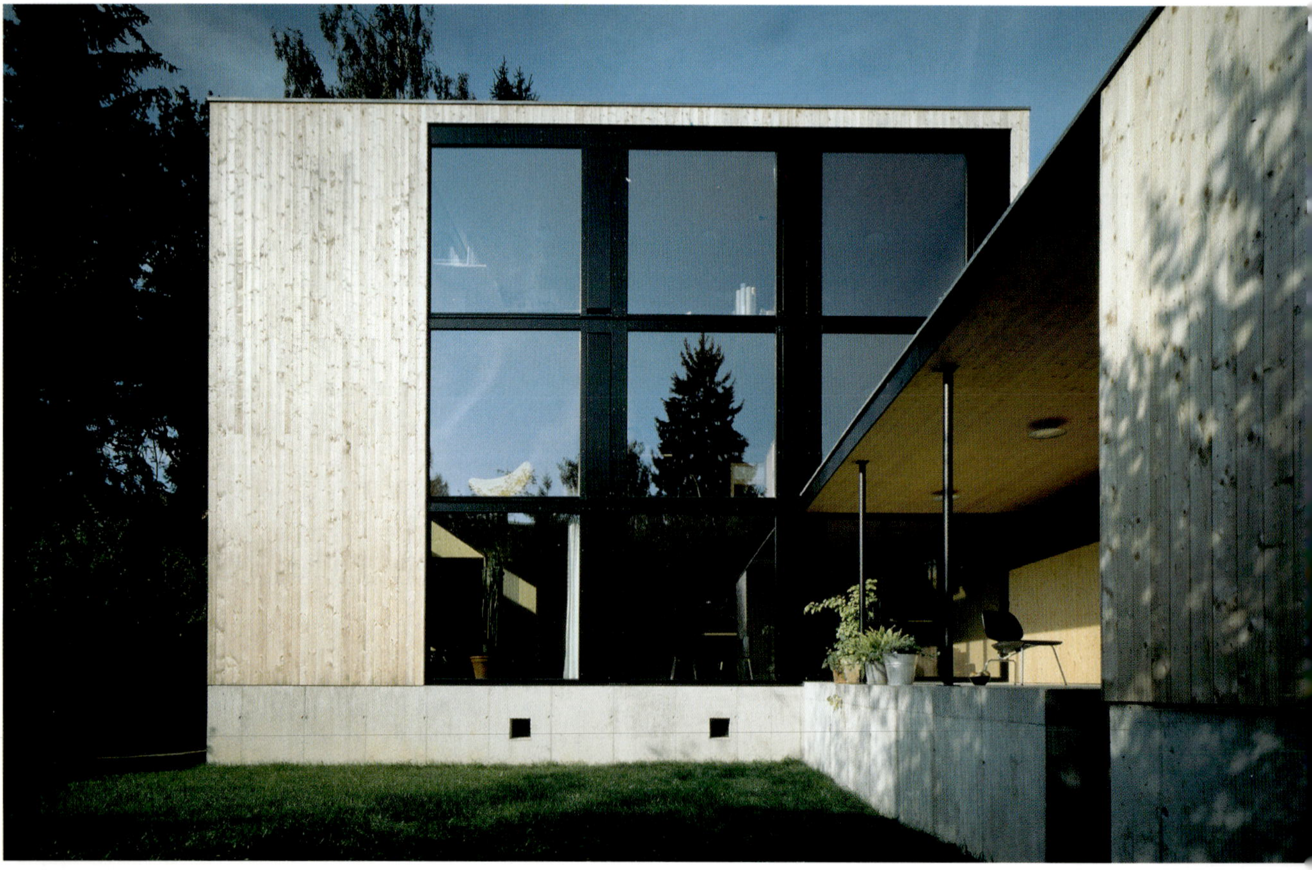

建物は非常に短期間で建てられたが、木質壁パネルを並べ、外壁をラーチ材の羽目板で被覆した木質パネル構法は堅固である。またこの住宅には、太陽熱利用機器、雨水の貯留と活用、地元産出木材の無公害利用など、エネルギー資源の節約という思想が織り込まれている。

Built with great speed, the dwelling consists of a tough wooden structure lined with panels and covered on the outside with larch wood slats. Energy-saving features are incorporated into the project such as solar energy devices, the collecting and use of rainwater and the pollution-free utilization of local wood.

07

Wood Interiors

Following, are some of the vast array of possibilities for the use of wood in interior design and decoration, presented in an orderly fashion. To facilitate comparisons, the groupings are by rooms and not by projects and they go from the more public to the more private rooms

インテリアとしての木材

以下は、インテリア設計、室内装飾における木材の可能性を示す膨大なプロジェクトから選りすぐったものであり、どれもきちんと整理整頓した状態を撮影したものである。比較しやすいように、ページ構成はプロジェクト別ではなく、リビング、キッチンなど用途別にしており、また共用スペースからプライベートな空間へと進んでいくようにしている。

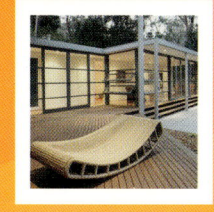

GREAT(BAMBOO)WALL

隈研吾建築都市設計事務所

撮影：淺川　敏

　万里の長城の傍で開催されたアジア若手建築家のためのコンテストに向けて、隈研吾率いる建築家グループが設計した作品。竹の象徴的な価値は、壁とパーティションに用いられるとき極限まで高められている。竹は空間になごみをもたらし、それはそのまま家の外まで流れ出している。

A group of architects led by Kengo Kuma designed this house near The Great Wall for a contest of young talents of Asian architecture. The symbolic value of bamboo is accentuated to the limit as it is used for the walls and the partitions, imbuing the atmosphere with a warmth that flows out to the exterior.

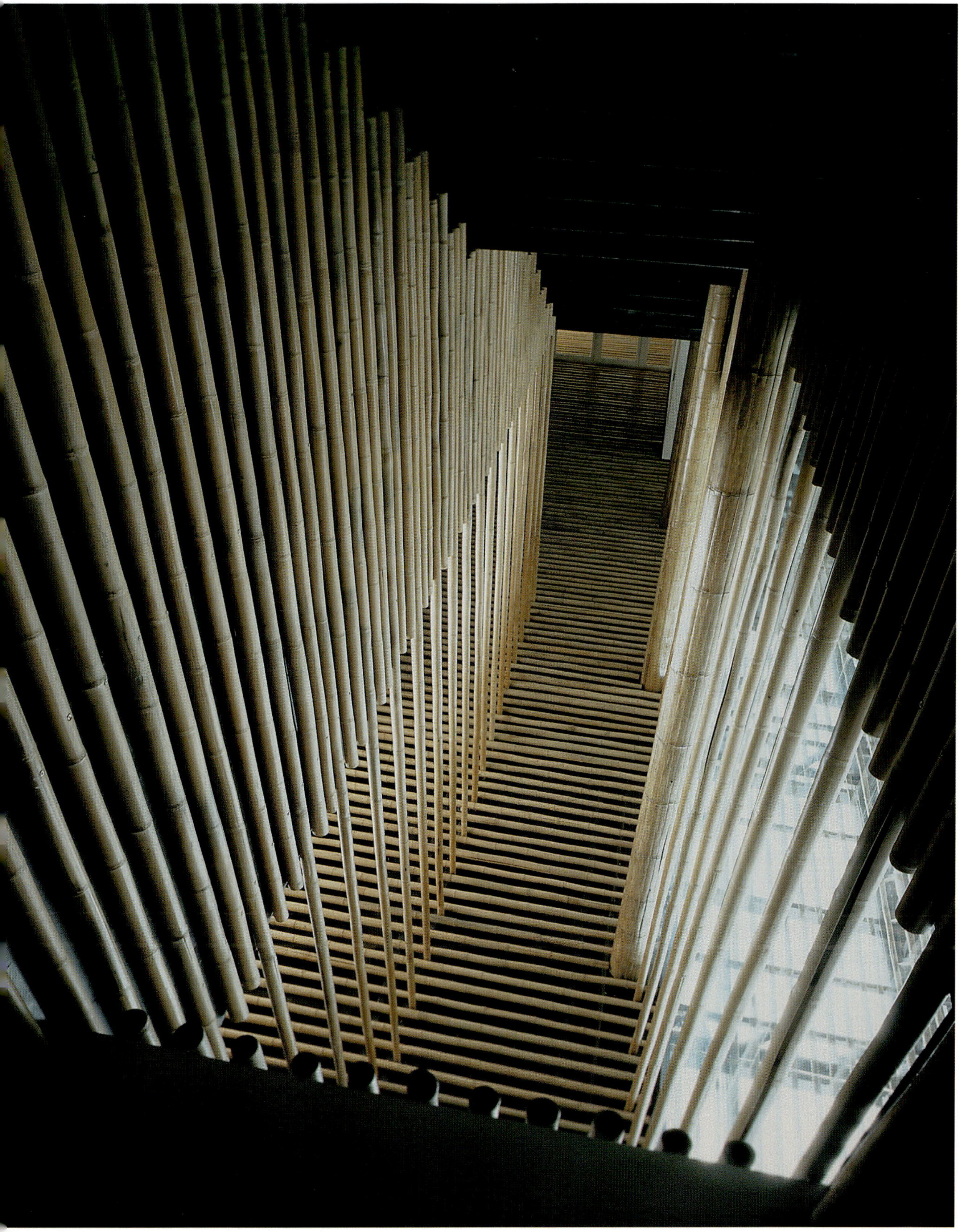

屋根の家

手塚建築事務所＆池田昌弘　　　　　　　　　撮影：木田勝久

　神奈川県にあるこの家の内部には周期的な景観が形づくられていて、家の内部空間はそれぞれの天窓で空と結合している。それらの天窓には梯子が掛けられ、各部屋から上れるようになっている。天窓から見える空は傾斜しており、この家の地政学的位置を示唆している。屋根は住める場所であり、ベンチ、テーブル、キッチン、さらにはシャワーまで備え付けられ、もう1つの住空間となっている。屋根は外側の梯子によって庭の地面と結ばれている。

In this dwelling built in Kanagawa, Japan, a cyclical landscape is developed that connects the internal space of the home to the sky of skylights that can be reach by the stairs from each room. The sloped sky responds to the topography in which it is placed. The roof is inhabitable and equipped with benches, a table, a kitchen and even a shower, as it is converted into yet one more space of the dwelling. It is connected to the earth of the garden by way of an exterior stairs.

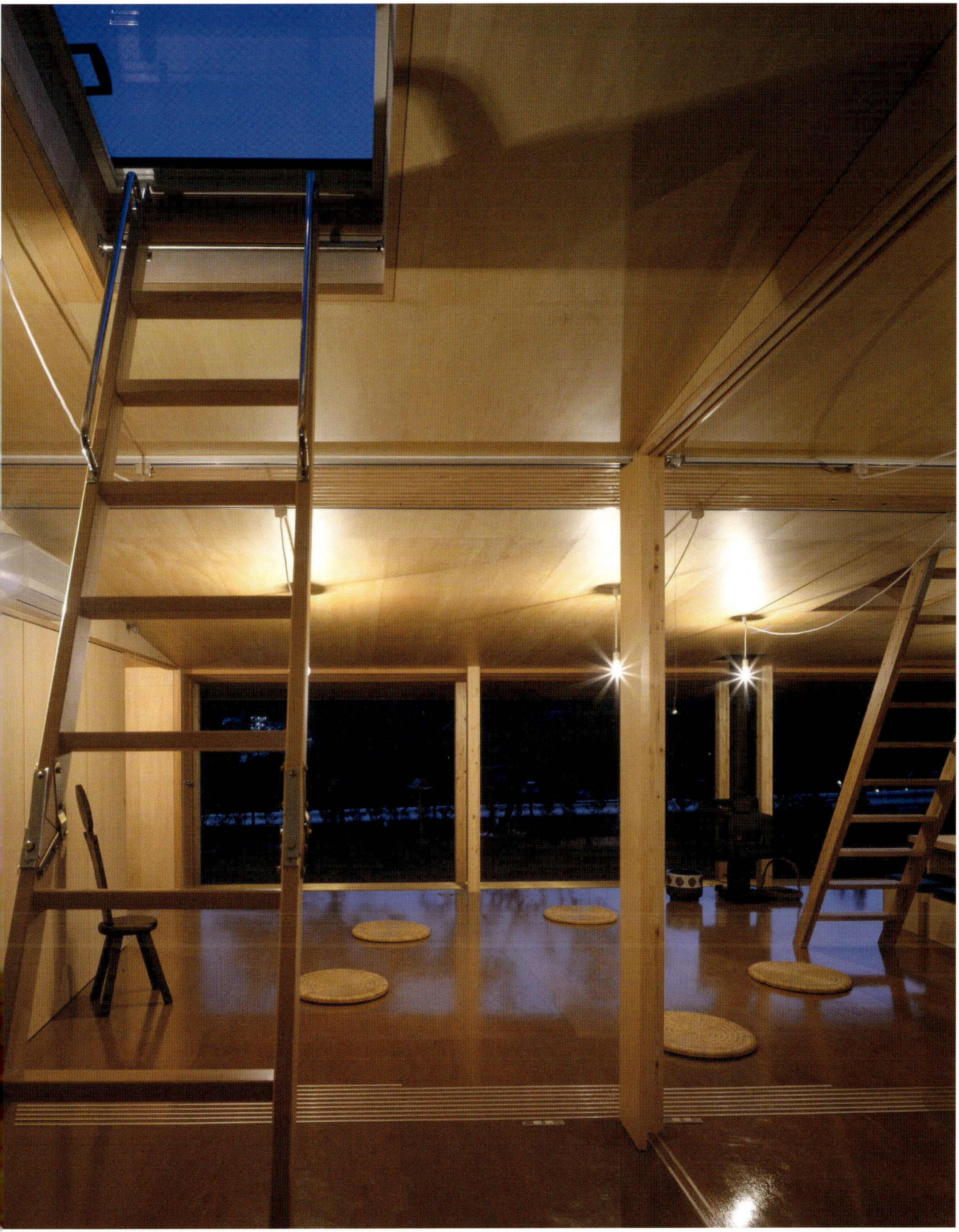

ミカエリス邸

ハリー・レビン アーキテクツ

撮影:パトリック・ビングハム—ホール

オーストラリア、シドニーにあるこの住宅は、2002年に建てられたものである。この住宅が誇るのは、心休まる、抑制された美しさに満ちた、広々とした魅力的なリビングルームである。ガラス窓が間口いっぱいに広がっているため、非常に開放的で、窓をあけると、外部のレッドシーダー、チェリー、タスマニアンオークと、室内のリサイクルウッド、そしてすぐ近くのウィロウビー湾、キャメレークリフの自然保安林の景観を占める老いた賢者の木、これらの間に対話が始まる。

This residence was built in Sydney, Australia, in 2002. It boasts a spacious and inviting living room that is comfortable and replete with discreet beauty. Open thanks to the windows running the full length of the exterior wall, there is a dialogue between the exterior red cedar, cherry, and Tasmanian oak trees and the recycled wood within, and the wise old trees filling the vistas of the nearby reserve in the Bay of Willoughby and the cliffs of Cammeray.

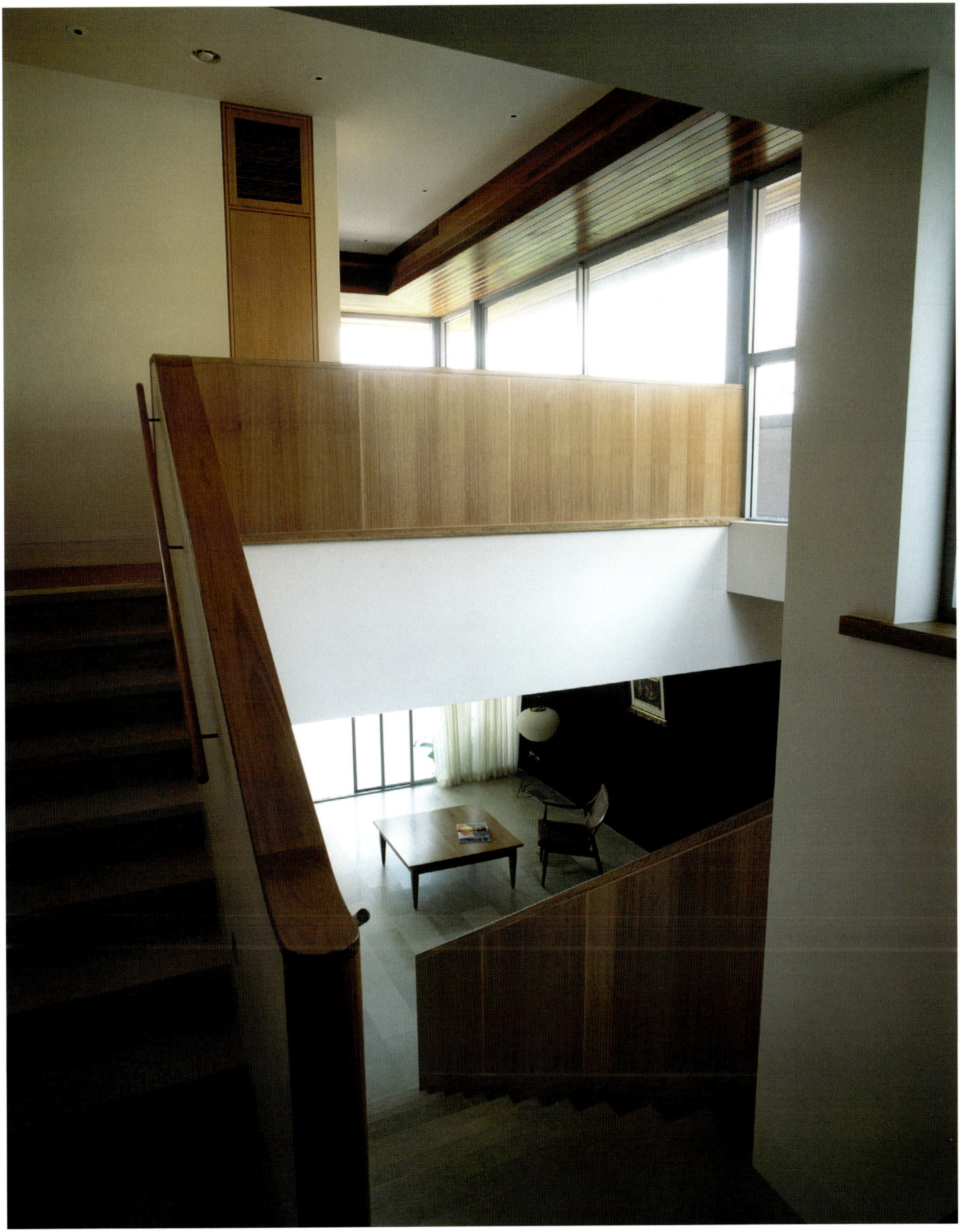

トレジャーパレス

エッジ・アーキテクツ

撮影:ジャネット・チョイ, ゲーリー・チャン

　台湾、台北市にあるこの家は、目に見えないハイテクシステムにより制御されたインテリジェントスペースを有している。部屋の代わりに、さまざまな「ストラータ」(階層)があり、活動はそれぞれのストラータに収められている要素に従って遂行される。常識的なリビングルームの概念は拒否され、代わりにこの家の中枢的な活動の場として「レイヤー」(層)が置かれている。ある時は、家の内部を走る玉石の通路を通って「グリーンレイヤー」に入り、そこで瞑想する。またある時は、「インフォメーションレイヤー」に入り、書物で囲まれた黄金色の木製の箱の中で隠れ家のやすらぎを感じる。

This house in Taipei, Taiwan, has intelligent spaces controlled by invisible technological systems. Instead of rooms, there are different "strata" where activities are carried out according to the elements contained within. The conventional concept of living room is rejected and instead "layers" are designed in that house vital goings-on. Thus, after following a cobblestone path running along the house we come upon a "green layer" where we may repose, or an information layer where we can feel sheltered lounging in golden wooden boxes surrounded by books.

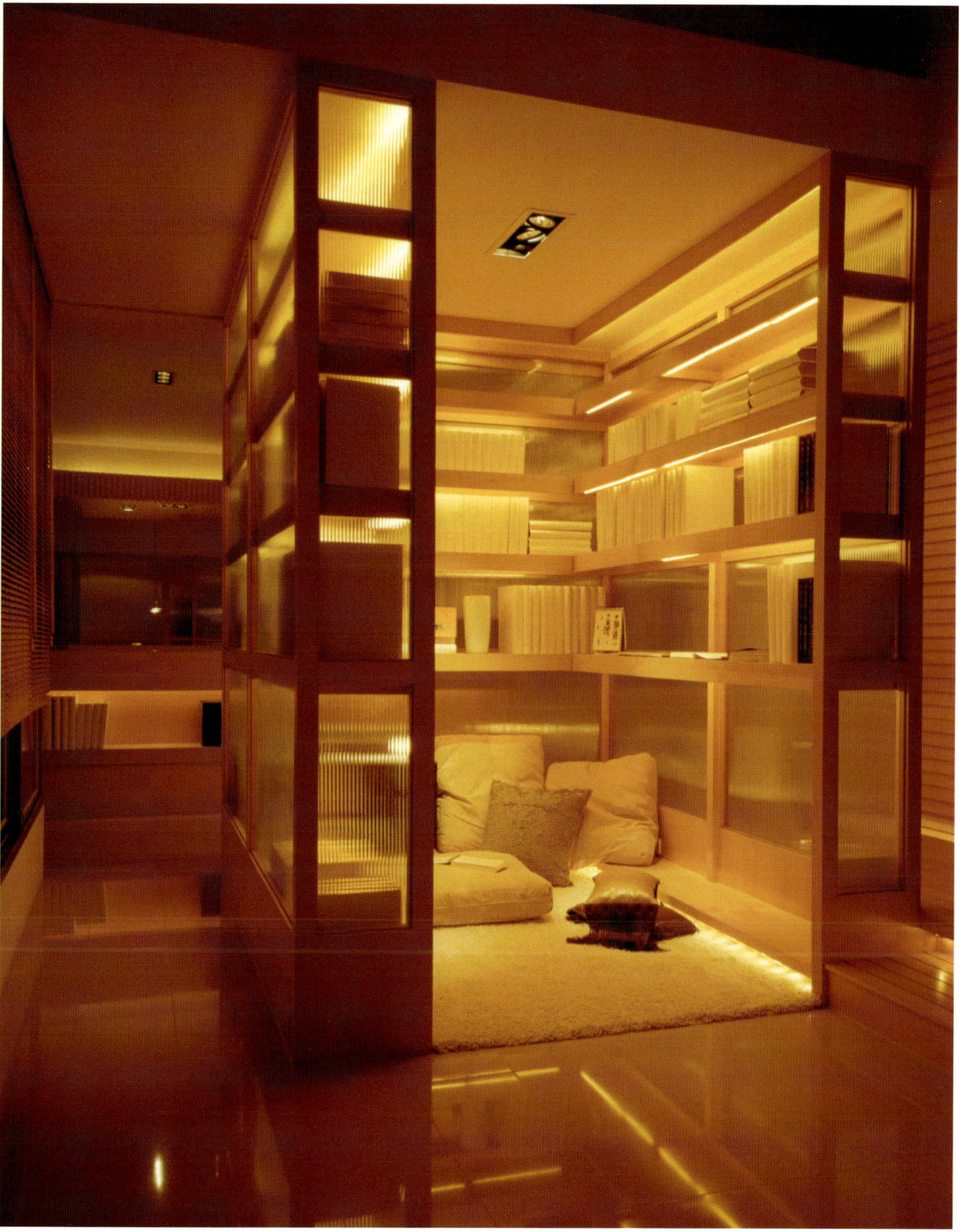

山あいの家

サイア・バーバリス・トポザノフ・アルシテクト　　　　撮影：マーク・クレイマー

　カナダ、ケベック州に位置するこの木造住宅は石積みの基礎の上に立ち、同じく2基の石積みの暖炉によって補強されている。1基はレストルームに、そしてもう1基はミーティングルームにある。室内はすべて木質パネルで覆われ、外界と同質の雰囲気が沁み込んでいる。天井は高く上方へと伸ばされ、それはまるで木が上へ上へと伸びていき、ついに空に達しているようである。側面は横に長く広がり、透明で限りないように見え、森の魅惑的な凝視に庇護されているようである。森はある時は小刻みに震え、あるいは大きく身体を揺らし、またある時はカサカサと囁き、あるいは悲しそうにすすり泣く。

Sited in Quebec, Canada, the wooden structure of the residence has a stone base and is strengthened by two stone chimneys, one for a rest area and another for a meeting area. The interior is completely covered with wood panels and imbues it with the same ambience as the exterior. The stretched height of the ceiling seems to reach upward like the upward growth of the trees that long to reach the sky. The width seems to spread out and on transparently and endlessly under the charming gaze of the forest, with its trembling and shuddering, its rustling and whimpering.

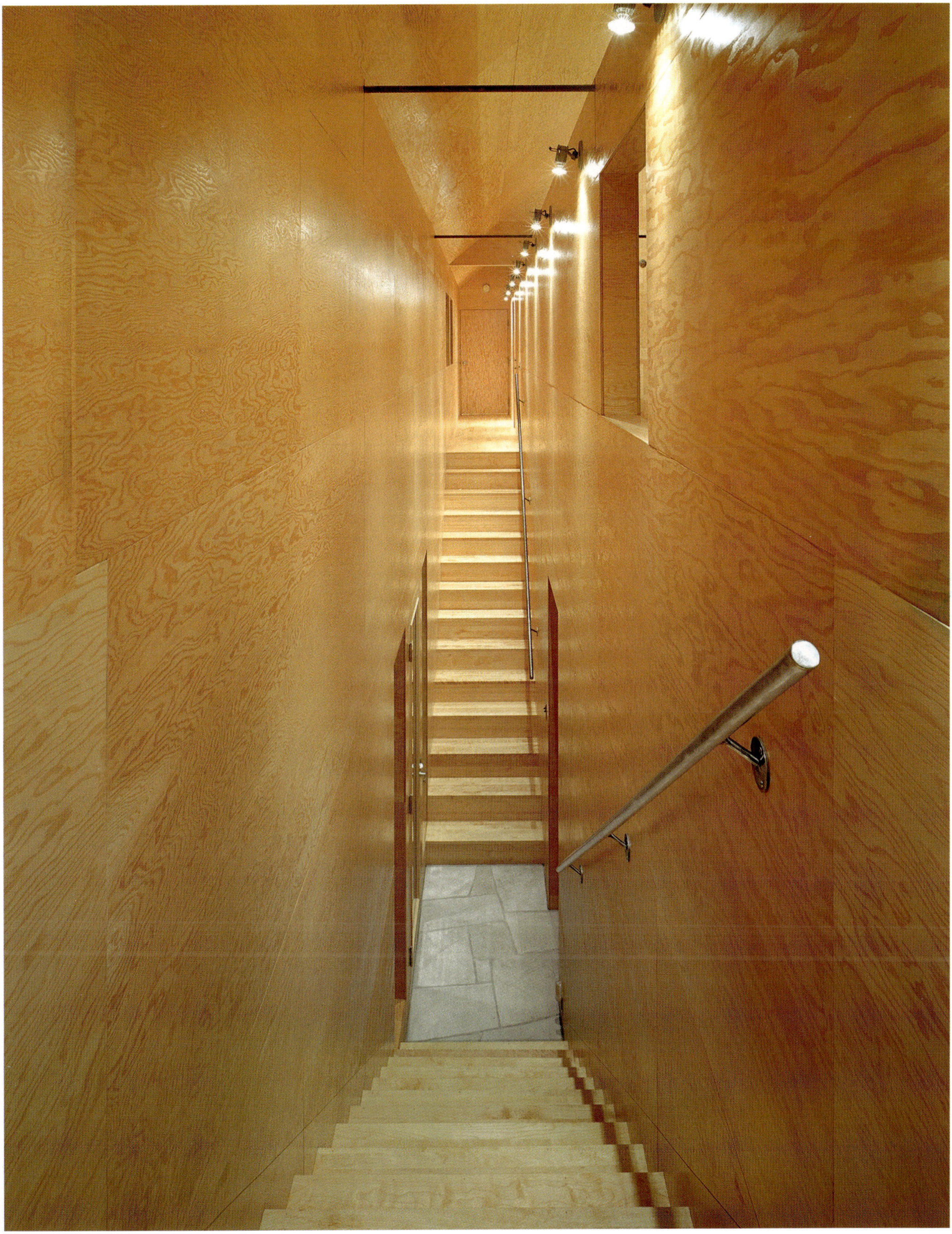

ランボー邸

オラヴィ・コポーネン

撮影：ユシ・ティアニエン

　フィンランドにあるこの住宅の設計思想は、人と自然を分かつすべてのバリヤーを取り去るということである。壁は限りなく透明であることを欲し、ガラスはただ寒さをしのぐために張られているだけである。窓の木枠は、上方へと大きく広げられた木々の枝が生みだす和音に加わり、楽曲を奏でる。家のまわりに張られたデッキの上を歩けば、それは森の散歩であり、チェアーに腰掛ければ、それは樹冠の天井の下に休むことである。

Set in Finland, it is designed so as to remove all barriers that could separate man from nature. The walls aspire to transparency, glass which is only there to keep out the cold. The wooden frames of the windows participate in the script of harmony composed by the outstretched rising arms of the trees. A walk around the house is to take a stroll in the woods and to sit to rest beneath the ceiling of treetops.

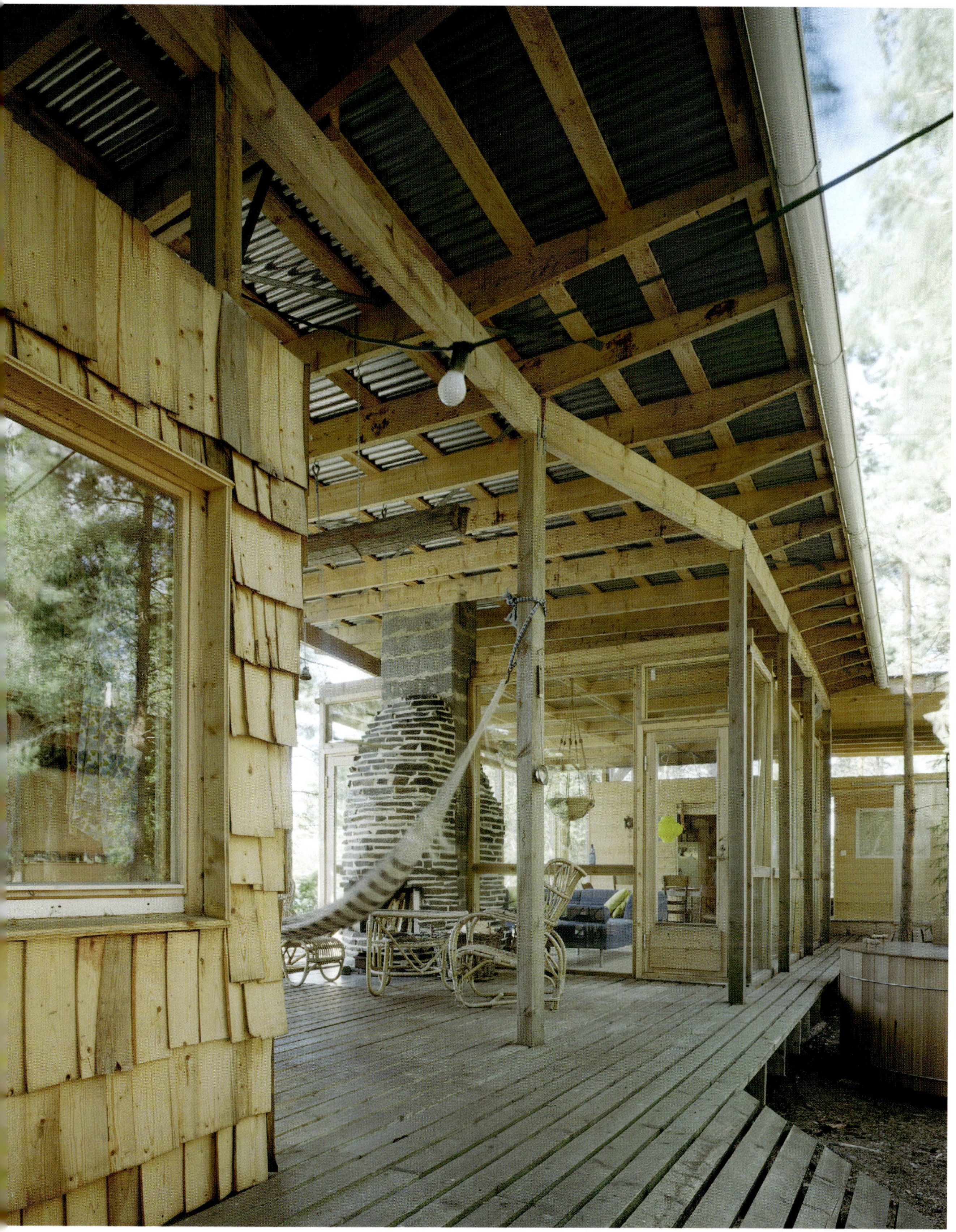

チュン・スタジオ

チュン・スタジオ　　　　　　　　　　　　　　　　　　　　　撮影：ティム・ストリートーポーター

　このカリフォルニア、サンタモニカにある住宅の外観については、先の章（p.28〜33）で詳しく述べた。室内は静謐で穏やかな隠遁者的な空間を創り出している。木と落ち着いた暖かみのある家具を用いることによって、外部の庭と同質の感覚を室内に翻訳しようと試みている。

The exterior is well described in the chapter on exteriors. This dwelling is located in Santa Monica, California. The interior generates reclusive spaces of calm and tranquility. By use of the wood and sober, warm furniture, it attempts to transpose the sensations of the exterior gardens to the interior.

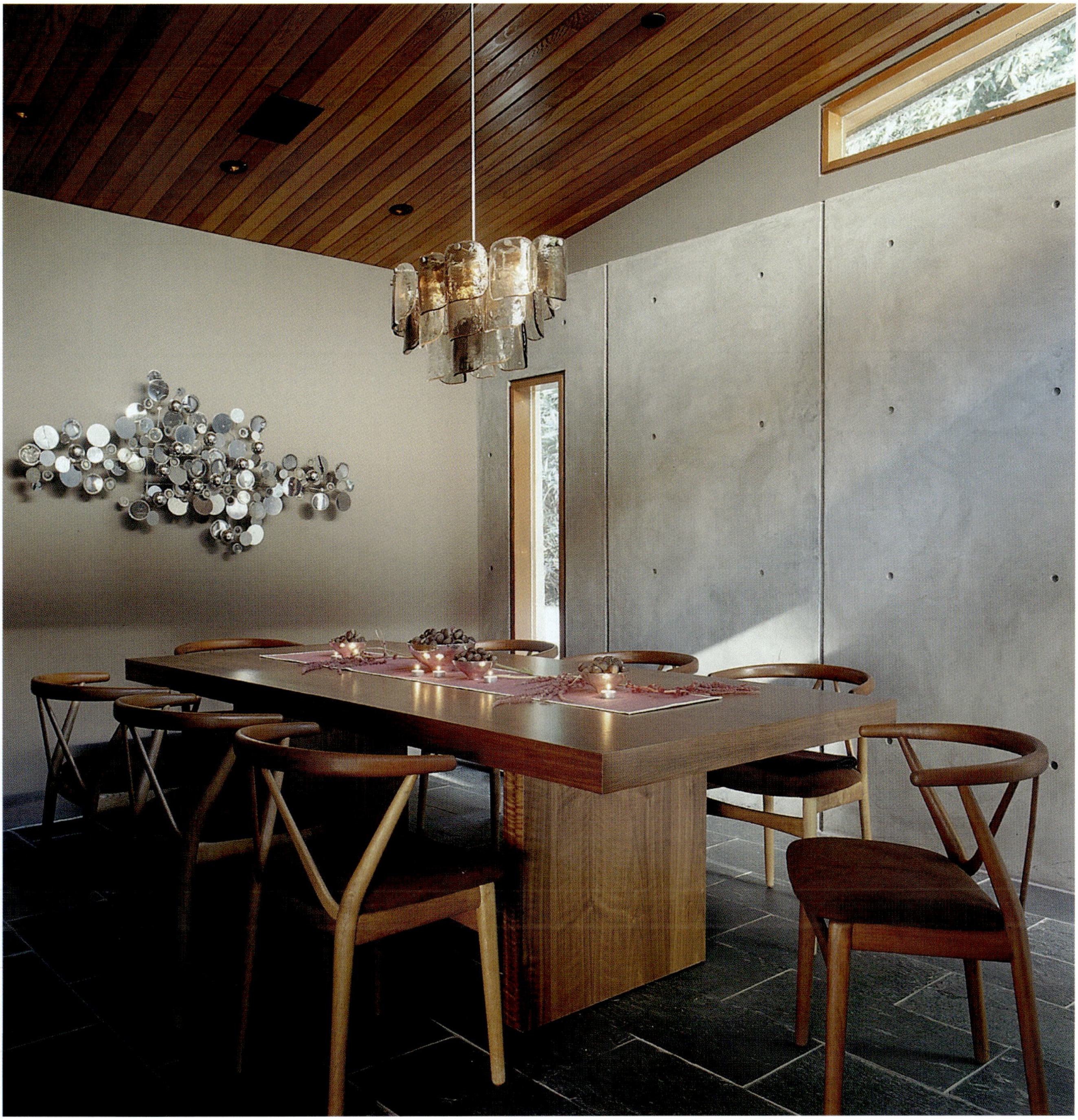

アカヤバ自宅

マルコス・アカヤバ

撮影：ネルソン・コン

　ブラジル大西洋岸の森の中にあるこの家は、森のもう1本の木になることを願って設計された。それは現場の地形にきわめて自然な形で植えられ、眼下に臨む海と、上方の山地へと続く一体となった空間を表現している。森の高さと同じ高さを持つことによって、住宅は樹冠のすぐ下にいるときのような、たとえようのない、特権的な心のやすらぎを与えてくれる。木がふんだんに使われた室内は、景観にすぐれた屋外バルコニーの連続のようである。

Placed in a forest on the Atlantic coast in Brazil, the residence is designed to be yet one more tree in its setting. It is inlaid in its topography in a natural way and is the expression of continuous spaces that lead to the ocean or to the mountain range. The height, as high as that of a woods, affords incomparable and privileged repose near the treetops. The interior which is rich in wood, is like a series of open balconies with vistas.

187 リビングルーム
livingrooms

バンデイラ・デ・メロの住宅

マウロ・ムニョス アルキテクチュラ　　　　　　　　　　撮影：ネルソン・コン

　外観に関する章（p.146〜151）でも紹介したとおり、ブラジル、イツーにあるこの住宅は繊細な豊かさを誇り、木材をふんだんに用いたリビングルームは、驚愕するほど感動的である。これらの共有スペースは、解放感と、かくも豊かな空間の連続性にもとづいて設計され、閉ざされた囲いとして使用されるのではなく、テラスとして使用されるものとして具現化されている。

Also described in the chapter on exteriors, this house situated in Itu, Brazil boasts a richness of subtleties and uses for wood in the living room areas which are absolutely astonishing. Designed with open character and such great spatial continuity, these common spaces personify more the uses put to terraces than to closed enclosures.

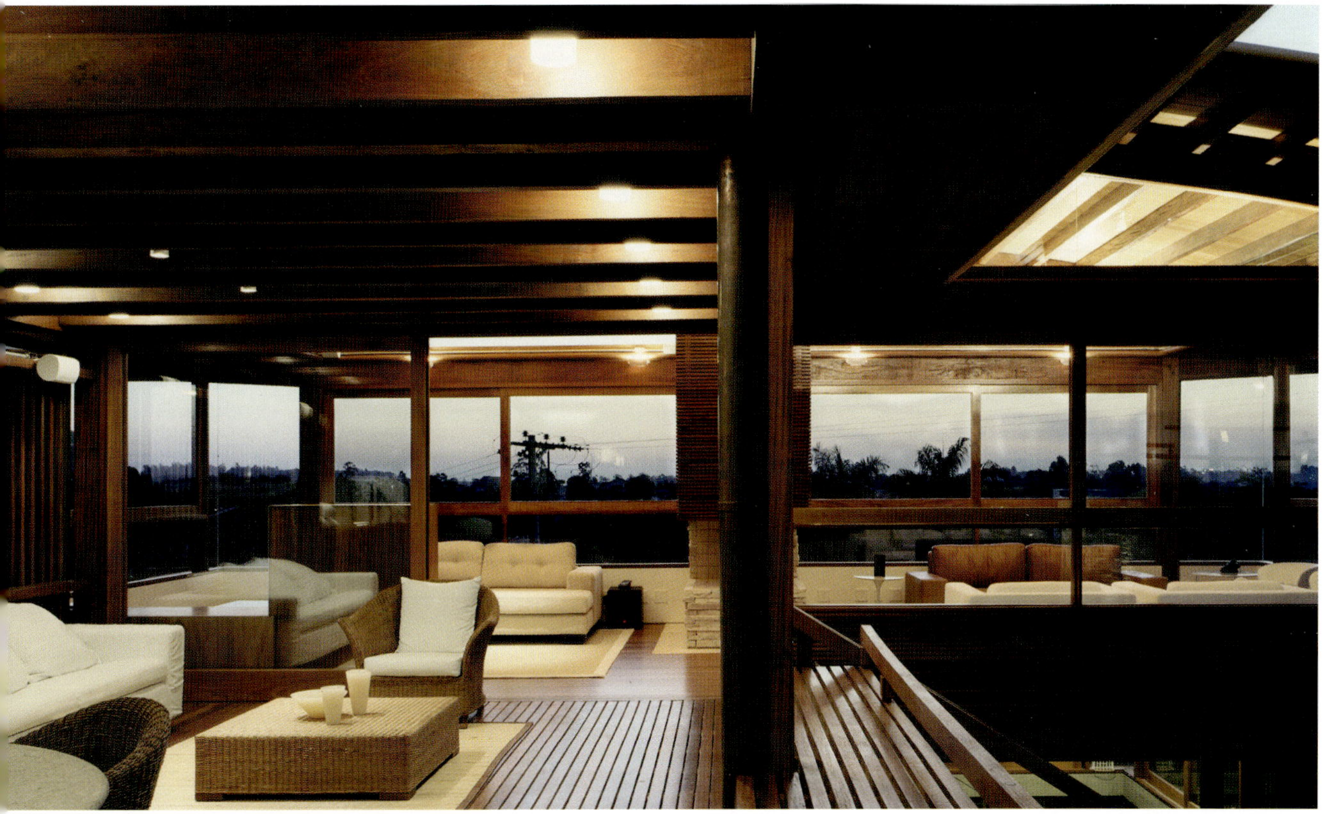

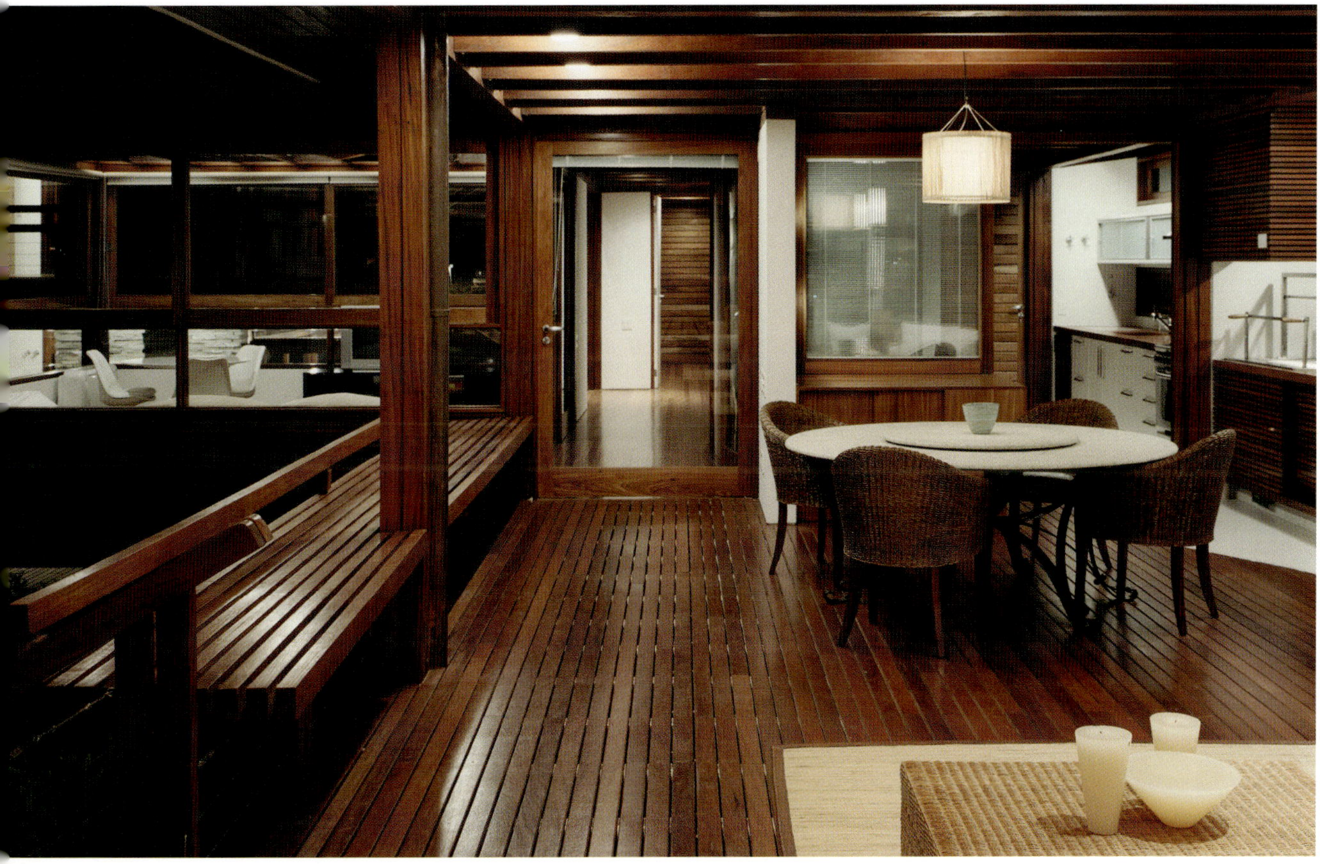

パインの森別荘

カトラー・アンダーソン アーキテクツ　　　　　　　　　　　　　　撮影：ウンディーネ・プレール

1999年にワシントンに建てられたこの小さな別荘は、規模をできるだけ抑え、環境への影響を最小限にとどめるひとつの試みであった。ベッドルーム、キッチン、バスルームなどの部屋はひとまとめにして、家の最も隠された部分に押し込められているが、その代わりに2階吹き抜けのデイエリアは目いっぱい風景の中に開放されている。木の支柱を組んだだけの簡潔なファサード、屋外部分を一体化した設計によって、内部空間は大きく広げられている。

The small cabin designed in Washington in 1999 is an attempt to minimize its dimensions and impact in its setting as little as possible. Rooms such as the bedroom, kitchen and bathroom are grouped together in the most concealed part of the dwelling whereas the day area, drawn as a double-height space, is totally opened out to the landscape. Fashioned with a simple facade with a wooden strut trimming, by drawing in the participation of the exterior, the interior space is enlarged.

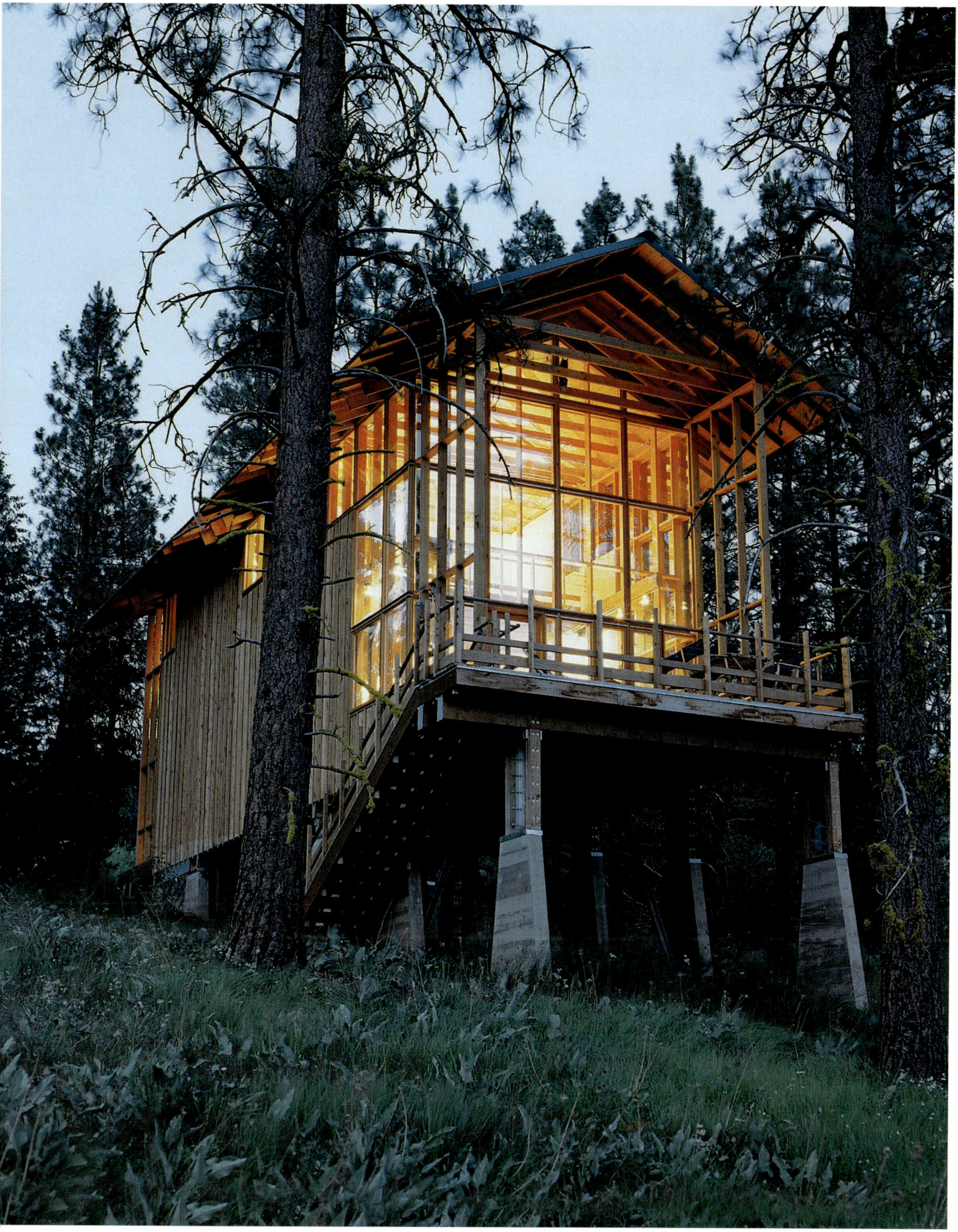

エッシンゲンの住宅

シュルーデ・アーヒテクテン　　　　　　　　　　　撮影：マルティン・ルーダウ

　2001年に建てられたこのドイツの住宅は、太陽輻射の受動的利用を行うことによって確固とした省エネルギーの提案者となっている。控え目であるが、親しみのある室内は、明快で簡潔な構成、抑制された純粋な線、建築に対する厳しい姿勢によって創りだされたものである。木材の豊富な使用は特に称賛されるべきである。というのは、それは持続可能で環境に害を与えない形で供給され、リサイクル可能で、無限の可能性を有しているからである。

This residential project in Germany in 2001 is an unwavering proponent of energy savings as it makes passive use of solar radiation. Sober yet inviting interiors are achieved by means of simple and compact volumes, restrained pure lines and rigor in the approach to construction. The abundant use of wood is noteworthy because of the sustainable and ecological way it is supplied, because it can be recycled and because of the numerous qualities it affords.

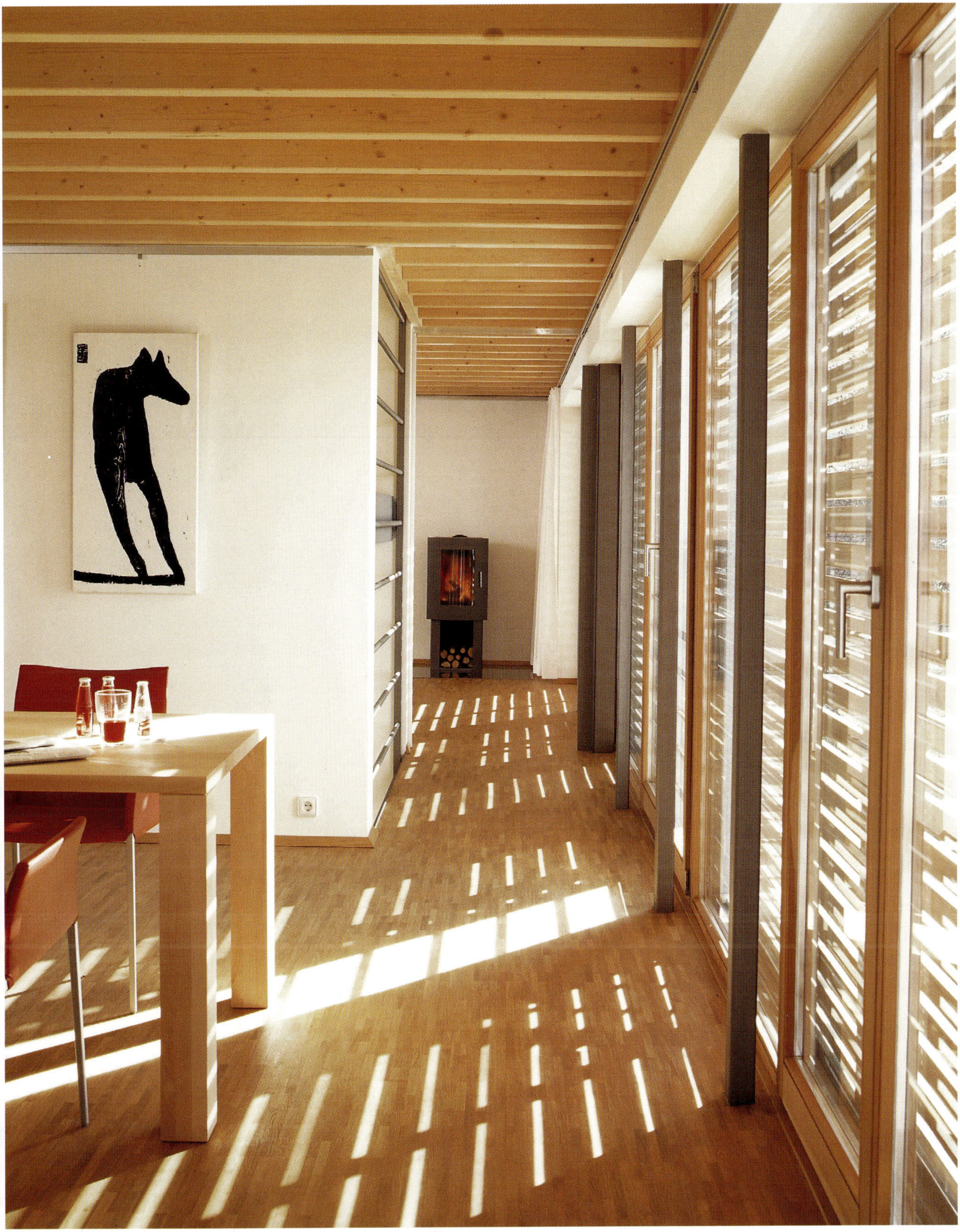

シュトゥットガルトの集合住宅

シュルーデ・アーヒテクテン

撮影：ユライ・リプタク,
ライナー・ブランク

　このドイツにある農家風の家には、大きく開放的な多機能空間が特権として与えられている。それは可動式パネルによって自在に変更することが可能である。濾過された光は日中を通して室内に漂い、豊かな透明感と親密さのなかに拡散していき、影が作る羽根板によって分節化される。木は外界の光を透過させるとき、さまざまな透明な影によって干渉し、階段の段板はそれを優しく撫でる。

This chalet in Germany is privileged with a large, spacious multifunctional space that can be redrawn at will thanks to movable panels. The filtered light that flows in all throughout the day diffused into a wide range of transparencies and intimacy, is fragmented by the slats of the shades. The wood intervenes in the diverse shades of transparency as it filters the exterior light while the steps of the stairs gently stroke it.

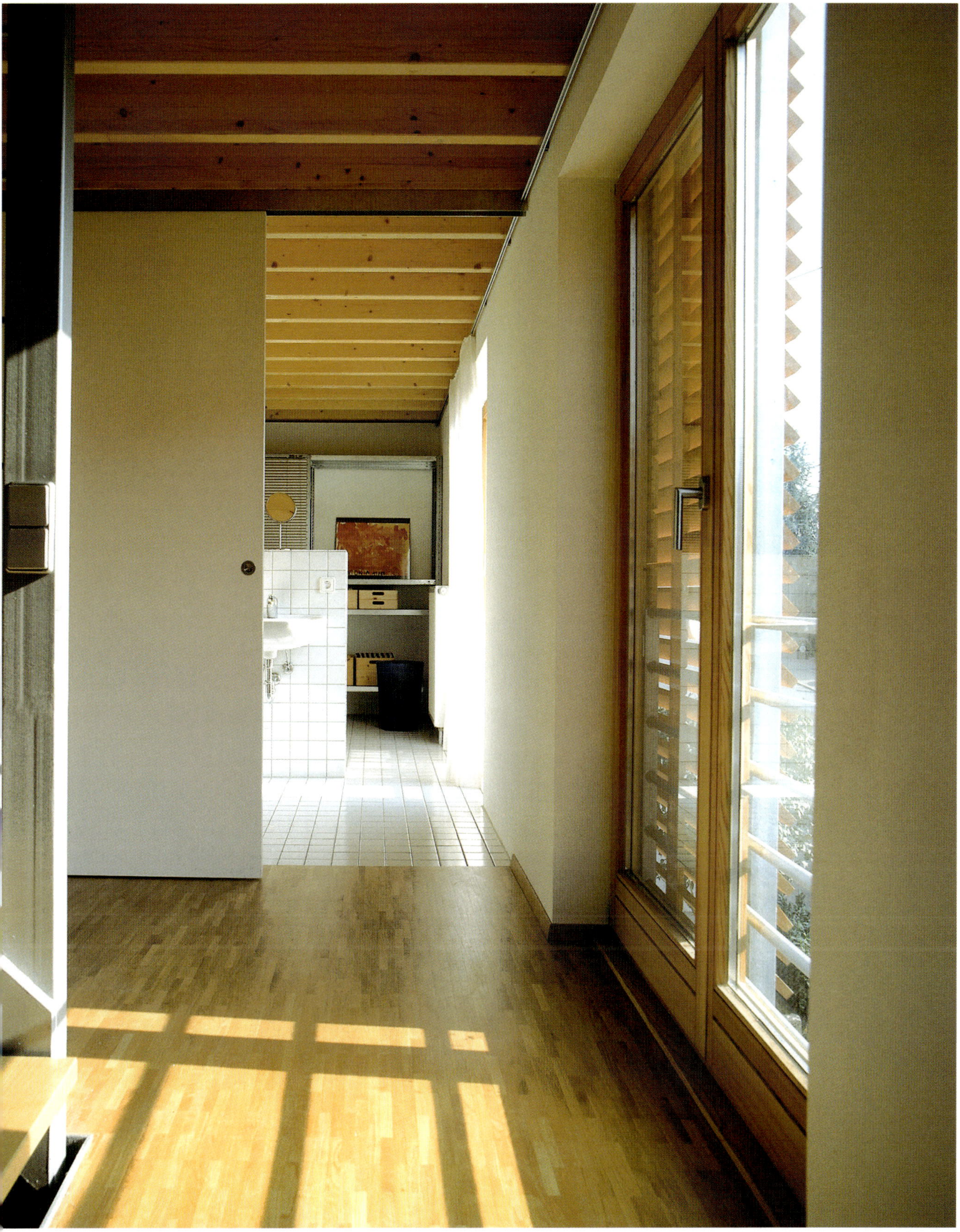

シャーレ・ピクテ

シャルル・ピクテ アルシテクト

撮影：フランチェスカ・ジョヴァネッリ

　この住宅は、1872年にスイスアルプスの山中に建てられたログハウスを、2000年に改修増築したものである。室内には、優しいが絶え間ない雨のしずくに似た、緩やかな時の流れが集積されている。歴史、歳月が現代的な家の中に組み入れられ、古い木材の風格が、製材されて間もない木材の若々しさと見事に調和している。そして過ぎ去りし時代の熟練の技が、現代風のリズミカルなビートと融合している。木がこの厚い壁で仕切られた空間を、温かく、優しく支配している。

This dwelling, erected in the Swiss Alps in 1872 and fashioned from logs, was restored and enlarged in the year 2000. It concentrates in its interior the slow passing of time like the drops of a gentle yet perennial rain. The oldness and aging is incorporated into the contemporariness of the house where the patina of aging wood is in harmony with the youthful emotions of recently cut wood. The skillful hands of yesteryear are fused with the rhythmic beat of the present. The wood, warm and friendly, dominates in this atmosphere of thick walls.

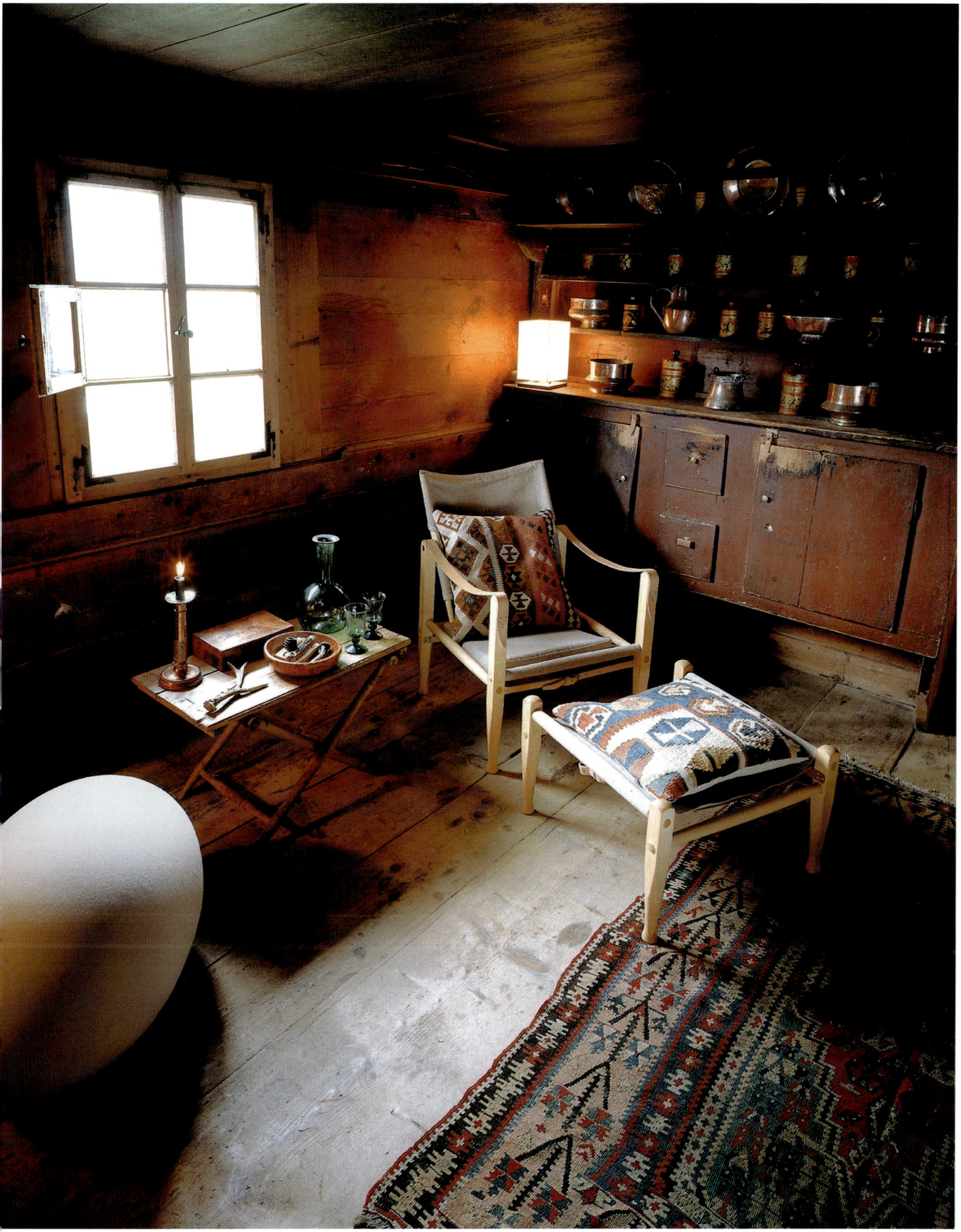

サヴォア通り重層式アパート

リトー・アルシテクト				撮影：ペッカ・リトー

　2004年に行われたこの屋根裏部屋付き住宅の改築では、後から付け加えられたり変更されたりした部分はすべて取り除かれ、木材が創りだしていた当時の雰囲気がそのまま再現された。木張りの天井は海面のようにうねりながら、静けさの波を放ち、それを支える陸地である床を優しく揺らしている。2つの水平線は木のつっかい棒によって垂直に結ばれ、それによって空間は2つの異なった部分に分かたれている。

The remodeling of this attic apartment in Paris in 2004 restored the original character of the wood by eliminating all posterior additions or modifications from the original. The wood ceiling sways like the waves of the sea as it gives off waves of calm that gently rock the land that sustains it. The horizons are vertically connected by way of the wooden bars that separate two differentiated spaces.

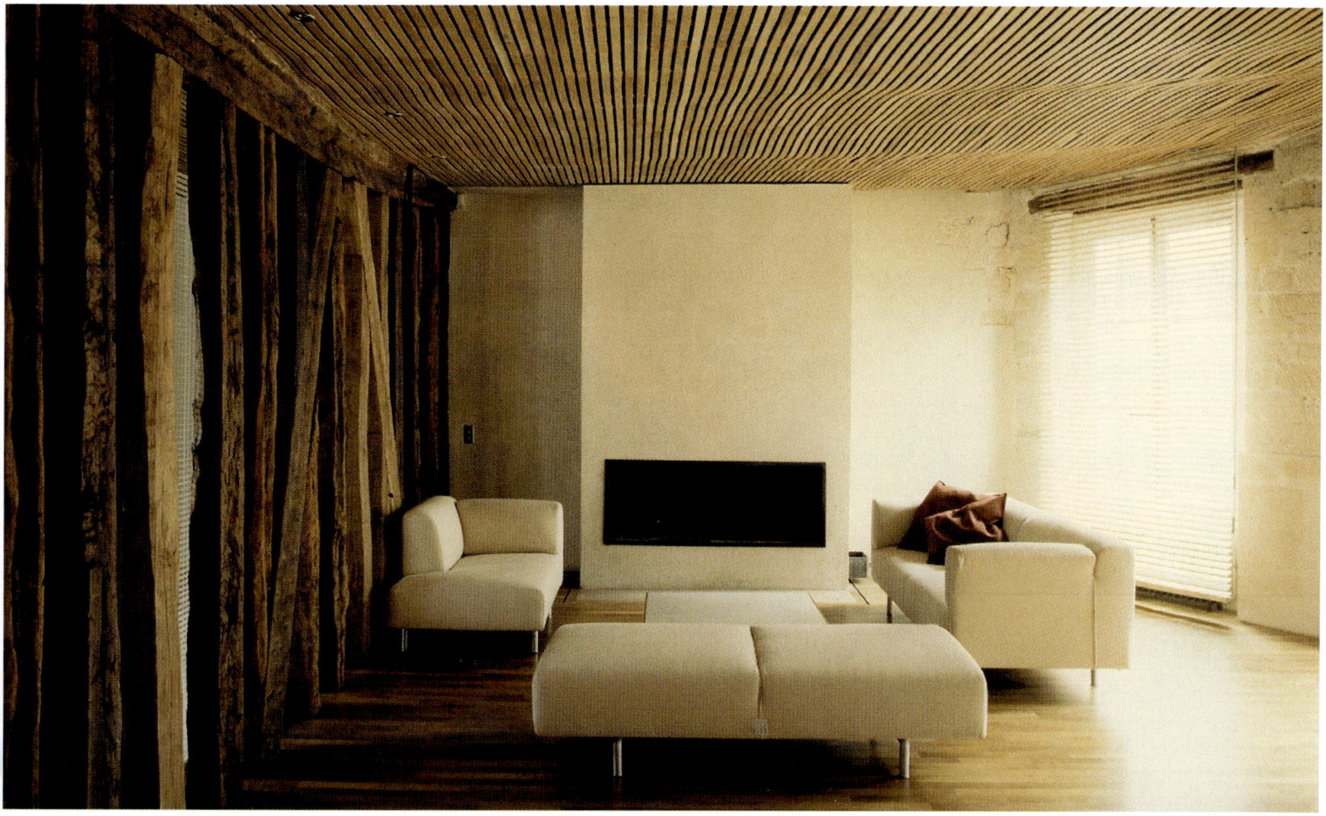
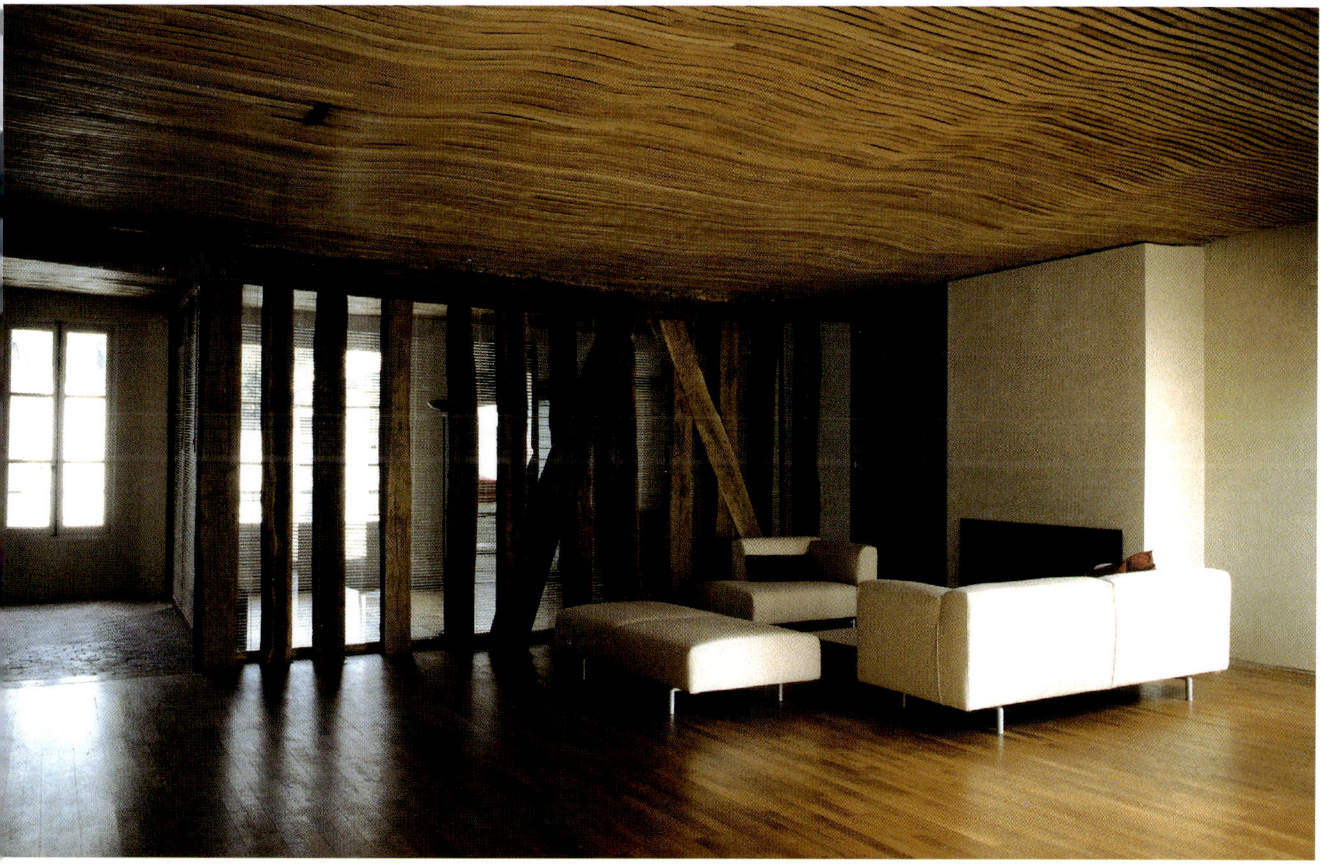

集合住宅 Ⅱ

ヴォークト・アーヒテクテン　　　　　　　　　撮影：ドミニク・ビュトナー

食器棚とキャビネットが、木材とリノリウムのさまざまな暗色の色と、背景色としての寄せ木張りの床を結合させ、落ち着いた優美なキッチンを創りあげている。それはとても小奇麗にきちんと整えられており、料理のための部屋というよりも、パーティーのための部屋のように見える。

Pantries and cabinets that combine a wide range of dark shades of wood and linoleum with a parquet floor as a backdrop, make up this sober and elegant kitchen that is so neat and prim that it seems not ready for cooking but rather, ready for a party.

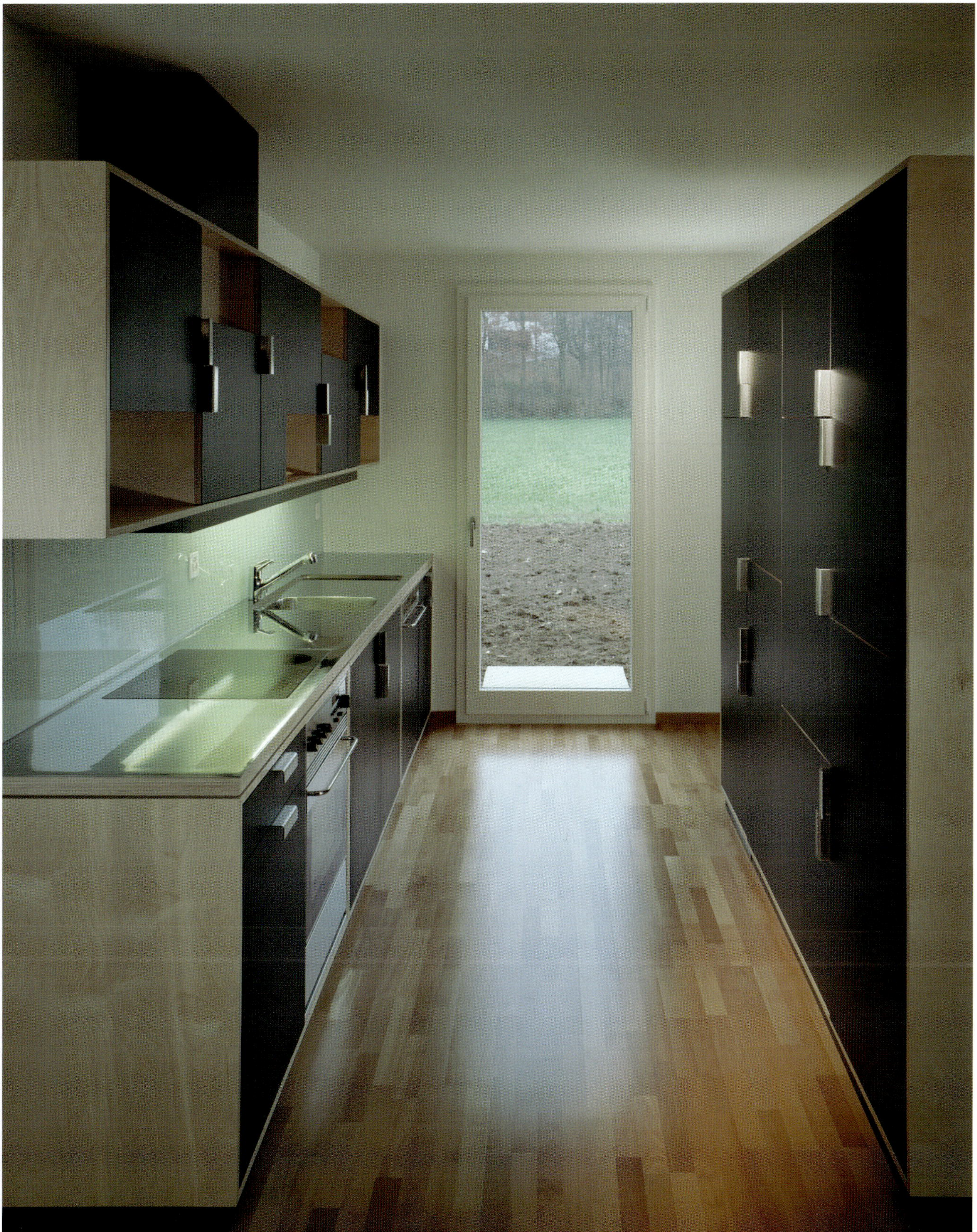

シャーレ・ピクテ

シャルル・ピクテ アルシテクト　　　　　　　　　　　　撮影：フランチェスカ・ジョヴァネッリ

　この修復された住宅の自慢は、木で覆われたキッチンである。そこはまるで離れ小島のようで、時間が止まっているように感じられる。ぐつぐつと煮える料理の熱や、ゆっくりと時間をかけて調理される料理の豊潤な香りが、それを温かく見守る格調高い無垢材の壁の中に沁みこんでいくようである。

This restored residence boasts a kitchen wrapped in wood which is like an island where the passing of time seems of little concern. The heat from simmering dishes and the aromas of food slowly cooking seem to perpetually permeate the solid rotund walls with their watchful eyes.

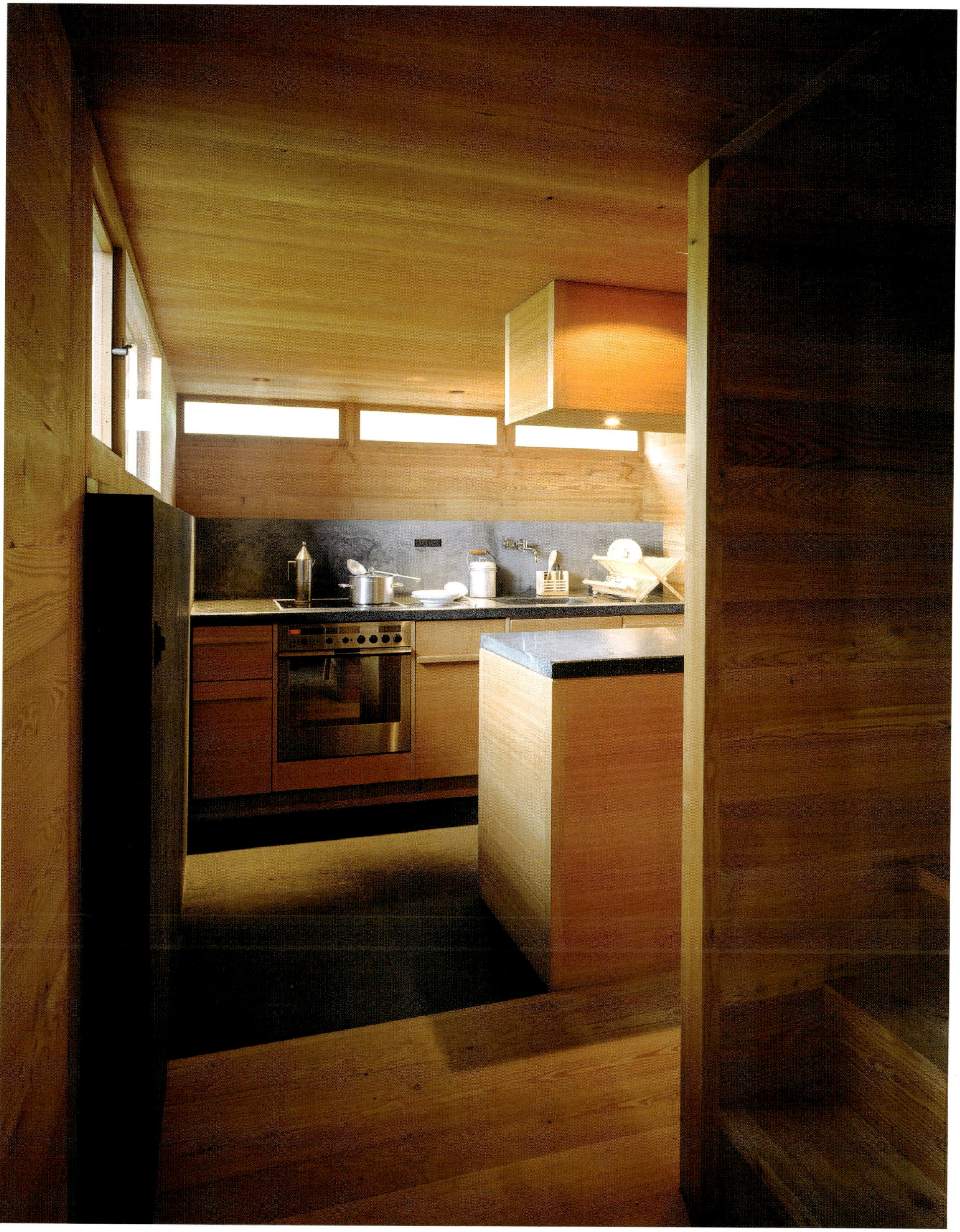

ラトーレ邸

ギャリー・カニンガム アーキテクト

撮影：オンディーヌ・プレール

　ダラスにあるこの家には、他にはない活気に満ちた現代的なキッチンがある。それは簡潔なモジュールの組み合わせによって構成され、効率の良さを感じさせるが、同時にスポットライトの使用に見られるように、それに反発するような遊び心も感じられる。天井を支える木の梁がこの空間に不可欠のエレメントとして活躍しており、棚やその他のキッチン用品がそこから吊り下げられている。

This Dallas home affords us an agile and contemporary kitchen made up of compact modules that convey a sense of efficiency, but also a ironical playfulness as exemplified by the use of the spotlights. The wooden beams that support the ceiling form an integral part of the space as shelves and other kitchen utensils are hung from them.

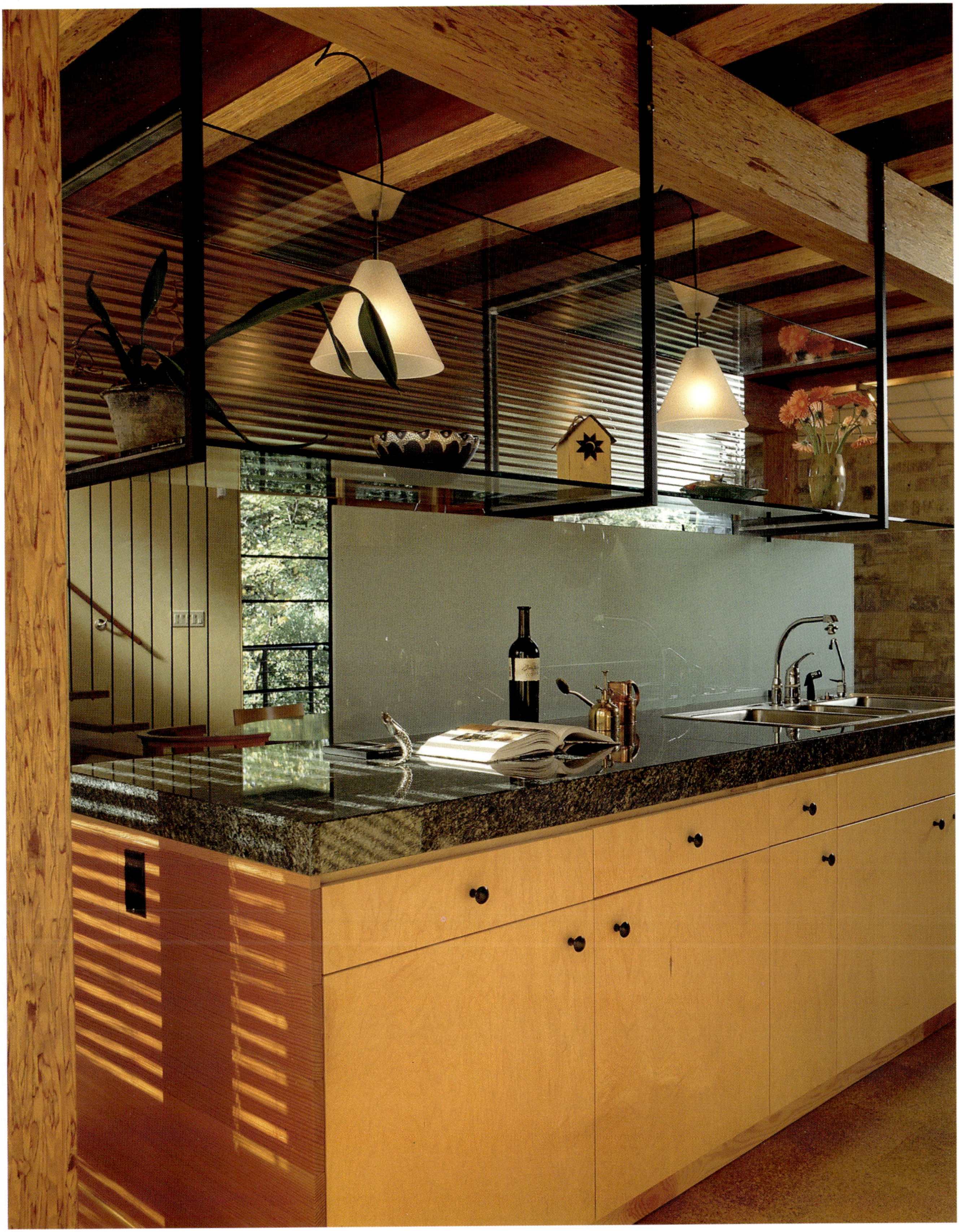

ウッドハウス

カトラー・アンダーソン アーキテクツ   撮影：オンディーヌ・プレール

　リビングルームとダイニングルームが一体となった連続した共有空間の奥にキッチンはある。空間は2つの異なった雰囲気を楽しげに誇示し、薪ストーブが温もりをもたらしている。その空間を歩行すると、さまざまな木が繁る森林の奥深くへ入り込むような錯覚を覚える。キャビネットは小鳥たちの巣箱のようであり、梁は辛抱強く小鳥の飛来を待っているようである。時間はゆっくりと穏やかに、暖色と柔らかな光の中を流れる。

The kitchen is at the back of a continuous unbroken shared space that is for the living and dining room. The space sports two different ambiences which the fireplace imbues with warmth. A walk in it is like penetrating the depths of a forest with a wide variety of trees. The cabinets seem to be the refuge for birds and the beams seem to be patiently awaiting the flight of a bird while time placidly and calmly passes by among warm colors and soft lights.

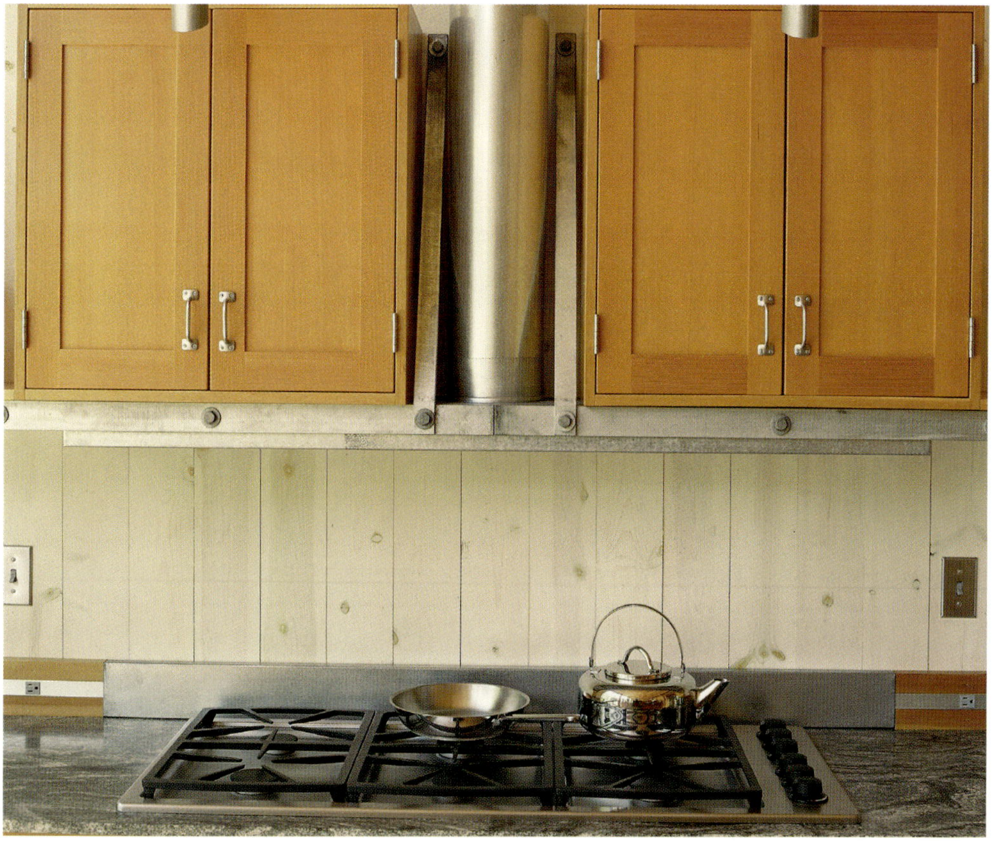

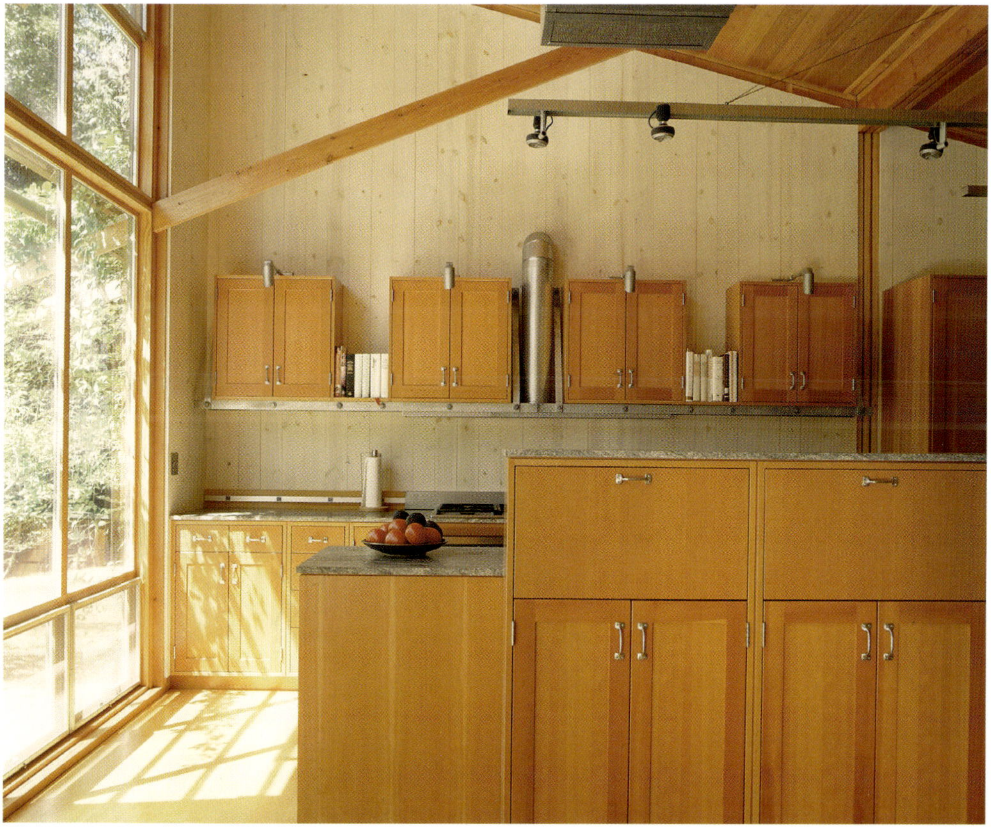

ミカエリス邸

ハリー・レビン アーキテクツ　　　　　　　　　　　撮影：パトリック・ビンガム・ホール

　オーストラリアのとある住宅のキッチンである。木製のキャビネットと棚でできた横枠が、「キッチンの通路」という題名の絵の額縁となっている。豊かな自然光をもたらしている窓はまた、キッチンで使う日常の食器類をディスプレイする棚の支えにもなっている。

Situated in a residence in Australia, a kind of bar of cabinets and shelves made of wood frame the picture which is the passageway of the kitchen. The windows that provide it with ample natural sunlight are also used to support shelves that display everyday objects for use in the kitchen.

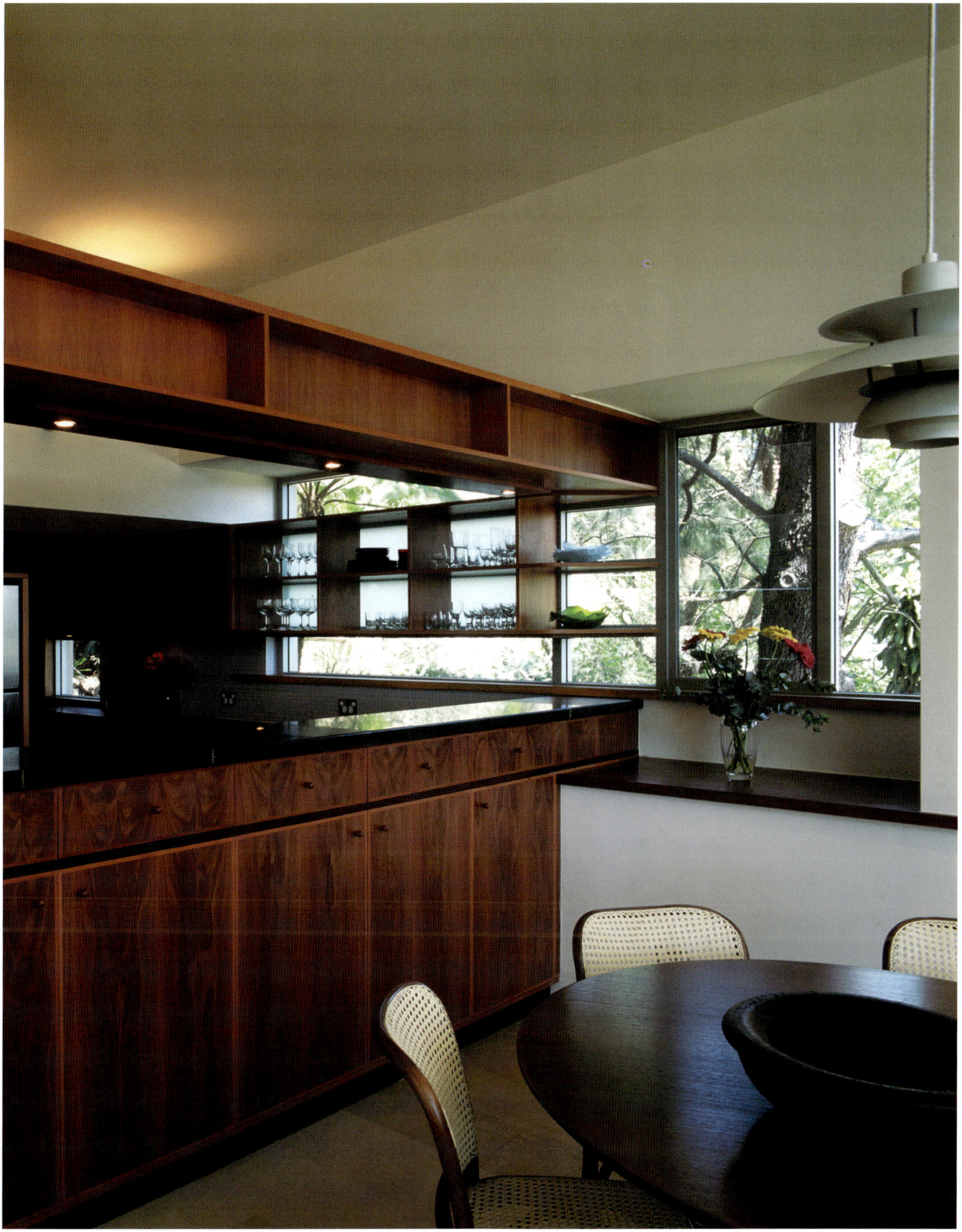

山あいの家

サイア・バーバリス・トポザノフ・アルシテクト

撮影：マーク・クレイマー

　リビングルームの章でも見たように（p.180〜181）、ここキッチンのデザインでも、特別な関心は、壁用の木質パネルの豊富な使用である。石積みの壁は天井まで切り開かれて、キッチンへの入口となり、訪問者はカウンターバーで迎えられる。それは大自然の真ん中、家全体をつらぬくガラスと木の長い通路の一部である。

Also appearing in the chapters on interiors, of special interest here is the abundant use of wood panels for the walls. A stone wall opens up to afford entry into the kitchen which receives the visitor with a bar. It is part of a long path of glass and wood throughout the house, in the middle
of nature.

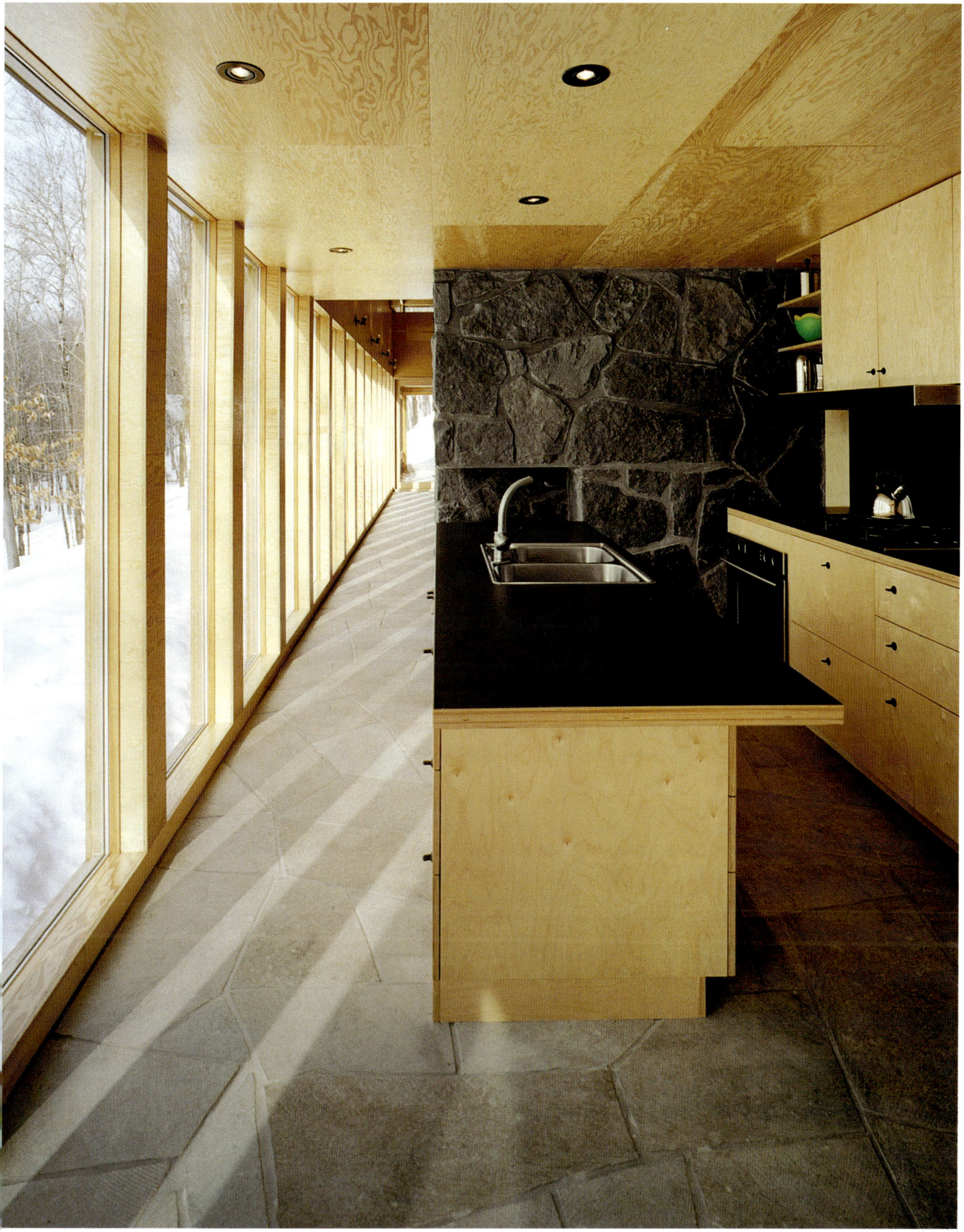

アイランドハウス

アルキテクトスタジオ　ウィッジェダル・ラッキ・ベルガーホフ　　　　　撮影：オーケ・エリクソン・リンドマン

　この家では、キッチンは家族が集う最も重要な場所である。そこからは窓越しに、オークの枝が作り出すほつれ髪と岩陰の間に海を眺めることができる。無垢材で構成されたキッチンは、壁、天井そして床と、同じく家全体を覆う無垢材と溶け合い、若い貴婦人のようにつつましやかで、静かな優美さをたたえている。

The kitchen is an essential meeting place and from it one may gaze out the window to the ocean, among locks of hair made of oak trees and the silhouettes of rocks. Built in and melded with the wall and the wood that clads all of the house, it is as discreet and silently elegant as a fair young lady.

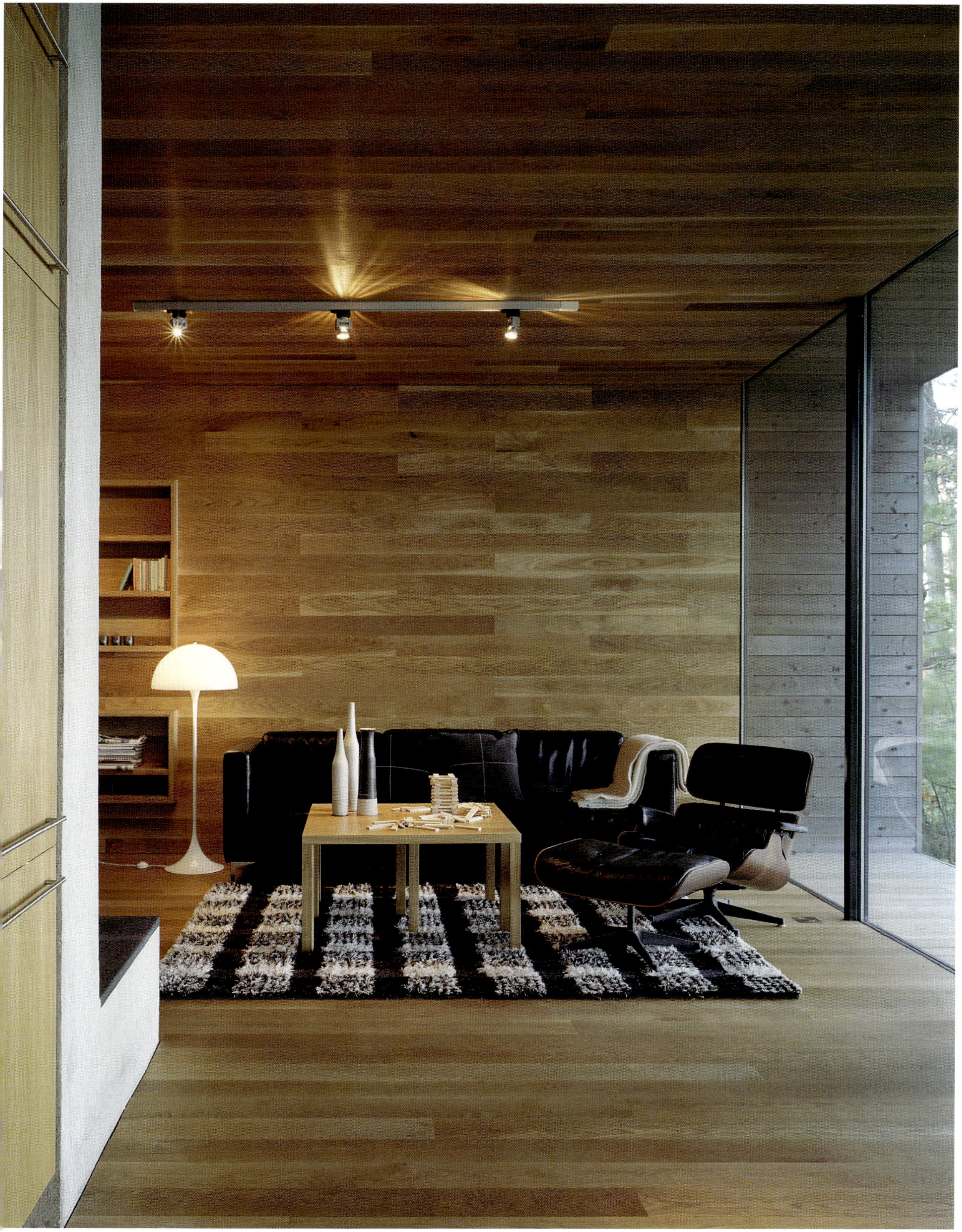

スタジオ3773

ドライデザイン　　　　　　　　　　　　　　　　　　　　　　　　撮影：オンディーヌ・プレール

ロサンゼルスのこの住宅のような狭い空間では、有効な空間を最大限活用する発明の才が要求される。この小さな家にベッドルームをどう置くかという問題に対する解は、リビングルームの上方、大梁の間に半分隠れるように、小さなロフトを設けるというものであった。この遊び心に満ちた微笑ましい介入は、精巧に仕上げられた木の存在により空間を豊かにしている。

In tight spaces, such as this residence in Los Angeles, ingenuity is needed in order to make maximum use of available space. The solution for the bedroom in this small home is to fashion a small loft over the living room area, half-hidden among the structural beams. This pleasant and cheerful intervention enriches the space with the presence of wood that is skillfully elaborated.

JOHN LE CARRÉ
THE CONSTANT GARDENER
DIAMOND
MATTHEW HART
ER-HORSE

サヴォア通り重層式アパート

リトー・アルシテクト　　　　　　　　　　撮影：ペッカ・リトー

　パリの屋根裏部屋付き住宅がリフォームされ、ベッドルームは屋根の真下に置かれた。伝統的木構造は剥き出しにされ、修復された。そして空間に温もりをもたらした。そこにあるのは、万物は流転するという感覚であり、それはベッドを置くことによって一層強められた。ベッドは床の上に直接置かれ、頭上の窓からの明かりに照らされて、修道院のようである。

The remodeling of an attic apartment in Paris allowed the bedroom to be placed directly beneath the roof. The wood structure was stripped and restored, which grants warmth to the space. There is a sense of everything being provisional which is accentuated with the placement of the bed; directly on the floor, almost monastic, illuminated by the windows overhead.

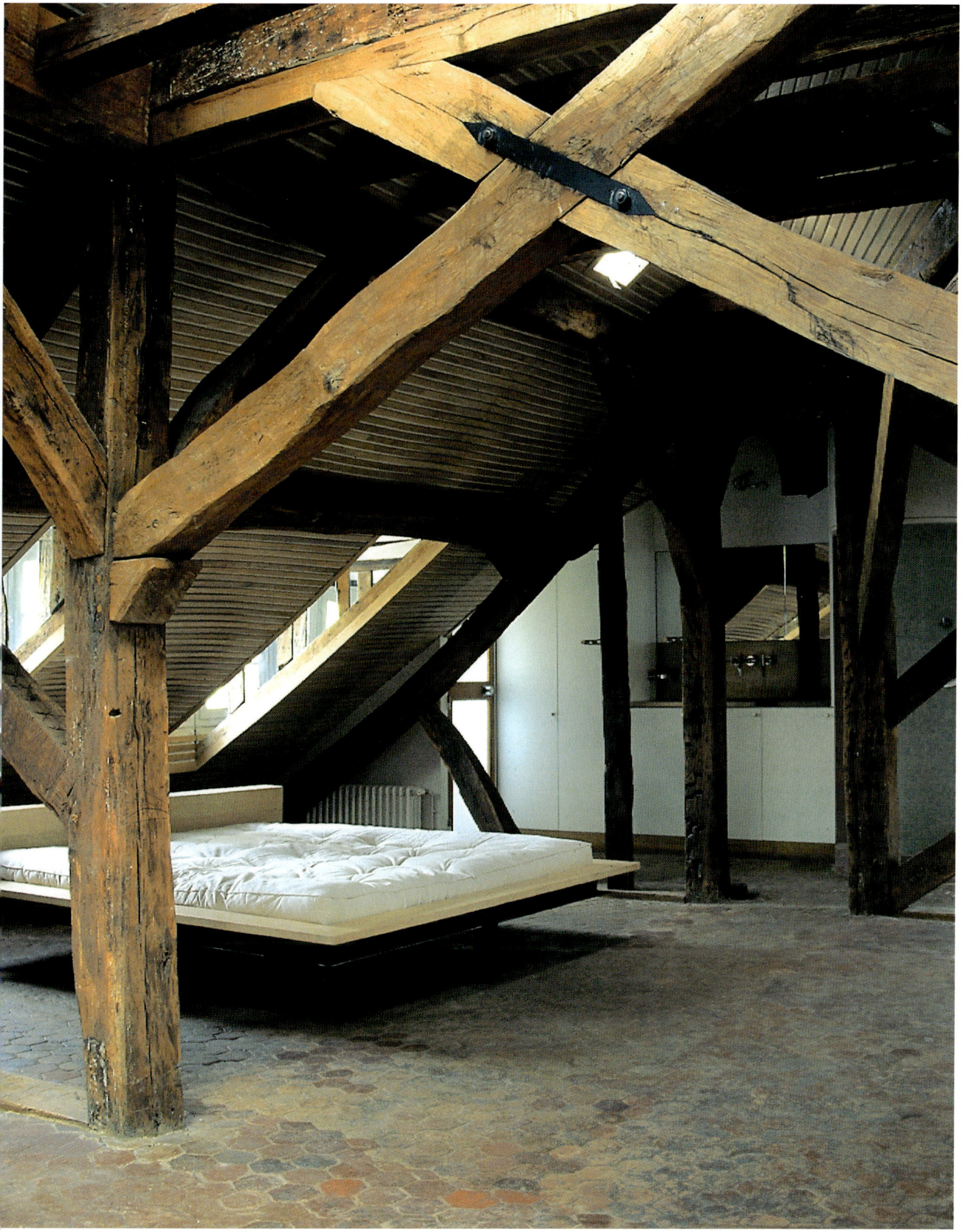

シャーレ・ピクテ

シャルル・ピクテ アルシテクト　　　　　　　撮影：フランチェスカ・ジョヴァネッリ

　どれも同一の住宅に属するベッドルームであるが、3つの部屋それぞれが、独特の木の使い方を示している。右ページは、波状になった板で壁面を飾ったものである。板を木理と色調に合わせてカットし、円を描くようにモザイク状に貼り合わせたもので、機能性と装飾性を満足させている。また別の部屋では、古びた、そして古びつつある木材が使われ、その無垢な存在は謙虚で簡潔である。また現代的なセッティングに合わせて用いられている木材もある。そのすべての持ち味を引き出され、木材は簡潔さを創造し、室内を独特な空間に変えている。

Three bedrooms belonging to the same residence exemplify three different uses for wood. Present is sinuous wood for dressing a wall which is both functional and decorative, a mosaic of circular forms drawn by the grains and tones of the material. There is aged and aging wood, whose rustic presence is humble and simple. And there is wood adapted to modernity. Taken in its entirety, all of this creates simplicity and transforms the interior into a unique space.

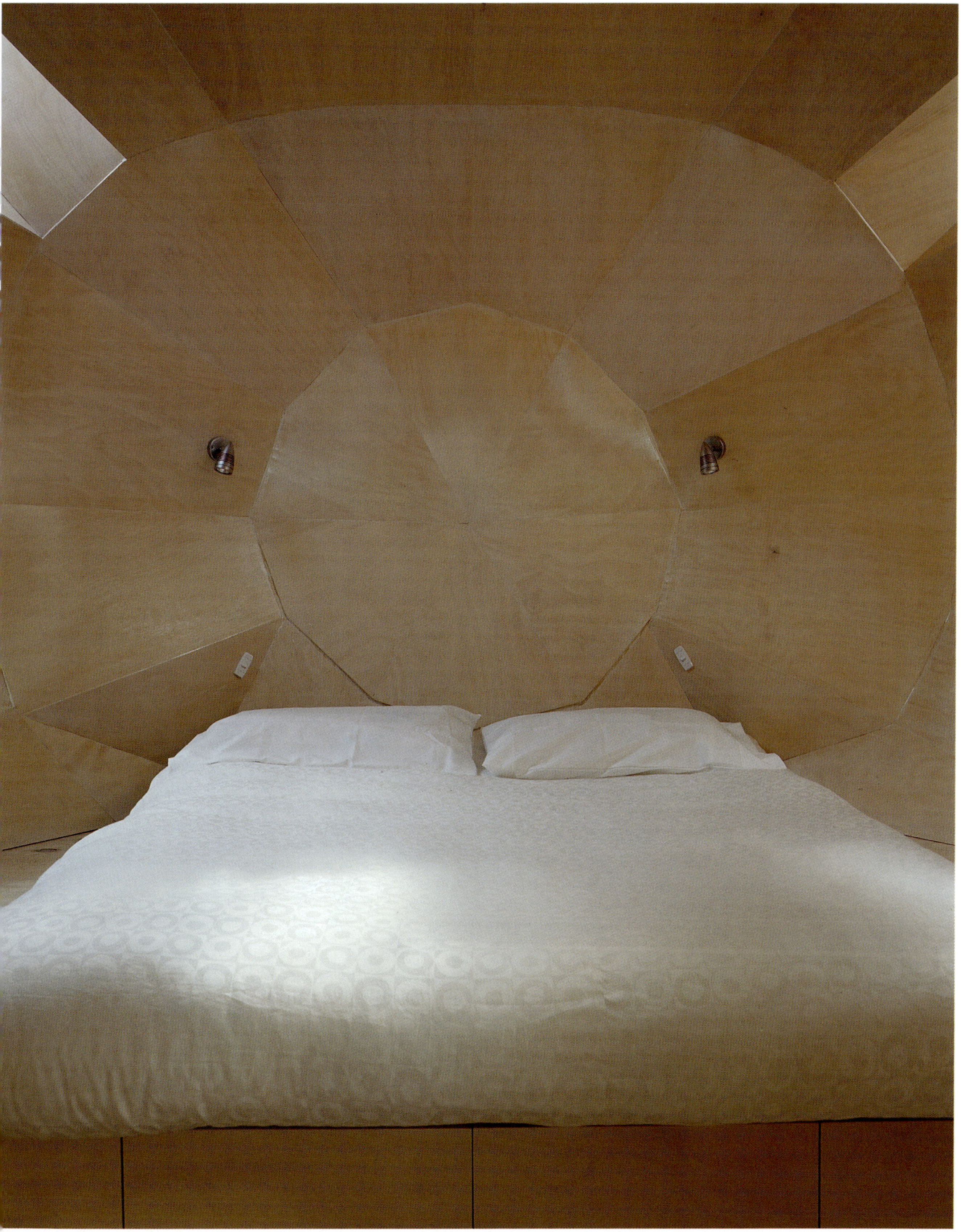

トレジャー・パレス

エッジ・アーキテクツ　　　　　　　　　　　　　　　　　撮影：ジャネット・チョイ, ゲーリー・チャン

　このベッドルームの設計思想は、東洋の室内空間のとらえ方と同じである。休息所は厳密なプランに基づき、空間を規定するものは壁ではなく建具であるという考え方にもとづいて、連続性の下に分割されている。この前提は究極まで推し進められ、ベッドルームとホールを仕切る壁さえ、ただの形式的な境界になっているだけである。それは平縁で作られており、ベッドルームに柔らかな光を流れ込ませることによって、美しい像を創りだしている。

The approach to decorating this bedroom is akin to the way interiors are designed in the Orient. A strict plan distributes the dorm in continuity so that it is the furniture that defines the spaces more than the walls. This premise is taken to the limit as even the wall that separates the bedroom from the hall becomes a simple formal limit as it is made of fillets that allow light to flow in, which creates a beautiful image.

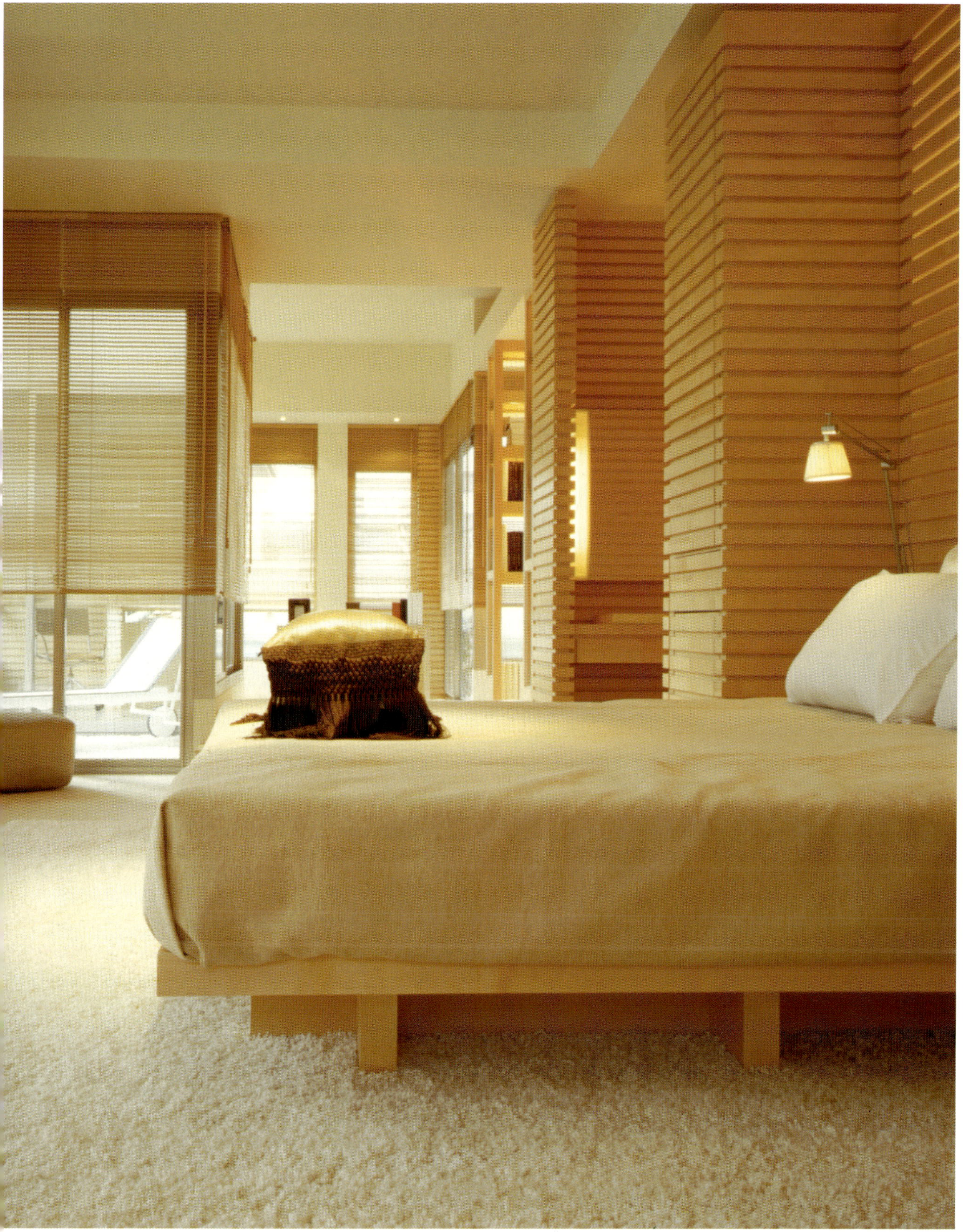

山あいの家

サイア・バーバリス・トボザノフ・アルシテクト   撮影：マーク・クレイマー

　細部の装飾を省いた明快な幾何学的空間が、ベッドルームの領域である。ベッドは1個の大きな木製の箱の中央に置かれ、光の小さな切れ目が、ベッドを包む無限を切り取っている。ベッドは平穏と沈黙の中に沈み、唯一それのみがこの部屋の機能を示唆する物体となっている。同時に、まわりを取り巻く重厚な厚板と静寂との終わることのない対話が延々と続く。

A simple geometric volume totally lacking in details is the domain of this bedroom. It is on display in the center of a wooden box and tiny apertures of light slice the immensity of what surrounds it outside. The bed, bathed in serenity and quiet, is the only object that hints of the function of this room. At the same time, an unending dialogue of silence with the setting of hefty trunks continues on and on.

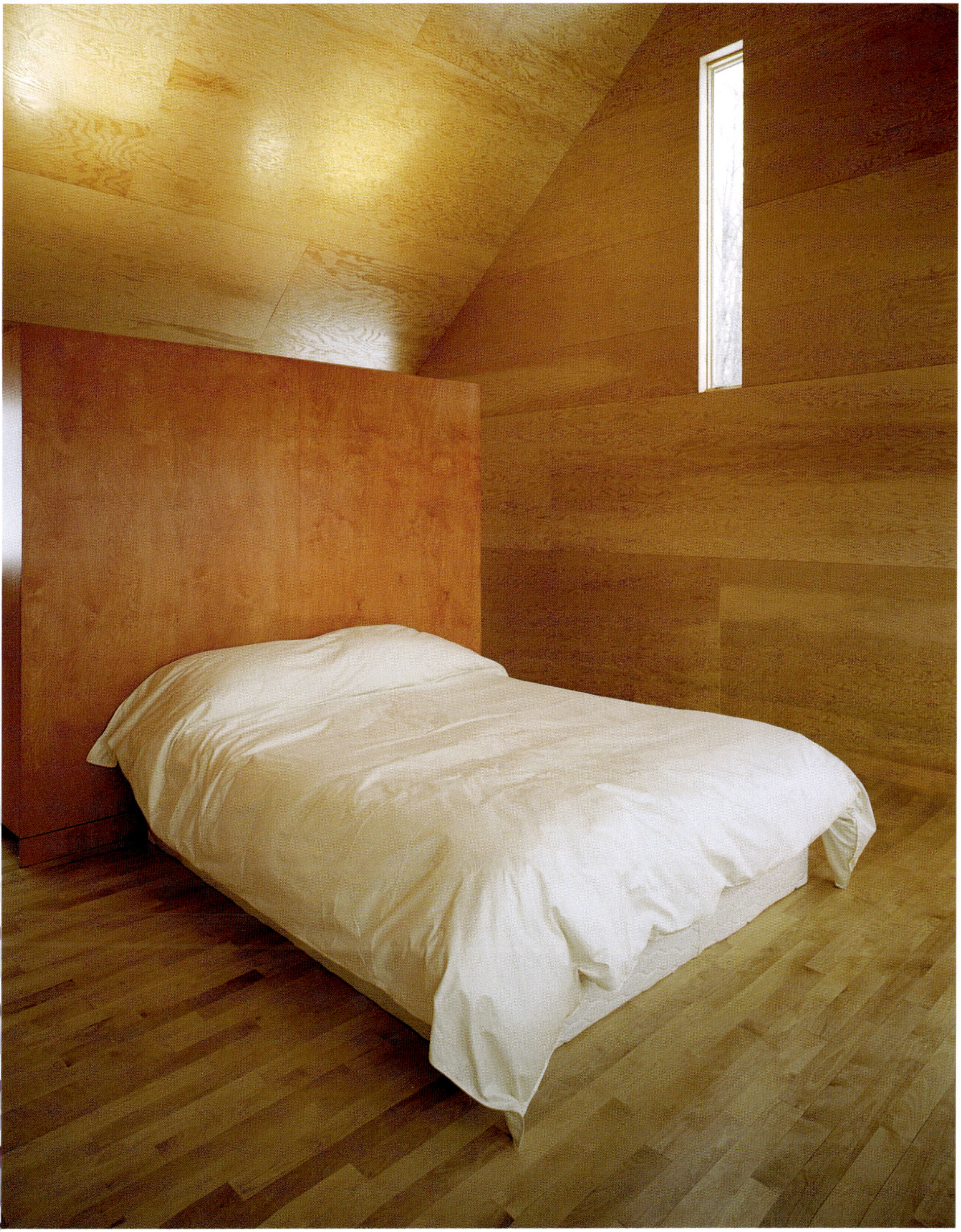

水没する家

GADアーキテクチュア

撮影:アリ・ベックマン, サリー・ククチュナ

　過去の遺産を拒否することなく建設すること、過去を繰り返すことなく歴史を継承すること、模倣することなく、遺物の中の使えるものを蘇らせ使用することによって新しいものを創造すること。何世紀も離れた、しかも非常に異なっているいくつもの文化の表象が現在のイスタンブールの豊かさを構成している。そしてこれらのベッドルームにもそれは見いだされる。このページのベッドは、あるトルコ人の家の屋根小屋組みの下に置かれているもの。左ページの壁に寄り添うように置かれたベッドは、3世代にわたる人々の起居を見守ってきた。

To build in our present century without rejecting the heritage from the past, to continue history without repeating the past, to create, without imitating, by recuperating and using what is usable from an aging body. The signs of the cultures, separated by centuries but also very distinct, which now make up the riches of the city of Istanbul, can be found in these bedrooms. A bed that reposes beneath the frame of an Ottoman house, and another, snuggled up against a wall, that has seen the sleeping and the awakening of three different generations.

3つの時代にまたがる家

フィンランドの住宅

ウッドフォーカス・フィンランド

撮影：エスコ・ジャムサ,
ミッコー・オーエルニーティー

2002年に完成したフィンランドのある住宅のベッドルームである。壁と天井には、ブルーに塗装された天然木ウッドシートが張られ、海上にいるような雰囲気が創りだされている。家具やレイアウトから生ずる垂直な線と水平な線が交差し、この休息の部屋にいると、まるで海図上の線の交点にいるような感覚を覚える。

In one of the bedrooms in this house in Finland completed in 2002, the walls and the ceiling are made with sheets of wood painted in blue so as to convey a marine ambience. Like a meeting point is the sensation one gets for this place for rest thanks to the criss-cross of vertical and horizontal lines stemming from the furniture and layout.

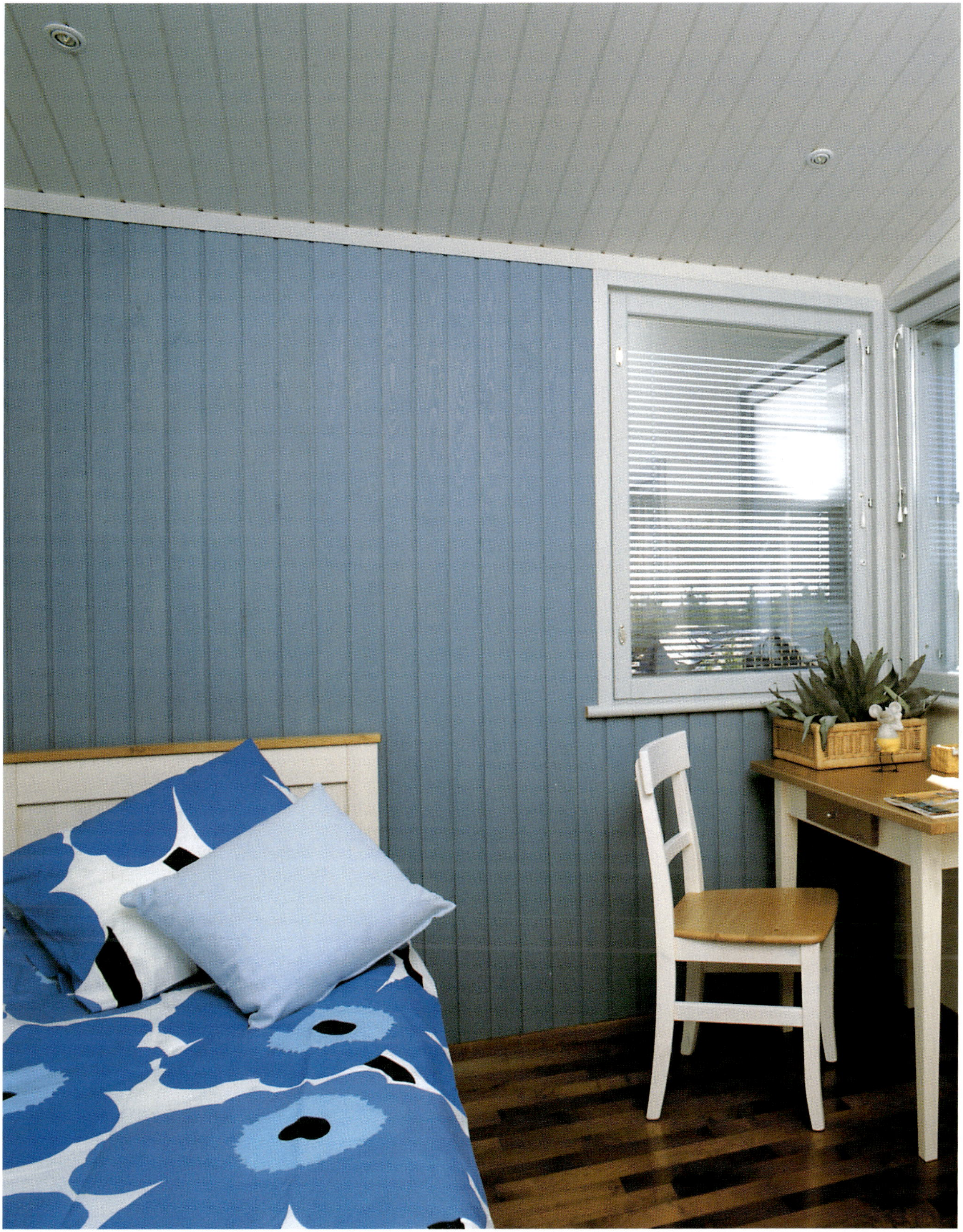

トレジャー・パレス

エッジ・アーキテクツ　　　　　　　　　　　　　　　撮影：ジャネット・チョイ, ゲーリー・チャン

やすらぎと愉悦の無限の広がりの一隅、見事な黄金の輝きを放つ木の豊かさのただなかにバスルームはある。それはこの家で最も大切に保管されてきた宝物である。多すぎもせず、少なすぎもせず、この場にふさわしい数の物体だけが、さまざまな線が織り成す美しさを最高にひきたてる位置に置かれている。

In one of the corners of this immense field of comfort and pleasure that this palace is, midst the richness of wood shining in all of its golden splendor, is the bathroom, one of the best kept treasures of this house. Here, there are just the right number of objects and they are ideally placed to maximize the aesthetics of the different lines.

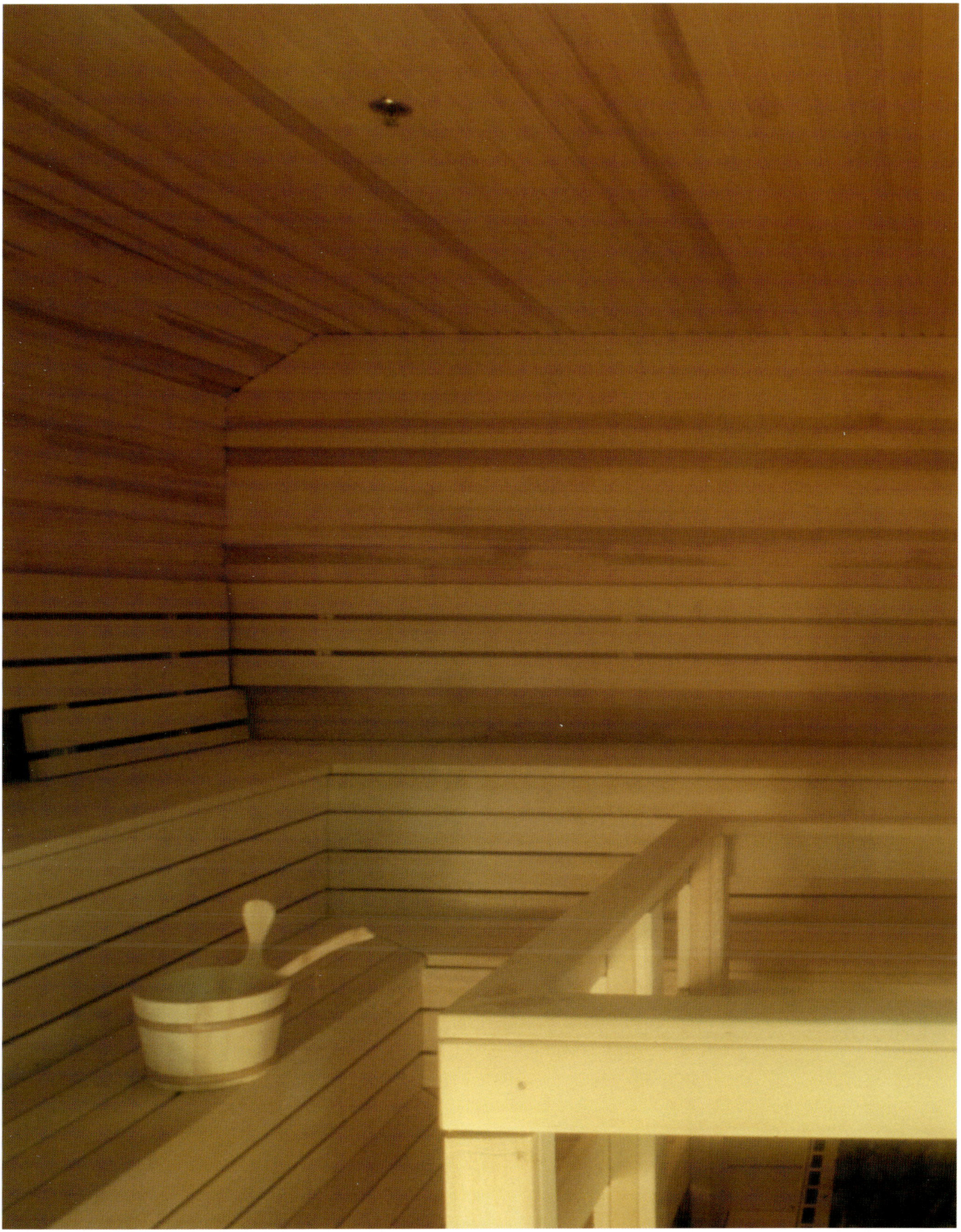

スーツケース・ハウスホテル

エッジ・アーキテクツ

撮影：ジャネット・チョイ,
ゲーリー・チャン

万里の長城の傍に建てられた可変式住宅の大きな連続した空間の半地下に、そのバスルームはある。その存在は訪問者には手がかりとして与えられているだけである。それは木製の扉でもある床の下にあり、その扉を開けたり閉めたりすることによって、現れたり消えたりする。そうすることによって、それは必要なプライバシーを満たし、また新しい雰囲気をもたらす。

Semi-underground in a large continuous space of this changeable house designed next to the Great Wall of China, we are given a clue as to the presence of the bathroom. It appears and disappears under a floor of wooden doors that open and close so as to afford the necessary privacy, or to provide a new ambience.

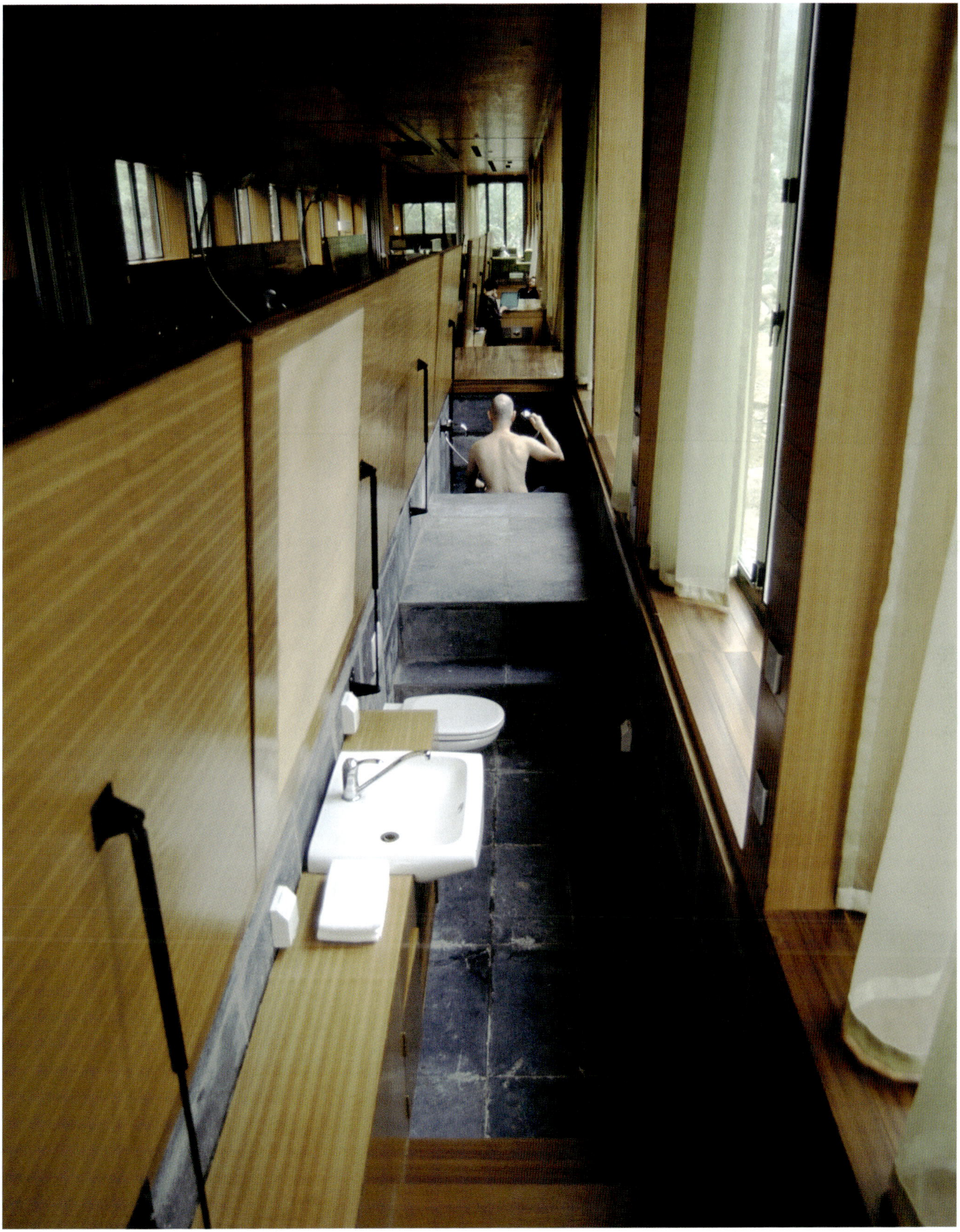

バンデイラ・デ・メロの住宅

マウロ・ムニョス アルキテクチュラ　　　　　　　　　　　　撮影：ネルソン・コン

　住宅の地政学的条件により、広いガラス窓を持つこのバスルームは、だれに遠慮することもなく満喫することができる。それは明快で温もりにあふれている。それとは対照的に、右のアイランドハウスのバスルームは控え目で内省的である。優雅で慎ましやかなそのプライバシーを知っているのは、唯一スウェーデンの空だけである。

Thanks to the topographical characteristics of the setting where Bandeira de Mello lies, this bathroom with its large windows can be thoroughly enjoyed. Its simplicity and warmth contrasts with the soberness and introversion of Island House which only unveils its privacy with elegant discretion to the skies of Sweden.

アイランドハウス

アルキテクトスタジオ　ウィッジェダル・ラッキ・ベルガーホフ　　　　　撮影：エイク・エリクソン−リンドマン

3つの時代にまたがる家

GADアーキテクチュア

撮影：アリ・ベックマン, サリー・ククチュナ

　石、土、木、れんが、コンクリート、これらが一体となってこのバスルームに秋の気配をもたらしている。刻まれた溝と線は拡張する空間を創造し、最小限の物だけが宙吊りにされている。この囲まれた空間は、さまざまな素材と色の幾何学的層によって構成された1個の抽象画である。木は決して目立つことなく、時に印象的に現れ、他の素材と心地良く調和させられている。

Stone, earth, wood, bricks and concrete imbue this bathroom with autumn hues, grooves and lines which creates a field of extensive spaces and minimal objects hanging in the air. The ambience of this enclosure is a composition consisting of a mosaic of geometric layers of different materials and colors. Without taking prominence, the wood appears striking at times and is well-coordinated with the other materials.

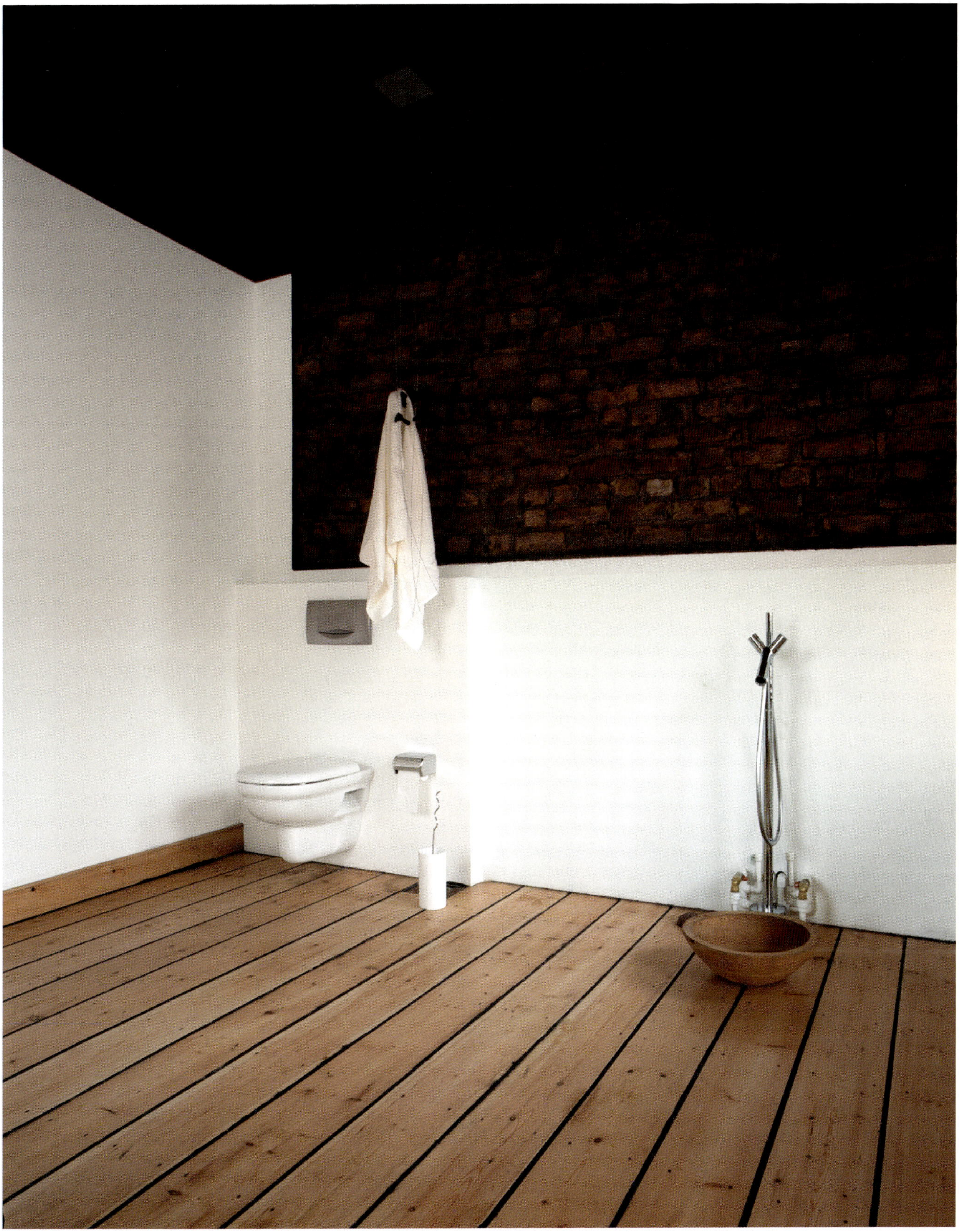

R邸

フェイファリックーフリッツァー アーヒテクテン　　　　　　　　　　撮影：ポール・オットー, グラーツ

　屋内のバスルームは、暗く、閉所恐怖症的な空間になりがちである。2002年にオーストリアで完成したこの住宅は、その問題を、バスルームを仕切る壁を本棚に変えることによって解決した。その結果外部からの光がバスルーム内に流入することができるようになった。本の置き方を戦略的に変えることによって、プライバシーと光の量を自分の好みに加減することができる。木との対照的な美しさを考え、備品には磁器が選ばれた。

Interior bathrooms are often dark and claustrophobic spaces. In this project completed in Austria in 2002, these problems were overcome by replacing walls that delimit it, with shelves, which allows the exterior light to flow in. By strategically placing the books, the user can satisfy his needs for more or less privacy or light. To contrast with the wood, white ceramic bathroom fixtures are the choice.

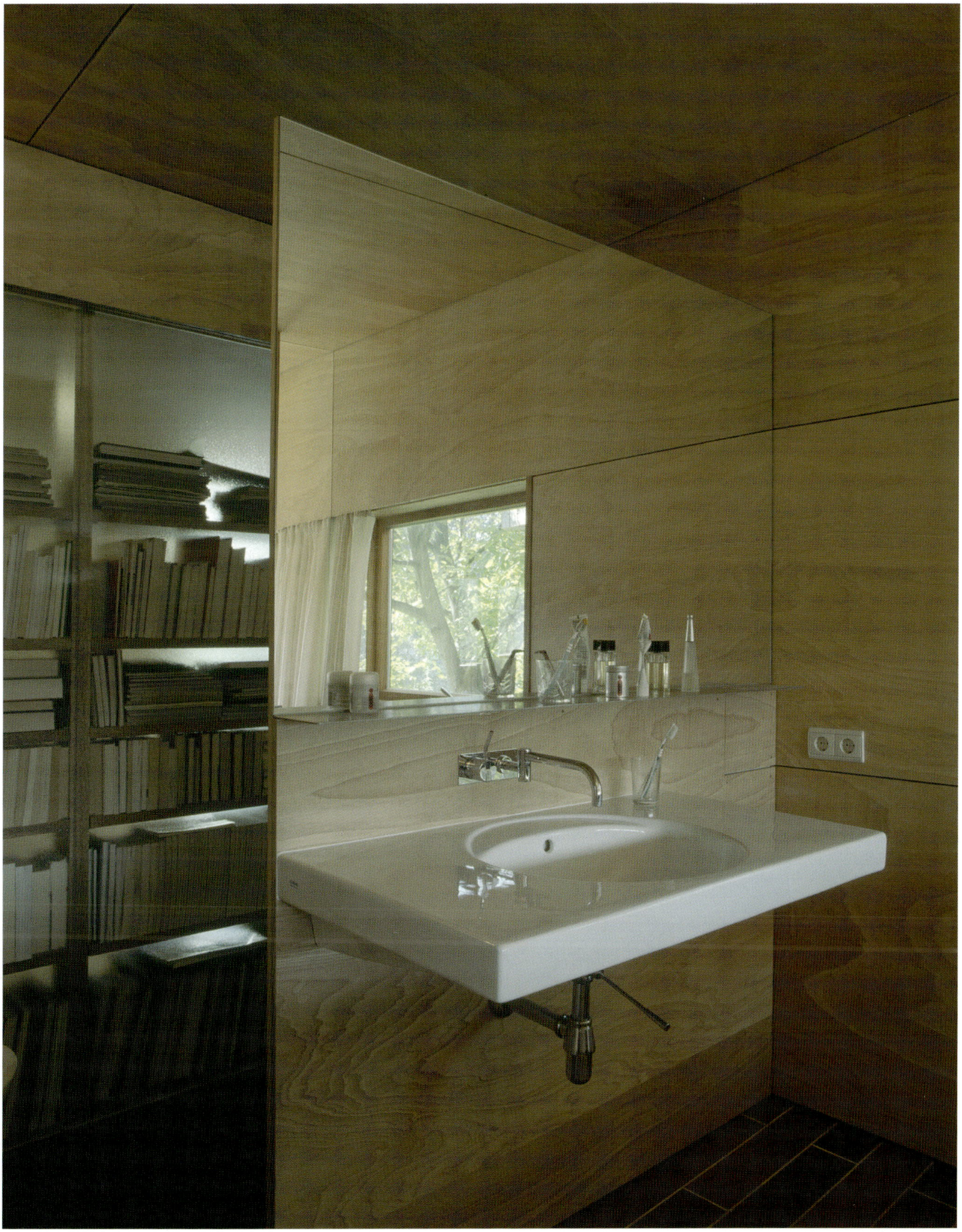

フィンランドの住宅

ウッドフォーカス・フィンランド

撮影：エスコ・ジャムサ、ミッコー・オーエルニーティー

このバスルームに入ると、誰もが木でできたサウナに注意を引かれる。バスルームの調和を持続させているその扉を開けると、落ち着いた温かな空間がわれわれを誘う。ここでも木の質感は、白色の磁器でできた手水鉢と完璧に結び付けられている。窓が空間の広がりを与えている。

On entering this enclosure our attention is drawn to the wooden sauna, as we are beckoned to enter in its calm and warm interior as we open doors that continue the harmony fashioned by the bathroom. Once again, the hues of the wood combine perfectly with the white bathroom fixtures. The windows grant a feeling of spaciousness.

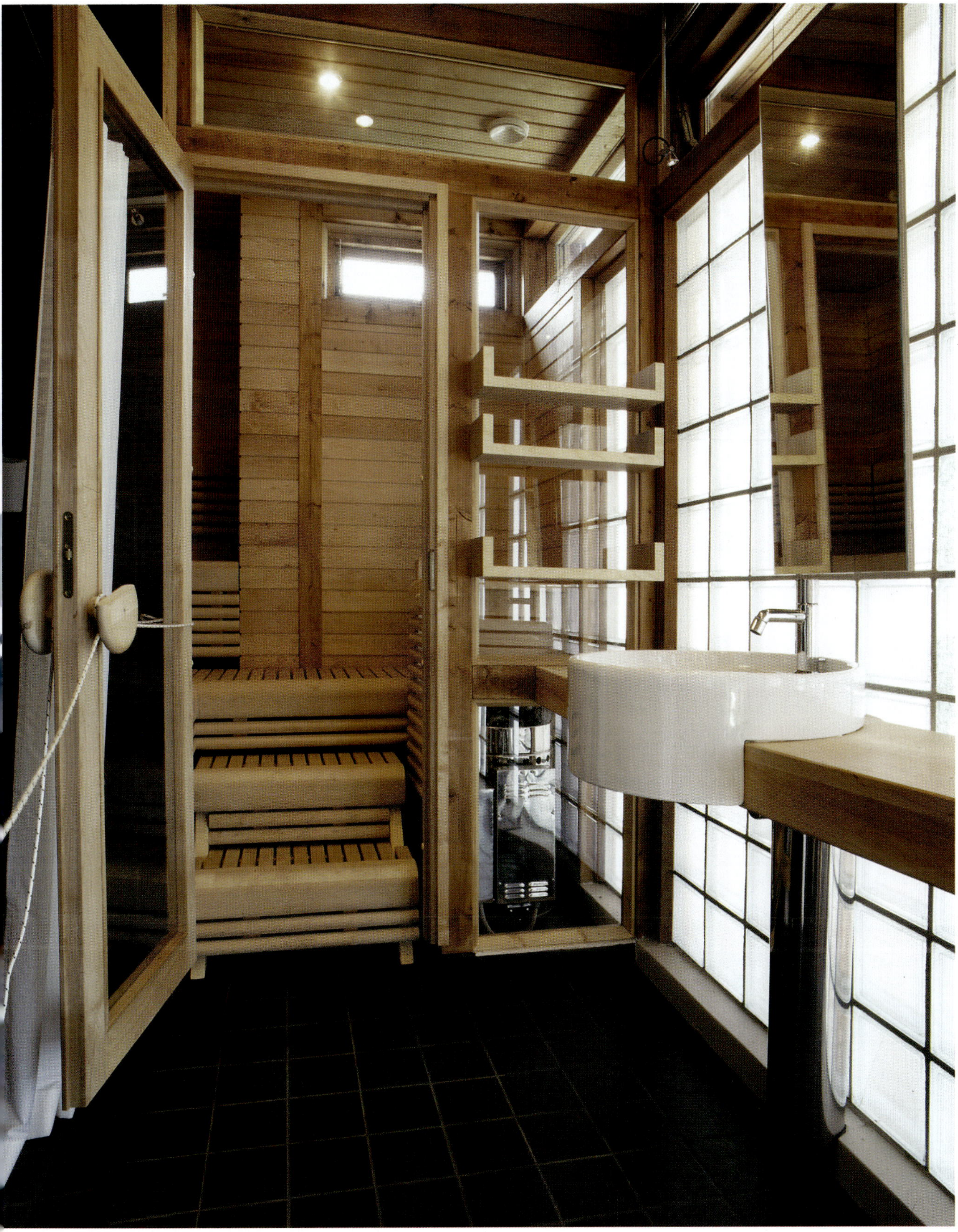

シャーレ・ピクテ

シャルル・ピクテ アルシテクト　　　　　　　　　　　　　　　　　　　　　　　　撮影：フランチェスカ・ジョヴァネッリ

スイスアルプス地方のこの家の改築に際しては、ここバスルームでも、改築前の使い込んだ木の温もりと柔らかな質感はそのまま残され、黒っぽい石の荒々しさとの間にコントラストが生み出されている。それにより、バスルームの温かさはさらに一層強調されている。

Once again in the remodeling of this house in the Swiss Alps, the warm hues and the softness of the texture of the smooth wood, present before the restoration, contrast with the roughness of the grayish stone, which strikingly accentuates the warmth of the bathroom.

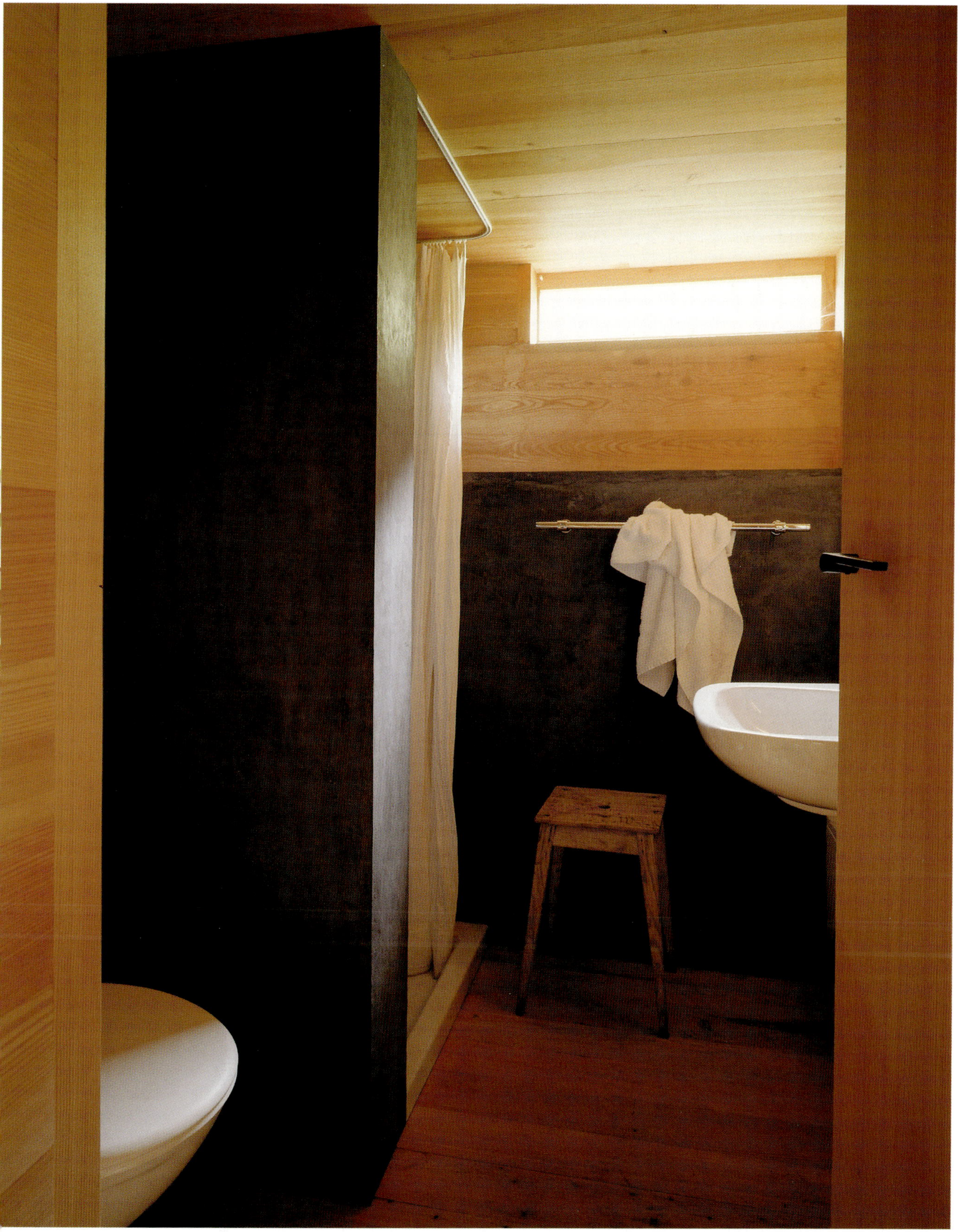

縁側の家

手塚建築事務所　　　　　　　　　　　　　　　　　　　撮影：木田勝久

　屋外は室内となり、室内は屋外となる。家全体が1個の大きな縁側となり、周囲の環境は一層身近になる。一陣の風は生き物が呼吸するための酸素であり、日光は部屋の奥や隅のモノクロ画に彩色する光である。寒さや暑さを感じることなく開かれた空間で生活するため、満天の星の下で身を寄せ合うため、雨の中で湯浴みするため。

Exterior is interior, and interior is exterior. All of the house is one huge porch which brings the setting in closer to us. A gust of wind is the oxygen that the inhabitants breathe, and sunlight is the light that paints the chiaroscuro of the nooks and crannies. To live in the open air without feeling cold or hot, to snuggle up under the stars and to bathe in the rain.

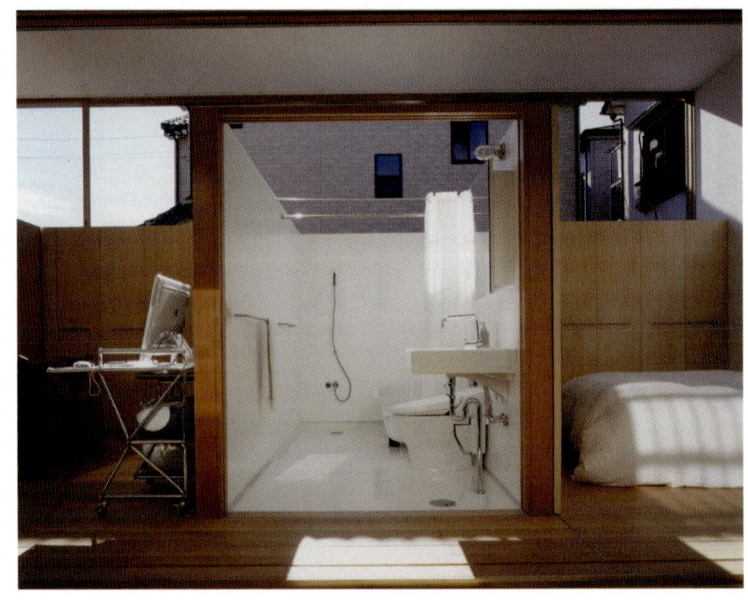

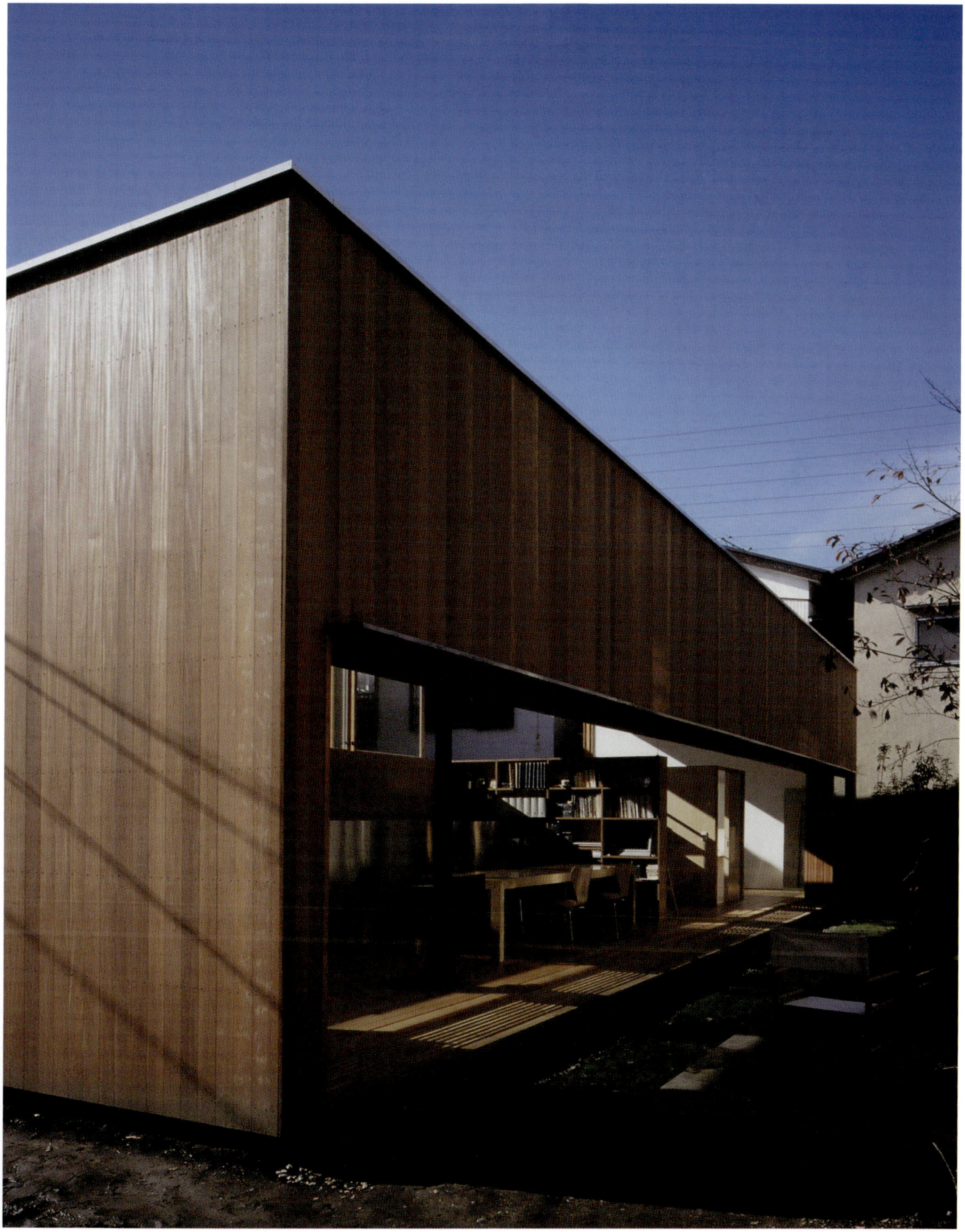

アヴァロン邸

コナー−ソロモン アーキテクツ　　　　　　　　　撮影：ピーター・スコット

2003年にオーストラリアに建てられたこの住宅は、小さなテラスをいかに効果的に用いることができるかということを教えてくれる最高の例である。ファサードを透明なガラス窓にしているため、狭いテラスでもひときわよく目立ち、実際よりも広く感じられると同時に、それは室内へと延長されている。地面からほんの少し立ち上がっている間口いっぱいに走る大きな平面は、人々を温かく迎える空間となっており、周囲の環境とのより密接な調和をもたらしている。

This house built in Australia in 2003 is a poignant example of how a small terrace is efficiently exploited. A narrow terrace gains in prominence thanks to the transparency of the facade, which broadens it, while at the same time, it expands the interior. A large surface that runs the breadth of the house, slightly elevated from the ground, gains for the home inviting spaces in close harmony with the setting.

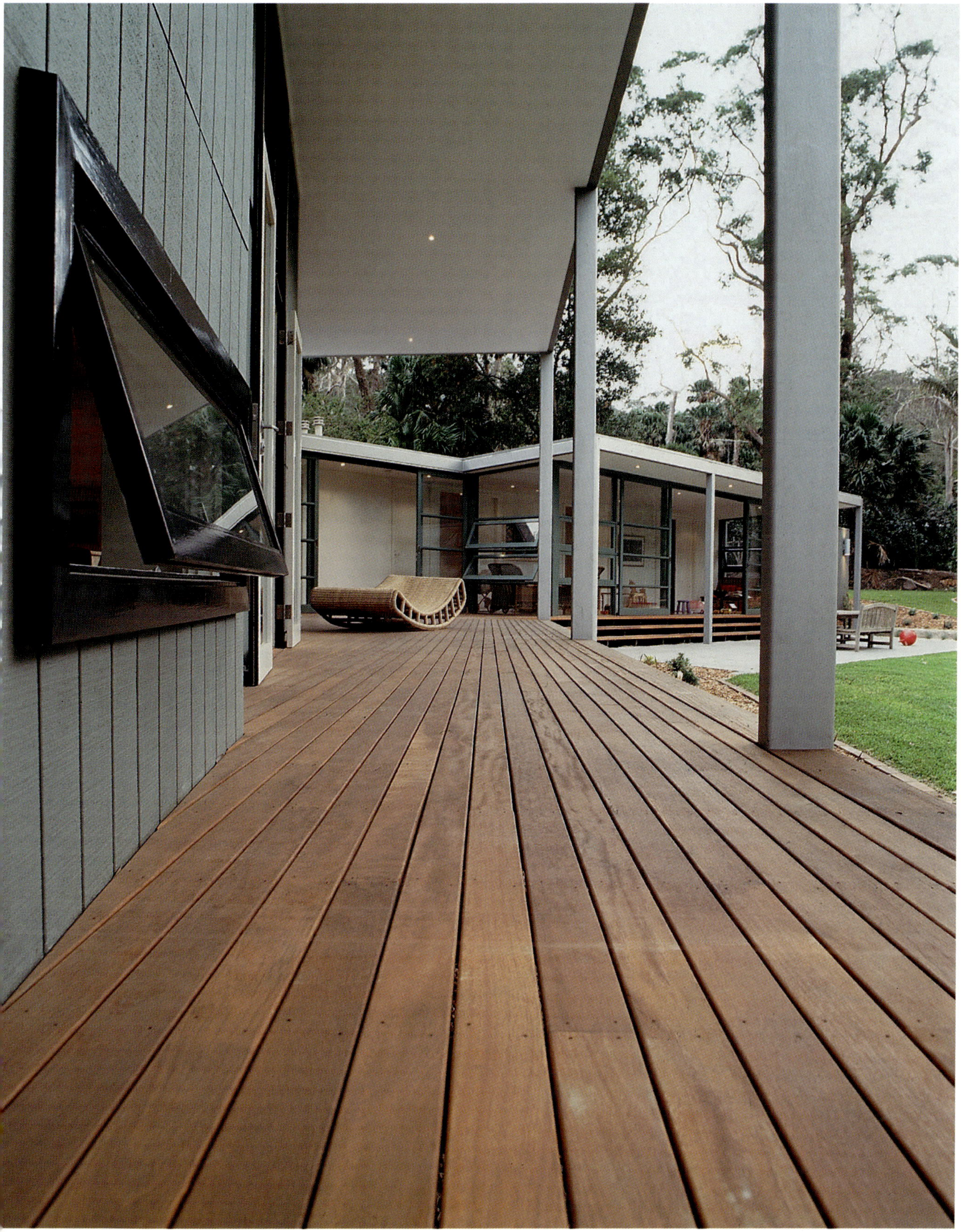

ネンニングの住宅

クックロビッツーナハバール アーヒテクテン　　　　　　　　　撮影：ハンスピーター・シース

　2004年に建築されたオーストリアのこの住宅では、外部空間は透明なドアと木枠の窓でできた大きな箱の中に閉じ込められている。住人はそれを通して、一日中つねに変化している光の揺らめきを感じ取ることができる。窓とドアはショーウィンドーのように全面に開かれ、あらゆるものをふんだんに陳列するが、それは買うことはできない。それはただ与えられるだけである。木はこの媒介的な空間を温かい光で彩っている。

In this residence built in Austria in 2004, the exterior space is contained in a box with transparent doors and wood frame windows, which allows in flashes and streaks of changing light all throughout the day. The windows and doors open up like a shop window to generously display all that can not be bought, but can only be given away. The wood colors the intermediate ambience with warm light.

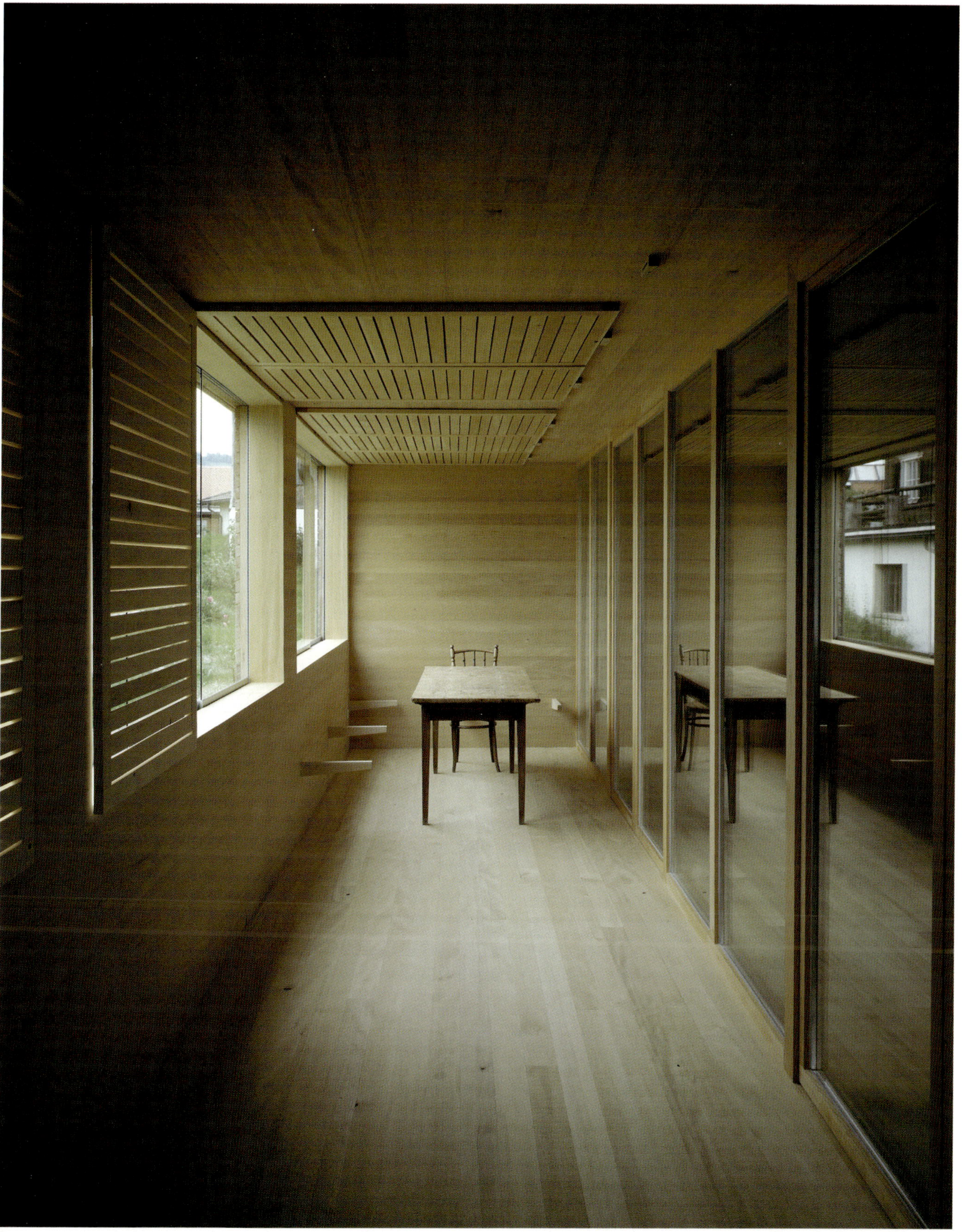

ハイン邸

クックロビッツ−ナハバール アーヒテクテン　　　　　　　　　　　撮影：アルバート・シュナベル

　伝統的な美しさを持つこの住宅には、現代的な味付けがしてある。それがプラットホームである。それはこの家の賛美者を風景に向けて発射する。テラスは建物の垂直なラインに対して、水平なラインを代表する。そこには頭上に屋根をいただく部分もあれば、空中に浮いているようにみえるバルコニーもある。床は連続した線となり、おのずと視線を水平線へと向かわせる。そこは山脈が主人公となって繰り広げられる舞台を観劇する王様の椅子である。山脈は遠ざかりつつあるように見えるが、視界から完全に消えることはない。

This house of traditional aesthetics was given a contemporary twist thanks to the platform which launches the admirer towards the vistas. The terrace represents a horizontal line on the verticality of the building. There is a corner with a roof overhead and a balcony that seems to hold up the sky. The floor is a continuous line that directs our gaze out to the horizon. It is a king's seat overlooking a stage with the mountains as the protagonist, which seem to be distancing themselves but never completely disappearing.

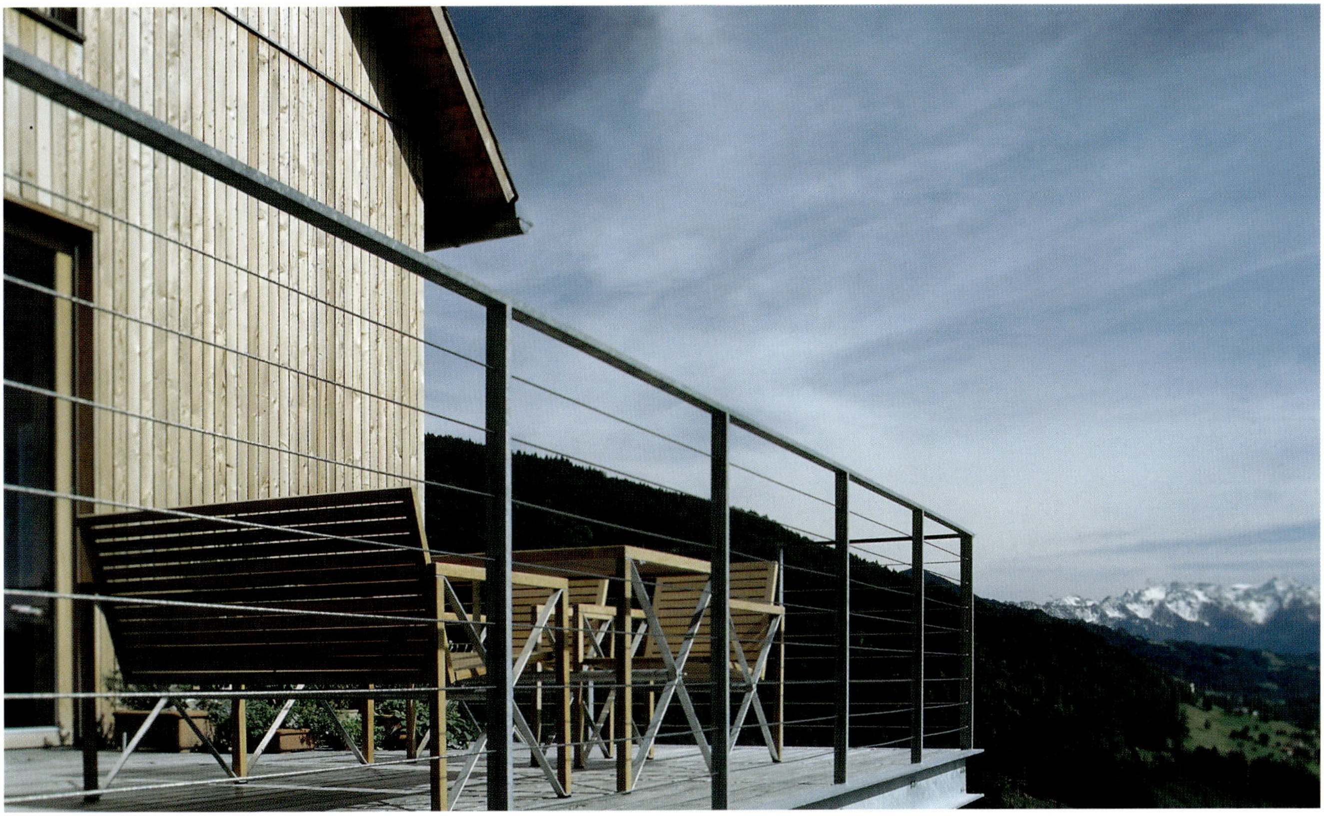

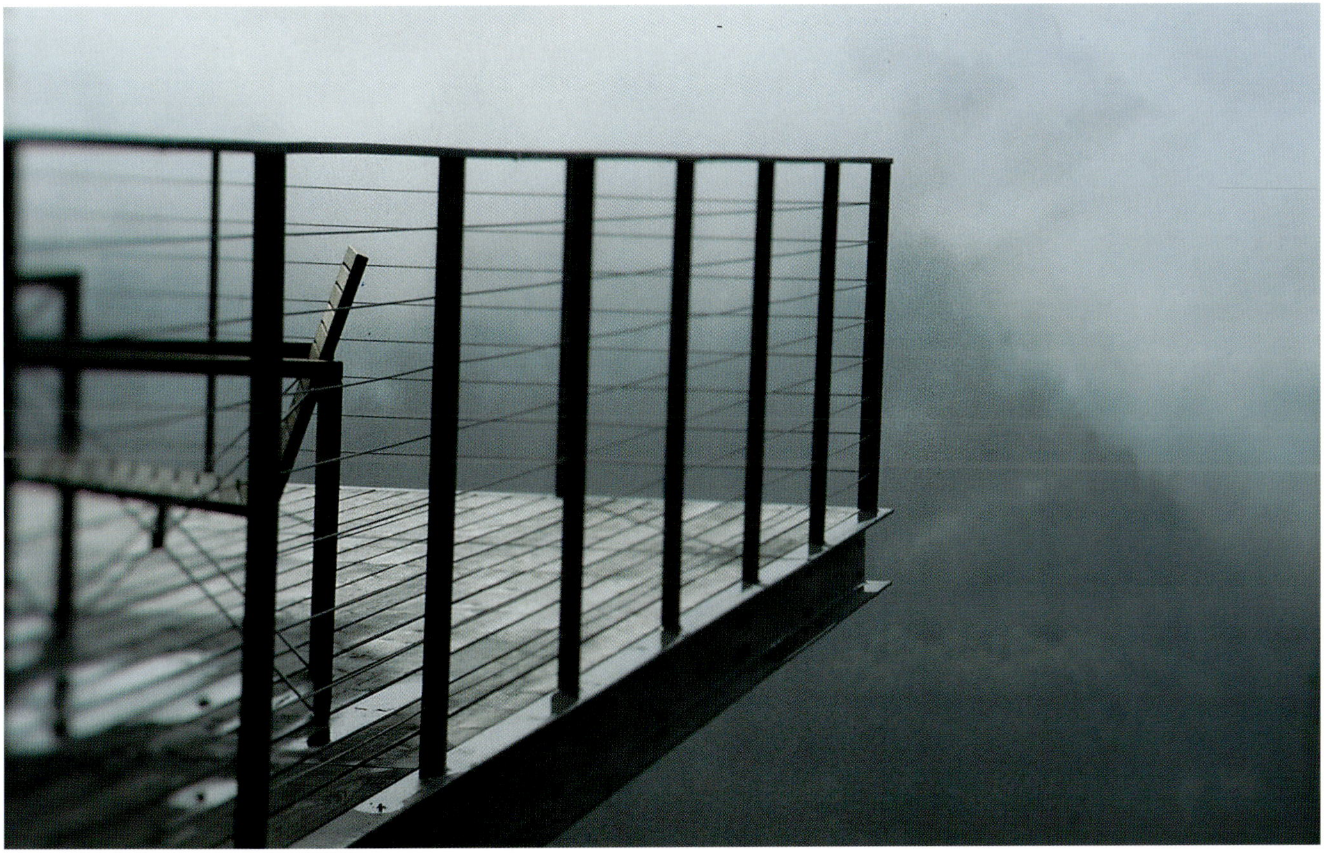

水没する家

GADアーキテクチュア

撮影：アリ・ベックマン，
サリー・ククチュナ

　ヨーロッパとアジアを分かつボスポラス海峡の岸辺に、ふたたびこの威風堂々とした建物の骨格が姿を現したとき、われわれは否応なしにあのオスマントルコ帝国の栄華を思い出した。それはよみがえった幽霊のようである。その住宅は2つの海と2つの大陸を、そして過ぎ去った歴史と新しく迎える歴史をまたいで建っている。テラスとポーチからは、大型船が海峡を航行する様子を静かに見守ることができる。その海峡の水は、家のすぐ近くまで満ちてき、地下のプールに収まりきれなくなるとき住宅内部に浸水する。

On the banks of the Bosphorus between Europe and Asia, we are reminded of the splendor of the Ottoman period as the majestic skeleton of this house reappears, like a ghost coming to life again. It reposes between two seas, two continents and among centuries of history, and centuries of history to come. The terrace and the porch are a calm space for witnessing the navigation in the strait. That same water, so near and unable to be duly contained in the underground pool, causes the seepage into the interior of the dwelling.

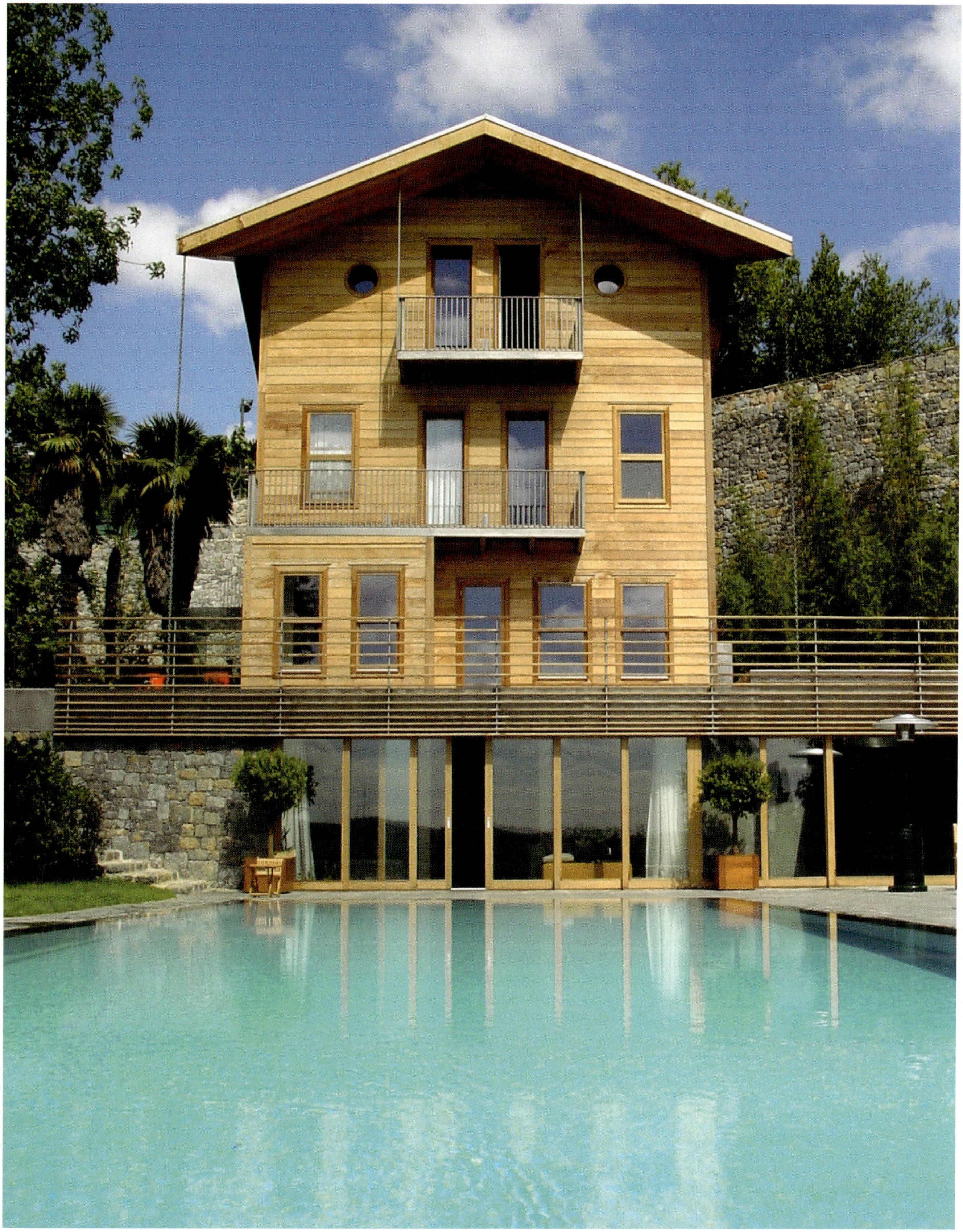

Great(Bamboo)Wall

隈研吾建築都市設計事務所　　　　　　　　　　　　　撮影：淺川　敏

　竹の持つ繊細さ、そして中国と日本の文化的交流において竹が果たした象徴的な意味、それが堅固で不可侵に見える万里の長城に侵入するための掛け橋となる。竹は組み合わされ、繋がれて、家と外部との境界を形づくる。内部から見るとき、それは控え目で、白紙の上に捕らえられた刷毛のひと掃きのように、厚さはなく、障害物ともならない。

The subtlety of bamboo and the symbolism it has regarding the cultural exchange between China and Japan, is a kind of bridge that penetrates the solid, seemingly impenetrable, Great Wall. The interconnected rods of bamboo are joined to delimit the exterior of the dwelling. Inside, it is restrained, like brushstrokes that are trapped on white paper, without obstacles nor depth.

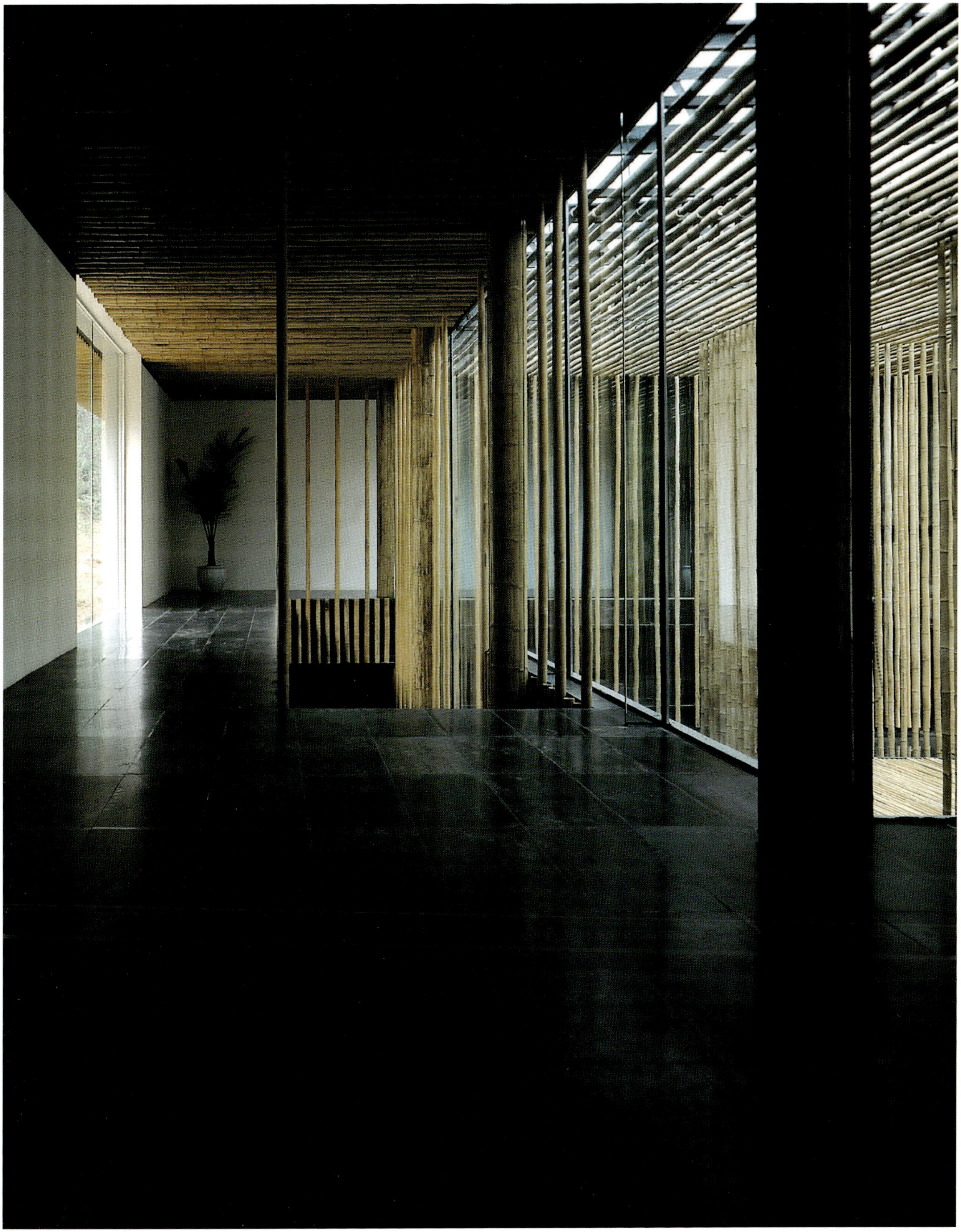

マシューズ邸

JMAアーキテクツ　　　　　　　　　　　　　　　　撮影：ジョン・メインワーニング

オーストラリア、バードンにあるこの家は、2002年に完成した。住宅は2つの突き出したバルコニーで飾られているが、それらは2本の斜めになった柱によって美しく支えられている。その形は、バルコニーが家を取り巻く森に向けて投げ戻されていることを示唆している。すなわち、それが元々あった場所に。

In 2002 the construction of this house in Bardon, Australia, was completed. It is embellished with two balconies that project out, which are beautifully braced by two slanted pillars. This feature suggests that the balconies are being tossed back into the forest that surrounds the house, thus returning to their place of origin.

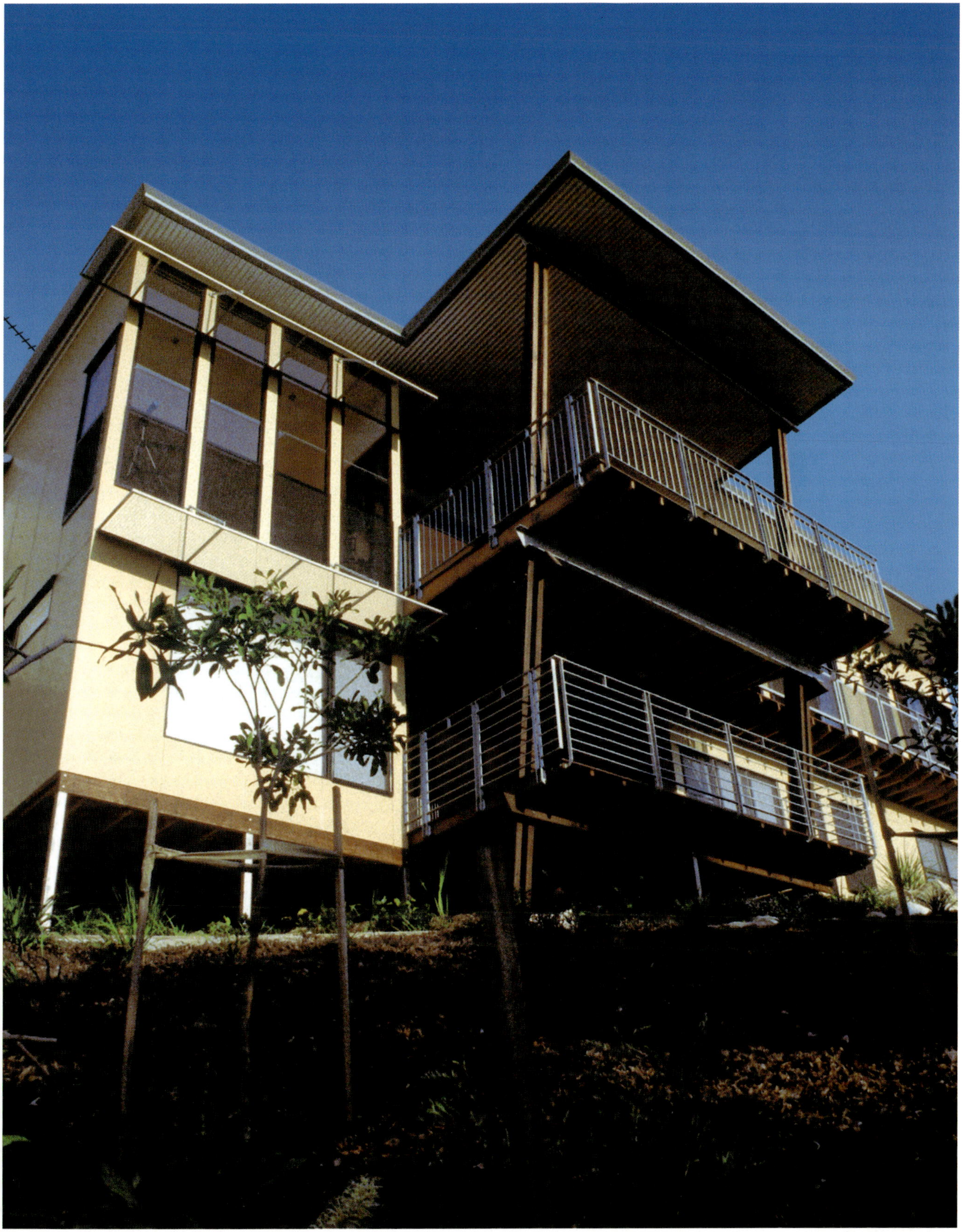

08

To Have a Dream

After an eventful journey, we return to our starting point: wood on wood. Tree houses make our childhood dreams of independence, having a hideout and having contact with nature, come true. Here are three examples. One is clearly oneiric, the second is rationally entertaining, and the third is practically residential

夢を持つため
(ツリーハウス)

実り豊かな旅を終え、われわれは出発点に戻った。そう、木の上の木。ツリーハウスは、独り立ちし、隠れ家を持ち、自然といつも触れていたいという子どもの頃の夢を現実のものとする。ここに3例を紹介する。最初の例はあきらかに夢幻的なもの、2番目は理知的な喜びを満足させるもの、そして最後は実際に住居となっているもの。

ポール・ミード・ツリーハウス
新しい生命

ハワード−フーティット−ミラー
撮影：メリッサ・ムーアー

PAUL MEAD TREEHOUSE
new life

ビスレー―グロスターシャー―イギリス―2003

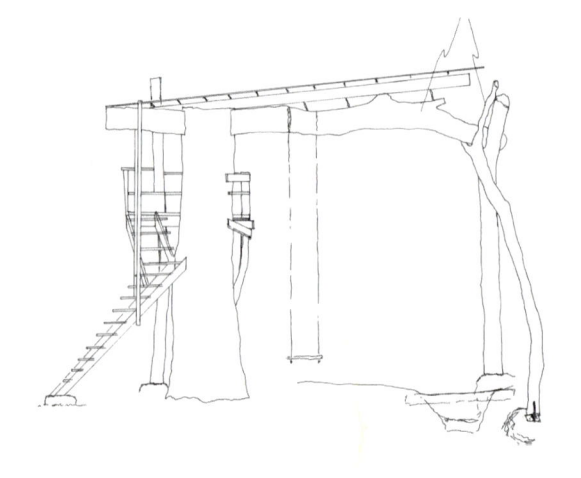

　このツリーハウスの根底にある考え方は、すでに樹幹のみをさらすまでに老いたオークの木に活力を与え、大地から引き離すことなしに新しい生命を注入する、というものであった。全体の構想は、主に子どもたちとそのお祖母さんによって練られた。オークの木の樹幹は柱となって、この夢幻的な空間を支えている。そこはおとぎ話と長い間失われていた感覚の隠れ場所である。

The ideas that guide the premise of this project are to recuperate an old oak tree which can now only offer its skeleton, and to inject new life into its remains without tearing it out from the ground. It is designed mainly with the children and the grandmother in mind. The tree trunk becomes the pillar that holds up a volatile place, a refuge of tales and long-lost sensations.

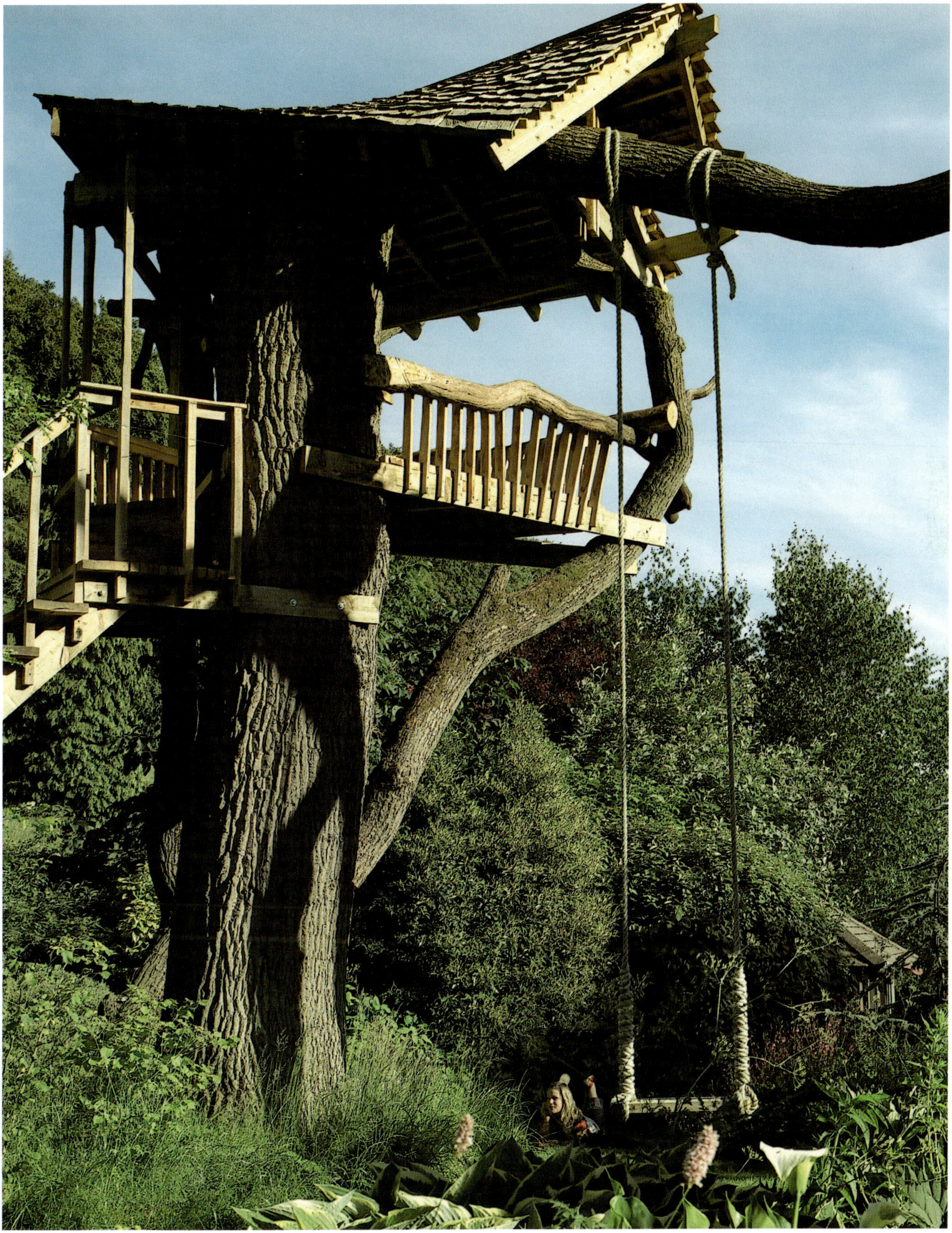

かろうじて1本の手すりによって囲まれ、小さな日除けで蔽われているだけのこの小さな小屋は、梯子のてっぺんに作られている。そこは夢が離陸する滑走路である。壁のない作りになっているが、屋根は十分雨をよけてくれる。内部は思いがけない訪問者を招待できる十分なスペースがある。

A small dwelling, barely enclosed with a railing and covered with a scanty parasol, was designed at the top of a stairs. It is a runway where dreams can take off from. Though built without walls, the roof is broad enough to afford protection from the rain. The interior grants sufficient space to accommodate impromptu visits.

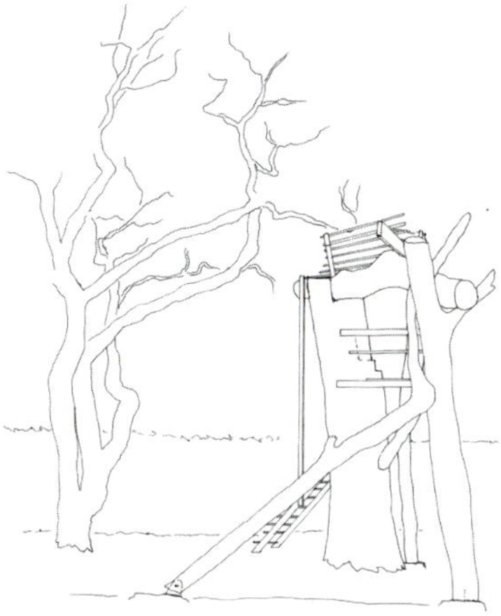

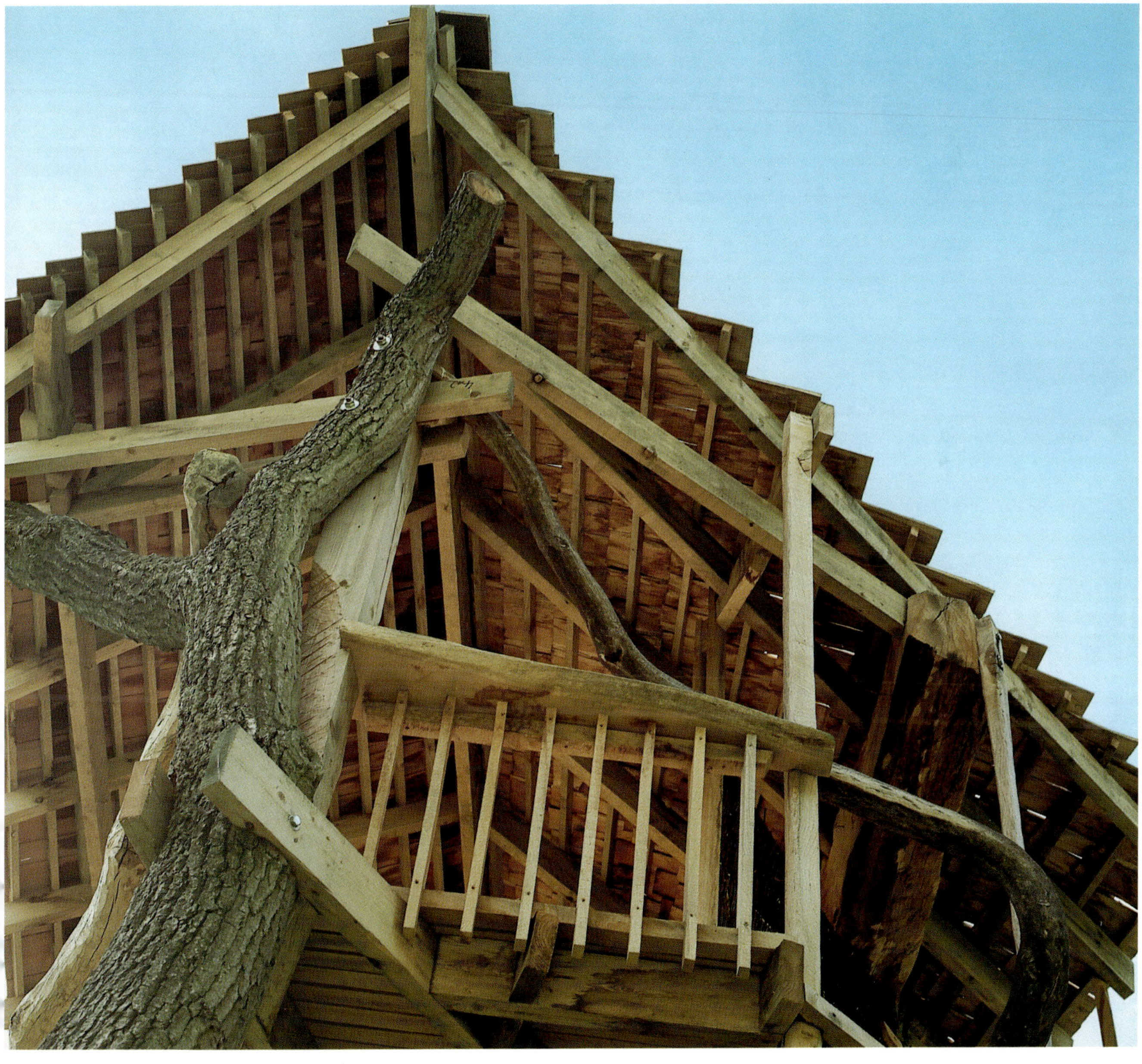

新たにすぐ横に植えたエルムの木が、やがてこの家にむかって、それを囲むように枝を伸ばすであろう。さまざまな花々が、その色と香りと新しい息吹でこの小さな家を覆うだろう。鳥たちはすでにこの家の中に巣を設けている。眼下に広がる植物の海は、神秘に満ちた夢幻の世界を創造している。枝の1つにぶら下げたブランコが揺れる。

With the passing of time the newly planted elm beside it will grow branches towards and around it. Blossoms and flowers will cover it with color, smell and new life. The birds are already building their nests in it. The sea of vegetation at the base is creating an oneiric image of mystery. A swing is hanging from one of the branches.

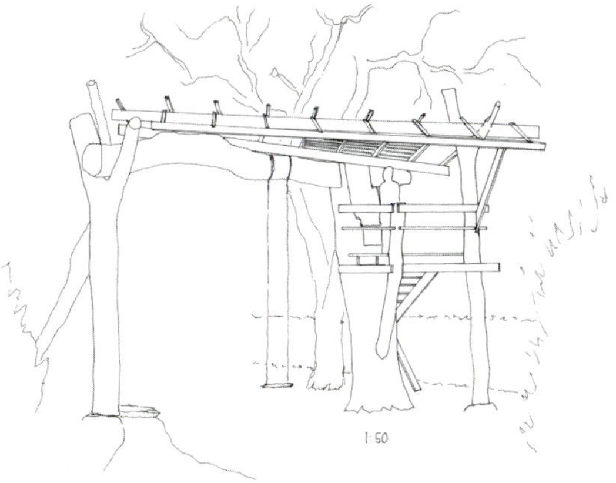
1:50

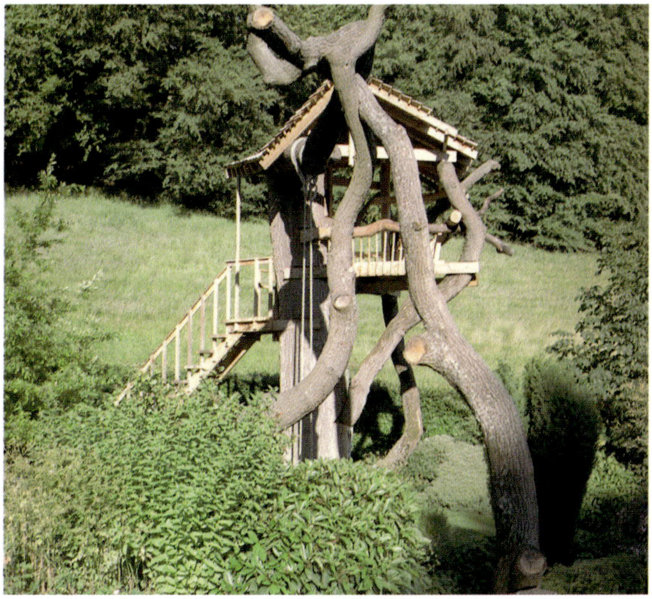

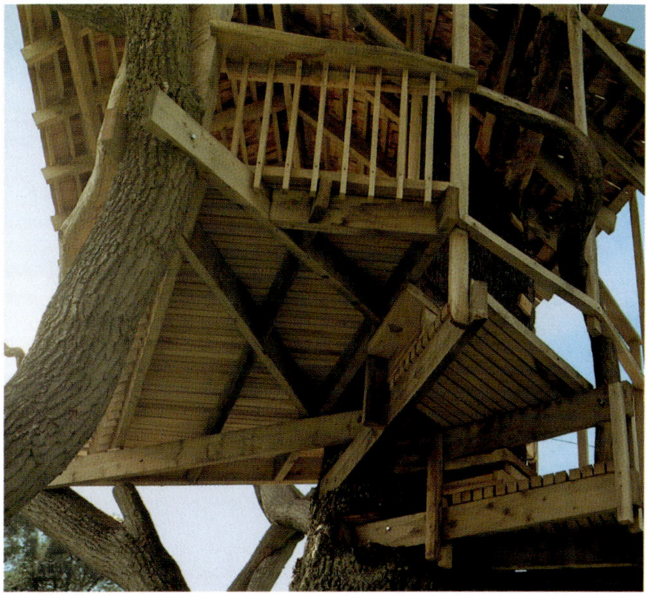

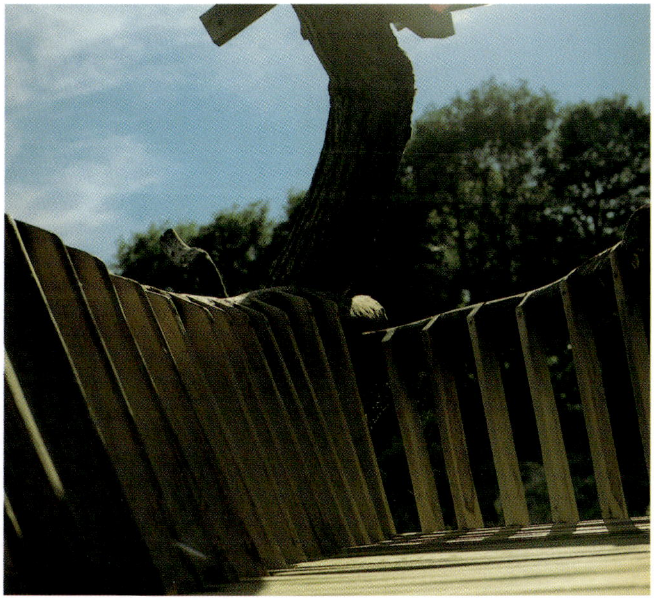

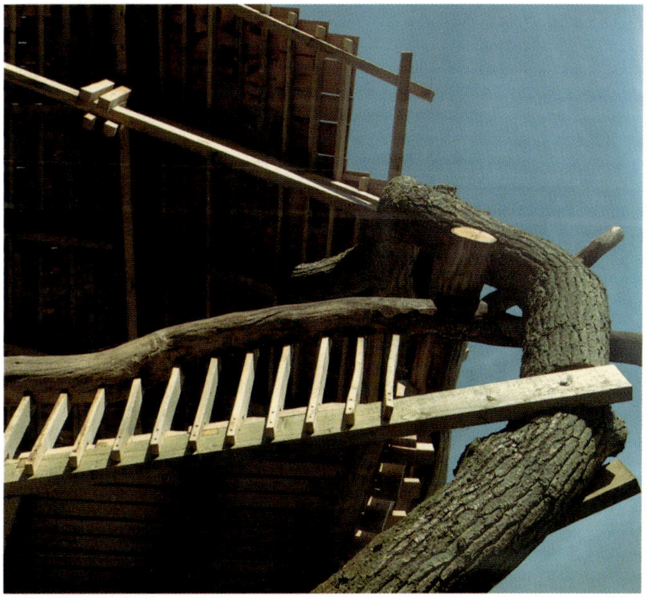

リー・ツリーハウス
共に生きるための交渉

ジョセフ・リム アーキテクト
共同設計：C.I.ヨー, ライ・ウェ・ホン
撮影：イスマーニー・キャヨン

LEE TREE HOUSE
negotiating living together

ギャロップパーク―シンガポール―2002

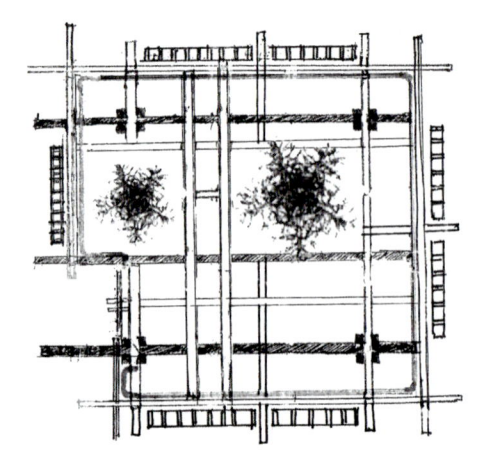

　このプロジェクトにとっては、2本の樹木が演じる演技を鉄と木の構造物がしっかりと受けとめるということが何よりも大切であった。2本の樹木は彼らの生きる道程を提示し、それは細心の注意を払って尊敬されなければならなかった。そのためプロジェクトはまず、2本の樹木を念入りに調査することからはじめる必要があった。

For this project a metal and wood structure that totally bears in mind the role of the two trees is of utmost importance. The trees impose their rules and these must be religiously respected. The first step was the thorough study of the trees.

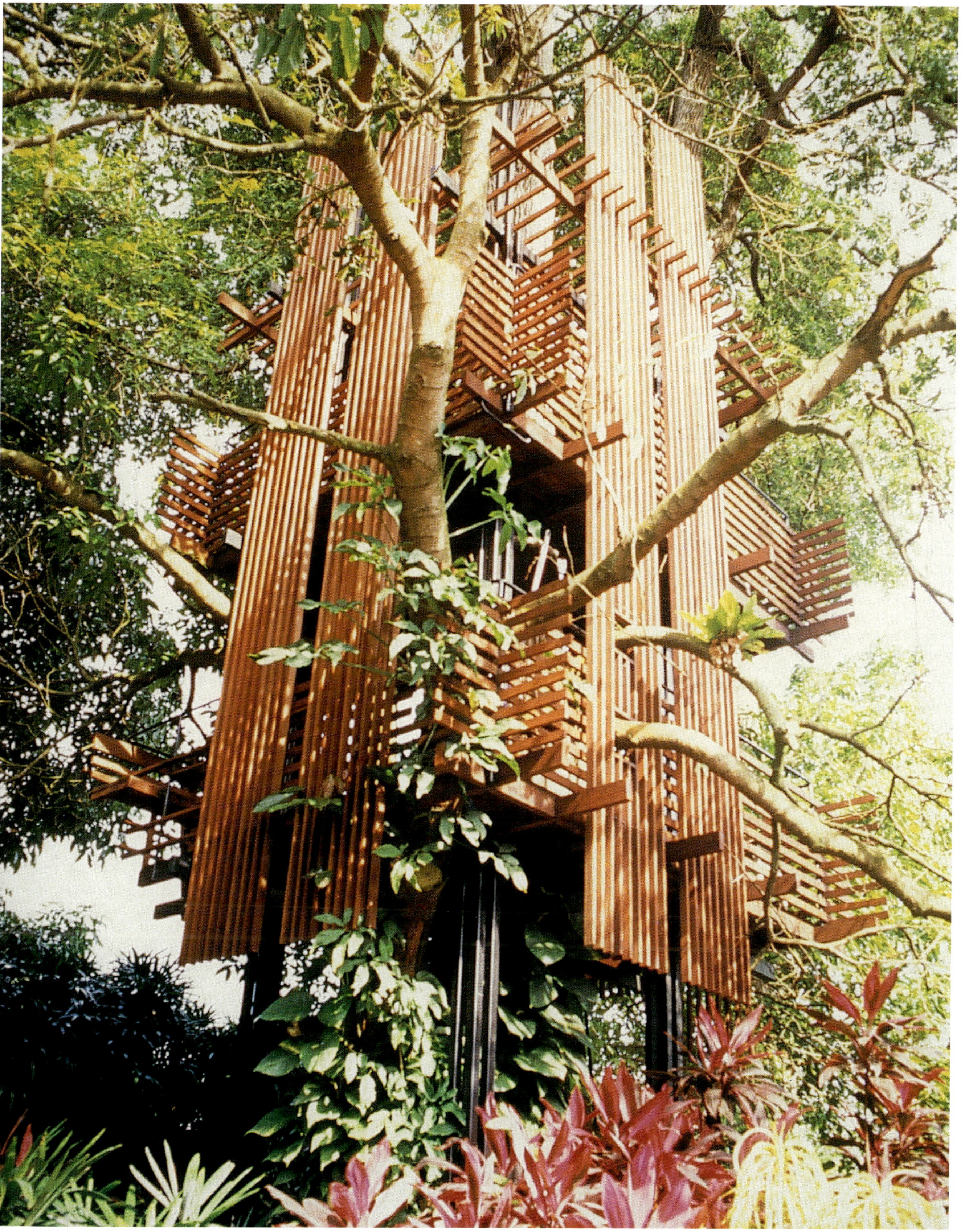

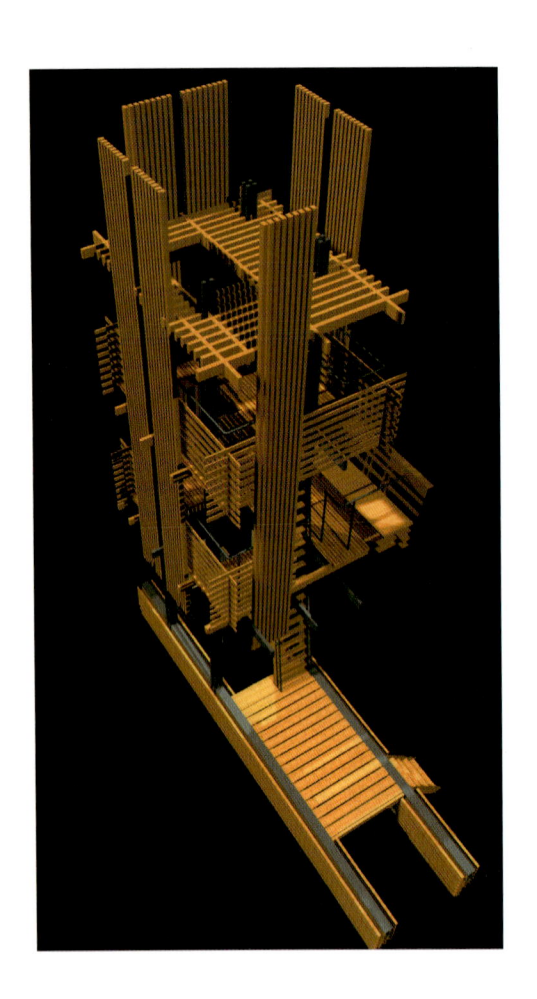

樹木は徹底的に精確に図面上に写し取られなければならなかった。それによってツリーハウスが樹幹の死んだ部分から自然に「発芽」し、樹木に生命を吹き込むことができるように、その支持基点の位置が決定された。樹木が、現在、そして未来永劫に自然との美しい交感を形成することができるように、木と鉄を巧みに組み合わせた立体的な柵がそれを優しく抱擁している。

The trees must be thoroughly and precisely mapped to decide on the basic points of support so that the tree house can "sprout" from the dead trunks, thus breathing life into it. A juxtaposition of wooden and iron bars embrace the tree to form an exquisite communion with nature, now and in the future.

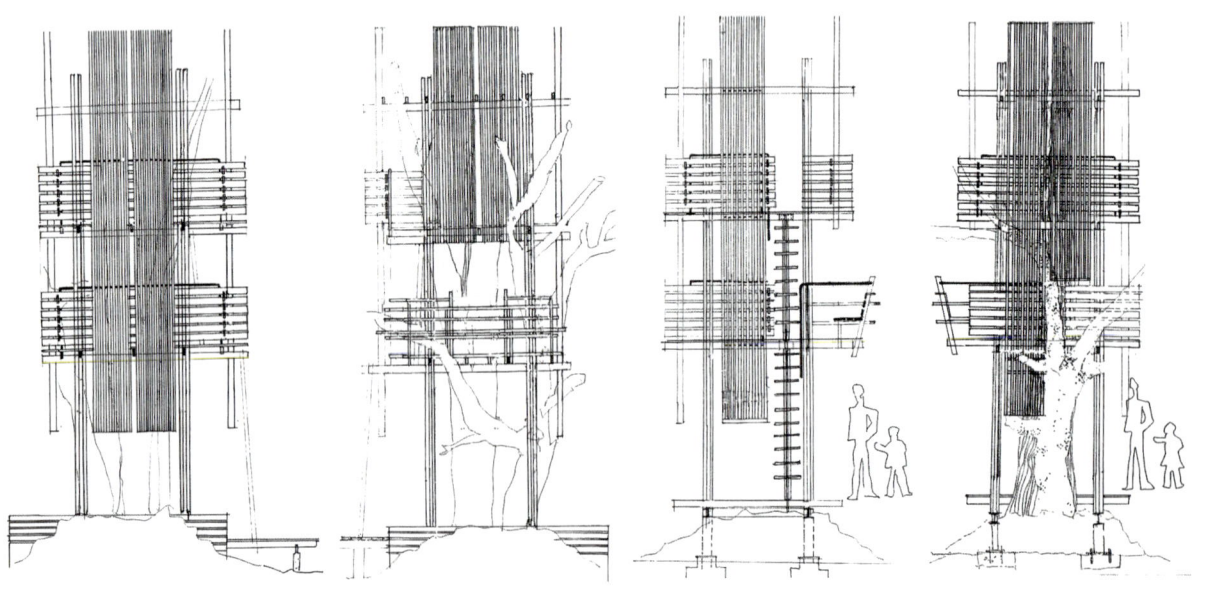

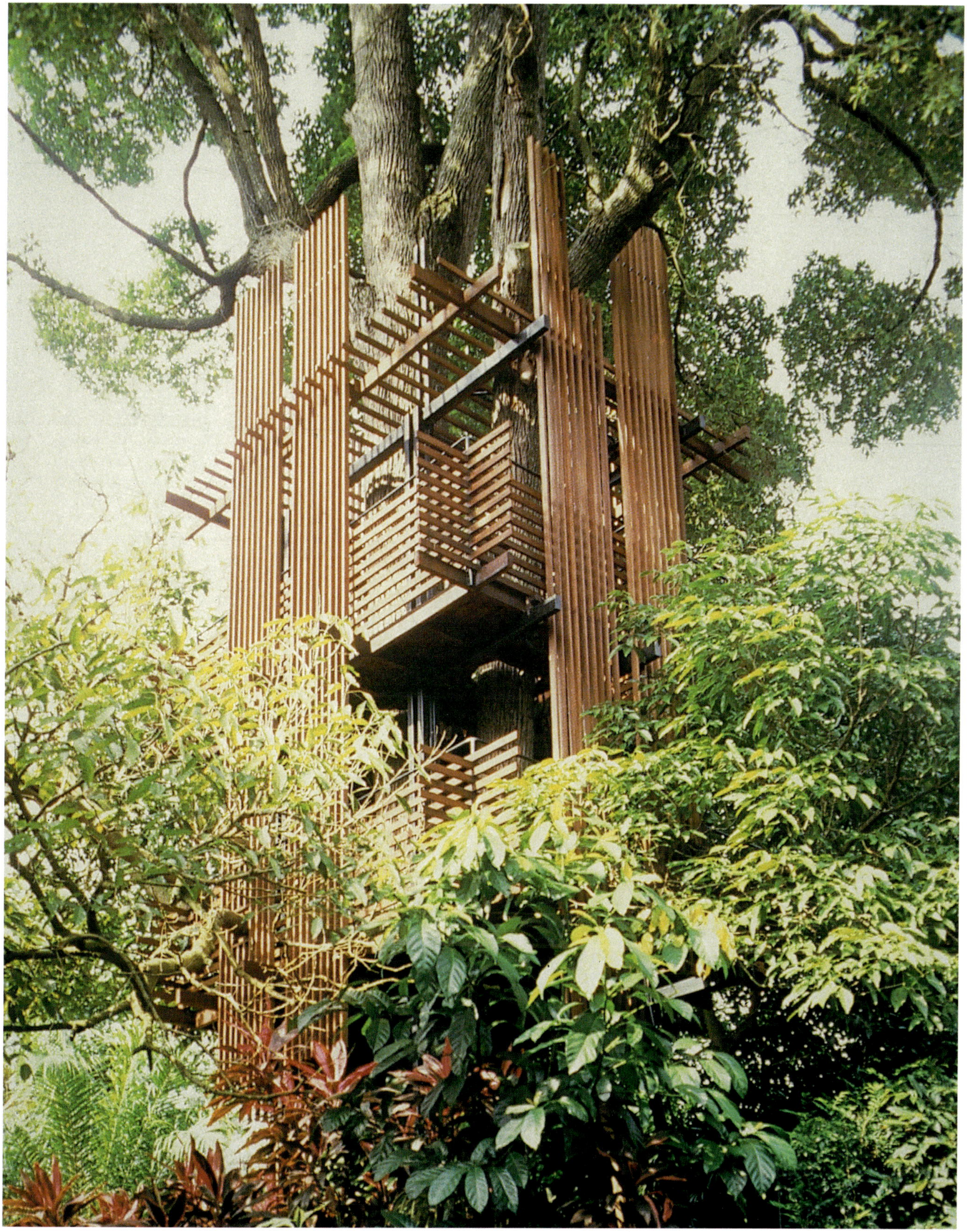

秘密の隙間や割れ目がいっぱいある迷宮の内部には、自然の中に隠れ家を作り、そこでさまざまな空想をはばたかせたいという子どもの頃の夢が閉じ込められている。建築家はもう一度子供時代と向き合い、それに確かな形を与えた。ツリーハウスの頂上で魔法の絨毯が広げられ、望む所どこへでも飛んで行ける。高齢の人でも子どもと夢を共有することができるように、だれでも昇れる構造になっている。

In its labyrinth interior full of secret nooks and crannies are kept the dreams of a child who wants to find a place in nature where he can let his imagination wander. The architect plans a reencounter with childhood and gives it a solid foundation so that the magic carpet can be unfolded atop it and can begin to fly to any place that it wants. One is never too old to climb trees to accompany your children who share your dreams.

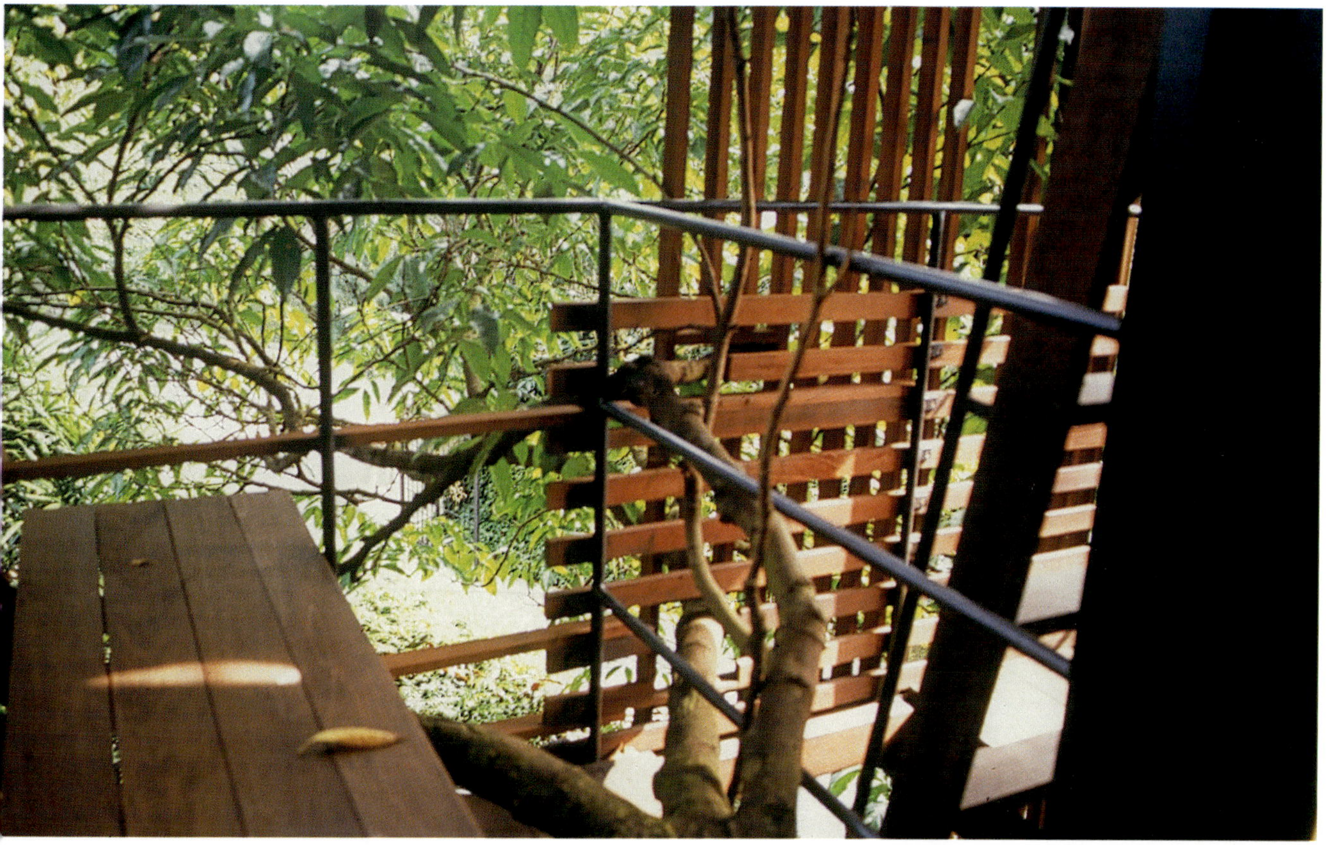
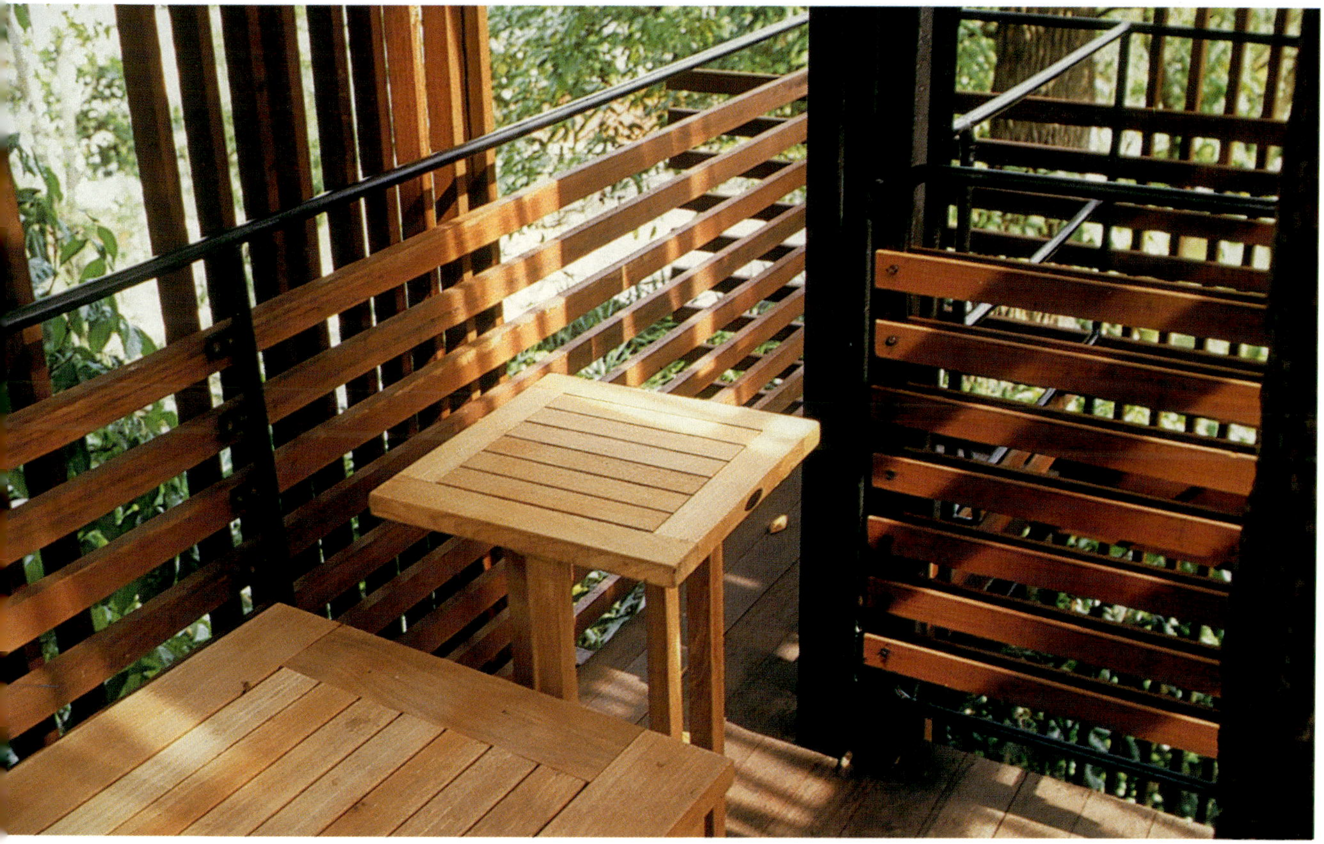

ハーディー・ツリーハウス
2階建ての家

ユー・クワン エリア
撮影：リオ・ヘルミ

HARDY TREE HOUSE
double level

バウン―バリ―2002

　自然と共にその1つであろうとし、その意味の永久不変の一部となること、これは人類が誕生して以来変わらず持っている潜在的な願望である。鳥の目で地上を眺めること、雲の上から人々の行状を傍観すること、人から見られることなくさまざまな出来事を目撃すること、これらが、この樹幹と枝に抱かれた家に込められている願望であろう。

To be one with nature, to become an indissoluble part of its meaning, has been a latent desire of mankind from the beginning of time. To see the earth from a bird's-eye view, to watch the goings-on from atop a cloud, to witness events without being seen, could all be wishes contained In this house entangled with trunks and branches.

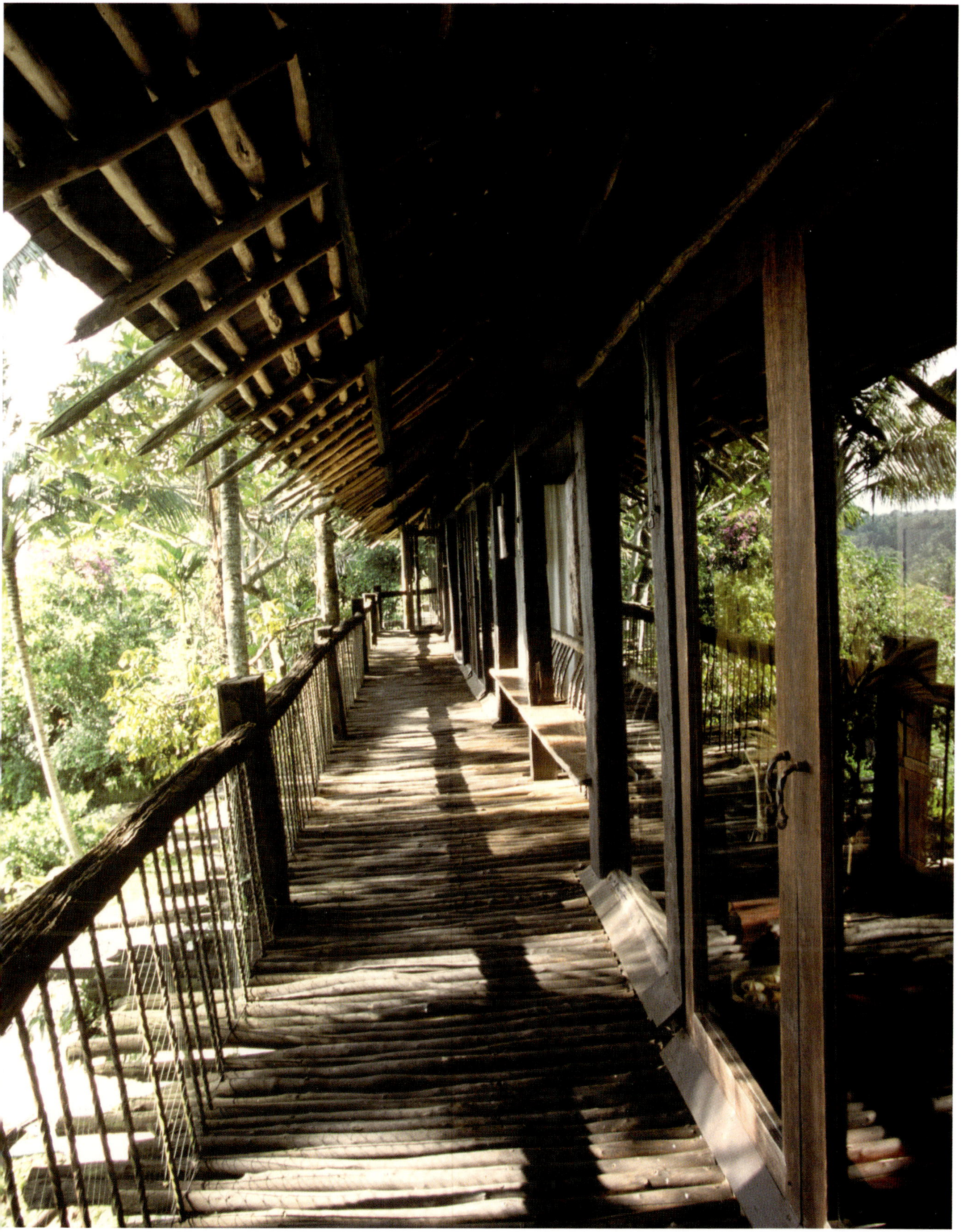

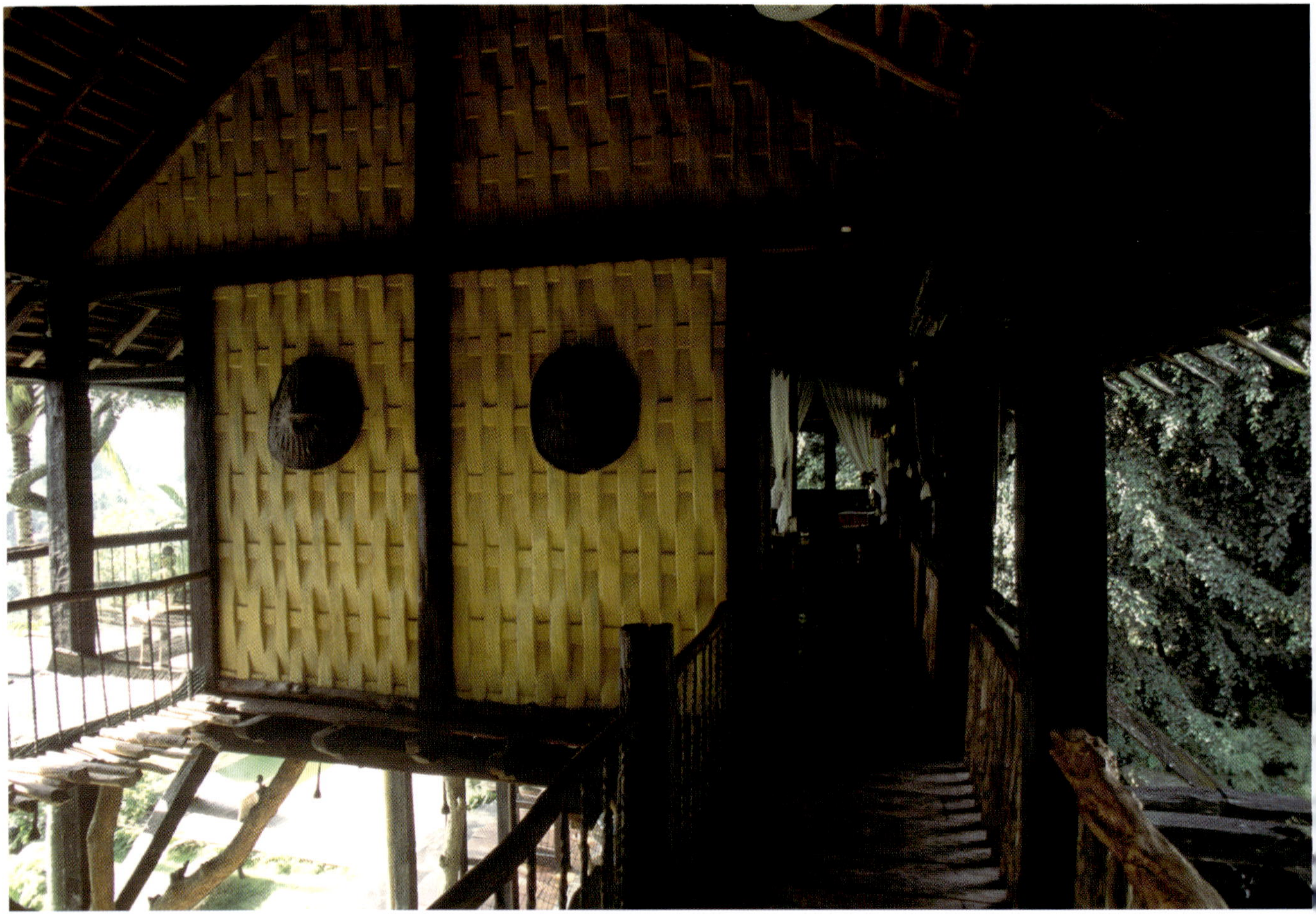
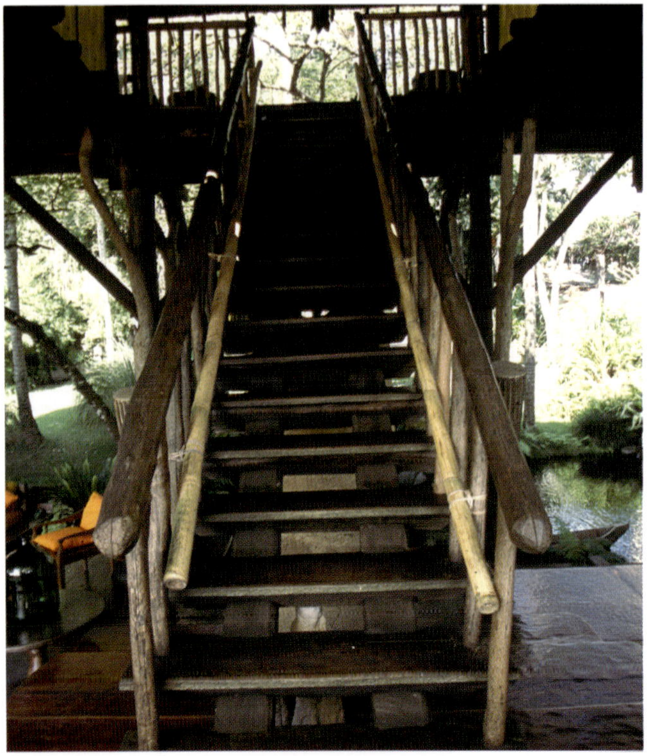
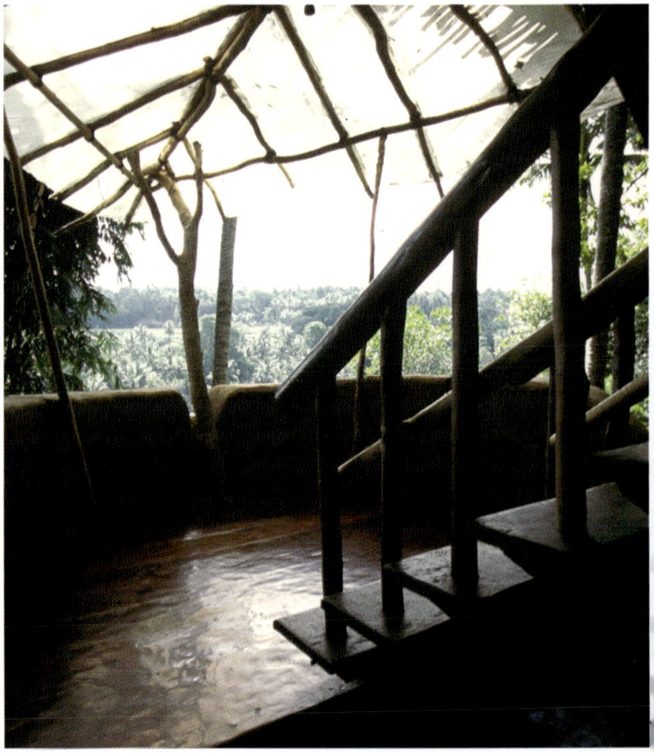

中空に浮かぶ蜃気楼のように、横に長く延びた水平な建物が木々の垂直な線をさえぎるように建っている。丸太と生木の枝でできた構造は、ところどころ木材で補強されている。なにか幽玄な層がこの超然とした家を支えているようである。この家は住むことが完全に可能である。それは一見粗雑な入れ物のように見えるが、無骨だが優しい手のような入れ物なのである。

Like a mirage suspended in mid-air, we see the elongated, horizontal body that cuts the verticality of the trees. The skeleton, made of logs and live tree branches, requires reinforcement with wooden props at certain points. A layer of subtlety seems to sustain this untamed house, which is perfectly inhabitable, in this seemingly rough holder, a holder that seems like coarse yet tender hands.

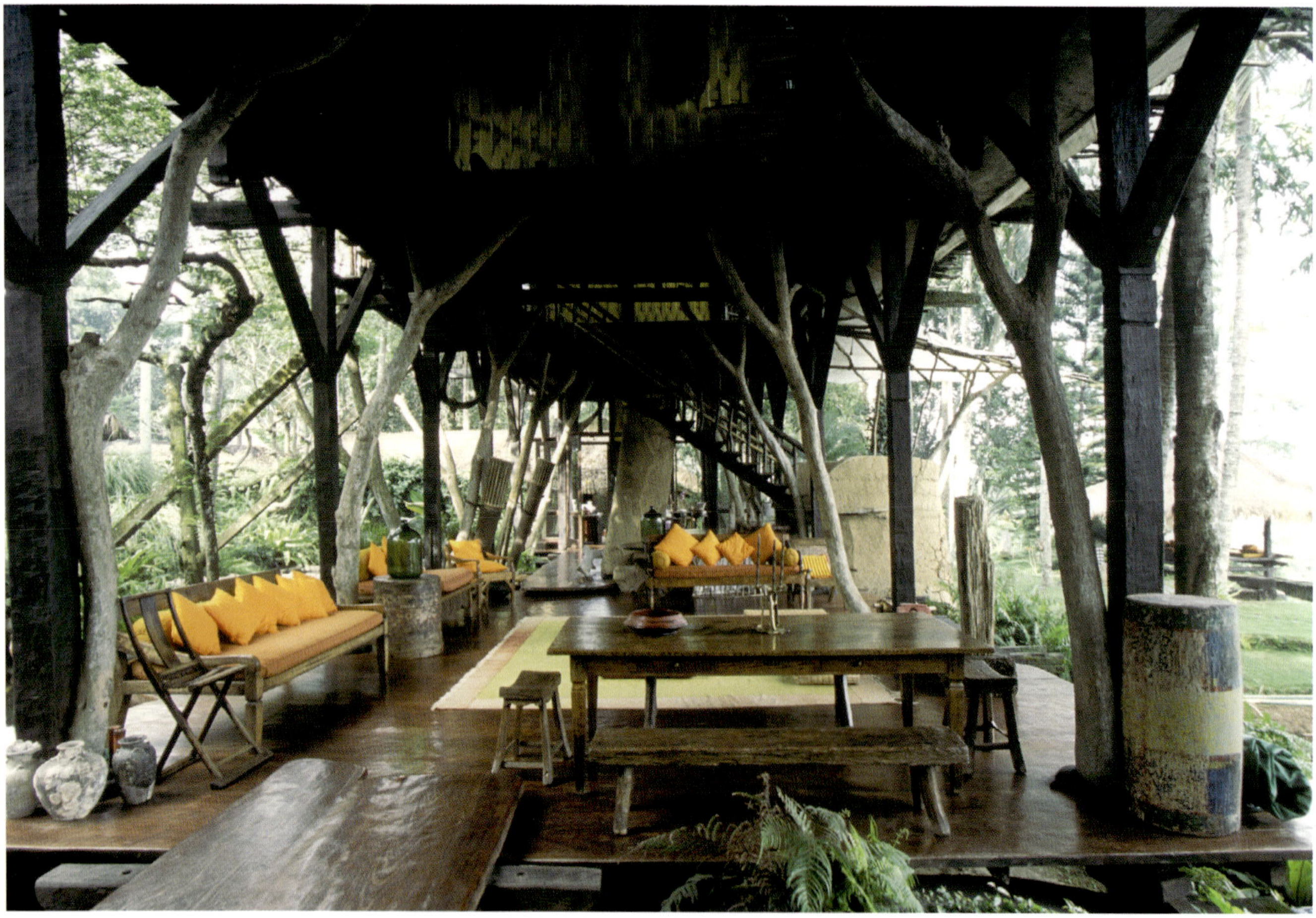

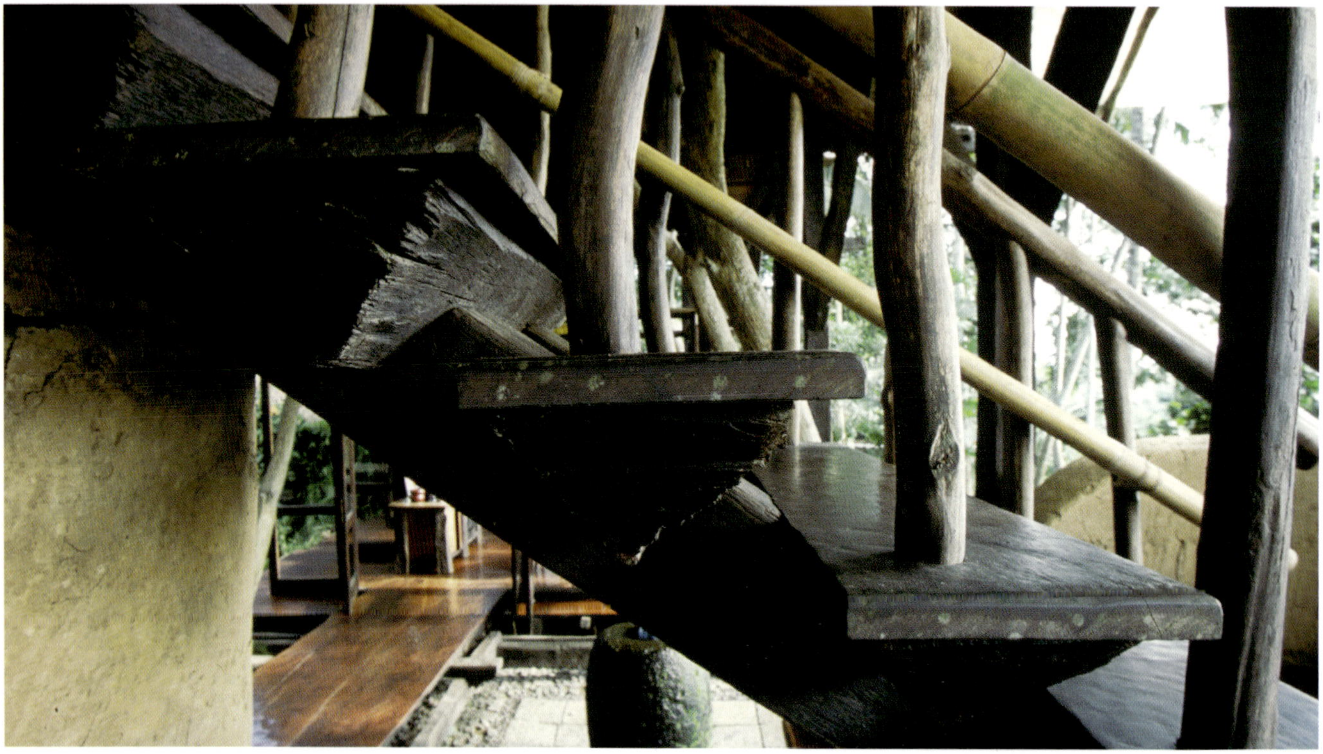

この家は、自然住宅を建てるという明確なプランのもとに建てられている。1階は壁はなく、ポーチで蓋われた共有スペースとなっている。ポーチの上にある2階は、プライベートな空間になっている。木の色と、織物や家具の暖色のこげ茶色との絶妙な組み合わせが、この家にやすらぎ感をもたらしている。

With a clear nature house plan, the lower floor is open and covered with a porch, which is for the common areas. A second floor, atop the porch in fact, houses the private quarters. The subtle combination of wood tones, fabrics and furniture in warm and toast-brown tones, endows it with a sense of comfort.

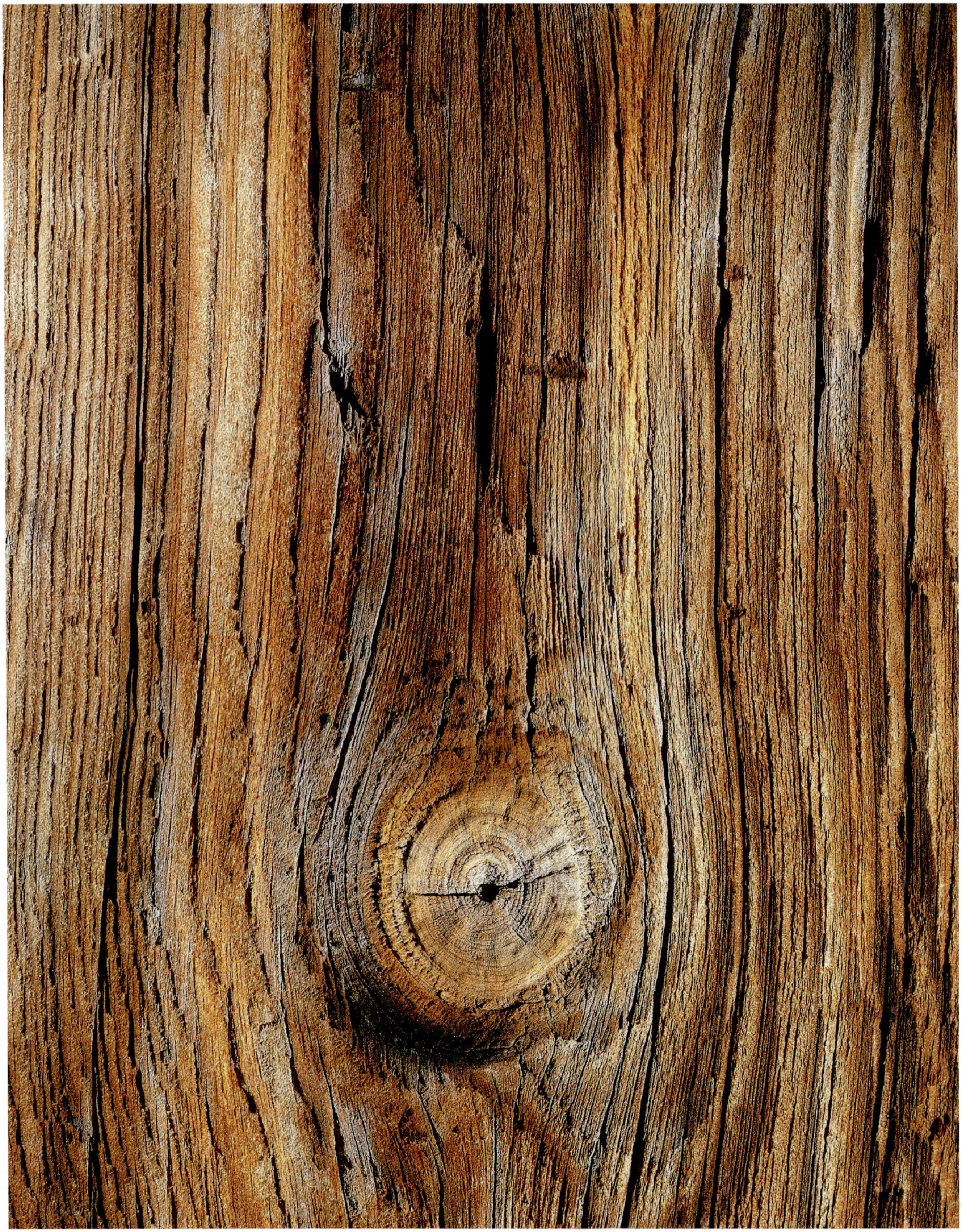

主要木材カタログ

次ページ以下は、木造建築に用いられる主要な木材のカタログである。それぞれの木材の外観、分類、主要特性、用途について概説している。

用語解説

- **辺材**：樹幹の外周部にあり、養分を輸送したり蓄えたりする生きた細胞からなる部分で、心材にくらべ淡色、多孔性で、腐朽しやすい。
- **心材**：樹幹の内心部にあり、樹木を構造的に支える部分で、生きた細胞の見られない材部。

微視的特性

- **木理**：樹軸に対する木繊維の方向を表す。樹軸に対して木繊維が平行に走っている通直木理は加工しやすいが、波状、交錯、旋回、斜行木理は加工が難しい。しかしこれらの木理のほうが美的可能性は高い。

物理的特性

- **比重**：含水率12%のときの重量と体積の比で、kg/㎥で表す。針葉樹材は、400(非常に軽い)から700(非常に重い)で、広葉樹材は500～950である。
- **硬度**：ある物質の他の物質に対する貫入度を示す指標で、研磨、切削に対する木材の抵抗性を表す。
- **吸湿性**：大気中、または木材が挿入されている媒体から、湿気(水分)を吸収する能力。
- **収縮**：水分の減少にともなう縮小。
- **収縮率**：含水率1%の変化に対する収縮量の割合。収縮率と比重の関係から、概して以下のようにいえる。

 低比重：(0.15～0.40) 家具製作に適している。
 中低比重(0.35～0.49) 建具製作に適している。
 中比重：(0.40～0.55) 建築工事に適している。
 高比重：(0.55～0.75) 放射状建造物に適している。
 超高比重：(0.75～1) 常に水分のある環境に適している。

挙動特性

- **亀裂または割裂**：貫通、釘打ち、ネジ止めによる破壊に対する抵抗性。

化学的特性

- **加工性**：樹脂、油分、蝋などを多く含む木材は加工が困難である。土壌に由来し材中で結晶化した石油成分、鉱物なども加工性を損なう。
- **耐朽性**：破壊的作用を及ぼす媒介物の攻撃に対する抵抗性。木材を含水率18%以上に達するおそれのある状況で使用する場合重要である。媒介物としては、真菌、シロアリ目の昆虫(甲虫、シロアリ)、水生シロアリなどがある。耐朽性は心材の特性であり(辺材は常に害を受けやすい)、耐朽性に優れる、害を受けやすい、耐朽性に劣る、などに分類される。
- **含浸性**：薬剤の浸入に対する木材の抵抗性。耐朽性は劣るが、含浸性が高い木材はシロアリの攻撃に対して耐性を持つことができる。

 高含浸性：加圧含浸装置により容易に薬剤を含浸できる。
 中含浸性：2～3時間の処置により平均的な含浸が得られる。
 低含浸性：3～4時間の含浸によっても表面しか含浸できない。
 非含浸性：実質的に含浸が不可能。

WOOD CATALOGUE

The following is an index for different types of wood in which the appearance, nomenclature, physical properties and uses are outlined.

GLOSSARY

- **Alburnum** (or sapwood): The part of the tree with living cells that transports or stores nutrients. It is a lighter color and more porous than the duramen, and can rot.
- **Duramen** (or heartwood): The mature part of the wood that is the structural part of the tree. It is without living cells.

Microscopic Characteristics

- **Grain:** The direction of the wood fibers in respect to the axis of the tree. Straight grain wood, parallel to the axis, is easy to work with. Wavy, curved, spiral or slanted grain is more difficult to work with, but aesthetically affords more possibilities.

Physical Characteristics

- **Density:** The relationship between mass and volume with 12% humidity, which is expressed in kg/m³. In conifers it ranges from 400 (very light) to 700 (very heavy), and in broadleaves, from 500 to 950.
- **Hardness:** Indicates the index of penetration of one material into another and specifies the resistance of the wood to abrasion or chipping.
- **Hygroscopicity:** The capacity of the wood to absorb more or less moisture (water) from the atmosphere or from the medium that it is in.
- **Contraction:** Shrinkage due to a loss of moisture.
- **Ratio of unit volume contraction:** The change in volume that wood undergoes due to a 1% change in moisture. According to this ratio wood may have:
 Slight density (0.15-0.40), ideal for the manufacture of furniture;
 Fair density (0.35-0.49), good for carpentry;
 Average density (0.40-0.55), good for construction;
 Rather high density (0.55-0.75), good for radial construction;
 Very high density (0.75-1), ideal for environments with perpetual moisture.

Mechanical characteristics

- **Cracking or splitting:** It indicates the resistance to breakage if penetrated, nailed or screwed into.

Chemical characteristics

- **Workability:** Woods with high resin, oil or wax contents are difficult to work with. Petro accumulation and mineral salts originating from the soil that crystallize in the wood, also hinder workability.
- **Natural durability:** This is the resistance of the wood to attacks from destructive agents. This is important when the wood is to be found in conditions where there are changes to moisture that are superior to 18%. The agents can be fungi, xylophagous insects, (coleopterans and termites) and water xylophagous insects. Durability refers to the duramen (the alburnum is always vulnerable to attack) and is classified as durable, sensitive and non-durable.
- **Impregnability**: resistance of wood to the penetration of liquid. Wood that is not durable but impregnable may be resistant against xylophagous attacks. Classification is as follows:
 Impregnable: Easy to impregnate with pressurized mechanisms.
 Average impregnability: Average penetration attained after 2 or 3 hours of treatment.
 Low impregnability: Only superficial impregnation achieved after 3 or 4 hours.
 Zero impregnability (or non-impregnability): Practically impossible to impregnate.

ABIES alba Mill.（ABETE BIANCO）　シルバーファー（Silver fir）

ヨーロッパ原産の針葉樹材。入手は容易。

物理的特性：比重400kg/m³の中庸の緻密さを持つ木材。軟らかく(1.4)、切削は容易である。樹脂はほとんどなく、吸湿性も低い。木理は通直。

挙動特性：接着性は良いが、釘打ち、ネジ止めに際して裂けるおそれがある。表面仕上げは良好だが、仕上げ剤を均等に吸収しない性質があり、厚さと色にむらが生じることがある。

耐朽性：真菌に侵されやすく、シロアリの害も受けやすいため、あまり耐朽性は良くない。

含浸性：心材の含浸性は低から中庸で、辺材は中庸である。

用途：外装、化粧単板、家具、積層木材。

This is a readily-available conifer of European origin.

Physical properties: It is of average density with a density of 400kg/m³, soft (1.4), cuts easily, has little resin, is moisture resistant and has straight grain.

Mechanical properties: It glues well but is a bit delicate for nailing and screwing. It finishes well but does not absorb finishings uniformly but rather manifests different intensities and colors.

Natural durability: It is not very durable as it is fungi and insect sensitive.

Impregnability: The duramen has low to average impregnability and the alburnum average.

Uses: Exterior, decorative veneers, furniture, laminated wood.

ACER pseudoplatanus L.（ACERO MONTANO）　シカモア（Sycamore）

ヨーロッパ、アジアに生育する広葉樹材。入手は容易。

物理的特性：比重610〜680kg/m³の中庸の緻密さを持つ木材。中硬(4.7)で、研磨は非常に困難。木理は通直または波状。蒸し曲げ加工に適している。

挙動特性：接着性、釘打ち、ネジ止め、すべて良好である。表面仕上げは良好。

耐朽性：真菌に侵されやすく、耐朽性は不良。またシロアリの害も受けやすい。

含浸性：含浸は容易である。

用途：内装建具(床材)、化粧単板、家具、飾り棚。

It is a readily-available broadleaf from Europe and Asia.

Physical properties: It is of average density with a density of 610-680 kg/m³, semi-hard (4.7) and very abrasion resistant. It has straight and wavy grain. It is good for steam shaping.

Mechanical properties: It glues, nails and screws well. It finishes well.

Natural durability: It is not durable (fungi) and is sensitive to insects.

Impregnability: It is easily impregnable.

Uses: Interior carpentry (floors), decorative veneers, furniture and cabinetmaking.

ANCOUMEA klaineana Pierre　ガブーン

中央アフリカ産の広葉樹材。入手は容易。

物理的特性：比重430〜450kg/m³の緻密な木材。軟らかく(1.5)、木理は通直または旋回。

挙動特性：接着性、釘打ち、ネジ止め、すべて良好である。仕上げにウッドパテが必要な場合がある。

耐朽性：真菌に侵されやすく、シロアリの害を受けやすいため、耐朽性はあまり良くない。

含浸性：心材の含浸性は低い。

用途：合板、内装建具、化粧単板、家具、飾り棚。

It is a readily-available broadleaf from Central Africa.

Physical properties: density with a density of 430-450 kg/m³. It is soft (1.5) and has a straight or spiral grain.

Mechanical properties: It glues, nails and screws well. Wood putty can be used for finishing it.

Natural durability: It is not very durable as it is affected by fungi and is sensitive to insects.

Impregnability: The duramen has low impregnability.

Uses: Plywood panels, interior carpentry with decorative veneering, furniture and cabinetmaking.

BETULA alba L. (BETULLA BIANCA)　ホワイトバーチ (White birch)

ヨーロッパ産の広葉樹材。入手は非常に容易。

物理的特性：比重640〜670kg/㎥の中庸の緻密さを持つ木材。中硬（2.7〜5.3）で、木理は通直。その特性から建築用合板に最適である。

挙動特性：接着性は良い。釘打ち、ネジ止めに際しては、ドリルで下穴をあけておく必要がある。表面仕上げは良好。

耐朽性：真菌に侵されやすく、シロアリの害も受けやすいため、耐久性は不良。

含浸性：含浸性は中庸。

用途：合板、最高級建具、化粧単板、家具。

It is a broadleaf from Europe that is quite readily available.

Physical properties: It is of average density with a density of 640-670 kg/m^3, semi-hard (2.7-5.3) and has a straight grain. Its qualities make it an excellent choice for structural plywood.

Mechanical properties: It glues well. Drilling is required before nailing and screwing. It can be finished well.

Natural durability: It is not durable (fungi) and is sensitive to insects.

Impregnability: It affords easy to average impregnability.

Uses: Plywood panels, top-quality carpentry, decorative veneering, furniture.

BETULA alleghaniensis Britt.（BETULLA GIALLA)　イエローバーチ (Yellow birch)

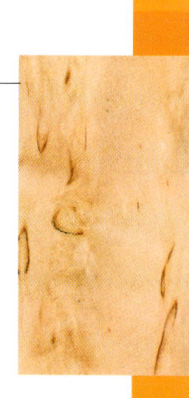

カナダ、アメリカ産の広葉樹材。入手はやや困難。

物理的特性：比重550〜710kg/㎥の中庸の緻密さを持つ木材。中硬（バーチよりも硬い）。木理は通直で加工しやすく、曲げ強さ、圧縮強さ、耐衝撃性も良好。

挙動特性：接着性は良いが、釘打ち、ネジ止めに際してはドリルで下穴をあける必要がある。表面仕上げは良好。

耐朽性：真菌に侵されやすく、シロアリの害も受けやすいため、耐朽性は不良。

含浸性：含浸性は中庸。

用途：合板、最高級建具、化粧単板、家具、床材。

It is a broadleaf from Canada and The United States that is a bit scarce.

Physical properties: It is of average density with a density of 550-710 kg/m^3, semi-hard (harder than birch). It has straight grain, it is easy to work and has good resistance to bending, compression and blows.

Mechanical properties: It glues well. Drilling is required before nailing and screwing. It can be finished well.

Natural durability: It is not durable (fungi) and is sensitive to insects.

Impregnability: It affords easy to average impregnability.

Uses: Plywood panels, top-quality carpentry, decorative veneering, furniture and floors.

CASTANEA sativa Mill.(CASTAGNO)　スイートチェスナット (Sweet chestnut)

ヨーロッパ産（地中海周辺）の広葉樹材。入手は容易。

物理的特性：比重540〜650kg/㎥のやや緻密な木材。軟らかく（2.1）、木理はかすかに波状。水分の多い場所では金属のさびを早め、青変する。

挙動特性：接着性、釘打ち、ネジ止め、すべて良好。仕上げに際してはウッドパテを使う必要がある。

耐朽性：真菌に侵されやすく、シロアリの害を受けやすいため、耐朽性はあまり良くない。

含浸性：心材の含浸は容易で、辺材の含浸性は中庸。

用途：建具（ドア、窓、床）、飾り棚。

It is a broadleaf from Europe (from around the Mediterranean) that is quite readily available.

Physical properties: It is of slight density with a density of 540-650 kg/m^3 and is soft (2.1). It has a slightly wavy grain. When moisture is present, it speeds up metal corrosion and turns blue.

Mechanical properties: It glues, nails and screws well. Wood putty should be used for finishing it.

Natural durability: It is not very durable as it is fungi and insect sensitive.

Impregnability: The duramen is easily impregnable and the alburnum is of average impregnability.

Uses: Carpentry (doors, windows, and floors), cabinetmaking.

CHAMAECYPARIS nootkatensis Spach.（CIPRESSO）サイプレス（Cypress）

北アメリカ産の針葉樹材。入手は非常に容易。

物理的特性：比重は430～530kg/㎥、やや緻密で中硬。木理は通直で、耐酸性がある。

挙動特性：接着性、釘打ち、ネジ止め、すべて良好。

耐朽性：耐朽性は中庸（真菌）、シロアリの害を受けやすい。水生シロアリに対する耐性がある。

含浸性：心材の含浸性は低く、辺材は良好。

用途：内外装建具、化粧単板、家具、飾り棚。

It is a broadleaf from North America that is quite readily available.

Physical properties: It is of slight density with a density of 430-530 kg/m³ and is semi-hard. It has a straight grain and is acid-resistant.

Mechanical properties: It glues, nails and screws well.

Natural durability: It is of average durability (fungi) and sensitivity (insects). It is durable against water xylophagous insects.

Impregnability: The duramen has low impregnability and the alburnum has good impregnability.

Uses: Interior and exterior carpentry, decorative veneering, furniture and cabinetmaking.

CHLOROPHORA excelsa Benth　イロコ

アフリカ原産の広葉樹材。入手は容易。

物理的特性：比重630～650～670kg/㎥の、中庸の緻密さを持つ木材。中硬で木理は通直。

挙動特性：接着性、釘打ち、ネジ止め、すべて良好。仕上げにウッドパテが必要な場合がある。

耐朽性：真菌、シロアリに対する抵抗性があり、非常に耐朽性がある。しかし水生シロアリの害を受けやすい。

含浸性：心材の含浸は困難。辺材は容易。

用途：建設用合板、内外装建具、化粧単板、家具、飾り棚、積層木材。チークの代替材となる。

It is a broadleaf of African origin that is readily available.

Physical properties: It is of average density whose density is 630-650-670 kg/m³. It is semi-hard and has straight grain.

Mechanical properties: It glues, nails and screws well. Wood putty can be used for finishing it.

Natural durability: It is very durable against fungi, and durable against termites. It is easily attacked by water xylophagous insects.

Impregnability: The duramen has non-impregnability and the alburnum is easily impregnable.

Uses: Structural plywood panels, interior and exterior carpentry, decorative veneering, furniture and cabinetmaking, and laminated wood. It can be a substitute for teak.

ENTANDROPHRAGMA cylindricum Sprague.（SAPELLI）　サペリ（Sapeli）

アフリカ原産の広葉樹材。入手は非常に容易。

物理的特性：比重640～700の中庸の緻密さを持つ木材。中硬（3.6～4.2）で旋回木理を持つ。樹脂の浸出があり、肌目は粗で粗い木目を持つ。

挙動特性：接着性、釘打ち、ネジ止め、すべて良好。表面仕上げも良好。

耐朽性：真菌に対する耐性は中庸。シロアリに対する耐性は非常に高いが、水生シロアリの害を受けやすい。

含浸性：心材の含浸性は低く、辺材は中庸。

用途：合板、内外装建具、化粧単板、家具、飾り棚。

It is a broadleaf of African origin that is quite readily available.

Physical properties: It is of average density with a density of 640-700 kg/m³ and is semi-hard (3.6-4.2). It has a spiral grain. It can ooze with resin and have a rough grainy surface.

Mechanical properties: It glues, nails and screws well, and has a good finish.

Natural durability: It has average durability against fungi, is very durable against insects and is sensitive to water xylophagous insects.

Impregnability: The duramen has low impregnability and the alburnum has average impregnability.

Uses: Plywood, interior and exterior carpentry, decorative veneering, furniture and cabinetmaking.

FAGUS sylvatica L. (FAGGIO)　コモンビーチ(Common beech)

西ヨーロッパ産の広葉樹材。入手は容易。

物理的特性：比重690〜750kg/㎥の中庸の緻密さを持つ木材。中硬(4)で、木理は通直。

挙動特性：接着性、釘打ち、ネジ止め、すべて良好。表面仕上げにはウッドパテを使う必要がある。

耐朽性：真菌に対する耐性がなく、シロアリの害も受けやすい。

含浸性：含浸は容易である。

用途：内装建具(床材)、化粧単板、家具、飾り棚(特に曲げ木細工の部分)。

This is a readily-available broadleaf from Western Europe.

Physical properties: It is of average density with a density of 690-750 kg/m^3, is semi-hard (4) and has straight grain.

Mechanical properties: It glues, nails and screws well. Wood putty should be used for finishing it.

Natural durability: It is not durable against fungi and is sensitive to insects.

Impregnability: It is easily impregnable.

Uses: Interior carpentry (floors), decorative veneering, furniture and cabinetmaking (especially for curved pieces).

FRAXINUS excelsior L. (FRASSINO)　アッシュ(Ash)

北アフリカ、東アジア、ヨーロッパに分布する広葉樹材。入手は容易。

物理的特性：比重680〜750kg/㎥の、かなり高緻密な木材。中硬(4〜5.3)で、木理は通直。曲げ木細工に適す。

挙動特性：接着性は良いが、釘打ち、ネジ止めに際してはドリルで下穴をあける必要がある。表面仕上げはおおむね良好。

耐朽性：真菌に対する耐性はなく、シロアリの害も受けやすい。

含浸性：含浸は容易。

用途：化粧単板、床材。

It is readily-available broadleaf of Northern African, Eastern Asian and European origin.

Physical properties: It is of rather high density with a density of 680-750 kg/m^3. It is semi-hard (4-5.3), has straight grain and good curve.

Mechanical properties: It glues well. Drilling is required before nailing and screwing. It can be finished well.

Natural durability: It is not durable against fungi and is sensitive to insects.

Impregnability: It is easily impregnable.

Uses: Decorative veneering and floors.

HYMENEA spp.　ジャトバ

南アメリカ産の広葉樹材。豊富にあるが、あまり製材されていない。

物理的特性：比重955〜970kg/㎥のかなり高緻密な木材で、硬く(8)、木理は通直だが、あて、やにつぼなどの欠点を持つものがある。

挙動特性：接着性は良い(内装)。釘打ち、ネジ止めに際してはドリルで下穴をあける必要がある。表面仕上げはおおむね良好。

耐朽性：真菌、シロアリに対する耐性はあるが、水生シロアリの害を受けやすい。

含浸性：心材の含浸性は低い。

用途：内外装建具(床、階段)、化粧単板、家具、飾り棚。

It is a broadleaf from South America that is abundant but production of it is scarce.

Physical properties: It is of rather high density with a density of 955-970 kg/m^3. It is hard (8), has straight grain and may have tension wood and pitch pockets.

Mechanical properties: It glues well (interiors). Drilling is required before nailing and screwing. It can be finished well.

Natural durability: It is durable in respect to fungi and insects but it is sensitive to water xylophagous insects.

Impregnability: The duramen has low impregnability.

Uses: Interior and exterior carpentry (floors, stairs), decorative veneering, furniture and cabinetmaking.

INTSIA bijuga O. Ktze. L.　メルバオ

東南アジアおよびオセアニア地域から産出する広葉樹材。入手は困難。

物理的特性：比重730〜830kg/㎥の中庸の緻密さの木材。硬く(6.4)、木理は通直または旋回。樹脂のせいで油質の触感がある。シリカや硫黄の堆積物を含む。金属と接触するとシミを生じる。

挙動特性：接着性は良いが、釘打ち、ネジ止めに際してはドリルで下穴をあける必要がある。表面塗装には適切な処置が必要。

耐朽性：真菌に対して非常に高い耐性を示す。シロアリに対する耐性は中庸。

含浸性：含浸性に非常に優れる。

用途：外装建具(窓)、内装(床、階段)、化粧単板、家具、飾り棚。

It is broadleaf that comes from Southeast Asia and Oceania that is difficult to obtain.

Physical properties: It is of average density with a density of 730-830 kg/m^3. It is hard (6.4), has straight or spiral grain and has an oily touch due to gum, silica and sulfur deposits. It stains if it comes in contact with metal.

Mechanical properties: It glues well and drilling is required before nailing and screwing. The surface must be duly prepared before finishing.

Natural durability: It is very durable against fungi and of average durability against insects.

Impregnability: Very good impregnability.

Uses: Exterior carpentry (windows) and interior (floors, stairs), decorative veneering, furniture and cabinetmaking.

JUGLANS regia-nigra L.(NOCE)　ウオルナット(Walnut tree)

北アメリカ、ヨーロッパ、アジア、北アフリカに広く分布する広葉樹材。入手は容易。

物理的特性：比重550〜680kg/㎥のやや緻密な木材。中硬(3.2〜3.6)で、木理は通直。

挙動特性：接着性、釘打ち、ネジ止め、すべて良好で、表面仕上げも良好。

耐朽性：真菌に対する耐性は中庸だが、シロアリの害を受けやすい。

含浸性：心材の含浸性は低いが、辺材の含浸は非常に容易。

用途：内装建具(羽目板、床)、化粧単板、家具、飾り棚。

It is readily-available broadleaf from North America, Europe, Asia and the North of Africa.

Physical properties: It is of slight density with a density of 550-680 kg/m^3. It is semi-hard (3.2-3.6) and has straight grain.

Mechanical properties: It glues, nails and screws well and has a good finish.

Natural durability: It is of average durability against fungi and is sensitive to insects.

Impregnability: The duramen has low impregnability and the alburnum is very impregnable.

Uses: Interior carpentry (paneling, floors), decorative veneering, furniture and cabinetmaking.

KHAYA ivorensis A. Chev.(MOGANO)　マホガニー(Mahogany)

西アフリカ原産の広葉樹材。入手は容易。

物理的特性：比重490〜530kg/㎥の中庸の緻密さの木材。軟らかく(1.9)、木理は通直。

挙動特性：接着性、釘打ち、ネジ止め、すべて良好。表面仕上げに際してはウッドパテを使用する必要がある。

耐朽性：真菌に対する耐性は中庸だが、シロアリの害を受けやすい。

含浸性：心材の含浸は不可能だが、辺材は中庸。

用途：合板、内外装建具、化粧単板、家具、飾り棚。サペリの代替材となる。

It is readily-available broadleaf of Western African origin.

Physical properties: It is of average density with a density of 490-530 kg/m^3. It is soft (1.9) and has straight grain.

Mechanical properties: It glues, nails and screws well and wood putty should be used before finishing it.

Natural durability: It is of average durability against fungi and is sensitive to insects.

Impregnability: The duramen is non-impregnable and the alburnum has average impregnability.

Uses: Plywood panels, interior and exterior carpentry, decorative veneering, furniture and cabinetmaking. It can be a substitute for sapele.

LARIX dedicua Mill.（LARICE）　ラーチ（Larch）

中央ヨーロッパ、北アメリカ産の針葉樹材。入手は容易。

物理的特性：比重470〜650kg/㎥のかなり高緻密な木材。中硬（2.2〜3.2）で、木理は通直だが道管が開いている。

挙動特性：接着性は良く、釘打ち、ネジ止めも先端の鋭いものを使用すれば良好。仕上がりに際して材面に樹脂が滲み出ることがある。

耐朽性：真菌に対してほとんど耐性がなく、シロアリの害も受けやすい。

含浸性：心材の含浸は事実上不可能。辺材の含浸性は中庸。

用途：合板厚板、羽目板、内装建具（床材）、化粧単板。

It is readily-available conifer from Central Europe and North America.

Physical properties: It is of rather high density with a density of 470-650 kg/m3. It is semi-hard (2.2-3.2), has straight grain and wide vessels.

Mechanical properties: It glues well and nails and screws well if fine tips are used. It has a resinous finish.

Natural durability: It shows little durability against fungi and is sensitive to insects.

Impregnability: The duramen is practically impossible to impregnate and the alburnum is of average impregnability.

Uses: Plywood boards, paneling, interior carpentry (floors) and decorative veneering.

MILLETTIA laurentii DeWild.（WENGÉ）　ウェンジ

アフリカ原産の広葉樹材。入手可能性は中庸。

物理的特性：比重700〜900kg/㎥のかなり高緻密な木材。硬く（9）、木理は通直で、耐朽性があり、樹脂が多い。

挙動特性：接着剤は合うものと合わないものがある。釘打ち、ネジ止めに際してはドリルで下穴をあける必要がある。仕上げ剤はワックス系のものを使用すること。

耐朽性：真菌に対して耐性があり、シロアリも寄せ付けない。

含浸性：心材の含浸は不可能である。

用途：内外装建具（床材）、化粧単板、家具、飾り棚。

It is broadleaf of African origin with average availability.

Physical properties: It is of rather high density with a density of 700-900 kg/m3. It is hard (9), has straight grain, is durable and resinous.

Mechanical properties: It is a bit delicate to glue and drilling is required previous to nailing and screwing. The finishing must be done with wax-based products.

Natural durability: It is durable against fungi and insects do not attack it.

Impregnability: The duramen is non-impregnable.

Uses: Interior and exterior carpentry (floors), decorative veneering, furniture and cabinetmaking.

OLEA europaea L.（OLIVO）　オリーブ（Olive tree）

地中海地域産の広葉樹材。入手可能性は中庸だが、ほとんど木材として加工されていない。

物理的特性：比重850〜1120kg/㎥のかなり高緻密な木材。硬く、木理は不規則で、油質の触感がある。

挙動特性：油脂のせいで接着剤の使用は困難。釘打ち、ネジ止めに際してはドリルで下穴をあける必要がある。仕上がりは良好。

耐朽性：良好。

含浸性：心材の含浸性は低いが、辺材の含浸は容易。

用途：内装建具（床材）、化粧単板、家具。

It is broadleaf that comes from the Mediterranean region, is of average availability but production is scarce.

Physical properties: It is of rather high density with a density of 850-1.120 kg/m3. It is hard, has an irregular grain and an oily touch.

Mechanical properties: Gluing is difficult due to its oiliness. Drilling is required before nailing and screwing. It finishes well.

Natural durability: Durable.

Impregnability: The duramen has low impregnability and the alburnum is of easy impregnability.

Uses: Interior carpentry (floors), decorative veneering and furniture.

PINUS radiata D.Don（PINO INSIGNE） ラジアータパイン（Radiata pine）

南東ヨーロッパ、ニュージーランド、オーストラリア産の針葉樹材。入手は容易。

物理的特性：比重500kg/㎥の中庸の緻密さを持つ木材。中硬（1.8）で、木理は通直。

挙動特性：接着性は良く（浸透性がある）、釘打ち、ネジ止めも良好。表面仕上げ前にウッドパテで処置する必要がある。

耐朽性：真菌に対してあまり耐性はない。シロアリの害も受けやすい。

含浸性：心材の含浸は事実上不可能。辺材の含浸性は中庸から低い。

用途：建設用合板厚板、外装建具（積層額縁）、内装（羽目板）、積層木材、家具。

It is a readily-available conifer that comes from the Southeast of Europe, New Zealand and Australia.

Physical properties: It is of average density with a density of 500 kg/m^3. It is semi-hard (1.8) and has straight grain.

Mechanical properties: It glues well (permeable) and nails and screws well too. Putty should be used before finishing.

Natural durability: It is not very durable against fungi and is sensitive to insects.

Impregnability: The duramen is practically impossible to impregnate and the alburnum is of average to low impregnability.

Uses: Structural plywood boards, exterior carpentry (laminated trimmings) and interior (paneling), laminated wood and furniture.

PINUS sylvestris L.（PINO SILVESTRE） スコッチパイン（Scots pine）

北アジアおよびヨーロッパ産の入手容易な針葉樹材。

物理的特性：比重500〜540kg/㎥のやや緻密な中硬（2）の木材。木理は通直。樹脂道から樹脂が滲み出てくる。

挙動特性：接着に際しては、樹脂に注意する必要がある。釘打ち、ネジ止めは良好。仕上げに際しては、完全に乾かすことが肝要。

耐朽性：真菌に対してはほとんど耐性がなく、シロアリの害も受けやすい。

含浸性：心材の含浸は不可能。辺材の含浸は容易。

用途：合板、内外装建具（ドア、羽目板、床材）、化粧単板、家具、飾り棚、積層木材。

It is readily-available conifer that comes from the North of Asia and Europe.

Physical properties: It is of slight density with a density of 500-540 kg/m^3. It is semi-hard (2), has straight grain and resinous vessels.

Mechanical properties: The resinous characteristic of it must be taken into account when gluing. It nails and screws well. To finish it well, it must be thoroughly dried.

Natural durability: It is little durable against fungi and sensitive to insects.

Impregnability: The duramen has zero impregnability but the alburnum is easily impregnable.

Uses: Plywood boards, interior and exterior carpentry (doors, paneling, floors), decorative veneering, furniture and cabinetmaking, and laminated wood.

POPULUS alba L.（PIOPPO） ポプラ（Poplar）

ヨーロッパ、アジア、北アフリカ産の広葉樹材。入手は容易。

物理的特性：比重420〜480kg/㎥の中庸の緻密さの木材。軟らかく（1.2〜2.6）、木理は通直。

挙動特性：接着性は良いが、釘打ち、ネジ止めは中庸。仕上げは木理と反対方向に行うこと。

耐朽性：真菌に対してはほとんど耐性がなく、シロアリの害も受けやすい。

含浸性：心材の含浸性は低いが、辺材の含浸は容易。

用途：合板厚板。

It is a readily-available broadleaf that comes from Europe, Asia and the North of Africa.

Physical properties: It is of average density with a density of 420-480 kg/m^3. It is soft (1.2-2.6) and has straight grain.

Mechanical properties: It glues well but nailing and screwing are average. The finishing must be done against the grain.

Natural durability: It is little durable against fungi and sensitive to insects.

Impregnability: The duramen has low impregnability but the alburnum is easily impregnable.

Uses: Plywood boards.

PSEUDOTSUGA menziessii Franco (DUGLAS)　ダグラスファー (Douglas Fir)

北アメリカ、イギリス、オーストラリア産の針葉樹材。入手は容易。

物理的特性：比重470〜520kg/m³の中庸の緻密さの木材。中硬(2.2)で、木理は通直。

挙動特性：接着性は良いが、変色する場合がある。釘打ち、ネジ止めは良好。仕上げには適切な前処置が必要。

耐朽性：耐朽性は中庸。シロアリの害は受けやすい。

含浸性：心材の含浸は不可能。辺材の含浸性は中庸から低い。

用途：合板、床材、内外装建具。

It is a readily-available conifer that comes from North America, the United Kingdom and Australia.

Physical properties: It is of average density with a density of 470-520 kg/m3. It is semi-hard (2.2) and has straight grain.

Mechanical properties: It glues well, though it may undergo coloration, and it nails and screws well. The finishing requires preparation.

Natural durability: It is of average durability and is sensitive to insects.

Impregnability: The duramen is non-impregnable and the alburnum is of average or low impregnability.

Uses: Plywood, floors and interior or exterior carpentry.

QUERCUS robur L. (ROVERE)　ヨーロピアンオーク (European Oak)

ヨーロッパ、小アジア、北アフリカ産の広葉樹材。入手は容易。

物理的特性：比重670〜760kg/m³の中庸の緻密さを持つ木材。中硬(3.5〜4.4)で、木理は通直。金属にさびを生じさせることがある。蒸し曲げ加工に適す。

挙動特性：接着性は良いが、釘打ち、ネジ止めに際してはドリルで下穴をあける必要がある。仕上げに際しては、パテを使用する必要がある。

耐朽性：真菌に対しては耐性があるが、シロアリの害は受けやすい。

含浸性：心材の含浸は不可能。辺材の含浸は容易。

用途：内装建具（床材）、化粧単板、家具、飾り棚。

It is readily-available broadleaf from Europe, Asia Minor and the North of Africa.

Physical properties: It is of average density with a density of 670-760 kg/m3. It is semi-hard (3.5-4.4) and has straight grain. It can corrode metal. It can be easily bent with steam.

Mechanical properties: It glues well and drilling is required before nailing and screwing. Putty should be used for the finishing.

Natural durability: It is durable against fungi but sensitive to insects.

Impregnability: The duramen is non-impregnable but the alburnum is easily impregnable.

Uses: Interior carpentry (floors), decorative veneering, furniture and cabinetmaking.

QUERCUS rubra L. (QUERCIA ROSSA)　レッドオーク (Red Oak)

北アメリカ産の広葉樹材。入手は容易。

物理的特性：比重650〜790kg/m³の中庸の緻密さの木材。中硬(3.5〜4.5)で、木理は通直。水分のある所で金属と接触すると脱色する。蒸し曲げ加工に適す。

挙動特性：接着剤との相性を確かめて使用すること。釘打ち、ネジ止めにはドリルで下穴をあける必要がある。仕上げに際しては、パテを使用すること。

耐朽性：真菌に対してはほとんど耐性がなく、シロアリの害も受けやすい。

含浸性：心材の含浸性は中庸から低い。辺材の含浸は容易。

用途：合板厚板、内装建具（床材）、化粧単板、家具、飾り棚。

It is a readily-available broadleaf of North American origin.

Physical properties: It is of average density with a density of 650-790 kg/m3. It is semi-hard (3.5-4.5) and has straight grain. It discolors on contact with metal and moisture and bends easily with steam.

Mechanical properties: Care must be taken with gluing as some glues work better than others. Drilling is required before nailing and screwing and putty should be used for the finishing.

Natural durability: It is little durable against fungi and sensitive to insects.

Impregnability: The duramen has low to average impregnability and the alburnum is easily impregnable.

Uses: Plywood boards, interior carpentry (floors), decorative veneering, furniture and cabinetmaking.

作品・建築家一覧 *directory*

ログキャビン
6　エステューディARCA
　　アーキテクチュラ
　　Freneria 5 pral 1.ª
　　08002 Barcelona, España
　　T (34) 933 107 160
　　F (34) 932 687 018
　　arc@coac.net

倒立する家
16　キロトーヴィチャード
　　4 Rue de la Prefecture
　　25000 Besançon, France
　　T (33) 03 81813131
　　F (33) 03 81619894
　　www.quirot-vichard.com

山あいの家
22　サイア・バーバリス・トポザノフ・
　　アルシテクト
180　339 est rue Saint Paul,
　　Vieux-Montréal
210　Quebec, Canada H2Y 1H3
222　T (514) 866 2085
　　F (514) 874 0233
　　sbt@sbt.qc.ca

チュン邸
28　チュン・スタジオ
184　4040 Del Rey Av., suite 5
　　Marina del Rey, CA, 90292 USA
　　T 310 821 0415
　　david@chunstudio.com

アイランドハウス
34　アルキテクトスタジオ
　　ウィッジダル・ラッキ・ベルカーホフ
212　Hornsgatan 79
233　SE 118 49 Stockholm, Sweden
　　T (46) 8 556 974 09
　　F (46) 8 556 974 39
　　www.wrb.se

スーツケース・ハウスホテル
42　エッジ・アーキテクツ
230　Suite1604, Eastern Harbour Centre,

トレジャーパレス
178　28 Hoi Chak Street, Quarry Bay,
　　Hong Kong
220　T 852 2802-6212
228　F 852 2802-6213
　　www.edgedesign.com

プトニー邸
48　トンキン—ズライハーグリア
　　117 Reservoir street
　　Surry Hills NSW 2010 Australia
　　T 02 9215 4932
　　F 02 9215 4901
　　www.tzg.com.au

ブレヌフ・ヴァル・アンドレの住宅
54　ドーフレスヌ,ル・ガレ・エ・アソシエ
　　5, rue Jules Vallees
　　75011 Paris, France
　　T (33) 01 53276464
　　F (33) 01 53276465
　　www.daufresne-
　　legarrec-architectes.com

ネンニングの住宅
60　クックロビッツーナハバール
　　アーキテクテン
246　Rathausplatz, 2

ハイン邸
248　6900 Bregenz, Austria
　　T (43) 5574 82788
　　F (43) 5574 82688
　　www.cn-arch.at

カーサDMAC
68　ナザール・アーキテクトス

カーサ　リサ/ビゲス
9　Trafalgar, 17, Prala
　　08010 Barcelona, España
　　T (34) 932955800
　　F (34) 932955801
　　nassarq@menta.net

ダニエルソン邸
74　ブライアン・マッケイーリヨン
　　アーキテクツ
　　2188 Gottingen street Halifax
　　Nova Scotia, Canada, B3K 3B4
　　T 902 429 1867
　　F 902 429 6276
　　www.bmlaud.ca

マウントヴュー・レジデンス
80　JMAアーキテクツQLD

マシューズ邸
254　Level 1,457 Upper Edward St.
　　Keynlynn Centre
　　PO box 380 Spring Hill, Brisbane,
　　QLD 4004 Australia
　　T (07) 3839 3794
　　F (07) 3839 6112
　　www.jma-arch.com

KFNパイロットプロジェクト
86　ヨハネス&オスカー・レオ・カウフマン

パッシブハウス
158　Sägerestrasse 4
　　A-6850 Dornbirn, Austria
　　T 43 (0) 5572 23690
　　F 43 (0) 5572 23690-4
　　www.jkarch.at

チルマークの住宅
94　チャールズ・ローズ・アーキテクツ
　　115 Willow Av.
　　Somerville, MA 02144 USA
　　T 617 628 5033
　　F 617 628 7033
　　www.charlesrosearchitects.com

ランボー氏別荘
100　オラヴィ・コポーネン
82　Apollonleath 23 B 39
　　00100 Helsinki, Finland
　　T 43 (0) 5572 23690
　　F 43 (0) 5572 23690-4
　　www.kolumbus.fi/olavi.koponen

ケーラー邸
106　サルメラ　アーキテクチャー&デザイン
　　852 Grandview Av.
　　Duluth Minnesota 55812 USA
　　T 218 724 7517
　　F 218 728 6805
　　dd.salmela@charter.net

アカヤバ自宅
112　マルコス・アカヤバ
186　Rua Helena, 170 – cj. 143
　　04552 Vila Olímpia Sao Paulo,
　　Brasil
　　T 55 11 3845 0738
　　F 55 11 3849 1045
　　macayaba@vol.com.br

軒の家
120　手塚建築事務所&池田昌弘
屋根の家
174　1-29-2 Tanattumi, Setagaya
縁側の家
242　Tokyo 158 0087 Japan
　　T 03 3703 7056
　　F 03 3703 7038
　　www.tezuka-arch.com

集合住宅II
126　ヴォークト・アーヒテクテン
200　Rötelstrasse 15
　　8006 Zürich, Switzerland
　　T 01 364 3406
　　F 01 364 3498
　　www.vogtarchitekten.ch

ギャロウェイ邸
132　ザ・ミラー—ハル パートナーシップ
　　Polson Bld. 71 Columbia sisth floor
　　Seattle WA 98104 USA
　　T 206 682 6837
　　F 206 682 5692
　　www.millerhull.com

チャマルティンの住宅
138　ギャリー・ニエト&
　　エンリケ・ソベヤノ
　　Rodriguez Marín, 61
　　28016 Madrid, España
　　T (34) 915 643 830
　　F (34) 915 643 836
　　nietosobejano@nietosobejano.com

バンデイラ・デ・メロの住宅
146　マウロ・ムニョス アルキテクチュラ
　　188　Av. Brigadeiro Luiz Antônio,
　　4919 Jardim Paulista
　　232　São Paulo, Brasil CEP 01401-002
　　T 55 11 3885 9353
　　F 55 11 3052 3858
　　mauro@mauromunhoz.arq.br

シュタインヴェントナー邸
152　ヘルトゥル・アーヒテクテン
　　Zwischenbrücken 4
　　A-4400 Steyr, Austria
　　T 43 7252 46944
　　F 43 7352 47363
　　www.hertl-arquitekten.com

マウラー自宅兼アトリエ
164　トーマス・マウラー アーキテクト
　　Melchnaustrasse 47G
　　CH-4900 Langenthal, Switzerland
　　T 062 922 10 11
　　F 062 922 10 11
　　imarch@bluewin.ch

Great(Bamboo)Wall
172　隈研吾建築都市設計事務所
252　2-24-8 Minami Aoyama
　　Minato-ku, Tokyo, 107 0062 Japan
　　T 81 33401 7121
　　F 81 33401 7778
　　http://www.so-net.ne.jp

ミカエリス邸
176　ハリー・レビン アーキテクツ
208　19ª Boundary Street
　　Rushcutters Bay NSW 2011
　　Australia
　　T 9380 6033
　　F 9380 6088
　　hl@harch.au

パインの森別荘
190　カトラー・アンダーソン アーキテクツ
ウッドハウス
206　135 Parfitt way sw.
　　Bainbridge Island, WA, 98110 USA
　　T 206 842 4710
　　F 206 842 4420
　　www.cutler-anderson.com

エッシンゲンの住宅
192　シュルーデ・アーヒテクテン
シュトゥットガルトの集合住宅
194　Kleine Falterstrasse 22
　　70597 Stuttgart, Germany
　　T 0711 765 2590
　　F 0711 765 2592
　　www.schlude-architekten.de

シャーレ・ピクテ
196　シャルル・ピクテ アルシテクト
202　13, rue de Roveray
218　CH-1207 Genève, Suisse
240　T 206 842 4710
　　F 206 842 4420
　　www.pictet-architecte.ch

サヴォア通り重層式アパート
198　リトー・アルシテクト
216　26 bis Rue des Peupliers
　　92100 Boulogne, France
　　T 33 (0)1 46 09 00 34
　　F 33 (0)1 46 09 04 82
　　littow@magic.fr

ラトーレ邸
204　ギャリー・カニンガム アーキテクト
　　918 Dragon Street
　　Dallas, Texas, 75207 USA
　　T 1 214 9150900

スタジオ3773
214　ドライデザイン
　　5727 Venice Blv.
　　Los Angeles, CA 9019 USA
　　T 1 323 954 9084
　　F 1 323 954 9035
　　www.drydesign.com

水没する家
224　GADアーキテクチュア
250　9 Desbrosses st.
3つの時代にまたがる家
225　GADアーキテクテン
234　T 1 917 345 0368
　　F 1 212 941 6496
　　www.gadarchitecture.com

R邸
236　フェイフアリック—フリッツァー
　　アーヒテクテン
　　Glacisstraße 7
　　A-8010 Graz, Austria
　　T 0316 34 76 56
　　F 0316 38 60 29
　　feyferlik@inode.at fritzer@iniode.cc

アヴァロン邸
244　コナー—ソロモン アーキテクツ
　　Warehouse 5, 37 Nicholson Street
　　Balmain East NSW 2041 Australia
　　T 612 9810 1329
　　F 612 9810 4109
　　www.coso

ポール・ミード・ツリーハウス
258　ハワードーフーティット—ミラー
　　Paulmead, Bisley
　　Gloucestershire, GL6 7AG,
　　England, UK
　　T 44 01 452770776
　　www.millarhowardworkshop.co.uk

リー・ツリーハウス
264　ジョセフ・リム アーキテクト
　　Departament of architecture
　　4 Architecture Drive, Singapur
　　117566
　　National University of Singapor
　　T 65 68743528
　　www.josephlimdesigns.com

ハーディー・ツリーハウス
270　ユー・クワン エリア
　　45, Cantonmrnt Road
　　Singapur 089748
　　T 735 5995
　　F 738 8295
　　area@indo.net.id

Architettura del Legno

Idea Mariarosaria Tagliaferri
Realization LOFT Publications
Editor Nacho Asensio
Editorial Coordinator Joaquim Ballarín i Bargalló
Documentation Mariona Villavieja i García, Joaquim Ballarín i Bargalló
Texts Maria Cinta Martí i Amela, Joaquim Ballarín i Bargalló
Graphic Design Argüelles Gutiérrez Disseny
Layout Anna Soler i Feliu

Edizioni Gribaudo - Redazione Varia - Illustrati
Corso Roma 35, Savigliano (CN)
Tel. 0172 712291 fax 0172 375319
e-mail: redazione@edizionigribaudo.it

Editing Vanina M. Carta, Francesca Ferrua
Printing Arti Grafiche DIAL - Mondovì (CN)

2005 © Edizioni Gribaudo srl
Savigliano (CN)
e-mail: info@edizionigribaudo.it

Originally published in 2005 by Edizioni Gribaudo

All rights in Italy and abroad reserved by the Publisher. No part of this publication may be translated, reproduced, stored in or introduced into a retrieval system, or transmitted, in any form, without the prior written permission of the Publisher.

産調出版の関連書籍

世界木材図鑑

本体価格
4,800円

世界中で最もよく使用されている
用途の広い木材150種を厳選

エイダン・ウォーカー：総編集
ニック・ギブス／ルシンダ・リーチ他：共著

序章では木の組織・生長過程や製材方法等、また森林保護について。木材一覧では、世界で最も使用されている樹種150種について豊富な情報を提供、精密な写真も掲載。木材の美しさを愛する全ての人々に捧ぐ総括的木材図鑑。

木材活用ハンドブック

本体価格
3,200円

最も使用頻度が高く人気が高い
主要木材の実践的ガイド

ニック・ギブス 著

木工家にとって価値ある木材150種以上を学名及び一般名、長短所は勿論生育・作業特性まで断面のカラー写真付きで解説。本書はまさに内容多彩、木材サンプルの優れたパレットとしてすぐに活用できる実用バイブル。

ニューナチュラルハウスブック

本体価格
4,940円

エコロジー、調和、
健康的な住環境の創造

デヴィット・ピアソン 著

健康的で調和がとれていてエコロジカルな家であり、美しい家。そんなナチュラルハウスの概念を健康と環境の両面から包括的にとりあげ、図版を用いながら表現。95年刊「ナチュラルハウスブック」の改題改訂。

ACKNOWLEDGEMENTS

We wish to thank all of the people who have collaborated (at times,
far beyond the call of duty) in finding and sending us
published material: proprietors, architects, designers,
photographers, and office staff
in architectural offices. Above all
we would like to give special thanks to Daniel Nassar,
a colleague
and friend, and an expert on wood.

OTHER PHOTOGRAPHIC CREDITS

The pictures of pages 6 and 7, corresponding to the
introductive chapter, are by the author of the
book; those
of pages 8, 9, 10 and 11 are by Daniel Nassar; pages 12
and 13 have been published by permission of the firm
Holza, and the pictures of natural
environments of pages 1, 5 and 276 are by Ricardo Vila,
and are also published in Colores, el paisaje iluminado
(Vila Editorial. 2003).

Architettura del Legno
現代建築家による木造建築

発　　行	2006年10月20日
本体価格	3,600円
発行者	平野　陽三
発行所	産調出版株式会社
	〒169-0074 東京都新宿区北新宿3-14-8
	TEL.03(3363)9221　FAX.03(3366)3503
	http://www.gaiajapan.co.jp

編 集 者：ナチョ・アセンシオ(Nacho Asensio)

翻 訳 者：乙須 敏紀（おとす としのり）
九州大学文学部哲学科卒業。訳書に『床材フロアマテリアル』『階段のデザイン』『屋根のデザイン』『世界木材図鑑』（いずれも産調出版）など。

落丁本・乱丁本はお取り替えいたします。
本書を許可なく複製することは、かたくお断わりします。

Copyright SUNCHOH SHUPPAN INC. JAPAN2006
ISBN 4-88282-486-8 C3052
Printed in Italy